BIBLICAL PARABLES
AND THEIR
MODERN RE-CREATIONS

SUNY series in Modern Jewish Literature and Culture
Sarah Blacher Cohen, editor

BIBLICAL PARABLES AND THEIR MODERN RE-CREATIONS

From "Apples of Gold in Silver Settings" to "Imperial Messages"

GILA SAFRAN NAVEH

State University
of New York
Press

Published by
State University of New York Press, Albany

Production by Susan Geraghty
Marketing by Anne Valentine

Cover photo by the author.

Printed in the United States of America

For information, address State University of New York
Press, State University Plaza, Albany, N.Y., 12246

Library of Congress Cataloging-in-Publication Data

Naveh, Gila Safran.
    Biblical parables and their modern re-creations : from "Apples of
gold in silver settings" to "Imperial messages" / Gila Safran Naveh.
        p.   cm. — (SUNY series on modern Jewish literature and
culture)
    Includes bibliographical references and index.
    ISBN 0-7914-4397-3 (alk. paper). — ISBN 0-7914-4398-1 (pbk. :
alk. paper)
    1. Parables—History and criticism. 2. Bible—Parables.
3. Jewish parables—History and criticism. 4. Literature,
Modern—20th century—History and criticism. I. Title.
II. Series.
PN56.P23N38 1997
809'.915—dc21   99-13726
                                                                   CIP

10 9 8 7 6 5 4 3 2 1

CONTENTS

LIST OF TABLES

LIST OF FIGURES

ACKNOWLEDGMENTS

Biblical Parables and Their Modern Re-creations emerged from, and was shaped by, my long-standing fascination with this recalcitrant yet seductive genre that spans from biblical to modern time. To Sarah Blacher Cohen, the editor of Modern Jewish Literature and Culture series at SUNY Press, my deep appreciation for her ongoing interest in my work. Her guidance and counsel were invaluable.

In 1995, while this book was well under way, Professor David Paterson had taken an interest in my study and awarded me a Skirball Fellowship at the Oxford Centre for Postgraduate Studies. The Centre provided me with the leisure, inspiration, and ideas I needed to shift from the study of ancient parables to modernity.

I wish to thank my colleagues and friends whose gentle attention and timely suggestions have played their part in the generation of the notions that inform this study. Two cherished friends, Jean and Matt Chimsky, were prolific of moral and technical help. So were Professors Michele Vialet and Ann Michelini, who read portions of my study and did not stint judgment. As is frequently the case, others have indirectly contributed; scholars and participants in institutes and my students who bore the brunt of my thought processes. Further back in time, but no less important, Alan Cohen, Ben Zion Waholder, Dan Miron, Michel De Certeau, Eugenio Donato, Zeno Vendler, Chaymi Alazraky, and Ita Sheres, have influenced my initial impulse to study parables. I wish to thank Alan Berger, Andy Gordon, Gloria Cronin, in the ALA and my dear friends in the SSA who have listened kindly to my complaints. Alice West, Joy Dunn and Alex Trunov have been wonderful. And finally, I am indebted to my husband Michael for his gentle presence and continual support.

This book is for our son, Dorian Aaron, and my parents, Sara and Itzhac.

I gratefully acknowledge the following for having given me permission to quote from published work:

Random House, Inc. Alfred A. Knopf, Inc. for permission to quote "On Parables," "The Sirens," "An Imperial Message," by Franz Kafka, copyright 1958.

Shocken Books, Tel Aviv, Israel, for permission to quote "Before the Kaddish," by S. Y. Agnon, translated by Goldin Yehuda.

New Directions Publishing Corporation, for permission to quote "The Parable of Cervantes and The Quixote," by Jorges Luis Borges, copyright 1964.

The Wylie Agency, Martin Secker, and Warburg Publishing for permission to publish "Cities and Signs," from Invisible Cities by Italo Calvino in the UK, and Commonwealth including Canada.

The Balkin Agency, for permission to publish "Two Kinds of Faith," collected by Martin Buber.

Martin Secker and Warburg Publishers for the use of "Cities and Signs," from Invisible Cities by Italo Calvino.

I am grateful as well to the editors of SUNY Press, who have been very helpful with the manuscript.

INTRODUCTION

The Zen master shows his disciple a stick with a snake and tells
him that he must choose wisely. If the disciple attempts to grab him
by the tail, the snakes bites him with his head, if he tries to grab
the snake by the head, the snake hits him with his tail. If he grabs
the middle, the snake hits him both with the head and the tail.

—Sun Tzu

Parables have fascinated students of the Bible for centuries, and lately
parables delight and preoccupy literary critics, in part because of their
formidable historical persistence as a literary genre and in part because
their overt simplicity is belied by their structural-discursive sophistication and resistance to exclusionist modes of interpretation. Parables continue to challenge our profoundest expectations to find meaning and to
make obvious the production of ideology by showing that reality can be
reproduced in the form of a sign that then functions as reality. Unique
as textual strategies, parables frequently place us in the position of the
Zen disciple.[1]

Unlike the narratives in which parables are frequently nested, parables present a particular problem in cognition and signification, because
they problematize even at surface level the inherent polysemy of a text.
Analyzing parabolic discourse presents, therefore, dilemmas far beyond
the usual difficulties encountered in narrative analyses.[2]

The widespread appeal of parabolic discourse is confirmed by the
multiple inquiries ranging from biblical and rabbinic exegeses to structural interpretations by scholars of postmodernity mainly in Europe, and
scholars of Judaic studies in Israel and in the United States. Of late,
investigations of parables in the Gospels and of the *mashal* (the generic
name for a classical parable in rabbinic literature) in *Midrash* attempt to
demarginalize parabolic discourse and give it back the honored place
among modern discursive practices.[3]

Extant studies of parables are lacking in several important respects.
First, the work is done within one social literary climate and shies away
from actually comparing texts across cultures. Lacking a comparative
perspective, these studies fail to show the multifaceted domain of parables, the culturally diverse milieu in which parabolic discourse is nested,

and, most importantly, its vast temporal range and transformations. While classical studies in the Gospel parables or exegeses of the *mashal* pretend to ignore each other but use similar, self-contained interpretative models and principles of investigation, the few structuralist analyses concentrate solely on the patterns of parabolic discourse, with little awareness or concern for the importance of overlooked premodern parables or the historical contextual milieu in which they developed; this sometimes results in the complete obliteration of the cultural and political climate mirrored in the parabolic text. The majority of extant studies favor exclusively the historical, allegorical, or eschatological dimensions of parables and leave unexplored those facets which offer clues about their rhetorico-poetic and narrational strategies. More importantly, these studies do not illuminate the parables' adaptation to new religious and sociocultural conditions. Specifically, existent studies leave out the unique "molecular structure" and architectonics of parabolic discourse, its transformational and seductive features, as well as its unique intratextual and intertextual strategies.[4] The end result is that the widely disparate approaches, with different scholarly traditions and educational backgrounds and goals, are seldom made to confront each other by contemporary literary critics.[5]

My book presents a cross-cultural analysis of representative parables from various social and historical climates. It contrasts what is ordinarily known as the *mashal*, the rabbinic parables commonly used to interpret the Scriptures, with synoptic Gospel parables, Chassidic parabolic tales, medieval philosophical parabolic discourse, and modern parables by Kafka, Borges, Calvino, and Agnon. I employ an interdisciplinary framework to conduct my study.

The conceptual innovation of my analysis lies both in the kind of parables chosen and in the methodology used. In bringing together, for the first time, parables found in premodern texts with modern parabolic discourse, my study encourages the reader to look at the internal and external transformations sustained by this unique literary genre. At the same time, my inquiry reveals a dramatic social, cultural, and political change in the way we envision the divine and in the way we witness.

As a result, my investigation illuminates the systematic drain, in modern times and in postmodernity, of competence and likelihood of decoding the meaning of a parable by its addressee/listener/reader. Moreover, it uncovers the steady depletion of construable meaning in favor of an elaborated form and sophisticated linguistic strategies, to the point of fascination, indeed obsession, with the word in modern parables. Finally, my analysis suggests that this unilateral preoccupation might have become a postmodern form of ritual.

In tune with the work on signs by Thomas Aquinas and John Locke, as well as that of modern semioticians such as Charles Sanders Pierce, Umberto Eco, Thomas Sebeok, John Deely, Jonathan Culler, Myrdene Anderson, Juliet and Dean MacCannall, Ita Sheres, Alain Cohen, and others, I probe the transformations of codes and the changes undergone by prototypical parables.[6] In an attempt to understand the reasons for the direction taken by this particular order of discourse in modern times, I deal with transformational processes by which the "transparent" scriptural parables, called by Maimonides "apples of gold in their silver settings," have gradually become a "secret speech," "cryptic," and with "undecodable messages." I also attempt to show how this shift culminates in "non-deliverable" Kafkaesque "imperial messages" and climaxes with Kafka's parables, "The Imperial Message" and "On Parables," two powerful meditations on the impossibility of knowing in modern times.

To reveal the movement that has occurred in parables, I choose a particular course. I examine the changes sustained by parabolic discourse at several levels: in deep narrative structure, architectonics, signification, function, and at the level of pragmatics. At the same time, I highlight the changes in the way parables are structured and the transformations that ensue in their meaning. I outline the reasons for which parables are traditionally written and present periodically the literary and sociocultural contexts in which they commonly occur. This simultaneous syntagmatic and paradigmatic look enables me to suggest that the path of transformation in parabolic discourse parallels not only sociocultural change, but a dramatic change in our cognition; and reading back through the networks of earlier parabolic narratives reveals in a particularly poignant fashion the patterns of this change.

Different from earlier works, my study combines a hermeneutic approach that looks at the steady decontextualization of parabolic discourse with clear awareness of current semiotic methods of textual investigations, and ponders the underlying reasons for the particular trend in the transformations of parabolic codes. By examining the unique transformational course taken by parables, my analysis evidences some illuminating facts about the genre in general.

To investigate the praxis of parabolizing from *within* the shifting grounds of the parabolic mode, I concentrate first on the change from simple, formulaic constructs, to complex, multifarious configurations. Second, I show a reorientation in parables from teaching wisdom by pointing the addressee to a higher truth and promising a universe of absolute presence, to theorizing about the futility and hopelessness of human cognition, even forewarning the reader in a muscular, oblique way of the possibility, even the actuality, of absolute absence. Finally, I construct semeio-narrative models for analyzing parables by probing the

selected parables' rhetorico-poetic dimension, their thematic, philosophical, and psychoanalytic components (similarities between parables and
dreams). My model reveals gradually a kind of genetic encoding that is
clearly a part of a long cultural chain, and that remains hidden because
of sophisticated rhetorical parabolic strategies.

To describe the characteristics of prototypical parabolic discourse
as well as trace some of the transformational trends from antiquity to
modern times, I draw upon a sample of representative parables from a
vast and culturally diverse literature: the Scriptures, classical Jewish
texts, premodern and modern literature. In each chapter, as a practical
application of my model, I submit a number of parables to a detailed
analysis.

My model for analyzing parables is a generative model. It takes
shape progressively in the production of preliminary models that imply
each other but also challenge each other in the process of being construed. As new empirical findings surface, the apparatus that accounts
for the changes in parables is itself amended while it amends the old
parabolic paradigms. The end result is that the analysis reveals, gradually, both the trend in transformation of parables and the underlying
reasons for these transformations, while it outlines its own boundaries.

The selection of samples is based on personal preference as well as
relevancy to the theoretical points made here, yet it must be said that
many other sets of representative parables would point very much to the
same transformational trends, even when a switch in samples will introduce additional variables to our paradigms.

The objective of this study is not to give an exhaustive, all-encom-
passing account—I leave this task to the more ambitious historians of
literature and exegetes. My hope is to puncture the thick semiotic web
enshrouding parabolic discourse and its unique transformations to facilitate further research. I chose to read closely parables by Kafka who
cleverly read back to Kabbalah and to Maimonides, who reads back to
the Scriptures and to the Rabbis who, in turn, read back to the Scriptures, in a long intertextual chain that links up and intertwines with
other texts to form the various subgenres of a most perplexing discourse.[7]

In the first part, entitled "In Pursuit of Wisdom," I provide a comprehensive investigation of the various dimensions of parabolic discourse: allegorical, pragmatic, pedagogical, psychological, ideological,
symbolic. I show the particular configuration of parabolic discourse,
indicate its affinities to other types of discourse, and bring examples
highlighting the specific problematic raised by this type of discourse.
This chapter is meant to facilitate the reader's further travel in the
domain of parabolic discourse.

The second part of my study, entitled "Apples of Gold," is organized around readings of Sriptural parables ("The Parable of the Ewe Lamb"), synoptic texts ("The Parable of the Marriage Feast"), rabbinic parables ("The Parable of the King's Banquet"), and medieval parabolic tales ("The Tale of the Two Kinds of Faith"). Inspired by the pithy simile in Proverbs 25:11, "A parable is like apples of gold in silver setting," I envision them chronologically, as "Apples of Gold," "More Apples of Gold," "Late Apples of Gold," and "The Last Apples of Gold."

The third part of my study, entitled "Imperial Messages," receives its name from Kafka's parable "An Imperial Message" and examines modern parabolic discourse. It, too, contains an introductory commentary and four chapters. This part provides an even balance to the second part of the book. Each of the chapters contains a substantial introduction about the author, his contribution to the genre, the transformations he has brought about, and his indebtedness to ancient parables. Here, I examine the distinctive features introduced by Kafka ("The Imperial Message"), Borges ("The Parable of Cervantes and *The Quixote*"), Calvino ("Cities and Signs") and pay tribute to Agnon's ("Before the Kaddish") revival of the ancient parabolic practice.

In "Toward a Conclusion," I assess the new insights regarding the way in which the changes over the years in our worldview and in our cognition affected parabolic discourse. I show that the path of change in parabolic discourse parallels a dramatic change in our *Weltanschauung* and in cognition, and reading back through networks of parabolic narratives reveals in a particular way the terms of change sustained by this genre. I title symbolically these observations about the accomplishments and limitations of my study, and the limits of interpretation in general, "Some Fabulous Yonder," after Kafka's parable, "On Parables."

Parabolic discourse is notorious for being comely, seductive, and demanding a robust "musculature of the spirit" from those who wish to gain access to the web of its coded communication.[8] At each turn in the helix of interpretation, less can be grasped by fewer decoders; more challenging impediments are placed to the more daring of interpreters, until at times, parables seem completely enigmatic to all. Yet, despite the fact that *"parabola, in qua ponitur impedimentum de audienda doctrina,"* despite their impediment, parables are a compelling, very basic substance of human communication that tells of its nature and engages its addressee to act, to interpret, and to understand. We keep coming back to parables and seek to crack their unyielding coded core, because, unlike the Master of Zen, who raises a real stick at the confounded disciple, parables raise only a false "stick" (narrationally) at the interpreter's questions.[9] Only apparently do parables flout implicature; the inferences made in the text, follow coded rhetorical or psychological laws, and rely heavily on preestablished social, cultural, and ideological frameworks. Unlike the Master of Zen, parables invite us continuously to make connections between text, the "metatext," and "outside-of-text," and learn that human communication is governed by laws, other than, and additional to, the laws of syntax and semantics.

In my study, I try to present the changes in parabolic discourse to specialists in semiotic discourse analysis and to nonspecialists. In order to facilitate all readers' access to parabolic discourse beyond its "pop" aspect, I have offered various examples of prototypical parables and, whenever possible, I have placed technical linguistic and semiotic interpretative observations in notes.

PART I

In Pursuit of Wisdom

CHAPTER 1

The Nature and Structure of Parables

בֶּן אָדָם חוּד חִידָה
וּמְשׁוֹל מָשָׁל אֶל בֵּית יִשְׂרָאֵל

Son of man, riddle a riddle and tell a parable to the people of
Israel

—Ezekiel 17:2

BACKGROUND

It is told of Solomon, the wise king considered by many the inventor of
dugma (illustration),[1] that in order to understand the words of the wise
and their dark sayings,[2] he said one parable after another and spoke one
word after another until he understood all of the words of the Torah.[3]
A thousand years after the destruction of the Temple in 70 C.E., when
Maimonides, the medieval Jewish philosopher, theorized about
parabolic discourse, he claimed that the key to understanding all that the
prophets have said and to the knowledge of truth is an understanding of
parables, of their import, and of the meaning of the words occurring in
them; he too went back to the saying of the ancient sages.[4]

Maimonides states that his goal is to explain the meanings of certain
terms in the prophetic sayings, and pointedly, he proceeds to theorize for
his reader about parables and parabolic discourse. To elucidate the matter further, Maimonides quotes the scriptural proverb: "A word fitly
spoken is like 'apples of gold in setting of silver' [*ketapuhei zahav
bemaskiyyoth shel kesef*, בְּתַפּוּחֵי זָהָב בְּמַשְׂכִּיּוֹת שֶׁל כָּסֶף]."[5] And even though
Maimonides claimed earlier that he addresses this treatise to the ones
who "have philosophized" and "have knowledge of the sciences," he
analyzes the saying very thoroughly, and uses the trope of the apples of
gold in the filigree to illustrate how parables should be understood. We
are told the following:

> Hear now an elucidation of the thought that the Sage has set forth. The
> term *maskiyyoth* denotes filigree traceries; I mean to say in which there
> are apertures with very small eyelets, like the handwork of silversmiths.
> They are so called because a glance penetrates through them; for in the
> [Aramaic] *translation* of the Bible the Hebrew term *va-yashaqeph*—
> [meaning, he "glances"]—is translated *va-istekhe*.[6] The Sage accord-

ingly said that a saying uttered with "a view to two meanings" [my emphasis] is like an apple of gold overlaid with silver filigree having very small holes.

Now see how marvelously this dictum describes a well-construed parable. For he says that in a saying that has two meanings—he means an external and an internal one—the external meaning ought to be as beautiful as silver, while its internal meaning ought to be more beautiful than the external one, the former being in comparison to the latter as gold is to silver. Its external meaning also ought to contain in it something that indicates to someone considering it what is to be found in its internal meaning, as happens in the case of an apple of gold overlaid with silver filigree having very small holes. When looked at from a distance or with imperfect attention, it is deemed to be an apple of silver; but when a keen-sighted observer looks at it with full attention, its interior becomes clear to him and he knows that it is of gold.[7]

Subsequently, Maimonides draws a parallel with what he calls "the obscure parables" in the books of prophecy that have two meanings as well: one with respect to the welfare of human societies and the other, an internal, more profound one which contains wisdom related to truth "as it is."[8] This particular distinction facilitates further speculations about the very act of telling someone *that* a narrative is a parable.

Insightfully, Maimonides observes that to tell someone that a text is a parable is like "removing a screen from between the eye and a visible object," but, disappointingly for us, he also cautions his reader "not to inquire into all details occurring in the parables nor to wish to find signification corresponding to all of them," because in so doing he either drifts aside from the parable's intended subject, or goes into what Maimonides calls "exaggerated fantasies." He assumes, that there is an *a priori* intended meaning and that digression is always ill fated. "Regarding parables," in the words of the great Jewish philosopher, Maimonides, the purpose should nevertheless, "always be to know the whole that was intended to be known."[9]

DELINEATION OF STUDY

Maimonides, known also as Rabbenu Moshe ben Maimon, promptly goes on to expound other philosophical matters and, unfortunately, never teaches to "the perplexed" how the latter could know "the whole that was intended for him to know" about parabolic discourse. And so, some nine hundred years later, we return to the genteel and painstaking art of deciphering "golden apples concealed in silver filigree," an art once mastered by our undisclosing masters and philosophers.

"Why don't our present leaders speak in parables?"

One wonders for a fleeting moment about such a matter and quickly realizes that parables remain, since very early times, as puzzling as they are suggestive and that they require uncommon skill to decode. When a parable is meant to remain cryptic for someone, it will remain so even after all the cycles of decoding. We mean to say that a receiver will not be able to make the correct connection between different parts of the parable, since the narrative's unity and coherence is actually construed by the parabolizer *in* space-time of the parable. On the other hand, if a parable is "intended" for an addressee, he will understand it and, at times, decoding will be easy, even become superfluous. For example, when the disciples ask Jesus why he speaks to "them" [his disciples] in parables, the answer is an additional parable:

> To you it was given to know the secrets of the Kingdom of Heaven, but to them it has not been given. For to him who has will more be given, and he will have abundance; but from him who has not, even what he has will be taken away. This is why I speak to them in parables, because seeing they do not see, and hearing they do not hear nor do they understand.[10]

An ancient narrative form, parables can be found in the African, the Hindu, the Chinese, and the Persian oral traditions. The Babylonian exile has been most assuredly a strong catalyst in the exposure of the Jewish people to the Hindu and Persian mythology and folklore.[11]

Early good parables, like the folktale, tend to be simple and concise with a clear beginning, a crisis, and a well-defined ending, as miniature tales told to educate the masses.[12] These early parables mirrored a mode of existence in the world that allowed man [and woman] to gain knowledge from the wise and instilled in him hope to enter the realm of absolute presence in the world to come.

Ancient parables were thoroughly interpreted by their addressor. In *Jesus and His Jewish Parables,* Bradford Young suggests that the *darshan*, the expounder of parables, reformulated many of the classic answers to the question he was pondering in new contexts and according to new teaching concerns. Following Flusser and Young, David Stern asserts that when the *darshan* was called upon to compose a *mashal,* a parable, for a particular verse he was able to draw upon stereotypical elements that his people enjoyed and understood, because his audience was part of an existing semeiosis.[13] The parabolist used parabolic speech mainly as an efficient tool to communicate a message, to "interpellate"[14] the listener, and point him in the right direction in regard to religious belief and to the art of living.

While I acknowledge the importance of parabolic tales to their respective cultures and their relevance for the study of folklore,[15] I focus here on a single path that traces the scriptural parables and their modifications up to modern times. Specifically, I investigate the transformation of the "apples of gold in their silver settings,"[16] into Kafkaesque, undecipherable "imperial messages" (termed so after of one of Kafka's parables[17]) and reveal changes in the scriptural parables, the synoptic Gospels, and modern parables. Against this backdrop, I read the medieval Kabbalist and Chassidic parables. In passing, I show that philosophers, medieval sages, and even some modern writers, such as Agnon, use at times parables as an embellishment to their personal style, and at times, simply as homage to the old sages and ancient cherished traditions.

The parables I examine in this study, many of which have ancient Near-Eastern sources, appear interwoven in the Hebrew Scriptures, in the New Testament, and, later, in modern literary texts. In dealing concomitantly with the complex cultural milieu of parables and the transformations incurred in this narratives over time, I reveal to the reader a number of insights about their specific nature and structure, while at the same time I illuminate narrative, thematic, and rhetoric differences as time progresses.

PARABOLIC ELEMENTS

Parables in literature have been defined as short allegorical stories designed to teach a moral lesson in an oblique way. Parables have been customarily defined in terms of three parameters: in terms of teaching, which places them next to pedagogical discourse, in terms of their allegoricity, which likens them to all tropological discourse, and in terms of obscuring a truth, which brings them close to rhetoric and to philosophical discourse. Yet, despite all similarities to other discourses, we simply "know" that parables are not philosophical texts, nor are they truly pedagogical manuals. Everyone seems able to recognize a parable for what it is, namely, a literary discourse with an easily discernable identity and a specificity of its own.

Thomas Aquinas claims that, "He speaks enigmatically who speaks by ways of parables." He also notices that, while these narratives present an impediment to understanding, the unlearned learn better through parables in many other ways.[18] Evidently, this graspable "doubleness" characterizing parabolic narratives has always been most confounding.

One realizes soon that at the core of their discursive makeup exists a signal that propels the addressee into two equally powerful, yet opposing, directions. One learns that on the one hand, parables, a primitive communicatory force, invoke elementary passions and short-circuit the path to understanding by putting the addressee in touch immediately with a primeval "ought," or "must do," an early, inbred in humans, deontic mode (performance as obligation). On the other hand, parables baffle the mind because, as David Stern succinctly puts it, "their messages are allusive and their means indirect."[19]

A paradox is invariably created in the mind of a parable teller. The parabolist must take the story from reality and refer to the real world. At the same time, he has to go beyond reality, and invoke the all-powerful "Other" authority (that of God and the Scriptures, in antiquity), in order to obtain what is needed, namely a moral lesson that will influence the listener.[20]

And yet, despite their inherent doubleness, in the past, parables have been a most efficient and convenient tool in the service of those who propounded them for ideological purposes. In ancient times, these narratives were used extensively when an important message had to be delivered, or a critical point had to be made and explicit, "straight," language did not suffice.

Why so?

Because, in essence, parabolic discourse proposes a "likeness" between two dissimilar elements (life events or phenomena and verses of the Scriptures) and disguises with linguistic craft the "seam" in its discursive texture. Understanding (extradiscursively) the pragmatic relation established between the two disparate narrative parts in the parable is therefore the crux of the matter. In fact, in a number of recent studies it was argued most convincingly that the *nimshal*, the moral lesson at the end of a parable, is actually primordial, preexists in fact the *mashal*, and in no way should it be considered only an ornamental appendix, an "epimythium," as some New Testament scholars like Jeremias, Jülicher, Via, Dodd have claimed.[21]

THE PARABOLIC MODE

The following parable (attributed in *Pesikta Rabbati* to Rabbi Berachiah Hakohen Berabbi[22] and elsewhere to a Rabbi Levi, a third generation Palestinian Amora rabbi considered a master of the *Aggadah*), we learn how the parabolist uses parabolic speech to convey a certain ideology to his addressee.

R. Berachiah Hakohen Berabbi said:

To what may Israel be compared?
    To one who had a son whom he placed on his shoulder and took to the market. There, when the son saw a desirable object, he said to his father, Buy it for me, and his father bought for him what he wanted

the first time he asked, the second time, and the third. But then, when the son saw someone whom he asked, Have you seen my father? He said to his son: You fool, you are astride my shoulder, whatever you wish I buy for you, and yet you ask that man, "Have you seen my father?" What did the father do then? He threw his son from his shoulder, and a dog came and bit the son. (This sentence dos not appear in this version but appears in *Pesikta de Rav Kahana*, where the parable is attributed to R. Levi an Amoraic rabbi.) Thus, after Israel went out of Egypt, the Holy One encompassed them with seven clouds of glory, as is said "He compassed him about, He cared for him" (Deuteronomy 32:10). They asked for manna: He gave it. For quail: He gave them. After he gave all that they asked, they proceeded to ruminate "Is the Lord among us, or not?" (Exodus 17:7) the Holy One said to them: You ruminate as to My presence in your midst? As you live, I shall make you aware of it. Here is a dog to bite you. And who was the dog? Amalek, for the very next verse in Exodus says, "Then came Amalek" (Exodus 17:8). Thus it is said, "Remember" (Deuteronomy 25:17).[23]

This is an original way of expressing an ideology which insisted on the special relationship between God and his people Israel. The parabolist first shows the ubiquity of God, and his paternal interest in his people, while Israel is depicted as an authentic brat who misbehaves and forgets his God. As in Jesus' parables (Matthew 7:7–11) and (Luke 11:9–13), the son makes demands upon his father and all of his demands are readily met. The parabolist invites the listener to make an inference. The argument is (קל וחומר, *argumentum a minori ad maius*), that if a father is so very generous, how much the more so will God be. This parabolic argument puts God in glorious light. The child [of God] on the strong and protective shoulders of his father [God]) forgets him [God], and so, the father throws him off. The dog who bites the child represents Amalek that is discussed in the antecedent homily. The addressee must have been persuaded. Clearly our sermoneur felt that, to tell of the intimacy between God and his people, he ought to speak in parable, a mode he found both elegant and poignant.

ETYMOLOGY

The term "parable" comes to us from the Greek *parabolē,* which is derived in turn from the verbal form *paraballō,* which can be translated as "put side by side," or "parallel to" or "comparing item 'a' with item 'b.'" The term designating the prototype midrashic parable[24] is *mashal,* and it was commonly rendered by the Greek *parabolē,* or *paroimia.* For other than synoptic gospels, the term *parabolē* is also used for allegory, riddle, exemplum or symbol.

The etymology of the word *mashal* was most pertinently derived by L. Koehler and W. Baumgartner from the Akkadian root *masalu*, which means to "resemble," or "be like."[25] The rabbinic midrashic word *mašal*, with its variant *matlā* can also mean any of the following: a riddle, an allegory, an oracle, a wise saying, or a proverb.[26] A shift in the connotation of the word must have taken place in rabbinic parables. The rabbis have extended the meaning of the word to encompass a story parable as well.

Presumably, early parables were designed to be told *aggadaically*, namely in the very process of storytelling. The earliest parables were spontaneous improvisations and were a part of the oral teaching. Only later did they become fixed and written. The Dead Sea Scrolls describe in detail the practice of the sect to have someone expounding regularly the teaching of the Scriptures in an unrehearsed manner. Parables were shaped upon the scaffold of artistry, *technē*, long before they became a literary genre to investigate.[27]

The etymology of the word *mashal* in Hebrew has two distinct sets of meaning: "to rule" and "to resemble." In Hebrew, to "tell tales" (למשול משלים), means definitely both to "rule," and to "illustrate," "liken," and "propound."[28] This double connotation must have doubtlessly frustrated the translators and later must have caused great interpretational complications and confusion among the Church fathers as well as the early scholars of synoptic gospels who had to read the texts already translated into Greek and interpret the word *parabolē* (obviously different from the Hebrew word *mashal* but with an equally complex connotation).

Early parabolic narratives were highly stylized and had a stereotypical format.[29] The classic parables, also called *meshalim*, had, commonly, two distinct parts following a short introductory formula: a story proper, and a moral lesson. The story proper in a rabbinic text is called in Hebrew a *mashal*, and the moral lesson is called the *nimshal*. In Hebrew, both words are derived from the same root *M.S.L.* and offer a graceful, categorial, and phonological unity. It must be noted that the English translation of these two words (the Greek version as well) fails to capture the elegance and the linguistic range that they capture in Hebrew by representing different aspectual forms of the same grammatical categories.

EARLY PARABOLIC DISCOURSE

Modern discourse analysts have, for a long time, concentrated their creative energies solely on the study of gospel parables, which date back to the first century C.E. and are attributed to Jesus. Yet, interestingly, parabolic discourse not different from the one in the synoptic narratives may be traced back to the Hebrew Scriptures. Tucked away among the verses of sacred literature, are early biblical parables[30] and some excellent early rabbinic parabolic narratives that quietly preexisted the synoptic gospels.[31]

With the destruction of the First Temple (586 B.C.E.) and then the Second Temple (70 C.E.), profound historic and ideological crises befell the Jewish people. Jews found themselves frequently cast out of the land but, even more tragically, they felt as though the "divine presence" had departed from Jerusalem.[32] The fulfillment of the *mitzvot* (commandments) became in many instances forbidden, or made very difficult, and worship in the Temple had ceased. Despite these hardships, most of the nation remained faithful to its religion and was frequently ready to rebel, or undergo martyrdom.

The continuous occupation by various conquerors and the distrust of those ruthless conquerors (the Romans in particular), necessitated a kind of language that could hide both the ancestral knowledge and the ancestral practice, while still allowing the people to learn about them (for example, the *amidah*, or silent meditation, signals to us the existence of coded speech and behavior).[33]

Early Jewish parables reflect the religious heritage, culture, language, and social concerns of the Jewish people during the Second Temple period. These ancient Jewish parables must have been used in public sermons on Sabbaths or festivals, and only later regularized and written down. Like the Greek *ainos*, a literary genre that includes fables like those by Aesop and several Odyssean stories, a number of *Midrashic meshalim* contain anthropomorphisms and were being told to forewarn the addressee of the real danger of certain actions, such as rebelling and protesting against the oppressors. Some parables have a certain pattern of association with lower orders.[34]

As Fishbane correctly asserts, exegesis and parable arise out of a practical crisis of some sort—the incomprehensibility of a word or a rule or the failure of the covenantal tradition to engage its audience, and parables, like annotations, allusions, and other synthetical reasoning, come to engage further the audience. A rich legacy of graspable parabolic symbols was available to the addressee who could select them freely when needed.[35]

Given the characteristic changes experienced in oral transmission, as well as a typical loss of material due to historical, sociopolitical, or even biological factors, some of the very early parables are lacking segments of the moral lesson, or the introductory formulaic structures, or both, a phenomenon quite prevalent in the evolution of an oral literary form.[36]

With the fall of Jerusalem (the land, the Temple and the king gone), when the only contact with the holy left for Israel was *the divine word*, the people yearned to reconcile themselves with the God whose word they had continuously violated. Repentance was conceived of now as compliance with YHWH's commands. Israel's religious self-confidence having been shattered, it was as if they could reestablish their relationship with God upon *the written word*.

This fear may also explain the sudden feverish compilation and canonization of sacred literature. One after the other, the Torah, the Prophets, and other sacred writings underwent canonization. For example, the Pentateuch was canonized during the Babylonian exile. Upon their return to the land, a group of scholars headed by Ezra brought to Jerusalem a new progressive attitude.[37]

During the Golden Age of Israel's creativity in pre-exilic times, the religion of Israel exerted no influence on its surroundings. Later, in the Second Temple, however, in its own fervor to find "grace," Judaism actually agitated the gentile world. Hence, its influence gradually spread, until by Hellenistic times there were myriads of converts and "God fearing" among the nations, as Kaufman calls them, and an ideological battle raged between Judaism and paganism.[38]

The Jews took up the task of eradicating idolatry from the world. After considerable struggle, proselytism evolved in Judaism religious. The belief in resurrection, in judgment, and divine retribution in the afterlife gradually came into being. Jews began to speak with passion of "the world to come" as the world of truth and oppose it to "this world." Jeremiah's words reflect this budding idea of a better man for a better world. According to the Scriptures, Jeremiah said there that the redeeming act of God waits upon man's initiative, man must first choose God.[39]

The split between those who conformed to this belief and chose God and those who did not is accurately depicted in various scriptural texts. The most poignant examples of synoptic text seem to be the parables related to Jesus's christological teachings, where he insists that one must choose God at every moment.

Jesus' preaching and his parabolic teachings of the vision of the New Covenant can be easily understood in this context. His parables, though thoroughly transformed and elaborated by the Early Church, can still be easily dated and related to the issue of choice of divinity and etched as part of the ancient Judaic practices of that time, which are reflected in other rabbinic texts as well.[40] Indeed, while a precise dating of these ancient Jewish parables seems almost impossible,[41] as narratives, they show a vitality and a sophistication that is hard to ignore, and an affinity to synoptic speech that is impossible to disregard.

Even a quick glance at an early parable reveals an architectonic very similar to those attributed to Jesus, with a few irregularities.[42] These parables do not have a scriptural verse as their ending, nor serve a specific exegetical function, the way the later rabbinic parables do. At the same time, one cannot help noticing that these narratives are of similar literary excellence and beauty. Below is an poignant example of how the Rabbis clothed the divine refusal to Moses's plea to enter the Promised Land in the form of a pastoral parable:

> The Holy One, blessed be He, said unto Moses: How canst thou desire to enter the land? This might be likened unto a shepherd going out to tend the royal sheep. The sheep were taken captive. When the shepherd thereafter sought to gain admittance to the royal palace the king said unto him, "If thou enter now will not the people [seeing thee unconcerned] say that thou art to blame for the capture of the sheep?" Even so was it here. The Holy One, blessed be He, said unto Moses: It is to thy praise that thou broughtest out 600,000 of them, but now that thou didst bury them in the wilderness and art bringing in another generation it will be said that the generation of the wilderness has no portion in the world to come [hence thou didst leave them behind]. Remain therefore at their side and enter with them, as it is written, "There a portion [i.e., a grave] was reserved for the Lawgiver that he might come of the Lord."[43] Hence Scripture says "Ye shall not bring *this* congregation into the land,"[44] but the congregation [sc. resurrected] that came out with thee from Egypt.[45]

Analyzing the linguistic characteristics mentioned above and the structural idiosyncracies of early parables such as this one may help us, in the future, to date with more precision the early rabbinic parables and to reclaim a parabolic tradition, which clearly has preceded and may have parented the acclaimed synoptic Gospels.

SYMBOLICITY

Parables are told to represent reality also "symbolically"; therefore, in order to proceed with our analysis, we wish to review for our reader the notion of symbol. In his classical essay entitled "On Symbols," Umberto Eco argues convincingly against the Peircean classical definition. To say that a symbol is "something" that represents "something else" by virtue of an anagogical correspondence or a continued system of terms, each of which represents an element of another system is, according the Eco, at best a very vague explanation for what a symbol is.[46] A symbol, claims Eco, must be seen primarily as a textual modality, because it is first and foremost produced textually. In other words, to Eco, a symbol is above all a (textual) replica. To the extent to which parables "symbolize," or represent an event "symbolically," it follows that parables too are mere textual replicas, or "textual strategies," and their symbolicity must be taken into account.

RHETORICAL ART AND PARABOLIC DISCOURSE

Parables are, above all, a fine rhetorical artifact. That a particular parable means something specific to someone is largely the work of auto-reflexivity. That is to say that the meaning of a parable is essentially the by-product of that parable's internal cohesion, and its cohesion, one should not forget, is the veiled artifact of a skilled craftsman of parables. In fact, parables, most vividly the *Midrashic* ones, assume that the reader/addressee/listener knows *a priori* the literal text as well as the metatext upon which the parabolist builds the parabolic system of tropes with its intricate system of transformations.

The parable's movement of displacement from one time-space frame to another generates an isotopic (analogical) world into which it implodes, and syphons in as it were, the addressee and keeps him occupied with complex processes of decoding. The parabolic movement is either a circular movement that eventually brings its addressee back to the parable's starting text, or it regresses into itself, and thus, as is the case in modern parables, it "absorbs" the reader (see analysis of the Parable of the City of Tamara). In both cases, the addressee enters a uniquely complex activity of interpreting.

The receiver of a parable is taken from one point to another and from one narrational segment to another in a chain of textual substitutions with the false understanding that all the segments are logically derived from one another. In reality, the propulsory force in the decoding "game," where a parabolist explains a text by offering a parable, is the receiver's own desire. And the syntax of that desire manifested in language as moving energy is made visible at the level of discourse.[47]

Parabolic narratives as adroit linguistic artifacts can be better understood in the light of Aristotle's views about rhetoric as an art. In *The Art of Rhetoric*, Aristotle claims that orators or, in this case the propounders of parables, usually persuade not by laying down their 'Art,' (τέχνη), literally 'tricks' or impersonations of rhetoricians, but by establishing "the true, or apparently true" from the means of persuasion applicable to each individual subject. Aristotle goes on to say that as a persuasive art, in the sense of craft, "Rhetoric assumes" (literally "slips into the garb of") the character of Politics, with all its implications.

All orators produce belief, Aristotle further claims, by employing "as proofs," examples (*enthymemes*) and "nothing else." Orators persuade, asserts Aristotle, because that which is persuasive "appears to be proved" by propositions that "are convincing."[48] In this respect, parabolic discourse belongs to the 'art' of rhetoric *par excellence*. We suggest that parables are the place where the competence of the pupil and that of the master is being construed. Indeed, parables convince only after the shrewd parabolist convinces, namely, after he brings in the examples that sway and seduce the addressee. In the parables attributed to Jesus, for example, quite clearly the seduction takes place only after the parabolist has evidenced in his persuasive speech his moral character in order to charm the addressee.

One can go one step further and claim, as Nietzsche does, that there is no non-rhetorical language. The concept of "truth," Nietzsche tells us, is "a mobile army of metaphors, metonymies, anthropomorphisms. Truths are illusions of which one has forgotten that they *are* illusions."[49] Eugenio Donato also reminds us that:

> Telle est la loi de la représentation ou de la représentation ici plus que jamais sont indissociable: s'y représent ce qui ne se présente pas et ne peut pas se présenter c'est à dire s'y représente ce qui s'est toujours déjà représenté.[50]

As rhetorical devices, parables produce desire in both the addressor and the addressee who become willing to continue their condition, namely to go on decoding parables. They instill in the addressee a genuine passion for the game of finding out their "truth" and put him in a state of desire. The addressee is seduced by the parabolist and his parabolic game of simulation in which there are no answers, only a rhetoric return to an "original text."[51] To Derrida, who forcefully assaulted our notion of origins, this is of utmost significance. "In the difference between the original and the second tablets[52] and the repetition . . . our own acts are secondary and exegetical," he claims. "Yet, this negativity in God, is our freedom, our transcendence and the verb which cannot find its originary purity except in the possibility of the Question."[53]

We suggest that the passion aroused in the seduced addressee in the process of parabolizing causes him to believe the truth of the parable, that is in actuality construed *in* the parable, and to perform *as* a believer. To that extent, the parabolic narrative creates the conditions of possibility of its circulation as a system of signs and as value.[54] That is to say, as a system of signs, a parable has the power to duplicate itself, to repeat itself, essentially become a "topos" without a center. At the same time, a parable "helps the addressor in his quest to escape the closure of the 'identical.'"[55]

In erasing the distance between the original text (the emitted narrative) and its own interpretation, parabolic discourse puts into question the entire apparatus upon which the discourse of knowledge is founded, namely the operation of immediate intuitive understanding with its internal lack (*prima facie*, the parable makes no sense) and the reactivation of the process in the shape of individual speech (the introductory question in rabbinic parables: "Why do we say that . . . ?").[56]

THEMATICS

Parables have very distinct thematics. Many of the themes present in parables reflect the intention of the particular parabolist to move, or to sway the addressee in a particular way, by focusing on a complaint (blame), apologia, or consolation (praise, eulogy), usually presented in a polemic context. A parable may be told to exonerate man before man, and man before God, or to exculpate God before man. An accusatory parable is written for the same purpose. "The Prince and His Nursemaids" can be interpreted as blaming Israel for not being close to the Torah:

> A parable, to what may the matter be compared? To a king who had a young son. He entrusted him to two nursemaids. One occupied herself with harlotry and the other with witchcraft. The king commanded them to give his son milk but not to teach him their ways. Thus the Holy One blessed be He warned Israel concerning the Egyptians and the Canaanites, "Do not learn from their ways," and He said, "Train up a child in the way he should go, and when he is old he will not depart from it."[57]

In this early parable, the first nursemaid is identified with the Egyptians and the second with the idolatrous Canaanites. One can read this parable as a disguised blaming of the people of Israel for having failed to observe the Torah and its precepts.[58]

Parabolizers craftily take into account the addressees' responses to their parables when construing them. Flexible rhetorico-poetical devices, their parables are made to mean different things to different readers. The parables are being "tailored" for a particular occasion by syncretizing (combining) many different disparate texts to produce the same effects. In this fashion, parables tell obliquely about underground ideologies or rituals, communicate secrets, dangerous opinions, are instruments of praise, blame, or reproof, apology, or eulogy.[59]

For example, in the desire to demonstrate that two particular verses in the Scriptures should indeed be placed together, Rabbi Akkiva composed the following blame parable and syncretized two completely disparate images, that of the daughter of the priest, and the centurion. The parables, "The Centurion Who Became a Deserter" reads:

Here is a parable. To what may it be compared? Unto a centurion who had served his term but failed to enter his primipilate (to which he would have been promoted in due time), and fled. The king commanded that the head of the deserter be cut off. Before the execution, the king said: "Fill a vessel with golden denarii and carry it before him, and say unto him: "If you had behaved like your colleagues, you would have received the vessel of golden denarii, and [preserved] your soul, but now, you have lost both your soul and your money!"

So also with the daughter of a priest who has played the harlot; the high-priest goes in front of her and says to her, "If you had behaved in the way which your mothers had behaved, you may have been found worthy to become the ancestress of a high priest in like manner [like me]." But now you have lost both yourself and your honor!"

Thus these two sections, "And the daughter of any priest . . ." (Leviticus 21:9) and "The priest who is chief among his brethren . . ." (Leviticus 21:10), are brought together.[60]

God and Man

"The Parable of the King's Banquet," attributed to the famous Rabbi Johanan ben Zakkai, thematizes the king and the kingdom:

Rabbi Johanan ben Zakkai said: This may be compared to a king who summoned his servants to a banquet without appointing a time. The wise ones adorned themselves and sat at the door of the palace, ["for,"] said they, "is anything lacking in a royal palace?" The fools went about their work, saying, "can there be a banquet without preparation?" Suddenly the king desired [the presence of] servants: the wise entered adorned, while the fools entered soiled. The king rejoiced at the wise but was angry with the fools. "Those who adorned themselves for the banquet," ordered he, "let them sit eat and drink. But those who did not adorn themselves for the banquet, let them stand and watch."[61]

The theme of the king and his kingdom can be found in numerous rabbinic parabolic texts and prevails in the Gospels as well. This theme, like many other popular themes in the Scriptures, is taken up later by medieval and premodern mystics and chassids (a new context and for different purposes). We use the concept of theme in Beardsley's sense, namely, as an idea relatable to the real world that can be extrapolated from a narrative.[62] This notion of theme is different from the notion of *sjužet* of a tale mentioned by the renowned Russian formalist Juri Lottman or the notion of *sjužet* investigated by Vladimir Propp in *The Morphology of the Folktale*.[63]

To illustrate a theme's function, we probe the parable attributed to Rabbi Johanan ben Zakkai that problematizes the relation between God and man. This parable indicates to the addressee the proper behavior man has to display vis-à-vis his God, and the proper preparations he should make in this life, in order to rejoice and encounter the divine in the world to come. Like dozens of other parabolic narratives with the same theme, this parable brings to the foreground the notion of an everlasting bond between God and his people.

The parable thematizes man's proper demeanor vis-à-vis the Lord and helps the addressee learn how to conduct himself correctly in this world. In this fashion, it empowers its addressee and guides him in his preparation (and in his quest) for the world to come, which appealingly and significantly is called in Hebrew עולם אמת, the world of truth. Finally, this parable thematizes the everlasting existence of God and of the world to come, which *is* the world of truth, and in essence reveals to man the wisdom in dealing with the Lord, even though it does it obliquely.

The World to Come

Scriptural texts tell very accurately about the circumstances in which each parable was told, thus greatly facilitating our task of establishing intertextual connections and disguised narrational correspondences. In the following example, we learn in the pre-parabolic text that the following parable was told by R. Johanan ben Zakkai on his deathbed. "The Parable of the Crossroads" has as its theme his predicament at the moment of his death:

> Then Rabbi ben Zakkai said: What is [my] situation like? It is like a man who was traveling all day on a highway. Towards dusk he reaches a crossroads, with one road leading to a settlement, the other to the wilderness, but he did not know which road to take.
>
> So with me אני כך: All my life I have traveled upon one road, and now I stand at a crossroads: One road leads to life in the world to come, the other to shame and everlasting contempt, and I know not where they are leading me—whether to life in the world to come, or to shame and everlasting abhorrence.[64]

The parable holds first a complaint by the learned rabbi who, at the end of his journey in this world, finds himself at crossroads and does not know how to decide in order to take "the right turn." But the parabolist also *praises* the rabbi at a deeper narrative level. He focuses his attention on the honesty and sincerity of the noble sage who is not afraid to be remembered by his pupils, as one who is pondering the impenetrable mysteries of the divine even as he dies. Lastly, the parable is meant *to console* the simple man who eventually finds himself afraid before his own death. By a typical scriptural induction קל וחמר implies the parable, if the great sage R. Johanan ben Zakkai was confounded before his death, how much more perplexed should we simple mortals be.

Such parables were told to provide the reader/addressee with strength at a crucial moment in life, when man senses a most profound alienation, at the moment of his death. The wisdom how to leave this world, how to part with our friends and foes, is possibly as difficult to attain as it is fundamental; therefore it needed to be taught by our great sages.

The editor who included the parable of Rabbi Johanan Ben Zakkai in the volume of *Semachot* wished to teach his addressee that, to a certain extent, we remain blind and lame in the King's garden and are required to learn how to transcend our inadequacies even on our last day in this world.[65]

In the congenial shade of this note we should mention that the same themes and rhetoric can be found in the parables of "the Kingdom," attributed to Jesus. Even a cursory reading of "The Parable of The Lamp and the Lampstand" (Matthew 5:14–16), "The Reed and the Wind" (Matthew 13:1–9; Luke 8:4–8), "The Parable of the Wicked Husbandmen" (Matthew 21:33–46; Mark 12:1–12; Luke 20:9–19), establishes multiple affinities with the rabbinic parables.

Of This World

We recognize in the parable of R. Johanan ben Zakkai a masterly narrative construct and a style altogether similar with "The Parable of The Great Supper" (Matthew 22:1–14, Luke 14:15–24), or "The Parable of the Sower" (Matthew 13:1–9, Mark 4:1–9 Luke 8:4–8) and other brilliantly construed parables attributed to Jesus.

"The Parable of the Sower" in the Gospel of Matthew brings to the foreground the theme of the proper posture when receiving wisdom. The parable belongs to the rhetorical mode of praise and blame, and speaks at the same time to different types of addressees. When Jesus is asked what the parable means (in the post-parabolic text, Matthew 13:53–54), he gives a perplexing answer: "After the parables which he spoke to the people which *only the apostles understood* [my emphasis]. . . ." In the Epistle of Barnabas XVII, 2, Jesus says, "of things present and things to come . . . you will not understand because they are hid in parables."

Yet, Jesus, like the other ancient rabbis who propounded parables, begins immediately to explain what he means by his comments, and to our mind, theorizes about parabolic discourse. First Jesus tells that "to those outside everything is parable," and "they may indeed see but not perceive, and may indeed hear but not understand."[66] This statement would seem strange and confounding had Jesus not proceeded immediately to explicate the parables in detail after the parabolic statement, and interpret thoroughly their meaning. We tend to agree with David Stern who contends that Jesus' claim that parabolic speech is "not-understood" was only a rhetoric ploy enabling him to distinguish his disciples from the non-disciples.[67] Jesus pretended and simulated to show lack of understanding by the "others." This modality of speech has been recognized in Semiotics and interpretative semantics as a clever elocutionary device and was termed *faire-croire*, or "make believe." A common logical-linguistic modality, "make-believe" is an important aspect of language use in the process of modalization of discourse.[68] The text of "The Parable of the Sower" reads:

> That very same day Jesus went out of the house and sat beside the sea. And great crowds gathered about him, so that he got into a boat and sat there; and the crowd stood on the beach. And he told them many things in parables saying: "A sower went out to sow. And as he sowed, some seeds fell along the path, and the birds came and devoured them. Other seeds fell on rocky ground, where they had not much soil, and had no depth of soil, and immediately they sprang up, since they had no depth of soil, but when the sun rose they were scorched; since they had no root they withered away. Other seeds fell upon thorns, and the thorn grew up and choked them. Other seeds fell on good soil and brought forth grain, some a hundred fold, some sixty, some thirty.
> He who hears let him hear.[69]

This parable thematizes yet another kind of wisdom. It deals with the proper way to acquire it and use it *after* it has been imparted to us. Jesus, our synoptic parabolist, teaches that it is not sufficient to "sow," namely to disseminate knowledge. That "the sower" went out and "sowed," does not mean yet that those seeds will "bear fruit," namely that wisdom will be acquired and that action will be taken by the addressee. In this light, getting wisdom requires the addressee's own assertion and energetic intervention by an explicit action. Moreover, wisdom has to be spread on fitting, "good soil" for it "to take root," a "solid root," declares Jesus.

The scriptural verse that organizes the texture of this parable, "He who hears let him hear," is told in order to intensify the double meaning sustained by the narrative, but also to bring support and authority to it. The listener is invited not to be a mere listener; he is called upon to be a "proper hearer" of the parable and taught to discern between parabolic texts and their divine metatexts. The addressee is asked to learn to "hear," namely understand and discern this parabolist's wisdom from that of others, that is to say "hear" Jesus's teaching as a very special kind of teaching: christocentric and eschatological, addressed to a particular listener who should become a disciple and a convert.

PARABOLIC TEXT AND CONTEXT

Parables commonly do not stand alone the way folktales do and parabolists, like other storytellers, had to access very quickly a preexisting pool of information.[70] Parables, therefore, were told or written in a special ideologico-political context and knowing the context and the metatext for a particular parable facilitated considerably the task of the interpreter.[71] It must be said, however, that being too intimate with a context caused the interpreter to have tunnel vision, and his interpretations seemed narrowed at times by his own ideology.

In looking over the text of "The Parable of the Spoiled Son" we distinguish a particular context that inscribes narrationally the events before the beginning of the parable. The introductory story deals with the reasons why Amalek could have been permitted by God to attack Israel, his chosen people. In this case, a *proem*,[72] the introductory part of a homily, sets the scene for the parable, which is attributed to a certain rabbi. The introductory formulaic structure found customarily in rabbinic parables follows immediately: "What may this [X] be compared to?" In addition to this introductory formula, one may see elsewhere the simpler structure: "What does it resemble?" (למה דומה הדבר)

The proto-morphic, the original morphemic particle, *it* (*zeh*, זה), or the *thing* (*hadavar*, הדבר) are made to be co-referential with a sentential or morphemic element in the introductory story. In prototypical early parable, next follows the story proper, also called the *mashal*, which is connected structurally to the second part by a morpheme. The [morpheme] particle *thus*, *therefore* (*lekhen*, כך) and other rhetoric-morphemic variants of the above introduce the second part of the parable, or what we usually call in Hebrew *the nimshal*, or the moral lesson.

Special attention needs to be given to the *nimshal*. We must deal with its primacy and its actuality, because parables use rhetoric to generate a connective chain of appearances. The cycle of rhetorical *faire-croire* (make believe) follows a well-known pattern. First, the story proper appears to create the moral lesson. In turn, the moral lesson becomes its proof, and both the story and the moral lesson become the vehicle of veridiction (being accepted as true) of yet another text, which, when veridified, or established as true, becomes the "voice of authority." It is easy to see how the addressor of parables as artist and manipulator generates "a truth" and "an authority" that is, in fact, the truth and the authority of the parable. In the connection established by the use of the morpheme "therefore," an entire rhetorical chain is put in function by the parabolizer and made to work.[73]

A typical rabbinic or Gospel parable concluded with a verse from the Bible, which interestingly, functioned both as the prooftext and the climactic point/reason for which the parable was told. That is to say that when a particular scriptural verse needed to be drilled into the listeners' psyche, it caused usually the invention of a parable which could teach it to them better and more swiftly.[74] For the interpretation of Jeremiah 23:7–8, for example, "The Traveler and the Perils" was elicited:

> R. Simeon bar Yochai says: One can illustrate it by a parable. To what can it be compared? to the following: One was traveling along the road. He encountered a wolf and was saved from him. So he kept telling the story of the wolf. Then he encountered a lion and was saved from him. So he forgot the story of the wolf and kept on telling the story of the lion. He then encountered a serpent and was saved from him. So he forgot the story of the lion and kept telling the story of the serpent.
>
> So it is with Israel. Later troubles cause the former to be forgotten.[75]

As one quickly learns here that the reason for telling this parable is to talk about the redemption of Israel, and that the parable was occasioned by a sermon in which the ancient sage wanted to illustrate the biblical verse actually quoted in the narrative:

> "Therefore, behold, the days are coming, says the Lord, when men shall no longer say, 'As the Lord lives who brought up the people of Israel out of the land of Egypt,' but 'As the Lord lives who brought up and led the descendants out of the house of Israel out of the north country and out of all the countries where he has driven them.' Then they shall dwell in their own land." (Jeremiah 23:7–8)

MODERN CRITICISM AND PARABOLIC DISCOURSE

Parables that come to us from antiquity display what Hartman has called "a macaronic" intermeshing of texts, namely, a robust intertextuality.[76] Indeed, it would be hard to conceive of what a parable would mean without the entire tradition to which it was harnessed and of which it speaks parabolically. Like the "blind" and the "lame" of the parable, interpreters could never get "to the fruit of the king's orchard," had the sweet fruit of wisdom in these narratives been decontextualized.

To get a better understanding of parabolicity one indeed has to look back and learn how and why these narratives intertwined and generated this parabolic productive chain. As Brad Young asserts, we need to do a comparative study, even though "the synoptic gospels more than other texts provide the opportunity for studying how the homiletical parable which was taken from the spontaneous animated teaching of Jesus was turned into the literary parable."[77]

We suggest that rabbinic parables were also used to understand how Jesus spoke to his contemporaries because they provided insights into the Jewish customs and culture and contained similar themes and motifs. We hope that by insisting on the change in the mode of propounding, the transitions from an oral to a written discourse, and by investigating parables up to modern days we may throw further light on parabolic discourse as a whole.

Even though it is difficult to associate now parables with "pop" literature, *midrashic* parables seem to have been very popular and perhaps the scribes and the editors did not see them as sufficiently "philosophical," or a "high enough" literature to write them down separately.[78] To our mind, these are precisely the reasons for which we do not find collections of parables per se. Unfortunately, many of the rabbinic *meshalim*, compositionally and thematically similar to those attributed to Jesus, were propounded orally by rabbis long before the destruction of the Second Temple, but were written down together with other scriptural material only during the second or third century C.E.

While in their *midrashic* guise parables remained governed by a special kind of metonymic displacement (in relation to an omniscient, divine law), we must remember that these narratives have always been syncretized texts, namely, have been artistically put together from disparate narratives brought together for persuasion purposes. To put it in current terminology, parabolic discourse has always been "polysemic" (many meanings) and "polyphonic" (many voices), two features that ought to have made it appealing to contemporary theorists.

Yet, unhappily, parables have not succeeded in captivating literary theorists until recent decades. With the exception of biblical exegetes, few modern critics have ventured into the ocean of rabbinic literature, partly because of lack of knowledge of the sources and partly because other types of discourses have captured their imagination. As a result, the great challenge posited to Western logocentrism by *midrashic* textual strategies was not understood until lately. Only in the mid-eighties, in analyzing open texts, did scholars like Geoffrey Hartman, Daniel Boyarin, and David Stern argue convincingly that *Midrash*, unlike other textual strategies, resists closure.[79] Unlike postmodern indeterminacy, Midrash is predicated upon the existence of a point of view from which to behold the empirical world and the flux of time; it is predicated upon the existence of an omniscient, merciful, and eternally present God. "Because of this feature, *Midrash* is one method that can destabilize all actuality but itself, one language to govern understanding. Most importantly, by presupposing the existence of God, in *Midrash* all contradictory interpretations can coexist"; all interpretations remain governed by the divine language that is also their veridiction. "In *Midrash*, without producing incoherence," writes Hartman, "the mode of existence of the text and the mode of representation, of mimesis, have fused beyond alteration, though not, of course, beyond analysis."[80] The exclusive attention given in continental literary criticism to synoptic Gospels until recently may have contributed seriously to the marginalizing of this interesting even if recalcitrant genre.[81] Beyond that, the fastidious but exclusive concern of extant literary criticism with the interpretation of synoptic narratives, or rabbinic parables alone, hindered not only the study of parables as a unique type of literary discourse, "this isolationist perspective" delayed our understanding of the limitations of literary criticism.

FABLES, SYMBOLS, ALLEGORIES, AND PARABOLIC DISCOURSE

Quite frequently, parables have been matched with fables and allegories for the purpose of description or interpretation.[82] Special caution needs to be taken, however, in establishing the differences and the similarities between symbol, allegory, fable, and parables since they are closely related.

Parables mostly resemble fables structurally. Both use tropological language, allusions, even anthropomorphisms, and both have a pedagogical dimension. Parables and symbols have in common a discursive gap between the disclosed and the undisclosed, the explicit and the implied, and are essentially auto-referential. Allegories and parables are both allusive and use indirect means to make a point. Like allegorical narratives, parables do away with the dogmatic search for "an originary truth." Williams successfully shows that, in Egypt, already in the Twentieth Dynasty (1200–1085 B.C.E.) there is evidence of fable-like structures.[83] According to Williams, La Fontaine, the French fabulist, already theorizes about fables in one of his own fables:

> Les fables ne sont pas ce qu'elles semblent être;
> Le plus simple animal nous y tines lieu de maître.
> Une morale nue apporte de l'ennui;
> Le contre fait passer le précepte avec lui.[84]

Fables "are not what they appear to be," insightfully claims La Fontaine, and "a naked moral will bring inconveniences, but a story will make the moral lesson pass."

Together with similarities, there are also many differences between parables and the other types of discourse. As a distinct narrative category, parables are made up of hermeneutic clusters, or segments, all of which demand immediate interpretation from their addressee, with no real "out-there." To read a parable means for the addressee necessarily to enter the interpretational mode. Each new cycle of clarifications brings additional interpretable information to the addressee, and new information means further interpretation: a kind of helical structure, drilling itself deeply into the text of the Scriptures, the *mater*-text, which the parable comes to illustrate, elaborate, or clarify.

Early parabolic narratives recounted the ubiquity of God, while postmodern parables bemoan God's absolute absence. Yet, both modern and ancient parables interweave polyphony, the many voices embedded in the text, with polysemy, the many possible meanings, and posit an idealized[85] internal interpreter, or what has been customarily called in Reader's Response theory "the narratee," "the imploded reader," or "the interpetant." The ideal addressee is presupposed to know well the metatext of the parable, and be capable of apprehending all the hints given in order to decode a given parable, or a parabolic tale.[86]

Unlike fables, parables suggest a set of parallels between an imagined fictional event and an "immediate real" situation with which both their addressor and addressee must contend. Given the religious and cultural vicissitudes suffered by the Jews and their perennial persecution by hostile authorities, Jewish parabolists offered a helping hand in the struggle for survival by teaching through parables.[87]

In sharp contrast with fables, which also teach (*fabula docet*) but allude to a "real-out-there," even if only in an oblique manner, parables are *only* a special teaching aid, an artifact to clarify or illustrate a point. Parables make use of ready motifs from a preexisting pool of fixed themes, and are the pure concatenations of a parabolizer. Because of this feature, parables have been always difficult to interpret, and presently have become enigmatic. Parables use anthropomorphisms quite infrequently, and when anthropomorphisms are used, they are not being used in the same manner as in fables.[88] Finally, as opposed to fables, parables are commonly embedded in a larger text. Only of late, are parables being clustered in collections of parables and appreciated for their aesthetic value.[89]

Allegory—and parabolic discourse is allegorical as well—has the relationships among its images determined by the "real life events, out there"—in other words, the metastory to which an allegory points exists in the real world. Any lack of coherence detected sometimes in the narrative is ironed away by "what-happened-in-the-outside-world."[90] To put it slightly differently, allegory demands the addressee to be initiated about the real life events to which it alludes. In the case of parable, however, the narrative may contain references to historical events and religious rituals that exist in real life, but its addressee must *primarily* make the connection intratextually and understand the relationship between various narrational sequences of the parable itself, in order to derive any significant message from it.[91] The essential criterion by which a parable is distinguished from an allegory is not, at least primarily, that parables have one central point, but that unlike allegory, their many elements relate first and foremost to each other *within* the spatiotemporality of the parabolic narrative.[92] The reason for the implosive quality of parables, the main trait that distinguishes them from fables (as well as other types of allegorical narratives), is the way in which parables are pieced together by the individual parabolist and not their connection with an outside reality. The use of age-old allegorical techniques permitted parables to continually change and acquire new significance.

Parabolic discourse has a particular kind of referentiality, which is different from fables and allegories; it is auto-referential (does not transfer from textual metaphor to life).[93] The moral lesson *is* the life, the "real" domain of that parabolic narrative. This is to say that in parables the interconnections exist solely as the aesthetic aggregations of an individual, the result of imaginative syncretic interfacing by a particular parabolist in a particular, creative mode. To be sure, the parabolic sign, as the allegorical, necessarily refers to another sign that precedes it, and, as Paul deMan so poignantly asserted, has renounced the "nostalgia" and the desire to coincide with a postulated origin, as is the case with the symbol.

In the world of the symbol it would still be possible for the *image* to coincide with the *substance*, since the substance and its representation do not differ in their being but only in their extension: they are part and parcel of the same set of categories. "The relationship between the image of substance and substance is one of simultaneity, which is spatial in kind and in which the intervention of time is merely a matter of contingency." In the world of allegory and parable, on the other hand, time is the originary constitutive category and the allegorical sign necessarily refers to the sign that precedes it. In parables, then, one refers to "another text," which in turn refers to yet another text, in a potentially infinite signifying chain. In essence, there is no "going out." We are being drawn in the parabolic text.[94]

Distinctly from symbols, going "back" to an "original discourse" in parables is possible only metaphorically. That is to say, that the regression to the "source text" is not really possible, nor literally applicable; parables are used only to suggest a resemblance. Because in parables the regression is only metaphorical, the text bursts as it were inwardly, and hints to an original trope, upon which it was predicated. This movement has been called by Derrida "the movement of a metaphor within a metaphor, all belonging to the text of metaphor and of communication."[95] In parables, the internal system of veridiction, with its syntactic and semantic components, is left in charge to tell the addressee whether his or her decoding is accurate or not.

PARABOLIC DISCOURSE AND MEANING

Parables are a coded discourse, thus, a singularly important task is to overcome the "impediment" in the way to understanding what is being told to us only allusively.[96] The reader/addressee/listener is uniquely challenged by the parabolic text to understand what is being implied narrationally and make the necessary connection so that he could proceed to construct on his own a meaning of the parable. Much like Oreste before the Sphinx, the addressee cannot understand the parable without decoding what is implied in the parabolic narrative.

The strength of a parable, and its beauty, lies in the way it seduces the addressee and makes him want to fathom its meaning/s and the way it eroticizes discourse in order to draw the addressee further in the text. To this end, parables construct and deconstruct metaphors, produce and deconstruct tropological language. At the same time, they generate a specific linguistic competence in the addressee and a unique expertise, that of decoding parables and understanding their hidden meaning.

The vigor of a parabolic narrative comes from its inherent polysemy. To impose one single meaning as the sole meaning of a parable is an act of violence to all other possible meanings, asserts Marin.[97] Indeed, parables are construed so that their meaning is never exhausted by its interpretational endeavors. Each time a particular meaning is chosen, *all* other possible meanings are necessarily eliminated and our reading of it limited.

Finally, parabolic discourse creates a hierarchy of proficiency in deriving meaning. The more competent the reader, the more he can understand, the more meanings he can derive. That is to say that parabolic discourse is anagogical, namely, it "transforms" and uplifts the addressee and changes his position vis-à-vis this discourse when he begins to understand its many layers.

PARABLES AND DREAMS

Parables have been likened to dreams, our "chaotic nightly aggregations," which Freud compares with palimpsests.[98] As parables, dreams remind us of an "old and precious communication" only when analyzed, decoded, and understood. Otherwise, they baffle and amaze, as parables do, because of the unexpected piecing together of the dream text in the complex process of dream *censorship, condensation*, and *symbolization*.[99]

In the 1909 edition of the *Traumdeutung*, Freud wrote in a footnote that nowhere in literature has he seen a more accurate description of dreams than the one offered by a Mr. J. Sully in 1893, in an article entitled "The Dream as Revelation" (in English in the original). Freud argues:

> It would seem, then, after all, that dreams are not the utter nonsense they have been said to be by such authorities as Chaucer, Shakespeare and Milton. The chaotic aggregations of our night-fancy have a significance and communicate new knowledge. *Like some letter in cipher, the dream-inscription when scrutinized closely loses its first look of balderdash and takes on the aspect of a serious, intelligible message. Or, to vary the figure slightly, we may say that, like some palimpsest, the dream discloses beneath its worthless surface characters traces of an old and precious communication* [pace Freud's text].[100]

The truths the dreams describe are complex and not fully accessible to consciousness because they undergo processes of transformations and condensation. Like dreams, parables are pieced together from disparate items, are the result of transformations, and possess an internal coherence. Like dreams, parables allude to real events in our daily lives in an oblique, cryptic fashion, and, just as the dreams are the "royal road" to the subconscious,[101] parables are the royal road to their metatext (the Scriptures, or other master texts).

The more divergent the elements encoded in them, the more puzzling the dreams and the parables become. As Lacan has noted, "one can speak of the code only if it is already the code of the Other." In other words, the message received in dreams, or obtained parabolically, always points covertly and "lackingly," to our intersubjective relations.[102]

In the medium of parables, the "lack" is its advantage because it allows for various shades of meaning. The *latent* meaning of the parable is supplied by the lacunae in it, by its "lack." Like dreams, parables always "say that they mean more" hence they lure the reader to reconstitute that which is not said and bridge the "gap" in the text. This lack, or gap in the text refers back to a "primordial lack of a fixed point" (the impossibility for desire to recover the lost object) toward which desire, and consequently the metonymic movement of discourse, is aimed. A dialectic is generated in parables between the injunction to interpret the lack and fill in "the blank" in the text, and the need to keep open a kind of "wound in the text," a reminder of that "other text" (the Torah, in the case of the *midrashic* parables) to which it alludes and which ought to remain always open to further analyses.[103]

Modern parables are closer than their ancient counterparts to the dream device; many modern parables, such as Kafka's, originated in dreams recounted in diaries. The same dreamlike quality can be noticed in parables by Borges, Peretz, Michaux, Agnon, or Gabriel Garcia Mar-quéz. Dostoyevsky's *The Dream of a Ridiculous Man*, Elias Canetti's first part of *Auto-da-Fe*, in *The Sacrifice of the Prisoner*, and Kobo Abe's *The Box Man*, also come to mind.

Revealing the connections between parabolic discourse and dreams may help us further our analysis of parables and of dreams. Many of the psychoanalytic insights about dreams may help us decipher some of the more stubborn parables and, in turn, a clearer understanding of how parables "mean" may help in our investigation of dreams.

PARABOLIC DISCOURSE, PSYCHOANALYSIS, AND SEMIOTICS

The "gap" in the parable (between what is said and what is alluded to and between the obscured and the revealed) is a perpetual invitation to name the signifier, or the thing (itself). This seduction with another text, the "metatext" to which parables allude, manifested on the surface of the narrative, like the neurotic symptom, is the work of an *overdeter-mination* (caused by more than one factor). The symptom and the lure are constituted in parables by a double meaning related to the symbolic representation of a past conflict and a (symbolic) present conflict.

When decoded, this symbolic expression of a doubleness (as in a psychopathology) eventually leads the addressee to make the connection with the metatext to which the parabolic text (or symptom) alludes but which it does not name explicitly. The said and the obscured correspond to gaps in the symbolic order where the voids are as significant as the plena.

Maintaining, in the text, the open gap between the signifier and the signified [the object and its representation], the thing and the like-ness of the thing, God, His Torah, and the commentary about the Torah, constitutes in parables a perpetual invocation of what Lacan calls "the Name-of-the-Father," the authority, which leaves a void at the place of the phallic signification in the "Other."[104] But the motion to reconstitute the gap left by the use of figurative language in para-bles is successively initiated and perennially subverted. This double movement is facilitated further, according to Lacan, by the fact that even when the symbolic identification is represented by a single indi-vidual, the paternal (God, in the Torah) function concentrates in itself both Imaginary and Real relations. This identification is more or less adequate to the symbolic relation that constitutes it. It is in *the Name of the Father*—or in the name of God, from the Torah's point of view—that we must recognize the support of the symbolic function which, from the dawn of history, has identified him/Him with the figure of the Law. To that extent, the signifier is not to be taken "au pied de la lettre, it *is* the letter."[105]

To our mind the parabolic "open wound" constitutes a primordial refusal to foreclose, a refusal to reject the fundamental signifier from the symbolic universe of parables. In this fashion, parables imply continuously the existence of and the appeal to a divine authority and an originary divine text. At the same time, this sustained duality in parables also brings back into focus the lack in the text.

The dreamlike condensation and distortion experienced in each narrative segment in parables, this "deflection" away from "the here and now," also indicates that parabolists attempt to efface the arbitrariness of their textual choices. By gliding over the whimsical nature of their selections, the ancient parabolizers seem very much in tune with modern linguists and semioticians, who expose the basic arbitrariness of linguistic signs and their discontinuous relationships.[106]

The notion of "token" emerges already in Aristotle. He talks about an utterance as a "token" (σύμβολον) or a "sign" (σημεῖον) both of which are the "likeness of things" (πράγματα) and not the things.[107] This *glissement*, or slippage of the signifier over the signified, that is to say, the shift from the thing to a "token of the thing," is not idiosyncratic to parabolic discourse, rather, it is a poignant example of the evolutionary process in language towards signifiers, "the likenesses of things," away from the "things" themselves.

Transitions inside parables are clearly away from the notion of "truth" as resemblance to the great book of nature and toward "notions" of truth *as* the *logos* of language, dependent upon the privileged verb "to be like," which, Michel Foucault tells us, in many of its uses corresponds or refers to nothing at all in nature.[108] Thus, when the ancient parabolizer craftily asks: "To what may 'this' be likened?" and replies "This is like the Kingdom of Heaven," this "likeness" is his textual strategy constructed upon the scaffolding of metaphorical language. Claiming that one thing *is* another, argues Cynthia Ozick, makes possible the transfers from one linguistic domain to another, and in doing so, transforms memory into a principle of continuity.[109]

To that extent, when we are told a parable and are made to believe that we have learned about the Kingdom of Heaven (in the examples above), in actuality, we have learned more about the rules of language and signification; when we believe that we know something about the things themselves, we possess the likenesses and metaphors of things, which do not correspond in the least with the original's essentials. In parables, we equate the equal with the unequal by an omission; "the thing" itself is left inaccessible and indefinable.[110]

PARABOLIC DISCOURSE AND TEACHING

Parabolists must have understood that sophistical teaching is a quicker way to operate modifications in the listener's faith; hence they opted to teach by offering parables. Offering a parable to illustrate, enhance, and vivify religious teaching, or to preach certain beliefs, goes far back in Jewish history. Parabolic speech seems to have been the most fitting mode to heighten the addressee's desire to understand.

As we have seen, the choice offered in parabolic discourse is a ruse, an innovative teaching technique that encourages learning through simulation. Parabolic reasoning disguises an injunction to deduce one parabolic sequence from another by inference, as if parables were valid inductive logical arguments. However, parables engender a logical distortion. This distortion, created by what I call "parabolic predicators" (*therefore, as, this is like, and so*), facilitates the transition from one segment of the parable to another, so that at the end, disparate elements are seen as logically and linguistically related.

Sophistic teaching in parables results thus from the fact that parables do not reveal a truth that exists "out there"; instead, parables proceed to generate a "vérité," a truth, that is their own truth, during the space and time of parabolic discourse. A parable never really answers the parabolic question being asked at the beginning of the narrative, it teaches the addressee only to proceed in the "right direction" (the direction desired by the parabolist) to solve the problems involving man and the divine.

Parabolic discourse generates fictitious analogies by means of parabolic predicators or shifters that indeed "equate the equal with the unequal." In this sense, parables are not truly pragmatic nor truly didactic, but rather play with the pragmatics of didactics through rhetorical moves. Their addressee is put continuously in a paradoxical position: he cannot decode the separate entities—sequential mininarratives—if he does not know the primal coding of the parable, and he does not know the global coding of the parable if he does not understand the encoding of the separate entities.

The parable of R. Elazar (or Eliezer) b. Zadok, a Tannaic rabbi whom scholars place somewhere between the second and the fourth generation, circa 80 to 165 C.E., might be helpful to illustrate these rhetorical maneuvers.[111]

> R. Elazar b. Zadok said: With what may the righteous in this world be compared? To a tree whose trunk stands entirely in a pure place, but its branches extend over to an unclean place. If those branches are cut off, then all the tree is in a pure place. And so God imposes suffering on the righteous in this world that they may inherit the world to come.[112]

The pre-parabolic question that prompted Rabbi Elazar's reply refers to the unfairness of the suffering of righteous people in this world. The shift from the human domain to that of botany and to the metaphor of the "tree and its cut off branches" is made to persuade the inquisitive faithful that just as the tree needs pruning away from the "unclean place" to be in a pure place, so does the righteous man. Rabbi Elazar equates in his parable "pruning" with "the unjust suffering of righteous men."

Yet a scrutiny of this shift discloses that the sage talks of two disparate worlds that follow different kinds of logic. The suffering of a righteous man does not remove the part of him that exists in an unclean place; it leaves him there. The addressee seems to have learned little about trees, righteous men, or suffering from this parable. Clearly, the parabolist aimed at transforming his listener's state of mind and change his position vis-à-vis his chosen text, rather than teach him about the "world out there."

The addressee is being placed in a new emotional state. The passion aroused by the act of questioning parabolically is mirrored vividly in the way the addressee attempts new decodings. A transformation (*passion*) occurs in the master who teaches parables as well. A seductive absorbing of the addressee and the addressor into the parabolic space and time, keeps both the propounder of parables and his listener in a heightened emotional state (impassioned state). The parabolist, as it were, enters a higher sphere of shared knowledge together with his freshly enlightened disciple/addressee/listener. Parables produce change: they uplift the master and the disciple to a higher level of understanding, to a realm where the competence of the master and of the disciple are being construed, a locus of enlightenment.

Wittgenstein has taught us that, "to understand the world and the explicit language" (explicit language is not adequate to undertake this task), "we must climb out of the realm of explicit language and the world and go to non-explicit language."[113] Understandably, parables, a non-explicit language *par excellence*, have been the most favored "other language" of teaching. For centuries they were used as the language necessary to instill desire to know, the special "other language."

If, as Edmond Jabès observed, the ultimate truth is the "void" and our daily awareness that in the end we learn nothing because in the end there is still another question to ask,"[114] parables emblematize the hopelessness of human endeavors by producing their own truth internally. This realization is akin also to Emanuel Levinas' assertion about truth: "Since there is no truth to tell any longer," the great twentieth-century philosopher contends, "one needs to produce one's own truth, not as a final truth, but as a temporary retreat in a book or in a conscience and respond to a human basic temptation which leaves us untarnished, that of knowledge in itself."[115]

What answer can we give to the question "What do parables ultimately teach us?" Even though there is some learning about a historical period, to assume that one learns much about the historical and sociocultural reality of that period from parabolic discourse is evidently a disappointing undertaking. Parabolic teaching is primarily not historical. We can know, for example, about the strong interest in the "feast" and the "protocol of the feast" indicative of that period's preference and preoccupation, but we certainly cannot get a realistic tableau of that society. On the other hand, finding the "key" and "cracking the code" to major images and symbols in parables that belong to various periods may enlighten us about the art of parable propounders during those periods and the craftsmanship they needed to convey knowledge, or lack of knowledge.

We suggest that in a world where the Jewish people were constantly threatened with extinction and cast off their land, the only way they could survive was by adhering stubbornly to the Torah and the Law. Parabolic discourse, with its legions of tropes and rhetoric, seemed uniquely appropriate to teach them the way how. Parables could operate the "transport" of the addressee from the world "out there" to the "other world" (of The Book and the Word), a well organized and properly regulated universe, uniquely capable to insure a nation's survival. To that extent, when Derrida said that the Jews have lived for two thousand years between the pages of a book, he indeed put his finger on the overwhelming significance of the grafting on to the Scriptures and to their interpretation; he recognized that The Book has unequivocally ensured Jewish survival.

PARABOLIC DISCOURSE AND CHANGES IN SEMIOSIS

The destruction of the Second Temple, the focal point of Jewish life, has meant the destruction of the entire semiosis of the ancient Jewish people. With the Roman conquest in particular, their ritualistic practices had to go underground, and the language needed to be encoded by the sages for protection against the oppressive Roman conquerors, who, unlike the Greeks, ruled with an iron fist.

Exiled from their once native land, parables also suffered a linguistic transformation, or a "discursive exile," namely, parables no longer "spoke natively," so they put on an exotic kabbalistic or metaphysical garb. Their "body" changed and the once slender (to indulge further in this metaphor), tight-lipped rabbinic parable becomes a heavy, medieval matron (the notion of *matrona* appears frequently in these texts) who talks of old times, with "an accent."

In the Middle Ages and premodern times, kabbalists (others were using mainly fables) talked of wisdom as already unknowable, and of *plēroma*, the realm of plenitude, reachable only asymptotically, from afar. Understanding a parable becomes thus a sign of "belonging," intended only for those initiated, for the few who know the proper preparation for its reading and reception. The proper preparation and delivery of parables clearly became a part of a complicated but very precise mystical ritual meant to open the doors toward another realm. A grand shift occurs in parabolic discourse, from a "downstairs" literature and praxis enjoyed and understood by the people, to an intellectual exercise of the "upstairs" literati.

For example, he who was not initiated in the doctrine of transmigration of souls and transvaluation, or in the relationship between being/meaning, inner/outer, reality/imagined, would never be able to gain access to it through kabbalistic parabolic discourse. In other words, the outsider always remained an outsider with no possibility to access the inside of that semeiosis. Perhaps, as a result, the moral lesson in parabolic discourse was either eliminated or became simply an appendage to the story proper.[116] Medieval Jewish philosophers, on their part, allegorized parables and used these allegorical narratives mainly to express their radical or obscure, philosophical opinions.[117] For instance, in order to convey his philosophical view that only a philosopher may come close to understanding the divine, Maimonides wrote his famous "Parable of the Palace":

> The ruler is in his palace, and his subjects are partly within the city and partly outside the city. Of those who are within the city, some have turned their backs upon the ruler's habitation, their faces being turned another way. Others seek to reach the ruler's habitation, turn toward it, and desire to enter it and to stand before him, but up to now they have not yet seen the wall of the habitation. Some of those who seek to reach it have come up to the habitation and walk around it searching for its gate. Some of them have entered the gate and walk about in the antechambers. Some of them have entered the inner court of the habitation and have come to be with the king, in one and the same place with him, namely, in the ruler's habitation. But their having come into the inner part of the habitation does not mean that they see the ruler or speak to him. For after their coming into the inner part of the habitation, it is indispensable that they should make another effort; then they will be in the presence of the ruler, see him from afar or from nearby, or hear the ruler's speech or speak to him.[118]

In modern times, parables are symptomatic of man's useless quest for meaning and knowledge, and the hopelessness of such enterprise.

From Agnon, for whom writing parabolically is both honoring the past and a way of invoking the "stable universe of meaning in traditional Judaism,"[119] to Borges, who generated a universal implosion with no destination,[120] to Calvino, who narrativized the incessant retreat of meaning, modern parabolic discourse deconstructs meaning as an ultimate ontological truth and tells us that wisdom is irremediably lost to modern man. Like the chassid, we are left only with the melody,[121] and, like Kafka's man in the parable "Imperial Message," we are left alone "to dream" the message to ourselves.[122]

Because modern parabolic discourse is incomprehensible to us, we shift toward interpreting it at different levels. In so doing, we encounter countless textual clues that, as Jonathan Culler claims, "none seems to encompass everything notable in the semantic universe" and are at the same time in conflict with each other.[123]

Modern parables become progressively elaborate and sophisticated in form as they become undecodable. In modern times, the parabolist laments our incapability of understanding parables, and the fact that we can no longer be taught through parables.[124] Franz Kafka's parable "On Parables" symptomatizes this radical incapability to accede knowledge and wisdom through parables:

> Many complain that the words of the wise are always merely parables and of no use in daily life, which is the only life we have. When the sage says: "Go over," he does not mean that we should cross to some actual place, which we could do anyhow if the labor were worth it; he means some fabulous yonder, something unknown to us, something too that he cannot designate more precisely, and therefore cannot help us here in the least. All these parables really set out to say merely that the incomprehensible is incomprehensible, and we know that already. But the cares we have to struggle with every day: that is a different matter.
>
> Concerning this a man once said: Why such reluctance? If you only followed the parables you yourselves would become parables and with that rid of all your daily cares.
>
> Another said: I bet that is also a parable.
>
> The first said : You have won.
>
> The second said: But unfortunately only in parable.
>
> The first one said: No, in reality; in parable you have lost.

Kafka's parable is a most effective illustration of modern man's anguish, because it expresses in a nutshell the impossibility of gaining knowledge (and wisdom) in modern times.[125] The parable tells the sage: "he really does not mean that we should cross over to an actual place, but to some fabulous yonder." In modern times, the allusions of the wise are incomprehensible and enigmatic to their addressees and the wise never come to interpret for them the meaning of these parables, the way Jesus did, for example. The chasm formed is abysmal. Our modern sages can "designate" that "fabulous yonder" but seem completely incompetent pragmatically, because they "cannot really tell us what they mean." The modern sage cannot perform two important tasks, according to Kafka's parable: "cannot designate more precisely" "the fabulous yonder," and cannot "help us here in the very least with our daily cares," the way the old sage and parabolist used to for their audience in the act of telling and decoding parables. In sum, Kafka's parable tells that parables are no longer useful in our daily life, because they do not help alleviate our struggle; it also tells that parables are no longer comprehensible, and even our wise are incapable of decoding them for us.

The moral lesson, "If you only followed the parables you yourselves would become parables and with that rid of all your daily cares," is also telling. What does the author mean by "becoming ourselves parables"? Are parables now a lesson about the impossibility of knowing?

To turn into a parable means, perhaps, to become the embodiment of a theory about existence. But this entails a loss: the loss of our aspiring "self"; our body turns into an actual "body" of a negative knowledge. It follows that to rid ourselves of the daily cares, namely, "win in real life," we must become a parable. But this in turn means to lose in parable, according to Kafka. In parables, he claims, we do not learn how to rid ourselves of daily cares, that is, our sages "cannot help us here in the very least." The end result is that we also necessarily lose in real life, exactly the opposite of what we had hoped to accomplish. Modern parables trap their addressee in a circular motion where there is no gain except for the realization of an absolute loss. Modern parables stand therefore in stark opposition to kabbalistic parables that taught one how to access the world of plenitude by esoteric gnostic practices.[126] Unlike the Zoharic (mystic) parabolizer, who, in attempting to illuminate a passage from Noah,[127] offers prior to the parable of the King's Special Feast an entire explanation for it,[128] the modern recipient of parables remains unenlightened about their meaning.

Modern parables do not offer wisdom; modern parables offer a circular ride for modern man.[129] The "sage" of Kafka's modern parable "does not really mean" for the addressee to "go over," thus, puts him in "a hermeneutical double bind."[130] This double bind compels the addressee of the parable to become himself a parable for human predicament.

In this sense, modern parable is a sign, a palpable symptom that signals the existence of an underlying pathology in modernity. As Robert Funk correctly assumes, modern parables must be seized as parable, namely as enigmatic. "The final frustration of rationality is to be wrong while being right, to lose while winning."[131] This is precisely the case with "the second man" who wins in Kafka's parable: he wins "unfortunately, only in reality."

That an assertion such as this is even possible, means that our modern addressee can never gain access to what Kafka called "the fabulous yonder." Modern man has lost forever the opportunity to divest himself of his "daily cares." For Kafka, to have won in reality means to have lost, irremediably, the ability to transcend the world of the literal, and to have lost the power to access to the world beyond literality.

In parabolizing, Kafka brings into sharp focus the crisis experienced by modern man, the plight that is vividly portrayed also by Louis Borges, Italo Calvino, Julio Cortázar, Gabriel Garcia Márques, S. Y. Agnon, and other giants of modern literature. Modernity, it seems, has irrevocably barred man's access to that "fabulous yonder" Kafka has yearned for. Modern parabolists, even the magisterially gifted like Kafka, can only decry their quandary in parables. With no way of satisfying their real ambition, modern parabolists concentrate on refining their linguistic deftness to the point of being consumed with "the word." Our representational image might have become the only Law and the ultimate authority to which we have recourse in modernity.

SUMMARY

The parabolic quest is unique because it simulates before the parabolic adventurer an entire epic chain of search and of findings. Parables offer a journey into an isotopic world of reward and discovery. The reward is learning how to decode a unique message and possess a competence in the parabolic game and a method. The discovery is the appalling realization of our fundamental incapability to go back to our linguistic and conceptual origins. Kafka's statement that parables are meant to remain parables, suggests that we always remain torn between the two dimensions of the letter: allegory and literality.

The ancient parabolic effort was a more successful attempt to bridge this gap, because ancient parabolizers and their communities held on to the divine Law as the ubiquitous guarantor of the truth of the parables they propounded. In modern times, like "the way" to Kafka's *Castle* that remained undisclosed while at a stone's throw from where the protagonist was, the gap in text remains unbridgeable, a "painful laceration" in the middle of the text, signifying that the fictive world is divorced from a final meaning in the real world. In Kafka's words, "the incomprehensible remains incomprehensible."

In modernity, "the *aggadah* is without a *halakhah*," that is, the elaborate narrative has no basic underlying law to invest it with the necessary meaning. We can no longer get to our ontological truths, therefore, like the messenger in Kafka's parable, we shout meaningless messages.[132] Eco most appropriately states:

> In modern aesthetic experience the possible contents are suggested by the co-text and by the intertextual tradition: the interpreter knows that he is not discovering an external truth but that, rather, he makes the encyclopedia work at its best. Modern poetic symbolism is a secularized symbolism where languages speak about their possibilities. In any case, behind every strategy of the symbolic mode, be it religious or aesthetic, there is a legitimating theology, even though it is the aesthetic theology of unlimited semiosis or of hermeneutics as deconstruction. A positive way to approach every instance of the symbolic mode would be to ask only: which theology legitimated it?[133]

Like Edmond Jabès' Rabbi Mendel, our sages say to the disciple "We will never know what we are trying to learn. True knowledge is our daily awareness that, in the end, one learns nothing . . . the nothing is also knowledge."[134]

To know in modernity is to know the nature of the void. Lacking the support of the divine myth expressed in the old days with the invocation a verse of the Holy Scriptures, modern parables generate their own fictional grounds by retreating into self-referentiality and self-canceling messages. Instead of bridging the gap between the signifier and the signified, modern parabolic discourse only punctures the natural cumulativity of language and offers as a kind of subterranean, punctual illumination, from the "bottom of Kafka's ravine,"[135] so to speak, the impossibility of perpetual illumination.

PART II

Apples of Gold

CHAPTER 2

Biblical Parables:
The Parable of the
Poor Man's Ewe Lamb

The transparency of the object
is beyond the object, it is its
ordinary fullness.
The transparency of man.
And R. Isaac: "I am listening, son.
And I see through you to the sky."

—Edmond Jabès

Let us get nearer to the fire
So that we can see what we are saying.

—Frenando Po

Why don't our politicians tell us a good parable now, when we are eager to be persuaded? Are they not familiar with the usage of this basic instrument of rhetoric, called art, or technē (τὲχνη) since Aristotle?

To sketch here our preliminary answers, we analyze a representative sample of parables. Our hope is that a scrutiny of texts that have come down to us in a particular form in modern times may help us understand more clearly the mechanism used to decode parables and other coded narratives. The linguistic and metalinguistic cues in parabolic narratives and the contexts in which these narratives appear since ancient times may uncover the process by which we make sense of allusive or tropological speech. Finally, cracking the core of ancient parables may also teach us how we construe meaning in general.

To proceed with our analysis, we use here tools from various disciplines that allow us to enter the microstructure of a narrative and learn more about the art of encoding and decoding texts. By isolating each of the building blocks, or parabolic units, that generate parabolic meaning, imply new connotation, and allude to other texts by means of particular narrative strategies, we reveal a parable's individual architectonics. As a result, we hope to get a better understanding of the nature of parables and their dramatic change over time.[1] At the same time, we hope to learn

41

about the extent to which ancient parables have served as linguistic and semiotic models to modern parabolic discourse. Lastly, in mapping the changes sustained over time by parables, we hope to explain how modern parables epitomize a kind of pathology in modernity and how modern parables express it "parabolically."

In comparing and contrasting old parabolic narratives with modern ones we notice that a serious crisis is manifest in modern parabolic discourse. Modern parables seem to mime and parody the early ones. They seem to imitate an ancient tradition without the power to reproduce it fully either in their new and intricate architectonics or in the way they address modern man. While modern parabolic discourse has acquired a sophisticated, complex form, it seems to lack the functionality and the vitality of ancient parabolic discourse. Semantically, it seems to be lacking as well.

To illustrate this great shift in parabolic discourse, we proceed to analyze below one of the earliest biblical parables.

Concealment and Revelation, Law and Lawlessness in Parable
THE PARABLE OF THE POOR MAN'S EWE LAMB

And the Lord sent Nathan to David. He came to him, and said to him, "There were two men in a certain city, the one rich and the other poor. The rich man had very many flocks and herds; but the poor man had nothing but one little ewe lamb, which he had bought. And he brought it up, and it grew up with him and with his children; it used to eat of his morsel, and drink from his cup, and lie in his bosom, and it was like a daughter to him. Now there came a traveler to the rich man, and he was unwilling to take one of his flock and of his own herd to prepare for the wayfarer who had come to him, but he took the poor man's lamb, and prepared it for the man who had come to him." Then David's anger was greatly kindled against the man; and he said to Nathan, "As the Lord lives, the man who has done this deserves to die; and he shall restore the lamb fourfold, because he did this thing, and because he had no pity."

"You are that man." Thus says the Lord, the God of Israel, "I anointed you King over Israel, and I delivered you out of the hand of Saul and gave you your master's wives into your bosom, and gave you the house of Israel and of Judah; and if it were too little, I would add to you as much more. Why have you despised the word of the Lord, to do what is evil in his sight? You have smitten Uri'ah the Hittite with the sword, and have taken his wife to be your wife, and have slain him with the sword of the Ammonites. Now therefore the sword shall never depart from your house, because you have despised me and have taken the wife of Uri'ah the Hittite to be your wife." Thus said the Lord, "Behold, I will raise evil against you out of your own house; and I will take your wives before your eyes, and give them to your neighbor, and he shall lie with your wives in the sight of the sun. For you did it secretly; but I will do this thing before all Israel, and before the sun." David said to Nathan, "I have sinned against the Lord." And Nathan said to David, "The Lord also has put away your sin; you shall not die. Nevertheless, because by this deed you have utterly scorned the Lord the child that is born to you shall die."

"The Poor Man's Ewe Lamb" has had a great impact on world literature for its poignancy and its sagacious style, but also for its rhetorical and pedagogical strategies.[2] Like other ancient parables, it lies entwined in the text of the Second Book of Samuel, between detailed descriptions of David's fierce battles with the enemies outside (Edomites, Syrians, Philistines, Hadadezer the king of Zobah, Amalek, and the Ammonites) and the passionate power-struggles within his house and his kingdom.

We wish to give our reader a few background details in order to contextualize this narrative. In the First Book of Samuel, we are told that "the Lord has grown more and more displeased with Saul,"[3] whom He anointed king over Israel by the hand of the prophet Samuel. God, we are told later, sends again the prophet to anoint David, the youngest son of Jesse the Bethlehemite, as king of Israel. We also learn that when Saul dies in battle, at Hebron, David is told by the tribes of Israel: "Behold we are in your bone and flesh . . . and the Lord said 'and you shall be shepherd of my people'" and that David makes a covenant with the people at Hebron, and "they anointed David king at Hebron, before the Lord."[4] The Scriptural text is also explicit about the fact that the Lord had said earlier to the prophet Samuel: "Arise anoint him [David] for it is he."[5]

It is also useful to add that throughout King David's tumultuous reign there shone the conviction that Israel was the people of the Lord and that His presence was at work in their history. Numerous biblical narratives, among which is the parable under scrutiny, mirror this belief. These passages relate in detail (despite the proverbial biblical conciseness) how the Lord had frequently intervened in battle on behalf of the Israelites and helped them in the long struggle against their enemies. After recounting some of King David's greatest feats, the biblical narrator introduces Nathan's parable and contextualizes it for the reader. The reader is informed that the parable is being said "in the name of the Lord."

Interestingly, "The Parable of the Poor Man's Ewe Lamb" appears in the text of the Second Book of Samuel at the height of David's power, when his kingdom has already been consolidated and his authority has become unquestionable.

A few questions will help us focus further on the text. First, why is Nathan, the courtier prophet, made to come and tell David the parable in the name of the Lord, at this particular time in the king's life? Second, has the prophet come only to inform David of God's punishment for the transgressions vis-à-vis Uri'ah the Hittite and Batsheva his wife? Is this parabolic story pointing to yet another alternative which has not been given attention until now?

To answer these questions, we need to explore more closely the biblical text and see why parabolic speech was chosen here for the delivery of God's indirect message. Finally, we need to question whether the parable was effective and why.

"The Parable of the Poor Man's Ewe Lamb," nested in the Second Book of Samuel 12:1–15, is in many ways very similar to the classic rabbinic parables in *Midrash*, which were written much later. The parable has many characteristics of a story parable: a well-defined beginning, a crisis, and a dénouement. However, this scriptural narrative does not match exactly the parables from the *Midrash*. The *nimshal* of this biblical parable, its moral lesson, is structurally quite different from the lesson in the classic rabbinic midrashim and the scriptural verse (to be pondered in Midrash) is missing. Likewise, the structure of the story, or what Propp calls the *sjužet* of this *fabula*, is less stereotypical.[6] While the midrashic mashal had a specific stereotypical, regularized pattern (introductory formula, main story, moral lesson and scriptural verse connected by a defined morpheme), this biblical parable is structurally lacking in several respects. While this parable has a number of features of a classic story parable—a beginning, a plot, and an end—its central character is not a king. Here, a "rich man" transgresses against a fellow man of a lesser status. For the reasons mentioned above, we may wish to call this narrative a *preclassic* parable, and inscribe it as an early link in the transformational parabolic chain.

"The Parable of the Poor Man's Ewe Lamb" is occasioned by King David's transgression. King David has taken Batsheva, the wife of Uri'ah, his Hittite loyal subject, for himself. Soon, when King David finds out that she is "with child" (the text never specifically states how soon), he orders Joab, his devoted general, to send Uri'ah to a certain death (the text never specifically mentions why the Hebrew king acts in this fashion either). However, we obtain valuable information from the pre-parabolic text. It states that:

> In the spring of the year, the time when kings go forth to battle, David sent Joab, and his servants with him, and all Israel; and they ravaged the Ammonites, and besieged Rabbah. But David remained at Jerusalem.[7]

The post-parabolic narrative is also of importance. Nathan says to King David:

"You are that man. Thus says the Lord, the God of Israel, . . . the child
that is born to you shall die.
    Then Nathan went to his house."

We note that the royal illicit behavior is rather brutally castigated by
Nathan, the court prophet and an intimate of the king. A very strange
action is displayed in the narrative. Nathan's unusually harsh reproof of
David, God's favored king, narrationally startles the reader. The Lord,
usually very kind to His people, is even more generous and kind to the
kings of His chosen people. This apparently anomalous behavior
depicted in the Biblical parables needs to be historically grounded and
contextualized further.

The biblical narrator states that at the height of his personal and
political strength, King David rules through a period of radical transformations in his kingdom and becomes visibly enmeshed in political
expansionist struggles and ploys. Surprisingly, in the midst of great
fighting with the Ammonites, David becomes immured in his palace and
this behavior must have elicited the ironic pre-parabolic comment "In
the time when kings go forth to battles David remained in his palace."[8]
King David, known once for his valiant fighting, leaves the combat to
his men and stays in the palace, but pursues no less bellicose activities
there. He gives heed to his concupiscence and uses shamelessly his royal
authority to cover up his criminal acts.

We also learn from the context that David's rebellious son
Abshalom plots ruthlessly against him. Abshalom is quoted to say: "Oh,
that I were the Judge of the land! Then every man with suit or cause
might come to me and I would give him justice."[9] This particular information will prove very important to our argument about David's intentions when taking Batsheva.

Uriel Simon and Joshua Guttmann, who label this a "juridical parable," discuss David's relation with his son and show the differences
between this parable and other parabolic narratives with juridical overtones.[10] While we acknowledge here their insights, we wish to move on
and concentrate on other, unexplored aspects of this rich biblical parable.

For example, the text's silence about Batsheva's own intentions and
her response to King David and her husband, Uri'ah's behavior toward
his wife and his king, and other textual ambiguities demand further
analysis. In the Scriptures, we are told only that Batsheva is the daughter of Eliam and the wife of a warrior.[11] When David "gets up from his
couch and walks on the roof of his palace,"[12] the story tells us that "he
sees a beautiful woman whom he takes and lays with her," despite the
fact that upon inquiring about her, his servants tell him that she is the

wife of another man (אשת איש). David transgresses at least at one level, because he takes "the property of another man."[13]

Given that women were considered in those days the property of their husbands, in taking Batsheva, David has taken unlawfully the possessions of Uri'ah, a man who is his subject and a loyal soldier. Now, considering the fact that in the pre-parabolic text we are informed of Uri'ah's excellent, but subalternate position at the royal palace, the parabolist is very astute in calling him the "poor man." The textual marker "poor man" enables the reader/addressee who is familiar with the biblical text to make the connection with the verses, "no man shall take the mill or the upper millstone to pledge; for he taketh a man's life to pledge."[14] These verses teach us not to abuse the poor.

In the following lines, a punishable behavior is implied. In preparabolic text, it is said that, "Now she was purifying herself from her uncleanliness."[15] This may be analyzed as cleansing herself after the menstrual flow, the way Guttmann and Simon propose. We suggest yet another interpretation. It might be the case that since מתקדשת (be in the situation of being purified), is a verbal participium that takes a circumstantial clause, Batsheva was merely obeying the law of post-copulatory cleansing. It might be the case that we are made to think of the post-menstrual ritualistic immersion, which means that she was at the most fertile period of her cycle, and that would explain her immediate impregnation. Gesenius proposes that David committed at this point a double sin in the eyes of the Lord.[16] We suggest that the words *tumah* (Hebrew: fem., impurity) and *nidah* (Hebrew: fem., impurity due to menstrual flow) are very skillfully intermeshed in the text, and add too much ambivalence to enable us to opt for one version of the meaning of the word over the other.

In the pre-parabolic text, King David appears to have had a very clear plan of attack. Interestingly, this narrative segment echoes in a negative way the earlier verse in which David is quite uncharacteristically and not very flatteringly away from the battlefield "while Kings and men go to battle."[17] This insinuation, which casts a negative light on the king, is further amplified by David's invitation to Uri'ah to "Go down to your house and wash your feet."[18] The request had clear sexual innuendo and sharply ambiguous overtones.[19]

The news of Batsheva's pregnancy must have prompted David to ask Uri'ah to go to his house and "wash his feet" (a disguised order for Uri'ah to have intercourse with Batsheva, his wife). This narrative sequence is placed right before the parable and enables us to speculate about the king's hopes that he could avoid taking further responsibility for his shameful action. But we suggest yet another reason. In the midst of intense power struggles, David badly needed another son, and an heir to the throne. The possibility of having a son with Batsheva seems thus to fit perfectly the king's present needs and appears to be of extreme importance to him. He is visibly anxious to assume the child's parentage.

Uri'ah, a rather high-ranking Hittite in David's army, proves to be free-spirited and devoted and loyal to his comrades in battle. He does not go home, but sleeps in the open field with them. The text tells of the king insistence: "Remain here today also, and tomorrow I will let you depart."[20] David is embarrassed again, because Uri'ah drinks and eats, but does not go to his wife's house.

Why does King David persist? Does he not know the battle taboos of his own people?[21] Why the narrational juxtaposition of King David with Uri'ah the Hittite who shows unexpected courage, moral fiber, and honesty? Why is David made to look so unworthy and disdainful here, when time and again God has promised to David that by his hand shall He deliver Israel?[22] The biblical narrator provides us with cues later in the text, but not before he shows David plotting Uri'ah's death with Jo'ab.[23]

The fact that David has Uri'ah himself bear the traitorous message is also very puzzling. The interpretation suggested by Simon and Guttmann is that the king is sure that Uri'ah is unaware of his betrayal and that the Hittite is so devoted and unsuspecting that he would not open the note containing David's scheme to send him to certain death.[24] To us, it also implies the respect Uri'ah has for his king and master, and David's abhorrent behavior makes him look even more vicious and lamentable. Jo'ab too is made to appear more humane than the great king of the Hebrews in the pre-parabolic narrative. This intensifies further the reader's negative view of the king's behavior.[25] When Jo'ab, fearful of his partial disobedience, sends word to king David of his servant's death, David observes only casually that "the sword devours now one and now another," a phrase both disconcerting and indicative of the king's state of mind.[26]

Notwithstanding the punishment inflicted on David, it appears that God is all the time on his side. Even the punishment itself, when scrutinized more carefully, seems more like a warning to God's favorite subject. Is God on the side of the rich in the parable? If this is true, what does the parable mean to teach its addressee? One is prompted to ask who guides Uri'ah's behavior and the behavior of the rest of the characters in this story, especially that of King David?

There seems to be a special encoding at a deeper level of the narrative. God forewarns David several times of his sinful behavior before he strikes him. Yet we cannot help noticing that God also brings the object of his desire, Batsheva, before his eyes, as though He is masterminding Himself their union.

In the extended text, we are invited to juxtapose God's behavior
with that of man. David, the man, does not warn Uri'ah, his victim,
while God, displeased by the king, sends David his prophet Nathan to
alert him of his transgression. Even Uri'ah's actions can be read as warning "signs" sent by God to David but ignored by the latter. Uri'ah's
character could be a mere "signifying sign" from God to a privileged
mortal, and Uri'ah's name, God is light, another "sign" yet.

It appears that God sacrifices Uri'ah, the Hittite. The question is
why. We suggest that this revolting divine deed is accomplished because
the Lord favors Solomon, the future great king of Israel, who is the
future son of Batsheva and David. However, the narrative provides no
overt statements to support this assertion. We learn much later in the
biblical text about the birth of Solomon to David and Batsheva.

Rhetorically this parable is a parable of blame. A complaint and a
warning by the parabolist meant to elicit repentance from the transgressor, King David. At the same time, the text has an additional, underlying message: God is more merciful than man.

To portray God's infinitely greater magnanimity, the text provides
numerous comparisons between man's actions and those of the divine.
Several narrative sequences illustrate this point. Very soon after "Batsheva makes her lamentations" and the mourning is over, we are
informed narrationally that David brings her to his house and makes her
"his wife." Two different semantic markers in the narrative posit Batsheva first as "Uri'ah's wife," and next as "David's wife," thus she is
inscribed textually at this point as the potential bearer of a rightful heir
to the throne of Israel.

Traditionally, David has married the women he desired and made
them his wives. To understand the significance of this gesture, it is
important to remember here the difference between a אישה (ishah, or
wife) and פלגש (pilegesh, literally, protected, or concubine) in those
days. A wife's children could become heirs to the throne while the con-
cubines' children could not. One realizes at once why the text shows
David in such a hurry to marry Batsheva and make her one of his wives.
Batsheva carries a possible heir to the throne, a rightful perpetuator of
King David's house; she thus has become a very desirable object.[27]

It has been argued convincingly that the order of the symbolic,
which is the order of language, of culture, of law, that is of the Name-
of-the-Father (in Lacanian terms), is especially difficult for women to
accede to, whether for historical or other reasons. Motherhood, which
establishes a natural link (the child) between woman and the social
world, provides a privileged means of entry into the order of culture and
of language.[28] It appears then, that while David's overt project was to
appropriate the woman who could provide him with a rightful heir, Bat-

sheva used a classical ploy (that of the powerless in a society) to enter David's house and gain admittance to power.

However, we are not told a single word in the narrative about Batsheva's own feelings or the actions that prompted her to bathe on the roof on the day King David was walking on the roof of his palace. In pre-parabolic narrative we learn about her only obliquely from King David's actions and her implied assent.

Should we view Batsheva as "the sacrificial lamb" once she is depicted in the parable as the "ewe lamb"?

In those days, a woman had not much input in matters of love and marriage. The fact that David is a king and a ravenous man only adds to the precarious situation of the women he chose for himself.[29] Yet, despite the difficult situation of a woman at the king's court, Batsheva appears to have her own secret agenda. She plots in a similar but covert manner, to become the progenitor of the next king of Israel. Moreover, given that she is described in the pre-parabolic text as the wife of one of David's devoted warriors, it stands to reason that she must have been "in" with the courtly intrigues and the royal politics. This may explain, for example, why she had made herself visible on that day on the roof of the king's palace, and later, available to the king's voraciousness.

The verses that describe the later events give the reader interesting new cues to consider. When David is "very old," the text portrays Batsheva as very assertive in asking the king to keep his promise (she suspects that he will not). She says to the king: "My Lord, you swore to your maidservant by the Lord your God, saying, Solomon your son shall reign after me."[30] Later we learn that, "She came and stood before the king," to hear when David promises before Nathan the prophet that "Solomon [her son] will be the next king," and that only next is she, "doing obedience to the king," and says "May the Lord King David live forever!"[31]

In this narrative sequence, a new element worth pondering surfaces. Batsheva says "The Lord *your* God," and not "*our* God." Is this only a quotation of one of David's earlier promises, or does this indicate that she is a foreigner like her husband Uri'ah?[32] If one wished to press the reading of the verse as revealing that Batsheva, like her husband, is a foreigner, one could derive other interesting shades of meaning. In the first place Batsheva is "other" as a woman, subservient but fear-instilling. Then, she is "other" as a stranger, therefore elicits in David two opposite impulses involved usually in xenophobia: extreme attraction and excessive fear.[33]

Is the reader challenged to see her as a sacrificial lamb as well? Uri'ah appears as one. Josephus claims that David's letter to Jo'ab must have been sealed, therefore the king saw no danger of being exposed or having his plan disrupted.[34] David must have had very good reasons to believe that Uri'ah was unsuspecting of his clandestine activities, otherwise David would not have sent the letter with him.

Parabolic tales commonly hark back to other texts, usually biblical, with which they have established a complex intertextual network of polysemy and polyphony. Because of this dense intermeshing, ancient parabolic narratives may imply, allude, or summon other biblical texts as evidence and proof for their own veracity. When investigating one narrative, the reader is driven to find out what parallels exist between that text and other biblical narratives.

"The Parable of the Poor Man's Ewe Lamb" too has embedded in its structure an injunction to "look around" in the biblical text for similar situations and learn by analogy. In the narration of the events leading to the sacrifice of Uri'ah we find, for example, strong overtones that suggest to us another biblical narrative, the story of the *Akkedah*, the binding, where another unsuspecting victim, Isaac, was going with his father Abraham to Mount Mori'ah to be slaughtered (and, in many narratives, we might add, a king is thought of very frequently also as the father of his subjects). Interestingly, Isaac too was carrying the source (device) of his own destruction: "And Abraham took the wood of the burnt offering and laid it on Isaac, his son, and he took in his hand the fire and the knife." However, unlike Uri'ah, Isaac seems more conscious of the peculiar situation and asks his father: "Father . . . where is the lamb for a burnt offering?"[35]

The clear difference in the behavior of the two men to be "sacrificed" invites those who analyze the parable to conclude that Uri'ah is textually inscribed in the parable as even more trusting than Isaac; his sacrifice by the king is made to appear even more abhorrent. To our mind, this is a rhetoric ploy and a subtle narrational invitation to do some inductive thinking (קל וחמר, *kal vahomer*).[36] The argumentation seems to be: if Uri'ah is so much more credulous than Isaac, the prototype for unsuspecting naiveté, and David, unlike Abraham who went to sacrifice his son at the Lord's behest, wants Uri'ah dead in order to satisfy his own lust, then David must become so much more odious in our eyes.

This and more. David kills Uri'ah twice. Given the statement in the Scriptures that "he who takes away the property of a poor man commits an act that is equivalent to killing him,"[37] and, given that Israel lived by the word of the Torah, from a legal point of view, David kills Uri'ah once by taking his only woman/property away from him, and the second time literally, by ordering Joab to lead him in the biggest battle and leave him there alone. Nathan's parable, following immediately after, invites interesting conjectures.

In proposing that a juridical parable is meant to induce the unsus-pecting hearer to accuse himself, Uriel Simon claims that such parable must assume a realistic guise and conceal that it is a parable.[38] "The Parable of the Poor Man's Ewe Lamb" presents indeed a realistic story about a violation of the law in a concealed fashion. Its covert purpose is to entrap the king who has committed a violation, so that he will be the one to pass judgment on himself.

But what is the real violation, and against whom? And the real pun-ishment? Finally, what is the relation between punishment and the trans-gression?

Given the special function of parabolic discourse, it should seem natural that a parable was used to tell the king of his transgression. What better way than to present the truth obliquely, and use parabolic rhetoric to disguise the intentions of the addressor and the real reasons for his intervention?

The reasons for the narrative choice is clear. In parabolic context, God sends his messenger, Nathan the court prophet, to tell the king that he will be punished, just as in real life David has sent Uri'ah with a mes-sage to his general and confidant Jo'ab to kill him (Uri'ah). The message, we understand, is about a double violation of the law: a villainous rob-bery, followed by the vicious murder of the robbed poor owner (of the ewe lamb).

On the surface, the offence is against Uri'ah, a man in the king's ser-vice. Yet, by looking closer at the text, we see the need to amend again our position. We read: "But this thing that David has done displeased the LORD,"[39] and "The LORD sent Nathan to David."[40] Further, Nathan says: "Thus said the LORD, God of Israel, 'I have anointed you king. . . . I gave you your master's house and your master's wives'" and "Why have you despised the word of the LORD, to do what is evil in his sight?"[41] To our mind, this places David's transgression on a differ-ent level. From a transgression against man only, his transgression takes the shape of a violation of God's commandments. In this light, David has first and foremost disobeyed the Divine Law, therefore, he is now subject to divine retribution.

Most confounding is the fact that the prophet diminishes so sig-nificantly the rich man's iniquity when he tells King David the parable. Instead of telling the king a tale about a murderer he tells him a story about a thief. Why the lessening of the offense? Several plausible answers come to mind. Our first answer is related to the prophet's pre-sent political status. Nathan is a prophet at the king's palace. That means he no longer has the unlimited power a prophet like Samuel had, who was sent by God to anoint Saul as king of Israel.[42] Or, when later, "God repented that he has made Saul the king of Israel" and again sends Samuel to inform Saul about it, and at the same time anoint David the youngest son of Jesse the Bethlehemite.[43] At King David's court, the prophet has now less power and therefore he needs to be much more astute politically. To protect his own interests, the prophet, who must deliver God's message to the royal guilty party, needs, at the same time, to cover up his intentions when talking to a proud and powerful king. Secondly, to encourage a just judgment and repentance from the king, without further arousing his wrath or suspicion, the prophet needs to disguise the offense and make it look considerably different, and more innocuous than the one committed by the noble culprit.

Indeed, in post-parabolic text, a laconic exchange occurs between Nathan and David: "Thou art the man," exclaims the prophet, and proceeds to enumerate in the name of the Lord all of His generosities to the king. Surprisingly, for no apparent reason, this is immediately followed by David's instantaneous and equally brief admittance of a higher guilt: "I have sinned against the LORD."[44] The offence against man is not even expressed, and in biblical textual configuration it is not needed, since the admission of transgression against God is acceptance of an immeasurably greater evil than a transgression against man.

In telling the king a parable, Nathan astutely uses the power of ruse[45] and succeeds to convey to David God's anger while accusing him of despising the Lord. By speaking in parables, the prophet induces the king to admit to the highest inequity, that against God; he helps him repent immediately thereafter. The post-parabolic reproof of the prophet, "Now therefore the sword shall never depart from your house," the reiteration of God's admonition "I will take your wives before your eyes and give them to your neighbor"[46] and the divine messages after the king admits his crime "the Lord has put away your sin; you shall not die . . . the child will die," all seem to reinforce the law of exact divine retaliation.[47]

The post-parabolic segment, "David lay all night upon the ground,"[48] inscribes the king's hope that the child will not die, and perhaps God will change his mind, and have pity.[49] This action of great self-debasement on the part of the king is also textually troublesome. The parable told by the prophet brings David to his senses, so to speak, and facilitates the immediate admittance of his guilt. Why then, when David is told of his punishment, does he still hope for a reversal of judgment from the Lord? Perhaps, because God has changed his mind before (in the case of Saul, for example). God has given David Saul's (his master's) wives and the House of Israel and of Judah. Should King David not have had good reasons to hope against all odds? The text implies that he should have. Was he not himself once a "poor man" whom God had anointed by the hand of Samuel?[50] David's actions of self-humiliation can be seen then not as a further self-degradation in order to appease God the way Simon and Goodman see it, but as David's real hope that the Lord will continue to be nice to him, since He had promised David to be the deliverer of Israel, and of His people.[51]

A psychoanalytic interpretation of the signs (of pathology) in this parable may help the reader unravel additional levels of signification in the narrative. For example, we may want to take a closer look at the signifiers "desire/want to have" and "make believe" (*faire-croire*) at work in the dense network of power plays in this parabolic narrative.

In *Traumdeutung*, Freud claims that, to decipher a dream and understand its metatext, which lead to the unconscious of the dreamer, it is imperative to elaborate the dream's rhetoric and the manipulatory and censorial apparatus at work in that dream. He insists on reading the intentions (ostentatious, dissimulating or persuasive, retaliatory or seductive) out of which the subject modulates his oneiric discourse.[52] Furthermore, he attributes a major role to language, to syntactic displacement (ellipsis, hyperbaton, regression, repetition, apposition) and semantic condensation (metaphor, catacresis, antonomasis, allegory, metonymy, and synecdoche). Following Freud, Lacan claims that the displacement resulting from connecting signifier to signifier in process of "referring back" to a hypostatized "original text" generates a linguistic bridge that dissimulates the "lack" in the text.[53]

The parabolist who created the narrative of "The Parable of the Poor Man's Ewe Lamb" made use, consciously and perhaps unconsciously, of a mechanism similar to that at work in dreams. The rhetoric of desire in the narrative is best expressed in psychoanalytic terms.

"Human desire finds its meaning in 'the desire of the other,' not so much that the other holds the key to the object desired, as because the first object of desire is to be recognized by the other in language."[54] It follows that because desire is inextricably linked to discourse, humans are forever at the mercy of language. Desire necessarily passes through a defile of signifiers, and therefore it manifests itself as the desire of "the Other":

> "Desire is born from the split between need and demand. It is irreducible to need, because it is not in principle a relation to a real object which is independent of the subject, but a relation to the fantasy. It is irreducible to demand, insofar as it seeks to impose itself without taking language or the unconscious of the other into account, and requires to be recognized absolutely by him."[55]

In this sense, desire is fundamentally a desire of recognition as a (human) subject by requiring the other to recognize his (human) desire.

It is also the profoundest desire to control the other to whom he becomes subjected. Essentially then, desire seeks to annihilate the other as an independent subject; thus, human desire is *a priori* impossible to satisfy. In this light, Batsheva, the object of David's lust in the parable under scrutiny, is in fact the object of a power phantasy to dominate her as object of desire, namely as the longed-for but unreachable Lacanian "Other," by a sort of covetous anthropophagy, a cannibalization of that which is desired.

The sociological dimension of the "object of desire" surfaces as well. Viewing women as use-value for man, an exchange value among men, in other words, as commodities, is common since biblical times. As commodities, women remain the guardian of material substance whose price will be established. As a "commodity," Batsheva has a well-defined "exchange value" and a definite "price."[56]

We like to bring to the reader's attention here that parallel with the commodification of Batsheva we find evidence in the text for an "effemination" of King David. The fact that immediately after Uri'ah's death David seizes Batsheva and makes her "his wife," allows us to propose that Batsheva is needed by him not merely to fulfill his momentous lust. Appropriating Batsheva also actualizes David fantasy of being one with her (being her), and of seizing the power of fertility she possesses—her phallic powers in a dominant phallic economy—and to which, paradoxically, but not unexpectedly, he has become subjected.[57] The desire to appropriate Batsheva who "is with child" expresses David's need to appropriate the *phallus/the phallic power* he lacks (he has no heirs), and preserve its referential status *in* the act of negating it.

Unlike Freud's phallocentric articulations that posit that the phallus *is* the woman's desire "inasmuch as she doesn't have one," this parable, interestingly, narrativizes the androcentric aspect of the power symbol.[58]

As the "Purloined Letter" belongs to the queen as a substitute for the phallus she doesn't have, the unborn child belongs to Batsheva *as* her phallic substitute and *it* "effeminizes," (castrates) King David who desires to appropriate her phallic power for himself.[59]

The two opposed but enmeshed desires, that of a woman (Batsheva) and that of a man (King David), meet here in an archaic form through the body of the "mother," through the active/passive extension of the Law of the father. The mother's sacrifice, or what Susan Sulleiman so pertinently calls "the passive gratification" is, in this instance, made easy by the fact that through the male child, Batsheva compensates for the one "great lack," the penis.[60]

From King David's point of view, on the other hand, the wished for result in this warlike game of subjugation is for him to gain the power of perpetuating the Davidic lineage, namely the power to procreate and produce his rightful heir, since as we know, he has abandoned "going like kings and men to the real wars." Ostensibly, this verse has an intriguing insinuation about David's prowess as well.

The struggle for dominance of the "other" circumvents language. The narration of the "taking" of Batsheva contains only three verbs, one of them repeated: *he saw, he sent, he sent, he took.* Batsheva has no language to articulate her position. The text read: *she came, she purified, she returned.*[61] Her actions are described in verbs which indicate reaction to a demand and not an agentive subject. She has no agency. No verbal exchange between the two is indicated in the text, until her statement: "*I am with child.*"

On the surface, David secures dominance over the object of his desire, Batsheva, in an aggressive *veni, vidi, vinci.* We suggest that in deep narrative structure, however, David is defeated; he suffers the inevitable defeat one suffers in language, which Lacan tells us is the "locus of the word," the place where the unattainable *Other* constitutes himself as well.[62] The prophet's unmasking of David in the utterances "You are the man. . . . Therefore the sword shall never depart from your house, . . . the child that is born to you shall die," and the prophetic reproof enunciate that defeat in the narrative organization of the text.

To see how the parable's rhetorico-poetic mechanisms "smooth" away the gaps in the narrative and makes them appear seamless, we must look at each constitutive segment in the parable's narrative trajectory[63] and analyze the *modalization* of the narrative in terms of its *actantial* organization, and the "passions" of the subjects (their *états passionnels*). We must also keep an eye on the general "sensitization" of discourse that is related to the transformation of the acting subjects (actantial subjects) into actorial ones (with thematic roles, pathemic roles related to thymic values). Finally, we need to follow the pathemic sensitization of discourse (the activation of emotions in subjects who then act upon them) and its narrative modalization, which are autonomous and governed by different types of logic. All of these shifts co-occur, and become properties of the entire discourse—a "semiotic style" that is projected on the subjects, the objects, and their junction.[64]

The elementary structures of signification in the parable, at the semio-narrative level of a discourse, are to be seen as the result of continuous discretization, or fragmentation of the undulatory continuum of becoming by successive transformations: conjunctions and disjunctions of subjects and objects.[65] These microdiscursive transformations inform us how parables generate the conditions under which meaning can be created and pondered by each individual perceiver who gets his own meaning-system.

Putting the narrative segments in Nathan's parable of "The Poor Man's Ewe Lamb" under a magnifying glass sharpens significantly the image we get from the parable.

To begin with, there are two possible [agentive] subjects:

$$\text{MAN}_{(rich)}, \text{ and MAN}_{(poor)}, \text{ are BE}^{(tense)}$$

These agents find themselves alternatively *in a state of conjunction* or *disjunction* with/from the *objects of desire*.

The alternate conjunctions and disjunction from the desired objects can be put in this formula:

$$[\text{WANT} + \text{HAVE}]_1 \cup \text{herds/flocks/power}$$

$$[\text{WANT} + \text{HAVE}]_2 \cup \text{ewe lamb.}$$

$$\text{MAN}_{(ATT)=(rich)} \cup \text{OBJ}_{|FLOCKS,HERDS,POWER|} \rightharpoondown$$

$$\text{MAN}_{(ATT)=(poor)} \cup \text{OBJ}_{|ONE\ EWE\ LAMB|}$$

The two men in the parable, the poor and the rich, are in a logical relation of the shape:

$$a:b::c:d.$$

The "state of being" (*état*) of the two subjects in the continuum of becoming (in the space-time of the narrative) is "fractured," or "discretized" when punctured by a "doing" (*faire*), an action by a third subject with whom the first man enters in a fiduciary relation (his desire to please the traveler). This action takes the shape:

$$\text{MAN}_{(traveler)(inchoative,\ CAUSE)} + \text{DO}^{tense} \rightharpoondown_{(come)}.$$

The traveler's action COME$_{(causative)}$ in the rich man

$$\text{MAN}_{(rich)} \rightharpoondown \text{ACTIONS}_{(takes,\ kill,\ prepares)=}$$

$$\text{MAN}_{(rich)} + \text{TAKE}^{tense} + \text{KILL}^{tense} + \text{PREPARE}^{tense} + \text{BEEN}^{(MAN)}_{traveler} \cup [\text{EWE LAMB}].^{66}$$

Representing "the states" and "the actions" in this way answers poignantly our question about David's gullibility. To the question why doesn't the king recognize himself in the parable,[67] interpretative semantics evidences how the interpolation of the actantial subject /traveler ("the agent" causing the rich man to violate the law) creates a believable divergence in the text, and sends the unsuspecting addressee (King David) on a deceptive narrative parcourse.

A very efficient mode of presenting these communicational networks is offered by François Rastier, who shows the systems at work in acts of communication.[68] The four universal constituents, which interplay, are the thematic, the dialectic, the dialogic, and the tactic components of communication. All the components interact in a reciprocal manner, and at least two are always necessary elements for any discourse.[69]

According to Rastier's universal constituents in the first narrative cycle, the rich man wants to please a third person. Tactically and dialectically, he /takes other's possession / does not want to take his own/.

We have been talking at length about the abundant use of scriptural texts to elucidate ancient parables. A metatext to this parabolic text, is surely the law of hospitality (Abraham demands that the traveler be "well fed"). The rich man of the parable wishes to please the stranger without parting with his possessions. In order to support his argument that "rich man" in the parable breaks the law of hospitality, Uriel Simon talks about the custom of *Adayieh* among Bedouins. He quotes from Araf-el-Aref, *The Bedouin Tribes in the District of Beersheva*. The *Adayieh* says that the Bedouin may take the sheep if the owner is not around, but after the deed is done he immediately needs to notify the owner, otherwise it will be considered theft. Interestingly, the cattle excluded is the ram (needed for breeding), the ewe that has a bell (a sign of attachment of the owner), the ewe reared in the tent (special affection), and the one earmarked for payment of a vow. Whoever takes any one of these sheep must pay back *fourfold*, and pay the *Zerkha*, the judge's fee as well. This metatextual information helps us understand the significance of the "fourfold" reimbursement to the "poor man" by David, and why the king is mortified.[70] The parabolic sequence is expressed formally in table 2.1. In the dialectic and thematic parcourse of the next sequence the rich man's actions and those of King David are juxtaposed with those of God (table 2.2).

In the semantic juxtaposition of the actions of man and those of God, the parabolic text makes God appear infinitely more compassionate and merciful then man. As opposed to man who "has no pity," God "puts away man's sin." The highest human authority, the king, is posited textually parallel to the divine. Rhetorico-semantically, the parable serves to accomplish at least two things: it becomes a device for indirect divine reproof, but also an indirect method of glorifying the magnanimity and the justness of the Lord. The narrator embeds semantically man's grave transgressions, and his merciless punishments, on the firmament of a continuing kindness of God. When the addressee of the parable enters its

TABLE 2.1
Divine Actions

In the WORLD OF MAN$_{(LOC)}$$^{(TENSE: FINITE)}$:

DAVID$_{(ATT/angry)}$ERGATIVE $\Rightarrow$

SAYS + CONDEMNS$_{(death/restore\ fourfold)}$ $\Rightarrow$

MAN$_{(ATT/rich)(ATT/no\ pity)}$.

TABLE 2.2
Divine Retribution

In the world of the divine, GOD$_{(ATT:eternal/generous/just)}$ Y

$\Leftarrow$(ERGATIVE)$\Rightarrow$ GIVE^{tense}$\Rightarrow$ /anoints king/
/gives the House of Israel and Judah/
/would add as much/
/delivers from the hands of Saul/
/gives his master's wives/

[In the WORLD OF GOD$_{(LOC)}$$^{(tense\ \infty)}$]$\Rightarrow$ $\exists$ divine retribution

GOD$_{(ATT:\ eternal,\ generous,\ just)}$ $\Rightarrow$ PUNISH/ERG$\Rightarrow$

/raise evil
/take wives
/the child die

/PUTS AWAY DAVID'S SIN/

rhetorical play of revelation and make believe, he is encouraged to look at himself and his deeds, and learn parabolically (table 2.3).

Guilt, anger, pity, and the implicit kindness of God (who gave David all his power, prowess, and possessions), are the *pathemic states*, the emotional states (passions) of the subjects of the parable in process of conjoining or disjoining with/from the desired objects. These become alternatively states of dysphoria or euphoria in which the subjects of the parable are posited (table 2.4).

We realize that in reading this ancient parable, we enter a contractual agreement to interpret and decode its narrative structure and mimetic tactics, which ultimately aim to teach and convert to a certain ideology. The parable ultimately promulgates an ideology aimed at preserving God and His Law as the ultimate and immutable authority. The parable does this in an allusive way, which facilitates its acceptance and absorption.

TABLE 2.3
Narrative Trajectory

DAVID $\Rightarrow$ /takes Batsheva/
/despises (the word of the) LORD/
/smites Uri'ah/
/slays Uri'ah with the sword of the Ammonites/

DAVID$_{(ATT, GUILTY)}$ $\Rightarrow$ /cowardice/
/murder/
/disobedience of the law of GOD/
/disobedience of the word of GOD/

SOURCE OF /ANGER/: DAVID $\Rightarrow$ /ANGRY/—Someone else was /injured/
GOD $\Rightarrow$ /ANGRY/—HE was /despised/

SOURCE OF /EVIL/: FOR THE POOR MAN—/outside/, /unknown/
FOR DAVID—/his own house/, /from GOD/
FOR GOD—/David/

REASONS FOR /EVIL/ FOR POOR MAN—/no transgression/
FOR DAVID—/transgression/

The parabolic shifter is: /NOW THEREFORE/

TABLE 2.4
Euphoric and Dysphoric States

1. GOD$_{(ubiquitous, eternal)}$ $\cup$ HIS PEOPLE $\Rightarrow$ ATT$_{(Euphoric)}$

2. GOD$_{(ubiquitous, eternal)}$ $\cap$ LAWFUL BEHAVIOR$_{(of his people)}$ = ATT$_{(Dysphoric)}$

3. DAVID$_{(sinful, criminal)}$ $\cup$ BATSHEVA $\Rightarrow$ ATT$_{(Euphoric)}$ $\Leftarrow$ MAN$_{(rich)}$ $\cup$ /FLOCKS/HERDS/POWER

4. DAVID$_{(sinful, merciless)}$ $\cap$ CHILD/WIVES/ $\Rightarrow$ ATT$_{(Dysphoric)}$

5. URI'AH$_{(innocent)}$ $\cup$ BATSHEVA$_{(?)}$ $\cup$ COMRADES/WAR/ $\Rightarrow$ ATT$_{(Euphoric)}$ $\Leftarrow$ MAN$_{(poor)}$ $\cup$ EWE LAMB

We saw how at first, the parable seduces and incites the reader/
addressee to act, to decode, and to gain a competence at understanding
parabolic hints. Only when the reader/addressee/listener is already in the
act of performing (of decoding) does the parable operate a tactical
"glissment," or slippage from one narrative level to another and "causes
one to do" (*fait-faire*), makes one act on its injunction. The parable
operates "a doing" through the morpheme "therefore" (the parabolic
shifter), only when it has already seduced its addressee. In our case, the
slippage occurs after the telling of the parable has elicited from David

the decree: "As the LORD lives, this man deserves to die."[71]

"The Parable of the Poor Man's Ewe Lamb," as we understand it now, is not told merely to chastise the king for the taking a woman or killing a man. Rather, the parable uses a rhetoric of seduction to captivate the king and to bring him "in" into the parabolic space-time, in order to communicate to him his offense toward God and His Law.

Unlike the Zen Master in Sun Tzu's *The Art of War*, the parable raises (narrationally) a false "stick" at the interpreter's questions. Only apparently does this parabolic narrative flout textual and conversational implicature. The inferences made in the parable follow rhetorico-poetic laws, and rely on pre-established social, cultural, and ideological frameworks. This parable invites the reader to make continuous connections between text, "metatext" (the other biblical texts), and "outside-of-text," revealing that human communication is governed by laws, other than and additional to the laws of syntax, semantics, and pragmatics.

The "lack-in-the-text" and the text "alluded to" in parabolic narratives produce the interplay between deïxis, conversational implicature, and pragmatic presuppositions, all pertaining to the complex interplay of linguistic domains in the act of communication. And it is this special interplay that lends parables their robust communicatory power. The intervention of pragmatics in parabolic narratives signals to us the various contextual assumptions made by these texts.[72]

On the formal plane, *deïxis* (the pointing in the right direction) takes care of the manner in which the codification of parables and grammaticalization of the linguistic features affect the content of the parabolic speech event, while conversational implicature signals contextual assumptions such as specific relations between a king and a subject, a man and a woman (in antiquity), a king and a prophet, a parabolist and his addressee, and all serve to show how the parabolic "co-operative interaction" occurs.

This "co-operativeness" that happens or does not happen in parables points to the fact that each one of the parabolic locutors generates inferences that go far beyond the semantic content of that which is said, and go, at times even against logical implications because these are grounded in "mutual knowledge," and "common grounds." Nathan's use of parabolic speech rather than direct speech to address David is based on the specific function implicature has in conversations, namely a kind of pragmatic inference that serves to "represent" the presuppositions of the two interlocutors in the speech event.

The volatile nature of the pragmatic presuppositions, their "defeasibility" within a certain discursive context ("presuppositional holes" and "presuppositional filters") explains the unexpected reaction elicited in King David by the story of a poor man and a rich man. The presuppositional holes, always present in parabolic discourse, support that, as rule, pragmatic presuppositions are volatile, and need to be redefined during communication.[73]

A special mode of communication, ancient parables are also a mode of producing a new text, and a particular mode for interpreting it—through the pragmatic decisions of the addressee. When one says that he reads parabolically, he utilizes a modality of textual *use*. And, as I showed earlier, this pragmatic decision to read a text "parabolically" produces a new sign-function at the semantic level by associating new content—as far as possible undetermined and vague—with expressions already correlated to a preexisting, coded content. In relation to the process of decoding in the parabolic mode, one of its main features is that the text, even when the parabolic mode is not realized interpretively, remains nevertheless endowed with sense—at its literal or figurative level.

A parabolic reading of "The Parable of the Poor Man's Ewe Lamb" allows us to understand that in the biblical tradition, the coded contents of the parable were suggested by a preceding legacy and the interpreter knew that the codes were not cultural units but *referents*, or aspects of an extrasubjective and extracultural reality. To that extent, beyond their educational value, ancient parables, like riddles, may have been an intellectual exercise, a brain sharpener, and an initiation into a game in which one gains, not a knowledge of how to construe the ultimate interpretation to a text, but becomes gradually wiser, and this illumination was cumulative. Ancient parables provided man with the humbling understanding that his search for the ultimate wisdom in the absence of God and His magnanimity is a hopeless undertaking. Perhaps the most apropos modern statement regarding this ancient understanding is provided by Edmond Jabès:

> "What is going on behind this door? A book is shedding its leaves."
> "I saw rabbis go in"
> They are privileged readers. They come to give up their comments.
> "Have they read the book?" "They are reading it."
> They foresaw the book. They are prepared to encounter it."
> "Where is the book set?"
> "In the book."[74]

CHAPTER 3

Synoptic Gospel Parables: The Parable of the Marriage Feast

He who knows does not speak
He who speaks does not know

—Lao Tze

The Gospel parables we examine below are aesthetic objects with well-defined narrative configurations with an implied understanding of existence and experience. Like other biblical narratives, these parables often communicate to us about the nature of faith and unfaith.[1] Synoptic parables, like the narratives in the *Midrash*, originated in a strong oral tradition that does not teach directly of God and faith but alludes to the divine in an oblique manner. The parables attributed to Jesus come to enlighten man, to teach him wisdom, and to point him, albeit indirectly, toward the heavenly Kingdom of God. In these parables, the holy dominion extends sovereignly over past, present, and future, as the realm of divine reward to the good, and divine retribution to evildoers.

Parables, notoriously "non-explicit" and "concealing," seem at the same time uniquely suitable to assist Jesus, the world's foremost parabolist, in leading his listeners to a realm beyond the limits of this world. Wittgenstein called such going beyond this world, "getting out of this world in order to be able to specify its limits,"[2] and Kafka, the founder of modern parables, has named it "going over to a fabulous yonder."

Synoptic parables are to a large extent a reflection of the poetic genius of the people who created them, and of the discerning eye with which they observed the world around them. Their unique sensitivity to natural phenomena and to the perplexing nature of man is illustrated by the multifaceted tropological language used to portray nature and man in the Gospels. Like the early Jewish sages, who were owners of vineyards and agriculturists,[3] Jesus and his disciples were close to the land and observed all the preparations of the soil, the sowing and the tilling, the harvesting and the gardening. The graceful imagery of the orchard and the fig tree, of the flocks and the herdsman reminiscent of a serene life in nature are a subtle, graceful background providing a fine narrative balance to the tumultuous circumstance in which this kind of parabolic discourse has come into being and has subsequently evolved.[4]

63

THE SYNOPTIC GOSPELS AS MIMETIC MODE

Northop Frye categorizes the synoptic subgenre as a low mimetic mode.[5] This means that the images we find in the Gospels are drawn from ordinary life experience and give a believable impression of "the outside world." Eric Auerbach too has noted that synoptic parables, with "their ruthless mixture of everyday reality with high and 'sublime tragedy,' break the classical rules of style."[6] Both prominent critics fail however to show that while in the low mimetic mode the divine is of no great importance, in rabbinic and synoptic parabolic speech the divine occupies a primordial place, even though its presence is obscured. To that extent, synoptic and midrashic parables offer a distinct kind of mimetic model that is encountered nowhere else in Western literature. Unlike modern parabolic discourse, Gospel parables claim at their very core an unparalleled interest in the relation between God and man in "this world" and in the "world to come."

ESCHATOLOGY

The place of eschatology in synoptic texts is fundamental and needs to be carefully probed. The eschatological dimension of the parables attributed to Jesus, as well as their specific sociohistoric relevancy to Christianity, has been thoroughly elaborated by scholars of the New Testament, and considerable strides were made to elucidate the relation between early rabbinic parables and the parables in Gospels.

Starting with Jülicher, there was a move away from the allegorical interpretation of parables favored before by the early Church fathers. The early views have been maintained by modern scholars such as Joachim Jeremias, C. H. Dodd, Dan Via, Fiebig, and others,[7] who have dedicated their creative energies to reconstruct "the original setting in life" of these narratives. These critics aspired to demonstrate in a definitive way that the parables attributed to Jesus were a unique appearance, an absolutely new and matchless phenomenon in the world; therefore, they must have a particular relation to Jesus's personal life, his teachings, and Christianity.[8]

RECONSTRUCTION OF GOSPEL PARABLES

The gargantuan effort to reconstruct the socio-linguistic milieu of these parables, their actual "*Sitz im Leben*," by culture, original language, and the struggle to establish clear interdependencies among different Gospels, came about as a result of serious distrust of the available sources. The debate over "the original language" of the synoptic Gospels has been quite intense. Some scholars believed that they were delivered in Aramaic; others, that they were told in Hebrew. While it is clear that the parables attributed to Jesus were delivered in the languages of the people, we concur with those who suggest that even if Jesus was speaking in Aramaic, his words must have been translated in Hebrew as well.[9]

Joachim Jeremias, one of the most committed reconstructors of synoptic parables, has asserted that much of the allegorical thrust of Jesus' parables is not original but the end result of various transformations and editing that has complicated immensely the task of those who wanted to reconstruct their original articulation. As we understand it, the numerous alterations and the complications have arisen from the fact that Jesus delivered orally his parables, and, most probably, in the languages spoken at the time: Aramaic and Hebrew. Only much later, upon their being written down, these parables underwent changes.[10]

Haim Rabin and David Flusser, two foremost scholars of the New Testament, have shown clearly that in the process of transposition from the oral to the written mode, much was altered and added by editors and compilers. Upon their translation into Greek, these parables underwent another cycle of change. In translation, the synoptic parables suffered emendations and transformations due to specific lexical incompatibilities between languages, as well as ideological differences. For example, the different meanings of *limshol* and *mashal* created serious problems when transposed into Greek. There seems to be a consensus now among scholars regarding the alterations by early Church fathers who transformed the parables further to fit their particular ideology.[11]

As a result of the complex changes to which the Gospel parables were subjected, the desire to reconstruct the "one authoritative version" may become an actual hindrance to learning more about them. To our mind, there is a serious risk involved, because in this feat we may also lose the very object of our quest. The process of getting back to the "authentic" parables is not unlike the unwrapping of the mummy that lies buried in layers of cloth in Melville's story. It takes time to unwrap the Egyptian king. By horrible groping, we come to the central room; with joy we open the sarcophagus: but lift and nobody is there. The process and the object have fused and have become one.

The work of reconstructing and reconstituting ancient parables is in many ways a frustrating, even impossible task. Due to the numerous layers of transformations, in order to learn more about the parables' original articulation and shape, we must perform at times a veritable archeological dig, and try to unravel one after the other, the many strata of change in order to get to what were once the original texts. Yet one can never be sure of the exact cultural, religious, and ideological conditions that have determined a particular linguistic output, nor can one fully grasp the complicated processes of compilation and creative concatenation of various texts that took place in the production of the synoptic parables.[12]

Jewish scholars of the New Testament, such as Jakob Petuchovsky and David Flusser, wonder in a quite vigorous tone, why would there be any doubt in the minds of those versed in the New Testament and in rabbinic texts, that the parables attributed to Jesus belong also to the creative genius of the Jewish people, as a particular literary type in the wisdom literature, but which took a separate path and underwent its own transformations over time.[13] We suggest that, by investigating the synoptic Gospel parables in a comparatist framework such our own and by following the transformations over time in parabolic genre, we accomplish two important things. First, the voices of these modern scholars naturally join those of other biblical scholars, and second, we can inscribe the Gospels parables in a long literary chain.

THE IDIOM AND THE OCCASION
OF SYNOPTIC PARABLES

We know that the Gospel parables were delivered in a Semitic language. The prevalent view regarding the language of the people in the first century is that some of the Jewish people spoke Aramaic but that Hebrew was extensively spoken and written in those days.[14] It has also been found that Matthew collected the Gospels in Hebrew ("it is said," and "he translated each as best he could" [Ματθαῖος μὲν οὖν Ἑβραιδι διαλέκτῳ τὰ λόγια συνετάξατο ἡρμήνευσεν δ αὐτὰ ὡς ἦν δυνατὸς ἑκαστος]).[15]

We also know in what circumstances these parables were told, because, as shown before, parabolic discourse informs the reader of the circumstances in which it was propounded. Here, the evangelists Matthew, Mark, and Luke tell that the parabolist (Jesus) "again will speak in parables."[16] Finally, it is clear that Jesus's parables were offered orally; they begin with the statement: "He went by the sea, and told his parable to the people."[17]

ORALITY

The manner in which Jesus' parables became written texts deserves our close attention as well. But first we wish to remember the functioning of orally transmitted myths. The process of mythicization of a history-making event, such as expressing in language the appearances of Jesus, is governed by a dialectic that frustrates researchers. On the one hand, there is a passionate desire of a people to recount and capture in language the events' importance, and thus secure their remembrance by future generations. On the other hand, an equally great compulsion to endow these occurrences with an aura of dignity that drives them to cloak these events in mystery and make them almost ungraspable.

To our mind, the many voices with their different viewpoints, the contradictions and the inconsistencies kept in the various narrative versions (and *midrashic* and synoptic narratives seem particularly good examples for keeping side by side all the versions), were meant to prevent a framing and limiting monopoly from hovering over memory.[18] It is as if events of such proportions were too important to entrust to the tyranny and fragility of one single voice and needed to be assigned to the "collective memory" of an entire people to preserve them when the original remembrance begins to fail, and falter, and fade away.[19]

This seems true of tradition preserving in general. In order to ensure our very existence as humans in the future, our collective memory must be entrusted with the retelling of our past and recounting tirelessly to each generation its feats, while keeping a delicate balance between covertness and overtness, between explicit language and non-explicit speech, allegoricity and literality. Oral traditions, built upon the primacy of the utterance, strive to maintain alive the polyphonic voices that link the generations in the memory chain, and only a growing fear before the disappearance of the weakened voice of the original witnesses promotes the final shift from the oral to the written text.[20] This shift, born of a desire to preserve, actually freezes the text-event at a particular linguistic stage and, therefore, mediates also, in a sense, its calcification and arrest.

WRITTEN SYNOPTIC TEXTS

In the shift from the oral tradition to the written text, a paradoxical situation emerged. Writing down of the tales meant to eternalize the spoken word, also threatened to silence in this process the original fluid and flexible voice. It seems that writing down a text and canonizing it neutralizes, what Derrida, our most recent "unraveler" of myths,[21] called the false feeling of "immediate presence" of the spoken word, which has been wrongly invested in Western tradition, he reminds us, with the "transcending dignity of an originary language."[22]

When the parables of Jesus were written down, several versions were kept in the Gospels. Much as in the midrashic texts of the rabbis, where the most diverse, even opposing opinions are kept side by side and carefully preserved, the texts of the Gospels of Mark, Matthew, and

Luke retell the parables attributed to Jesus with variation, modification, and embellishments that suggest to the literary critic a strong urge to preserve and immortalize this extraordinary event.[23]

SECRECY AND RELIGIOUS VIEWS

When delving into synoptic Gospels' parables, an important concept to be understood is their "secrecy." We know from textual inscriptions in the Gospels that Jesus invariably analyzed the parables he told to the people and that he thoroughly explained them in the following lines, or what we call "post-parabolic" text. Yet, in many instances, we also notice that, while he interpreted in detail his parables, Jesus also claimed that these parables will never be understood by the "others" and remain a "secret," or mystery, to them (the others). The linguistic marker /they/ gets different names at various times in the synoptic Gospels, but is consistently positioned as the "outsider" to the semiosis, namely, the hermeneutic community described in the parabolic speech attributed to Jesus.

For the sake of clarification, we wish to revisit the notion of "secrecy" attributed to Jesus' parables. Was his parabolic speech "secret," the way the kabbalists' parables were to the outsider, or was his secret language a rhetorical ploy meant to assign to his audience various strategic positions in the community of listeners: belonging/not-belonging, disciples/pharisees, insiders/outsiders? Was this "secrecy" just a "hermeneutical conceit," or something else as well?[24] If Jesus' secrecy were only an expression of hermeneutical conceit, it would be a rhetorical ploy among others. We suggest that it means more. To formulate an answer, we turn to those passages in the synoptic Gospels in which Jesus talks about "secrets" and "understanding" of "the hidden [truth]" and try to understand from the intimations made in his parabolic statements.

We read that "All this Jesus said in parables; indeed he said nothing to them without parable . . . : 'I will open my mouth in parables I will utter what has been hidden since the foundation of the world.'"[25] In the Gospel of Mark, we read:

> Then the disciples came and said to Him, "Why do you speak in parables?" And he answered, "To you has been given the secret of the kingdom of God, but for those outside everything is in parables; so that they may indeed see but not perceive, and may indeed hear but not understand; lest they should turn again, and be forgiven.[26] And he said to them, "Do you not understand this parable? How then will you understand all the parables?"[27]

In these passages, Jesus promises to his people to restore for them what Nietzsche called the "faded emblem on the coin" and help them come to grasp a mythical "originary truth."[28] However, since the "promises" made by Jesus to his addressees are made in language, we need to look at them as speech acts, and understand them as speech acts in a linguistic framework. Jesus, the parabolist, performs the elocutionary act of "promising." Now, as John Austin has shown, the act of promising, as a speech act, finds resolution in the very promise.[29] But this is also to say that, when Jesus "promises" to tell the "hidden [truth]," in the framework of speech acts, he points only to a relation of perfect adequacy between the statement he makes and its referent. But succeeding in speech acts is the pleasure of the speech act itself. In other words, since the speech act of "promising" is auto-referential, it follows that "promising" to tell "the hidden truth" is the deed and the fulfillment of that deed in one; the "promise" made by the parabolist is accomplished by and while making that statement. So, when Jesus opens his mouth, speaks in parables, and "utters what has been hidden since the foundation of the world," he also accomplishes his task (of promising) in the very statement. Linguistically, no further action is required on his part.

At the syntactic level the discrepancy between "the uttered" words and "the hidden truth" is generated by the incongruity between the two verbal forms: the lexical items "hidden" and "utter." These verbal forms are composed of phonemic and semantic micro-units that have no co-extensive or co-referential *sememes* (the most elemental intelligible linguistic particles). To utter implies a performative statement, while to hide implies an action of covering, which is not a speech act. It follows that any confusion or disappointment on the part of an addressee comes not from the statements themselves, but from a lack of understanding of the pure performative nature of the promissory act. A promise only simulates a dialogue between two orders that do not intersect here: the order of speech acts and the order of deeds.

In this light, Jesus, promising revelation in parables by "uttering" and by saying "what has been hidden since the foundation of the world," is *a priori* compromised by the performative nature of the act of promising. Revelation through the utterance is also jeopardized by the use of tropological language, which, as we have suggested earlier, does not allow us to go back to our "origins." When Nietzsche inquires about the possibility of our going back to our origins and asks "what is truth?," he answers:

> Truth is a mobile army of metaphors, metonymies, anthropologisms; in short a sum of human relations which became poetically and rhetorically intensified, metamorphosed, adorned, and after long usage seems to a nation fixed, canonic and binding; truths are illusions of which one

has forgotten that they *are* illusions; worn-out metaphors which have become powerless to affect the senses; coins which have their observe effaced and now are no longer of account as coins but merely as metal. . . . To be truthful, that is to use the usual metaphors, therefore expressed morally: we have heard only about the obligation to lie according to a fixed convention, to lie gregariously in a style binding for all.[30]

To "utter what has been hidden since the beginning of the world" is thus to forget that the original metaphors of perception are metaphors as well, in the sense that "our hidden truths" are themselves "coins with their emblems effaced, worn-out metaphors, and illusions of which we have forgotten that they are illusions."[31]

In analyzing Nietzsche's numismatic metaphor, Derrida suggests that any theory of metaphorical language is primarily a theory of meaning; therefore it presupposes that a certain "naturalité originaire" (an originary naturalness) belongs to the trope. To that extent, restoring "the original figure on the coin" is an act that "discolors the ancient fables while assembling its own."[32]

SYNOPTIC PARABLES AND IDEOLOGY

We claim that, when Jesus promises to his people the "truth hidden since the beginning of the world," in actuality, he aims to create a new mythology based on a new ideology. We suggest that the parabolic speech attributed to Jesus clearly aims to replace a set of functioning metaphors that belong to one hermeneutic order by a set of new metaphors belonging to a "new order." As the leader of a new religious order, Jesus was clearly not interested in uncovering "a truth hidden since the beginning of the world," but in replacing the old religious order with his own.

If we follow Nietzsche's claims that "only by forgetting that primitive world of metaphors, and only by the congelation and coagulation of an original mass of similes and precepts pouring forth as a fiery liquid out of the primal faculty of human fancy *does man live with some consequence* [my emphasis],"[33] the act of promising to let a person know "that which has been hidden since the foundation of the world" means also destroying his life on this earth. In this light, it is safe to claim that rather than just a "hermeneutical conceit," Jesus' parabolic speech launches his new doctrine—supported by the parabolic complex rhetorical and poetic apparatus—that prescribes embracing the world to come at the expense of life in this world.[34] We can also speculate that such parabolic discourse may leave many of its ingenuous addressees blundering, together with "the sightless" and those "who do not hear" in the parable, through a labyrinth of tropes, while "the hidden truth" necessarily remains hidden to all, undecodable, and irretrievable.

THE PARABLE OF THE MARRIAGE FEAST:
AT THE KING'S TABLE

And again Jesus spoke to them in parables, saying, "The kingdom of heaven may be compared to a king who gave a marriage feast for his son, and sent his servants to call those who were invited to the marriage feast; but they would not come. Again he sent other servants, saying, 'Tell those who are invited, Behold, I have made ready my dinner, my oxen and my fat calves are killed, and everything is ready; come to the marriage feast.' But they made light of it and went off, one to his farm, another to his business, while the rest seized his servants, treated them shamelessly, and killed them. The king was angry, and he sent his troops and destroyed those murderers and burned their city. Then he said to his servants, 'The wedding is ready, but those invited are not worthy. Go therefore to the thoroughfares, and invite to the marriage feast as many as you find.' And those servants went out into the streets and gathered all whom they found, both bad and good; so the wedding hall was filled with guests. But when the king came in to look at the guests, he saw a man who had no wedding garment; and he said to him, 'Friend, how did you get in here without a wedding garment?' And he was speechless. Then the king said to the attendants, 'Bind him hand and foot, and cast him to the outer darkness; there men will weep and gnash their teeth.' For many are called but few are chosen."[35]

This parable appears also in Luke 14:16–24. In the Gospel of Luke, the text reads: "Blessed is he who shall eat bread in the Kingdom of God," while the Matthean text reads "The Kingdom of Heaven[36] may be compared to. . . ." In Luke, a "man" gives a "great feast," and he send the servants to get the "the poor, the maimed, the blind," and the "lame," which reflects a change in ideology and rhetoric when we reach the text of Matthew. The man who is dressed improperly is completely absent. The parable also ends slightly differently: "for none of those men who were invited shall taste my banquet."[37]

The differences between the two versions of the parables point to the fact that more than one source was consulted in the process of writing them down and suggest that they were conflated and combined by editors and scribes. We notice in Matthew a number of transformations including the change of "the great feast" into a "king's wedding" and the introduction of the "son" of the king, which is non-existent in Luke. Such changes indicate processes of allegorization by the Church at a later date.

The version in the Book of Matthew seems construed with less style and contains a problematic embedded story of a man with an "improper garment" reminiscent of "The Parable of the Wedding Garment." Since the man in this parable was invited at the last minute,[38] the king's observation and punishment is stylistically out of place and suggest to us a mixing of at least two parables from different sources.

The contextual story in the Gospel of Matthew is slightly weaker. In the pre-parabolic narrative in the Gospel of Luke, the comments attributed to Jesus: "he marked how they chose the place of honor" and "when you are invited by any one at a marriage feast, do not sit down in a place of honor, lest a more eminent man than you be invited by him,"[39] solicit the parable following immediately after and lend it narrational balance in the context.

While the setting in the parable of the Gospel of Matthew reflects the cleansing of the Temple upon the entry into Jerusalem and the inquiry of the elders and chief priest about the authority by which Jesus performs his deeds, the setting in the Gospel of Luke is a Sabbath meal at the home of a Pharisee. Both scenes, obviously contrived, are believable nonetheless and create a realistic atmosphere for propounding parables, yet the version in the Gospel of Matthew is wanting in detail and technique.

The elegant, ironic style prevalent in the Gospel of Luke when citing the reasons offered by the guests for not coming to the feast, "I have got five oxen and I go to examine them,"[40] "I have married a wife, and therefore I cannot come,"[41] the graceful parallelism "go to the streets and lanes of the city,"[42] and the effective parallelism in enumerating, "bring the poor, the maimed, the blind and the lame"[43] are missing in the version of this parable that appears in the Gospel of Matthew. Yet, clearly, this verse alludes to the scriptural verse "The blind and the lame shall not come into the house."[44]

The statement attributed to Jesus stands in stark opposition with the statement made in 2 Samuel, and other scriptural passages where these people are left "outside," "because they . . . are hated by David's soul." We may say then that, in the synoptic Gospel those excluded from "the house of David," namely from the old tradition, are welcomed and most desirable in the new order.

Despite its shortcomings, to a linguist, the text in Matthew is interesting, because its visible redactional "seams" allow us a rare glimpse into textual manipulations done by a parabolic redactor who operates rhetorical shifts and combines disparate sequences of narrational units to lend the new story an aura of authenticity and credibility. For example, the sequence non-extant in the version in the Gospel of Luke, "The king was angry, and he sent his troops and destroyed those murderers and burned their city,"[45] offers insights into the national tragedy of the Jewish people at the hands of the Romans.[46] The shift from "the murderers of His servants" and "the lame," "the blind," and "the maimed," in Luke, to those whom "they found, good and bad"[47]—the change to the unwanted and rejected members of society supplies us with firsthand information about allegorization and transformations by the Church fathers.

Synoptic parables, like the scriptural parables, never stand alone, yet they are essentially autonomous narratives. Their idiosyncrasy affords one the use of almost identical parabolic discursive means in very different parabolic contexts. At the same time, it promotes a quick recognition of an original prototype, despite identifiable differences between any two versions of a parable. The essential independence of parabolic discourse is evidenced very clearly in the synoptic Gospels of Luke and Matthew. The demands of the time and the circumstances must have dictated the rearranging and reorganization of many parabolic texts, yet, since an original parable peculiarly remains identifiable, it allowed its parabolic messages to remain essentially unaltered.

Also unaltered remained the themes reflecting the special needs and the reality of that ancient community. The fact that so many of the themes in the synoptic parables are echoed in the rabbinic literature, and nowhere else, is also a strong indication that the impressive parables of the synoptic Gospels inscribe themselves as an adjacent link in a long tradition and point back to an old legacy of teaching to the masses a lesson that is hard to grasp, through an allusive parable.[48]

The structure of the parables in which Jesus claims to reveal what has been hidden since the beginning of the world, yet keeps it secret from the "others," like the structure of rabbinic parables, is symptomatic of the conflict-ridden society in which they appeared.[49] Moving among various religious factions in that society, an individual was bound to vacillate between diverse groups; hence he is at times posited as the "other," and knows that he is "other," vis-à-vis a specific religious group. In that sense, the rhetoric used by parabolists was transparent to all. "The Parable of the Marriage Feast" is a good example of a text that isolates, with the help of rhetoric, a specific community of believers from the "others" and grant the former a privileged status, "in parable," as Kafka says.

"The Parable of the Marriage Feast" is considered by all a sample of great narrative craft and may be analyzed as a literary and aesthetic object. The parable directs attention to an entire sociocultural and religious semiosis that aims to dislodge and reshape into a new network of relation. In this succinct parabolic narrative, the "old order" is being criticized for its deficient and corrupt religious institutions. At the same time, this "old order" is being displaced and replaced by an alternative religion, which is portrayed as more helpful and more tolerant. This intra-parabolic change, which generates surprise (or shock), permits the mundane to become extraordinary and allows it to be seen with renewed interest.

The synoptic parables have a well-delineated plot, with a beginning, a crisis, and a dénouement. At the onset of the parable, a simple wedding invitation to the king's marriage feast for his son is issued to all. The crisis is precipitated by the prospective guests who "made light of it" (the invitation) and "treated his servants shamefully, and killed them." The king "was angry and sent his troops and destroyed those murderers and burned their city."

In the first parabolic segment, the king sends the servants to the thoroughfares to invite as many as they find. They gathered all, both "good and bad." The next parabolic sequence takes place at the palace during the feast, when the king observes the man "with no wedding garment," orders his attendants "to bind him hand and foot and cast him into the dark." The last verse qualifies as an epilogue, "For many are called but few are chosen."

I show below the parable's narrational micro-structure. The actantial sequences, its thymic and phoric dimensions and the challenges (*défi*) to these actions.

TABLE 3.1
Euphoric and Disphoric States

I. THE KING$_{(+wants/+ready)}$ ⇒	my dinner
Euphoria	my oxen
	my fat calves
II. THOSE INVITED $_{(-want/-ready)}$ ⇒	come –they
Dysphoria	make light –of it
	want off⇒ –to his farm
	–to his business
	seized –the servants
	treated$_{(shamefully)}$
	killed$_{(the\ servants)}$
III. THE KING (angry) ⇒	sends –his troops
Dysphoria	destroyed –those murderers
	burned –their city
⇒	orders –to bind the man hands and feet
⇒	throw –him into the dark
IV. THE KING$_{(ready/wants\ to\ honor)}$ ⇒	his son
	himself
	his guests

In terms of Vouloir = Want to do and Faire = Do, we come up with the expression:

$$V.F._{king} + F._{king} \text{ vs. } (-) V.F_{subj} + (-)F._{subj}$$

V = Vouloir   F = Faire[50]

The actantial sequences are featured in Table 3.2.

"The Parable of the Marriage Feast" can be categorized as a king parable (its main character is indeed a king) and, rhetorically, as a blame parable. Typically, it posits the character "king" as the highest authority. The reader is being alerted right at the beginning that those invited to the king's feast do not consider it an honor and do not feel privileged by his invitation.

TABLE 3.2
Actantial Sequences

Action $I_{LAW} \Rightarrow INVITE_{guests}$

Challenge $I_{guests} \Rightarrow$ Ignore-invitation

Action $II_{Law} \Rightarrow$ invite second time

Challenge $II_{guests} \Rightarrow \left(\begin{array}{c} \text{ignore} \\ \text{kill} \end{array} \right)$

Action $III_{Law} \Rightarrow$ (kill burn) $\Leftarrow$ Challenge III_{Law}

Challenge IV = Ø

Action IV_{Law} Invites everyone $\left(\begin{array}{c} \text{good} \\ \text{had} \end{array} \right)$

Action $(V, VI, VII, VIII)_{Law} \Rightarrow \begin{array}{c} \text{Look, question} \\ \text{expel, bind} \end{array}$

Challenge $V_{murderers} \Rightarrow$ Ø

Action $IX_{Law} \Rightarrow$ Fortell

Challenge $V_{man/murderers} \Rightarrow$ Ø

$KINGDOM_{Earthly} \rightarrow$ Punishment $\rightarrow$ bind/throw-out

$KINGDOM_{HEAVEN} \Rightarrow \left(\begin{array}{c} \text{PUNISHMENT} \\ \text{REWARD} \end{array} \right) = ?$

The addressee of the parable is encouraged from the start to see an anomaly. As subjects of that king, those invited should have considered the king's request a command as well. Proper behavior would oblige those invited to acknowledge an invitation from such high authority differently than "not going" and "making light of it." Disregarding the king's invitation is, therefore, an element of shock in the narrative and represents an affront to the king, who is "ready" and "made ready his oxen and the fat calves." This improper behavior is sure to elicit his anger and vindictiveness.

The question we wish to ask is why are the consecutive invitations/commands of the king met with such disdain and clearly ignored? Were those invited not afraid of the king's wrath? Was partaking in the marriage feast of the son of that king so repulsive an action that they were ready to risk the king's anger? Even more puzzling in the text is the brutal treatment of the king's servants. To ignore a king's invitation is improper; to treat servants shamefully and to kill them is a transgression of the law, and a criminal act. The king's reaction is incongruous and incommensurable with receiving an invitation to a marriage feast. Similarly harsh and unbecoming actions are attributed later to the king. He "sends the troops and destroys the murderers and burns their city."

The following sequence in the parable is also odd. An entire city burned because a few men did not wish to come to his feast and engaged in brutal behavior? Besides, why would a king throw out a man with no wedding garment, bind him hands and feet and leave him in the dark? After all, the man has come to the feast because of a last-minute invitation, when he was found by the king's servants "in the thoroughfares"; he obviously did not have the time to prepare himself properly for the event.

Why does the king act with such lack of kindness? Why does he use such violence? True, the man may have been unwittingly disrespectful since he had no proper garment,[51] but it is important to mention that the king did not tell his servants to bring only the "well-groomed" guests. Could the king afford to be so particular when the others, whom he invited earlier, have plainly refused his invitation?

When the king asks the man "by [what right] did you enter here" (Πῶς εἰσῆλθες), and he addresses him in a direct manner, ἑταῖρε, an expression known uniquely as a Matthean expression, the man remains speechless.[52] Some scholars claim that the man knew that he was a transgressor of the law, and a great "sinner."[53]

The man's silence suggests that he must have sneaked in uninvited together with the others and he felt embarrassed before the king's direct question. He might be an undesirable "other" who "had no right to be there" (which would explain why, when addressing him, the king asks by what right he is there). If the latter is a correct conjecture, then, in saying to his servants get "as many as you find and bring them to the feast," the king either had a secret understanding with his "servants" about who is to be invited and most of those invited had an implicit understanding of how they should appear at the king's feast, or the king's general invitation to his son's marriage feast was insincere. In either case, the parabolic text suggests that something else is at stake and is only implied in the parable. On the one hand, the laws governing the actions of the protagonists are not stated and the reader can only guess what they are, and, on the other hand, the power of the existing law is severely subverted and intentionally jeopardized.[54] Clearly, the official law of the place is diminished, and its authority put into question in the parable by the fact that the law is transgressed by a lawgiver himself (the king kills the men who did not accept the invitation) and by the other characters in the story (they kill the servants who came to invite them, and the man comes dressed improperly).

Unlike in folktales where the punishment is commensurable with the evil deed and the law governing that place is clearly expressed to the people, we distinguish in this parable a pattern that is stylistically peculiar: the rules of behavior for that place are not known and not explained. Also different from the balanced action in a folktale, an unusually brutal behavior dominates the narrative beyond this uncommon disregard for the law.[55]

The radical transgression of the law in this parable takes us back to the equation established by Lacan between the law of man and the law of language. "No one is supposed to be ignorant of the law," claims Lacan, "this formula taken from the heavy-handed humor of our Code of Justice" nevertheless expresses "the truth" in which our experience is grounded and which our experience confirms. "No man is actually ignorant of it, since "the law of man has been the law of Language since the first words of recognition presided over the first gifts . . . uniting the islets of the community with the bonds of a symbolic commerce."[56]

Our negotiations in language of the truths that the law expressed show our cognizance of it at the deepest level:

> In language, as a way things have been expressed or spoken out, there is hidden a way in which the understanding of *Dasein* (being-there-in-the-world) had been interpreted. . . . The dominance of the public way in which things have been interpreted has already been decisive even for the possibilities of having a mood—that is, for the basic way in which *Dasein* lets the word "matter" to it. The "they" prescribes one's state-of-mind and determines what and how one "sees."[57]

The relation between "law" and "truth" in this parable can also be deduced by the isomorphic (similarly shaped) segments of narrative offered to the addressee. The addressee needs to infer from them which ones are metonymic relations and decipher, as a result, the special law that governs in this parabolic text. We distinguish the following narrational fascicles: the servants who come to invite are killed by those invited, those invited "make light of it," the city of "those murderers" is burnt, the man interpellated by the king remains speechless and is thrown out, and in the end, "many are called but few are chosen." We notice a pattern. The paradigm is that the characters who transgress or abuse the law, and the law of discourse in this parable, do so knowingly and intentionally. The relationship between transgression and punishment seems hard to comprehend to the reader only, because for him, the law of the place and the law of that discourse are not explicitly stated, in fact remain an enigmatic parable. Hence, his enlightenment and the enlightenment of the "insiders" must necessarily come from a source other than the parabolic narrative.

If this parable is not to be read as a mere prophetic text, namely as a text that tells that Jesus is the son of God and that he is capable of anticipating his death as a result of betrayal while in his prophetic mission, then the parable in the form we read it today, with its peculiar structural configuration, contains a coded and non-stated message.

In its discursive configuration, "The Parable of the King's Marriage Feast" contains a strong, implicit injunction to its prospective reader to draw a parallel that interprets the death of those invited to the king's marriage feast as similar to that of the Jews at the hands of the Romans and as the act of vengeance of an angry God whose son has been offended, and further to consider the burning of their city, an act of divine retribution. The parable encourages the reader implicitly to see Jesus *as* the son of the King, who is God, and blame those who "made light" of the invitation to the feast, namely who do not wish to be part of the new order, to be guilty also of his tragic end.

The parabolic shifter, "the Kingdom of Heaven," which, in this parable "may be compared to . . . ," generates an analogous topos, another place, where "many are called but few are chosen." Jesus' disciples must eventually make these necessary connections extra-parabolically.

Why must this be so? In our view, the addressee is told of a law, and of the transgression of that law by the king's subjects and by the king, the highest authority of the place. The characters act mysteriously and receive punishments that are equally enigmatic to the reader. Nevertheless, the addressee is encouraged to make a parallel and compare the Kingdom of Heaven with the marriage feast of that king. It follows that to know how the Kingdom of Heaven functions means to understand the laws of the parable. However, since the laws of the parable, as we have shown, are unknown and unknowable to the addressee, clearly the addressee will never understand the laws of the Kingdom of Heaven from this parable alone. We must conclude that knowledge of the divine law of the Kingdom of Heaven must be known prior to hearing the parable, or it will never be deciphered. To that extent, this parable remains cryptic, unless the addressees are already "disciples" and "know" *a priori* what the Kingdom of Heaven is like, by virtue of being part of that hermeneutic community and that semeiosis.

The modern reader of the "Parable of the King's Marriage Feast" must keep in mind that an interpretation also excludes all other possible interpretations. In interpreting we too syncretize elements from various linguistic vistas and bring them in relation to our context. In this respect, interpreting this parable in the present entails also a risk of corrupting it and of losing the thread that provides its own continuity.[58] At the same time, the process of interpreting, the effort to recover the primal voice of the tradition that generated the text in the first place, keeps the canon alive, by extending it, while purging it of stagnant voices.

The layers of new readings and new understandings, of interpretations and reinterpretations of Jesus' parables, intertwine and enter tradition. We might never really get back to the original, unique voice of Jesus, but only to the symphony of voices that kept his voice alive.

CHAPTER 4

Rabbinic Parables:
The Parable of the King's Banquet

THE RABBINIC PARABOLIC MODEL

Rabbinic literature developed in special historical circumstances and was propelled by a powerful ideology of cultural and religious affirmation. Rabbinic literature addressed itself to the pressing issues in land of the Hebrews during the third and fourth century C.E., in an exegetical enterprise we came to call *Midrash*.

Midrash, a Hebrew word derived from the verb דרש (*darash*), describes the body of exegesis of the scriptural texts, as well as the activity of inquiring and interpreting as it was practiced during and shortly after the formative period of rabbinic Judaism. Midrashic literature consists of the legal and homiletic *Midrashim* (the plural of *Midrash*),[1] and is based on actual sermons given by rabbis. Rabbinic exegesis follows the order of the biblical verses.

Rabbinic parables were customarily told to illuminate a particular verse in the Scriptures, therefore can be found in homiletic midrashim (sermons). In rabbinic Judaism, parables were a very important part of the instructional repertoire. Rabbis usually told parables on festivals and on the Sabbath, when they needed most urgently to clarify a scriptural verse, or bring a point home to their audience.

These flavorful narratives were relished by the audience whose rabbis summoned all their poetic, linguistic, and rhetorical skills to clarify a "rub" in a verse, to keep information secret from an enemy, to commend their people, condemn, caution, or celebrate. Propounding parables for the purpose of teaching was a vital part of this ancient communal semeiosis.

In rabbinic tradition, the scriptural verses come to life and communicate semiotically[2] and semantically.[3] When interpreting the text semiotically, the rabbinic addressees looked for the verses' system of signification, the circulation of signs, and the intentionality they expressed. To that extent, each reader could produce his own version of that scriptural text. On the other hand, when interpreting their semantics, the rabbinic addresses worked to include all the possible meanings of that verse. José Faur appropriately states that privileging a "single reading" excludes all other possible meanings, and, as a result, excludes intertextuality.

Faur contends further that, "while the semiotic and the semantic systems are vastly divergent, in rabbinic tradition, Scripture is meaningful at both levels."[4] The semiotic level in *Midrash* involves the *peshaṭ*, or the literal level; the semantic plane contains the *derasha*, or the interpretational level.[5] The *peshaṭ* can be investigated in terms of its structuration; the *derasha*, in terms of its poetics and rhetoric. At the level of *derasha*, each interpretation is subjective and depends entirely on the interpretational skills of the addressee and his approaches to the original biblical verse. Most importantly, the meaning of the parable construed by the addressee depends on the rhetoric maneuvers and the artistry of the rabbinic parabolizer.

RABBINIC MIDRASH AND MODERN CRITICISM

Midrash currently enjoys unusual attention from modern criticism in Europe and in the United States, because it is perceived as the embodiment of a radical alternative to Western conceptions of reality and to its logocentrism. Susan Handelman invites her readers to take note of a distinctively Jewish metaphysics that descends from the early rabbis to modern Jewish thinkers such as Freud, Derrida, Jabès, and Levinas.[6] Geoffrey Hartman and Stanford Budick too set up to find links between poststructuralist intertextuality and rabbinic practices.[7] Soon after, José Faur claimed, uncharacteristically, that:

> The object of *derasha* [the activity of midrash] is liberation from conventional reading, and dissemination of knowledge; more precisely, it is dissemination of knowledge through liberation from conventional reading. As did Jacques Derrida, the rabbis sought "a free play," amounting to a "methodical craziness" whose purpose is the "dissemination" of texts; this craziness, though "endless and treacherous and terrifying, liberating us to an *errance joyeuse*."[8]

In "The Hermeneutic Quest in *Robinson Crusoe*," Harold Fisch discusses more prudently the advantages of juxtaposing the midrashic and the poststructuralist models. He claims that bringing together these two interpretative models could provide an interdisciplinary touch, as well as "free the categories from formal boundaries and restrictions."[9] Contrary to Harold Bloom's controversial famous assertion that later poets invariably experience an "anxiety of influence" because of the greatness of earlier ones, Fisch notes that in uncovering the many similarities between modern models of reading and the *Midrash*, modern critics may experience "an alternative mode of belatedness," the "joy of recognition."[10] He insists that "the dialectic legitimated by the midrashic model is that of surprise and recognition—the unlimited possibility of new readings which never annuls the loving adherence to what is already known."[11]

Robert Alter, who wrote extensively about biblical poetry and literature,[12] disagrees with these "modern midrashizers," as he calls them, on the ground that the similarities they find with the Midrash are superficial. He claims that the similarities are only "one of those instances of the convolutions of cultural history in which a new loop exhibits surprising correspondences to a very old loop, and by so doing, shows certain instructive continuities in the diversity of cultural expression."[13] In antiquity, when the midrashic interpreters perceived "surface irregularities in the biblical text," they used techniques similar to those of poststructuralists, such as Paul de Man or Jacques Derrida.[14] However, while the rabbinic style is associative and unsystematic, and invites a proliferation of readings, rabbinic intertextuality, unlike the modern, is rooted in a firm understanding that the biblical canon is timeless, all-inclusive, and self-referential. Midrash is not mere free association; it is a textual system with fixed boundaries all divinely underwritten and follows fixed, homiletic conventions. Unlike current deconstructionist trends whose primary exercise is to detect and undo opposition in a text, *Midrash* has as its goal to teach and reaffirm rather than unsettle the "hierarchical opposition" between God and man, good and evil, redemption and exile, and so on.[15] To those who did *Midrash*, the Torah was given by God and remained present in the world concretely as the source of all authority, a source to measure by our own knowledge, accomplishments, and observations. And rabbinic literature in its totality comes to illustrate this worldview.

ORAL AND WRITTEN RABBINIC PARABLES

Like biblical parables, rabbinic parables are rhetorico-poetic narratives entwined in larger texts. Rabbinic literature as a whole comes from men who had no real interests outside religion and law.[16] Heirs to the early biblical sages, the prophets, and the psalmists, the early rabbis traditionally aimed to demonstrate the ubiquity of God and the infallibility of the Holy Scriptures. They had no interest in *belles lettres*, in poetry, or science (medicine excluded). The tradition of the rabbis who had one book upon which to exercise their wits was intended to be preserved and transmitted orally as a part of the *aggadah*, of storytelling.[17]

For a long time, to write down legal decisions and prayers, parables and arguments was considered impious, even tantamount to "burning" the Torah. In maintaining an oral tradition the sages must have aspired to ensure spontaneity in prayers, freshness in literature, and refinement of the law, which, they felt, had to be adaptable to the changing needs of a society permeated by ceaseless turbulence.

Under Roman occupation, the voices of the rabbis began to falter. When study was proscribed and ordination became punishable by death, when the danger of mass slaughter of scholars and the subsequent decay of tradition became imminent, the rabbis turned to the written word.[18] Thus began the long process of codification of the oral tradition and the canonization of Scriptures, which, while rescuing that tradition from annihilation, also produced its calcification. With the codification and canonization of rabbinic literature, rabbinic parables, inextricably woven, remained immured in it like ants caught in amber formations.[19]

An integral part of a highly stylized literature, rabbinic parabolic narratives were perfectly adapted to oral transmission. The traits most suggestive of an oral mode—the large number of mnemonic devices, stereotypes, and codes—demonstrate a clear intention to facilitate quick remembrance and easy dissemination and transmission.

Typically, rabbinic parables have highly formalized configurations and narrational characteristics.[20] They begin with a formulaic introductions such as "lemah zeh domeh"? ("to what does this compare," or "to what may this be likened?"), and continue with: "emshol mashal" ("To explain this, I will tell you a parable"). Commonly, these parables have a cast of protagonists in a play-like production. The application is introduced by a parabolic shifter such as "therefore" or "and so" ("kach"), to equate dissimilar domains of discourse and logic for persuasion purposes. Rabbinic parables commonly end with the scriptural verse that the parabolizer wished to investigate; usually, a part of the Torah reading for that specific week.[21]

To bring the rabbinic parabolic enterprise into better focus, we present here two examples. To highlight the transformations and the encodings that took place in later rabbinic parables and parable-like narratives, I have chosen first a text from *Ecclesiastes Rabbah*, which is essentially a compilation of midrashic commentary by rabbis on the Book of Ecclesiastes. The translation is my own, except for the biblical verses, where I have followed the King James Version, but for a few non-significant pronoun changes. In the next chapter, I investigate an eighteenth-century parabolic "tale" by the great Rabbi Nachman of Bratslav. In presenting the two parables side by side, I hope to evidence similarities between parables told over a thousand year span, while highlighting the transformations that took place in rabbinic parables over time. This will help us also understand the transformations and recodification in early modern parables and parable-like tales due to dramatic changes in the semiosis of Eastern European diaspora Jewry.

THE PARABLE OF THE KING'S BANQUET

R. Phineas, in the name of R. Reuben, told this parable:

> A king made a banquet, and he invited guests to it, and he decreed that each guest should bring what he was to lie on. Some brought rugs, some brought mattresses, some brought coverlets, others sheets, others chairs, and some brought logs and some stones.
>
> The king examined everything, and said, "Let every man lie on what he brought." They that sat on logs and stones were angry with the king, and said "Is it fitting for a king's honor that his guests should lie on logs and stones?"
>
> When the king heard what they said, he said, "Not enough that you have polluted my palace, upon which I spend so much, but you are impudent and accuse me. I did not injure your honor; you injured it yourselves." So in the world to come, when the wicked are condemned to hell, they will murmur against God, and say, "We hoped for thy salvation and now this has come upon us." God will say, "In the other world were you not quarrelsome, slanderous, evil doers, men of strife and violence, as it says, 'Behold, all ye that kindle a fire, that compass yourselves about with sparks: walk in the light of your fire, and in the sparks which ye have kindled.' Do ye say that this is from my hand? Nay, you did it to yourselves; therefore: 'in pain shall ye lie down'."[22]

I call this parable "The Parable of the King's Banquet," because of its beginning and to facilitate interpretation. As indicated in the first line, it was told by a certain Rabbi Phineas, in the name of R. Reubin. The parable is a blame parable embroidered upon the biblical verse from Isaiah.[23] The sermonizer uses parabolic rhetoric to show that the unfaithful Jews are to blame themselves for the afflictions that come upon them.

Fortunately for the investigator of parables, in rabbinic texts we are customarily informed of the identity of the specific parabolizer and told of the circumstances in which the parable was narrated. In the rabbinic *mashal* under investigation, Rabbi Phineas apparently wished to interpret for his addressee the meaning of the biblical verse from Isaiah, where God says "This shall you have from my hand: you shall lie down in pain," a verse that must have caused puzzlement to the rabbinic addressee. As was the custom, the parabolic narrative ends with the biblical verse the parabolizer wished to elucidate, "in pain shall you lie down." We note, however, that the rabbi gives only a fragment of the verse from Isaiah at the end of the parable, a seemingly unimportant omission, but one that deserves our attention.

At the figurative level, the king in the parable is representing God and the king's guests, the people of Israel. While the two images are quite popular in parables in general, a significant change is introduced in this rabbinic tale. Customarily, banquet parables talk about the food, the appearance, or garments of the guests. A discursive shift is being made, and honor (*kavod*, בבוד) becomes the focal point of the parable. This categorial difference and lack of linguistic relatedness between *banquet* and *honor*,[24] together with the ambiguity inherent in the word *honor*, encourages multiple interpretations.

The tension maintained by the rabbinic parabolizer even after the parable has been "explained" points to the fact that the parable is structured by strict conventions of fiction. Its internal rhetorico-poetic mechanisms enable it to produce parallelism and similarities where, in reality, there are none.

"The Parable of the King's Banquet" is preceded by the semantic marker "*classème*,"[25] "parable," to alert the addressee about the kind of structure and information the follows. Unlike in modern parables, where the reader is left to establish on his own whether a given text is parabolic or not, the rabbinic midrash is *ḥaviv*[26] or "user-friendly." Indeed, in defining itself "a parable," the narrative tells *a priori* that it intends to offer the addressee/reader/audience a moral lesson in an oblique way.

By cutting up the narrative trajectory of the parable into chunks of texts that interconnect to generate meaning, we can unravel the parable's semiotic wrapping and its metaphorical mapping. In pointing to the transfers (linguistic remapping) along the narrative path from one linguistic domain to another and from one semiotic level to another, we can understand how analogies are being concocted and maintained in this parable. For example, by inserting the parabolic shifters "כך" ("therefore," "and so," etc.) between two segments, the rabbinic sage suggests analogy even though the two narrative sequences are visibly not analogical.[27]

In the parable under investigation, we distinguish four narrational sequences, or segments, corresponding to a number of *isotopies* (meaningful chunks of text). The parabolizer shrewdly uses these parabolic shifters and maneuvers the scriptural material to create associations in the mind of his addressee. He hopes that with the aid of rhetoric, changing the emotional state of the parable's subject—the *guest* of the king (in our parable), he will also make a change in the real world; he will persuade his audience/addressees to become strong believers.

To be analogous with each other, the four narrational cycles of parable should each have four subsequences (as the first one). Yet even a casual look at the diagrams below reveals many empty sets (Ø) in place of narrational subsequences. We notice that subsequence b_1 beginning with "so in the world to come" points to a lack and generates a semantic void we marked $ß_1 = \emptyset$. Moreover, the parabolic deflective shifter "as it says" is grafted on to subsequence b_4, in order to generate a third semiological isotopy C. The gaps in sequence C are even longer and omissions point to further semantic voids. Five out of the seven possible subsequences are missing. Sequence D, assumed to operate the return to the original narrational cycle, is the most anomalous of all and lacks all the isotopic subsequences except part d_4, and d'_2 and d'_2 differ from its potentially analogous c_2, which is void.

Paradigmatically, false isotopies in the parabolic narrative blur the distinction between heterogeneous texts that have been "stitched" together for the particular sermon. Syntagmatically, the division is even more difficult to make, because unlike poems, where the stanzas are often heavy demarcations of isotopic sequences, parabolic discourse tends to obscure its semantic markers.

The schemata below show the function of each subsequence in the narrative: conjunctive, disjunctive, consequential, subsequential. At the same time, they show the emotional "sensitizing" of the discourse (*état pathémique*): euphoric, dysphoric, violent, impudent, quarrelsome, loving, and so on.[28]

The first narrative sequence (A) of the parable is made up of three narrative subsequences, which begin respectively with: "A king," "the king," and "when the king." The parabolic shifter *so* helps the parabolist to equate the first narrational sequence of the parable with the second sequence (B), which changes from the perspective of *this world* to the landscape to the *world to come*. The parabolic shifter establishes a surface semiological isotopy, thus enabling Rabbi Phineas to transport the addressee from "this world" to "the world to come" and from "the here-and-now," to the "here-after."

The second narrative sequence, "When the wicked . . ." is followed by another shifter, "as it says," which creates a new semiological isotopy between the second and the third sequences. Sequences B and C are also divided into subsequences. Sequence B, which embraces the third sequence, ends with "Do you . . . yourselves." The fourth sequence D is introduced by an additional parabolic shifter, "therefore." This parabolic shifter assists Rabbi Phineas to take the addressee back, "to transport" him emotionally and narrationally to the biblical text in the fourth sequence, and end his parable with a fragment of the verse from Isaiah: "In pain shall ye lie down."[29]

But while the biblical verse is meant literally as an eschatological statement, the dénouement is here part of fiction. The parabolizer's craft in overcoding and code-switching causes the listener not to notice the double valence inherent in the parable. Before his seduced audience, Rabbi Phineas leaps from the past tense directly into the future, to a fictional timeless time when men who "in the other world were . . . quarrelsome, slanderous, evil doers," are now "condemned to hell." Yet this "now" is parabolic, namely, a discursive artifact.

The mastery of Rabbi Phineas is this: In establishing in parable a bridge to the world-to-come, R. Phineas succeeds in cautioning his audi-

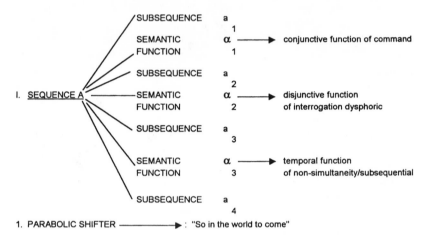

FIGURE 4.1
Structure of First Narrative Sequence

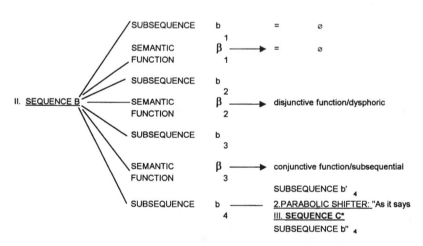

FIGURE 4.2
Structure of Second Narrative Sequence

ence, who complained about their present lamentable state, about the hereafter, and, at the same time, bring solace to those who act honorably toward God in "this world."

The parabolist claims an isomorphism between sequence A and sequence B of the narrative, in order to facilitate the logical inference in sequence C. Thus from A —> "so in the world to come," to —> B; from B —> "as it says," to —> C + Support from biblical text; from C —> "Therefore," D and returns to the original biblical text to complete the circular discursive trajectory taken by a questioning disciple/narratee/audience of the rabbinic midrashist.[30]

The unstated initial question, "Why does God say in the Book of Isaiah, 'This shall you have from my hand; you shall lie down in pain?,'" is the "rub" of this scriptural verse because it puts God in an unfavorable light. It is only partially invoked at the closure of the last sequence of the parabolic narrative to bring the audience back to the Scriptures and to the "story above," but, this time around, in a new disposition vis-à-vis it. This new inclination toward the scriptural text is instilled by the rabbi's art.

The question could have been triggered by a confused student of the Bible who read in Isaiah that God, whom all believers assume all-merciful, says to his people Israel, "By my hand shall you have this." The question might have been also initiated by the parabolizer himself in his *proem*, or *petiḥta*, a mini-sermon told as an introduction to the lec-

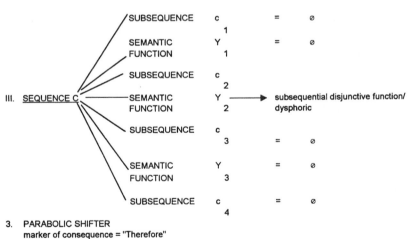

FIGURE 4.3
Structure of Third and Fourth Narrative Sequences

tionary-verse that began the weekly reading of the Torah, which frequently contained parables elaborating on that particular biblical verse.[31]

In the first narrational sequence, the "king," a signifier of power and unquestionable authority, "invites guests," another discursive subject, to a "banquet" he "makes." The power coordinates are set up from the beginning. Customarily we associate the "king" with complete authority over his subjects, "his guests," and they, in turn, are bound to him by unquestionable obedience.

The verb "decreed," in the subsequence, "the king decreed that the guests should bring," duplicates the relation of power set up at the beginning of the parable between the king and his "guests" and shows to the addressee of the parable that the king is cognizant of his power and uses it. He makes further use of his power when he "examined everything" and again when he decrees that "every man lie on what he brought." The king in our parable uses a ploy. "His guests" must provide for their own accommodation: "Each guest should bring what he was to lie on."[32]

Importantly, none of the guests in the narrative transgresses. Each one of them does bring something: "some brought rugs, some mattresses, some coverlets, others sheets, others chairs, and some brought logs and some stones." At the surface level, they have all obeyed the order of the king, hence, from the point of view of the narratee/audience, there was full compliance with the law of the king, the power holder.

In the following subsequence, however, a dysphoric event is introduced to alert the audience: First, "they that sat on logs and stones were angry with the king," and next, they ask: "Is it fitting for a king's honor that his guests should lie on logs and stones?" The lexical item "angry" is syntactically and semantically supported in the deep structure of the adjacent narrational sequence, where the "guests" proceed to complain openly to the king. The unhappiness and disappointment with the king's law, which is accepted (they do what they were told), has triggered "anger" on the part of his guests.[33]

The "guests" seem incapable of aiming overtly at the "king's" power. They do not overthrow him, refuse his invitation, or leave when he tells them to sleep on what they have brought with them. Their attack is indirect; the "angry guests" aim at one of his attributes, at his "honor." They say in protest: "Is it fitting for a king's honor?," which indicates also that they are afraid of the king and his wrath.[34]

In order to explain why God appears vengeful and malicious toward man, cleverly, the rabbinic parabolizer operates a rhetorical pirouette and makes the discursive subject talk about honor (that of the king and of his guests). While in deep narrative structure the parable deals with relations of power, its overt hypercode and focal point is honor.

The guests' choice of honor as the target attribute of the king, in their wrath against him is not innocent. The Bible is seasoned with abundant references to "honor."[35] We read that the Lord declares: "Far be it from me: for those who honor me I will honor, and those who despise me shall be lightly esteemed."[36] Accordingly, the rabbinic commentator expounded on this biblical verse:

> Who is honored? He who honors others. For it is said: "For those who honor Me I will honor and those who despise Me shall be held in contempt" (Isaiah 50: 11). It is the most common thing that people who seek honor for themselves behave towards others with reserve bordering on arrogance, and that they make very much of themselves but very little of others. Such conduct, they think, is the surest way to secure the respect and esteem of others. But this Mishnah knows otherwise. Honor, genuine honor, is just another one of the great gifts deriving from God, and it has a way of going to him who covets it least. He who does not despise any of his fellowmen, but respects them all as בריאות, as "creations" of God, giving them due honor for the sake of Him Who created them, actually honors God, the Creator of them all. And of such a man, God says, "Him who honors Me, I shall honor." Conversely, he who despises his fellow men God will let him sink into oblivion.[37]

The verse, "everyone who is called by my name, whom I created for my glory, whom I formed and made,"[38] has been commented upon thus in Ethics of the Fathers 6:11:

> Whatever the Holy One blessed be he created in his world, he created for his glory, as it is said: "Everything that is called by my name (God's), it is for my glory that I have created it; I have formed it I have made it" (Isaiah 43:7). It says also: The Lord shall reign forever and ever" (Exodus 15:18). And R. Hananyah ben Akashyah said: "The Holy One, blessed be he, desires to purify Israel" (Isaiah 42:21).[39]

Honor, as stated in the Bible and commented upon further by the rabbis, comes to an individual from two separate sources: from his deeds toward his fellow men and from honoring God. The honor that comes to an individual from honoring God, say the sages, is the highest honor a man could aspire to, since as cited above, "for His own glory has He created them."

To illustrate this point in his parable, Rabbi Phineas connects God, man, and honor in a particular order. He then argues, parabolically, that if man is dishonored by God, it is because his evil deeds dishonor God's creations, and not because of God's malevolence.

Rabbi Phineas introduces in the parable first the guests' protest and attack on the "king's honor." In saying that the king's deed is not fitting for "his honor," the guests induce a paranoid state in the king. He is put in the position to react to their accusations, reaffirm his power, and proclaim his actions just, so that "his" honor remains intact.

The honor of the king is encoded in the parable as reflexive and transitive, and is mirrored in the "king's" retort: "Not enough that you have polluted my palace, upon which I spend so much, but you are impudent and accuse me. I did not injure your honor; you injured it yourselves." In this fashion, the "king" turns the tables around and, after accusing them of polluting "his palace," of "being impudent," and "injuring their own honor," he exonerates himself. It is not *his* honor at stake now, but that of the "impudent guests."

Syntactically, the narrative functions are indicated by figures 4.4 and 4.5.

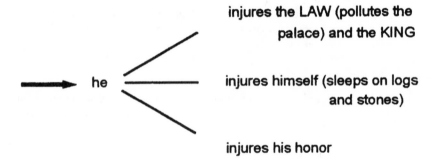

FIGURE 4.4
Narrative Function Expressed in the Third Person

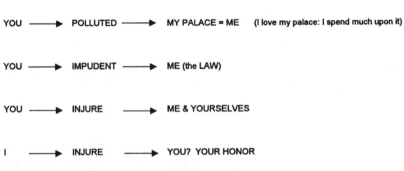

FIGURE 4.5
Narrative Function Expressed in the First and Second Person

Why is this exculpating gesture by the king brought into the story by our parabolist when the narrative begins with a happy event, a banquet given by someone in power, who apparently is obeyed? Furthermore, why the demand upon the guests to "bring what you lie on"? After all, the *king* in the parable is obviously rich: he has a "beautiful palace, upon which he spends so much." In asking these questions, I want to underscore that there seems to be something disquieting at stake that is not overtly stated. In the parable's symbolism, the misgivings of the guests, and the criticism they voice against the king indicate an underlying questioning of God and *his* treatment of *his guests,* the "chosen" people. In showing that the *wicked* will be punished, the parabolizer instills fear in those who transgress and, with the same rhetorical gesture, brings hope to his faithful audience in "this world."

The king's reaction to the guests who are putting into question the justice of his law ("they must bring what they lie on") is abrupt but unambiguous: each guest who has used it incorrectly and "polluted the palace," was "impudent," and "accused him," has brought upon himself his own dishonor, namely, he must now "sleep on logs and stones." The king's law is just; it is the guests who have misused it. Thus the parabolist disculpates the "king" in this parable. Symbolically, the rabbinic parabolizer exonerates God's actions toward Israel, while indicting "His people," who have drifted away from "His Law."

In the following sequence, the verbs "pollute," "behave impudently," "injure," and "accuse," point syntactically an accusatory finger at the guests, even though the king has actually not told them *what* to bring, but only, *that* they should bring "something to lie on." No guest has transgressed the *decree* of the king: each guest lies on what he has brought. No transgression of any kind seems to take place at this level either. Why, then, this attack by the king of the parable upon their expressing "anger" with him?

The rabbinic midrashist brings the point home by entwining full obedience to the king's law with honor rather with power. He arrives at the central images in the narrative, the pollution of the king's palace and the impudence of the guests, and intimates that there is a more serious danger foreseen by the king in the parable: a distrust in his *law.* Rabbi Phineas insinuates that there is a similar distrust of *God and His Law,* by the people of Israel.

The king has discovered *from* the actions of his guests that they did not take his decree seriously. They have polluted his palace with all kinds of unsuitable objects, because, in his view, they did not believe that he will actually make them sleep on what they "brought with themselves." Hence, he accuses them of not having taken his law seriously and of having, thus, transgressed.

With the parabolic shifter "so in the world to come," produces an eruption in the narrational cycle. The new sequence is semantically different, but syntactically parallel to the first. And it is this syntactic parallelism that is responsible for generating the illusion of similarity. The "wicked are condemned to hell by God." No narration of their transgression is being offered, nor do we find an explanation of how the divine law has been misused by them; there is only their condemnation to hell.

As the guests became angry with the king in the first sequence, in the "world to come," "the wicked murmur against God" in this next sequence. Yet, while in the first cycle there is a syntactic and semantic identity between the king who decrees and the king against whom they are angry, we find no textual evidence that the lawgiver who proclaimed the wicked's "condemnation to hell" is identical with "God" against whom "they (the wicked) murmur." There is no syntactic co-referential antecedent in this segment to God to establish the sameness of the "condemning law" and God whom they "murmured against." Instead, the passive voice is being used: "when wicked are condemned to hell."[40]

This discrepancy is reinforced further by the statement: "we hoped for thy salvation and now this has come upon us." The expression of anger and disappointment acts as a syntactic double to the complaint of the "angry guests" in the first cycle. While in the first sequence the addressee (Ae) is agent and patient of the same action X, in the second sequence, the addressee is agent of actions $X_1, X_2, X_3, \ldots X_n$: "quarrelsome, slanderous, evil doers etc.," but the addressee is semantically *and* syntactically the patient of an action Y, by another agent A', different from the addressee, and not marked textually.

A new shift occurs with the marker "as it says," whose parabolic function is equivalent to that in sequence A, in the last subsequence. The sequences "You are so impudent and accuse me, I did not injure your honor; you injured it yourselves" drive back to the statement at the end of the text, "Do ye say that this is from my hand? Nay, you did it to yourselves." The parable concludes with a fragment of the biblical verse, introduced by the shifter "therefore" and the *nimshal*, or the moral lesson, "In pain shall ye lie down," the biblical reference to Isaiah 50:11. The moral lesson, whose primacy is argued by Daniel Boyarin, David Stern, and others,[41] is a new narrative, whose primary role is to highlight the special covenant between God and Israel.[42]

The meaning of the parable cannot be deduced from any one sequence. It is encrypted in the thick layers of signs we discover at each shift from one sequence to another, and from the narrative proper to the moral lesson. The addressee has to construe the parable's meaning *in* the helical motion that this parable draws him in.

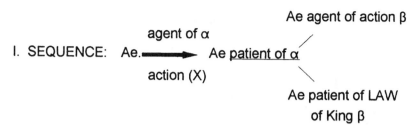

FIGURE 4.6
First Narrative Sequence in Terms of Agent Patient Relations

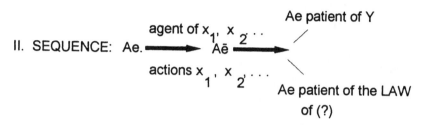

FIGURE 4.7
Second Narrative in Terms of Agent Patient Relations

There are three topoi in the parable. The first, "the king's banquet," the topos of the "world to come." This is a "utopos," since if it is yet to come, it is not yet here, that is, it is not. This topos is analogical to the king's world in parable. The third topos, "this world," is analogical to the first two; "world to come" implies (even though it is not stated) "this world."

The discursive coordinate most manipulated by the rabbinic parabolizer is temporality. Parabolic temporality is suggested by the past tense in the first and second narrational cycle. The future tense is used for the biblical reference only: "shall lie down" and no actual present features in the parable. The past is being projected by the rabbinic parabolist *directly* into the future. This shows his concern with the past and the future, rather than with the here-and-now, and mirrors the rabbi's desire to make his audience look at the future rather than look at its present condition of suffering and subjugation. Below are sequences:

THERE   IN THE PARABLE
IN THE WORLD TO COME
vs. IN THE OTHER WORLD

THEN   NO-TIME/ALWAYS(All verbs in the past)
        NOW (This has come)
        vs. SHALL LIE DOWN (future)

Temporal adverbs *then/now* creating the before and after:

THEN   YOU POLLUTED
KINDLE FIRE
before vs. after
NOW   YOU ACCUSEWALK IN THE LIGHT OF THE FIRE
THEN   YOU INJURED
before vs. after
NOW   YOU ARE
        IMPUDENT

Distribution of the noun phrases (NPs) and verb phrases (VPs):

NP	NP OF VP
King	Banquet/guests
He	Logs, coverlets, stones, . . .

The isotopies related to lexical configurations:

NP	VP	NP
we	lie on logs and stones	king's honor
_____/	_____/	_____
guests	now this has come on us	thy salvation

Further lexical distribution:

NP	VP	NP	VP	NP
You	polluted	I	spend	
You	are impudent			
You	accuse			
		me		
		I		
	injure			your honor
You	injure	your		honor

The spatial components equivalent to the temporal adverbs:

In parable (parabolic world) _____ here vs. there

In the other world
In the world to come

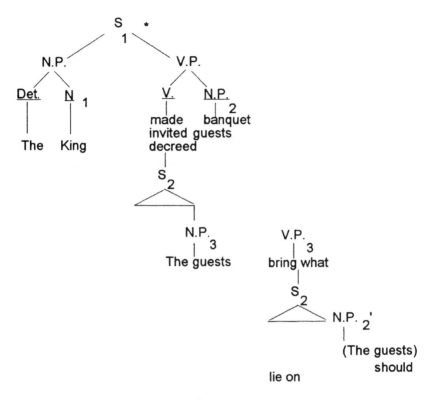

FIGURE 4.8
First Sequence Syntactic Deep Structure

We find that the discursive makeup of this rabbinic parable comments upon its logical structure, and conversely, its logic dictates its syntax. Paul de Man has termed it "a rhetorization of grammar, and a grammatization of rhetoric."[43] To reconstruct this parable's encoding, we look at these two domains. Scrutinizing the lexical items' anomalies in each sequence as well as its rhetorical play, gives rise to multiple interpretational possibilities.[44]

The following are transformational schemes for parallelism.

II.   a) Is it fitting for the king's honor that his guests should lie on logs/stones?
b) We hoped for thy salvation and now this has come upon us.

III.   Sequence A, subsequence a₃: Not enough that you have polluted my palace, upon which I spend so much, you are impudent and accuse me. I did not injure your honor; you injured it yourselves.

Sequence B, subsequence b₃: In the other world were you not quarrelsome, evil doers, men of strife? Do ye say that this is from my hand? Nay, you did it to yourselves;

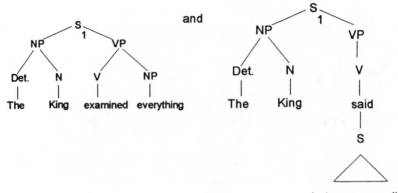

FIGURE 4.9
Syntactic Deep Structure of Two Parallel Sequences

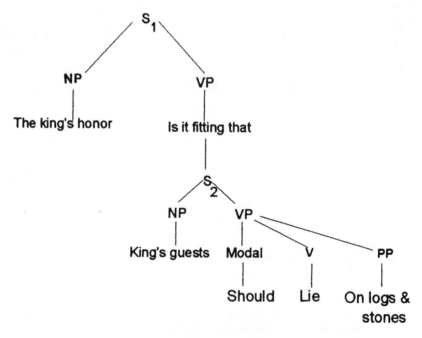

FIGURE 4.10
Syntactic Deep Structure of Parallel Sequences

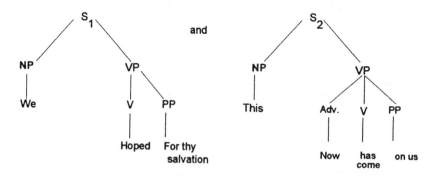

FIGURE 4.11
Syntactic Deep Structure of Parallel Sequences

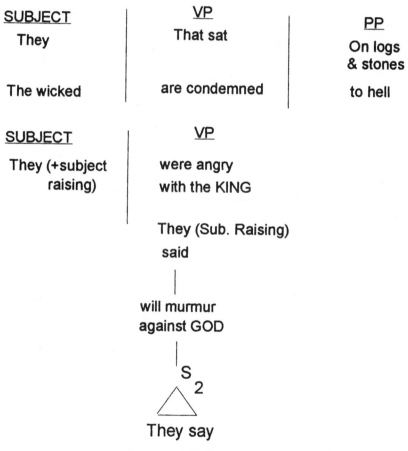

SUBJECT	VP	PP
They	That sat	On logs & stones
The wicked	are condemned	to hell

SUBJECT | VP

They (+subject raising) | were angry with the KING

They (Sub. Raising) said

|

will murmur against GOD

|

S₂

△

They say

FIGURE 4.12
Example of Equivalent Syntactic Structures

See equivalences:

you have polluted . . .	=	you were evil doers . . .
my palace upon which I		
spend so much	=	the other world
You are impudent		
and accuse me	=	Do ye say that this is from my hand?
I did not injure		
your honor; you		
injured it yourselves	=	Nay, you did it yourselves

Prepositional phrases forming isotopies are shown in Figure 4.13.

While isotopies create illusions of similarity and facilitate the sequential transitions in the parable so that its addressee is caught in the play of equivalences, semantic discrepancies insinuate themselves in the narrative and generate gaps at the level of transitions and within transitional sequences. For example, note the semantic differences in the following sequences:

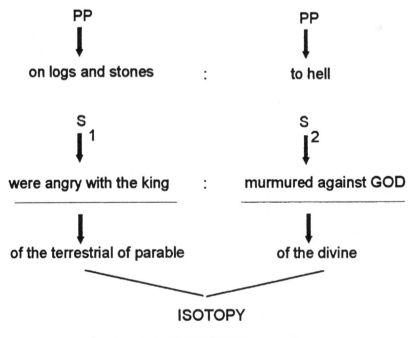

ISOTOPY

FIGURE 4.13
Examples of Phrases Forming Isotopies

Sequence A: obedience to the command of the king
Sequence B: disobedience of the command of (?)
Sequence A: complaint because of obedience to the law
Sequence B: complaint because of punishment by the law
Sequence C: complaint because of disobedience of the law (?)

At the pathemic, or emotional level, we notice shifts in the emotional states of the king and that of his people, indicative of additional modal and aspectual transformations. Parabolic images, such as the "banquet," change from euphoric to dysphoric. The "banquet" is at the beginning "conjunctive" and euphoria inspiring between the "king" and his "guests/subjects," but becomes "disjunctive" in the end of the first cycle, because it generates the guests' "anger" against the "king." In a similar fashion, the verb "invited" acts first as a conjoining element but serves later as a disjunctive element between the king's "decreeing" (that X) and the guests "bringing" (X'), which is displeasing to him.

The syntactic makeup of the narrative belies a further distortion in the parabolist's rhetoric. Rabbi Phineas implicitly tells his audience that their actions in "this world" cause God's reactions to be good or bad in the "world to come." But the reactions of the king in the parable are antecedent to the actions of the guests at every point of the narrative. Every action of the king's guests is in reality a reaction, and the king remains always in a position of power.

His position of power is expressed in an interesting way. If we concentrate on the use of the verb *say* throughout the parable, we find that there is an interesting tense distribution.[45]

See figure 4.15 for the distribution of the verb "say" and figure 4.16 for the shifts in grammatical subjects.

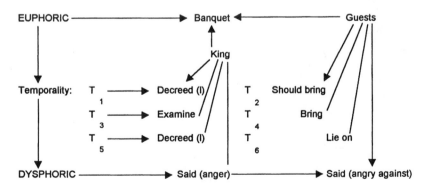

FIGURE 4.14
Examples of Dysphoric and Euphoric Elements

The king examined and *said*

They _____ angry and *said*

They _____ *said*

He _____ *said*

/

They _____ will murmer and *say*

God _____ will *say*

/

AS IT SAYS

FIGURE 4.15
Distribution of the Verb "Say"

King   King/God_____Ar = power

                                                          obedient
Guests   guests/you_____Ae = <
subject   disobedient
God

You/they/ye/ye

King	guests
decreed	lie on logs and stones

God		wicked		ye
____	vs.	_____	vs.	_____
says		came (this)		walk in
(condemns)		upon us		your fire

FIGURE 4.16
Shift in Grammatical Subjects

dysphoria	____	lie on logs/condemned to hell/walk in fire/lie in pain
euphoria	____	banquet with king/ walk with God/ salvation

The rhetorization of grammar, as anticipated by de Man, serves to create, in the narrative, symmetries that lead the addressee of the parable to believe in the existence of analogies in the parable. "Rhetorization ends up in indetermination, in a suspended uncertainty that was unable to choose between at least two models of reading,"[46] whereas the lexical symmetries, the grammatization of rhetoric, becomes a device for searching the truth, albeit through deception and simulation that obscure logical tensions.[47]

A transformation has occurred in the codic inscription. This parable's unique contribution is not its portrayal of the omniscient divine power, nor necessarily its commentary on man's honor, but the appeal to the people of Israel to part with their "polluting ways" that injure God, and become faithful again.

The illusion of freedom of choice before the Divine Law is created by artistic manipulation of language. The king proclaims that the guests should bring with them what to lie on, and when they do not bring what is pleasing to him, he accuses them of polluting his palace. Similarly, God, in the "real world," condemns those who question his judgment (the wicked) to hell. The fact that the parable has generated a fiction of freedom from a binding law called the "real world" and the "world to come" is revealed in the last sequence, which brings us back, parabolically, to the Bible and to the Divine Law. The rabbi states at the end that *it* (the Bible) *says* unquestionably and immutably to that community, and thus, brings the audience back to the reaffirmation of the eternal power of God's law. That the "Bible speaks" remains for the rabbinic parable the final and irrefutable authority to which one refers.

Between the sequence "let every man lie on what he has brought" and the verse "In pain shall ye lie down," from the Book of Isaiah, this parable enacts its own exegesis of the biblical verse "Therefore, in pain shall ye lie down (die)" and tells us of its own theorizing moment. In establishing parabolically the analogy between the king's guests who are sentenced to lie on logs and stones, and the wicked, who are condemned to hell, the parable acknowledges its own purpose to persuade its addressees of an ideology by which, in the "world to come," "those who kindle the fire walk in the light of their fire" (the part of the biblical verse that is not mentioned in the text of the parable).

To secure success in teaching this ideology, the parabolic narrative becomes "purloined,"[48] namely, when analyzed as narrative, it speaks of being "exegesis," and when looked upon for its exegetical moment, it teaches belief. Like the "purloined letter," parables are meant to circulate.

They come to us through "double or even triple filters, and are not the consequence of a fortuitous arrangement."[49] Parabolic rhetoric suspends logic and opens up possibilities of auto-referentiality. To that extent the rhetorical, figural potentiality may be equated with literature itself.[50]

What then of the assertion *in pain shall ye lie down*? The seduction of the text comes into being only when "honor" and "dis-honor" move from "this world" to "the world to come," with the reference to the Bible. The parable asserts this transfer in its concluding sentence "in pain shall ye lie down." The transfer is a didactic and anagogical exercise that we call parable. Their rhetorical model does not offer help in positing the question "why" from outside the narrative.

Still, does the incursion into rabbinic parables lead us to some certainty? We noted that it deconstructs the authority of its own rhetorical mode. In the vacillation between the "world of the parable," which is fiction, the "real world," and the "world to come," the reconciliation of fact and fiction occurs as a textual assertion and produces further parabolic text. The addressee remains in a state of ignorance, never able to deduce whether *he will lie in pain*. He cannot deduce narrational sequence D in a logical manner from A, B, and C. Instead, he learns about parables and how they change him in "this world."[51]

Since the decoding of the parable offered by the addressor contains a textual gap, clearly, the rabbinic parabolist demands of his addressee a competence outside the parable, a praxis and a know-how of decoding parables that help him fill in the gap:

> Behold, all ye that kindle a fire, that compass *yourselves* about with sparks, walk in the light of your fire, and in the sparks *which* ye have kindled. *This shall ye have of mine hand* [all emphases are mine]; ye shall lie down in sorrow.[52]

The riddle of the missing antecedent "by my hand/ (God's)" is not to be solved *in* the parable. The midrashist's/addressor's (Ar) work is

$$\text{Ar.: (SAVOIR X) w (VOULOIR FAIRE FAIRE)} \quad \text{w (FAIRE SAVOIR)} \quad \text{w (SAVOIR X')}$$
$$\text{Ar} \qquad\qquad\qquad\qquad \text{Ae}$$

EQUATION 4.1

$$\text{Ae} \underline{\quad\quad} \text{CROIRE SAVOIR X + SAVOIR X'}$$

$$\text{Ar} \underline{\quad\quad} \text{SAVOIR X + VOULOIR FAIRE FAIRE} \quad\text{+ FAIRE FAIRE} \quad\text{+ FAIRE SAVOIR}$$
$$\text{(Ae)} \qquad\qquad \text{(Ae)} \qquad\qquad \text{(Ae) SAVOIR X'}$$

EQUATION 4.2

not only to exculpate God and show that his deed is a result of man's impudence, but to teach his listener/addressee (Ae) to decode his messages and possess the same kind of knowledge with him. The manipulation of the parabolical discourse is the seduction operated by the addressor on the addressee (equations 4.1 and 4.2).

To the question "Why, rabbi, would the all merciful God strike us, and by 'his hand' shall we lie down in pain?" The entire rabbinical parable is a reply. Or is it not?

CHAPTER 5

Chassidic Parables:
Two Kinds of Faith

You have the void for face . . .
You have the void for voyage.

—Edmond Jabès

Even a casual look at the chassidic and geonic literature reveals that the parables and sayings by the chassidic sages and the *Geonim*[1] have preserved to a great extent the spirit in which rabbinic parables were propounded by the ancient teachers. In examining below one of these "parabolic tales," I hope to show that despite visible changes and deviations from the original model in the *Midrash*, early modern tales and parables represent a clear link in this vast undertaking.[2]

The Chassidic parables frequently depart from the rigid linguistic pattern of the rabbinic discourse, but are visibly suffused with stereotypical material and follow established practices. I suggest that, while the intermeshing of Scriptures with the chassidic rabbis' own interpretations is not at the core of the Chassidic tales, eighteenth-century rabbinic works[3] and many tales of the Vilna Ga'on and of his contemporary and friend, the great Maggid of Dubno,[4] or the eminent Rabbi Nachman of Bratslav,[5] are strongly influenced by ancient rabbinic parables and have been read as parables. Furthermore, while the transformations are noticeable and the new garb in which these narratives appear are largely the outcome of the sociocultural climate of Eastern European diaspora that has produced them, quite visibly, eighteenth- and nineteenth-century Eastern European rabbis have continued the rabbinic parabolic tradition.

The popular communal variety of Jewish belief, better known as Chassidism, and its spirited geonic rabbis, have left to us a wealth of parables and tales that have maintained the mood as well as the intentionality present in early rabbinic parables, if not their distinct style and precise configuration.

In tracing the transformations that have occurred in parables and parable-like narratives with their move to a new language and a new political and cultural climate and with the passing of centuries, we notice that their changes mirror these equally dramatic shifts in the semioses of the communities that have produced them. In following the changes in parables told by the chassidic rabbis, we learn how the Chassidic community communicated and what were its messages to its successors. We also get a better picture of the cultural processes that made possible the unique reorganization of signifying systems among Eastern European Jewry.[6]

To pierce through the semiotic web of the communities whose parables we investigate here, we revisit the phenomenon of Chassidism and Geonism whose new spirit is of significance here.[7] Chassidism sets the undivided wholeness of human life in its full meaning; the understanding that it should receive the world from God and act on the world for the sake of God. In times when the oppressed Jews began to question their "choseness," Chassidism, with its charismatic leaders who championed merriment and action, offered a more attractive life orientation than the stagnant, dogmatic traditional rabbinism. Chassidism perceived man as an active participant, whose role was to improve himself and ameliorate his relation with the divine.

The radical ideas behind Chassidism have been clearly delineated by Martin Buber: "Chassidism is not a category of teaching, but of life; the chief source of knowledge of Chassidism is its legends and only after them comes its theoretical literature."[8] The Chassidic message was that the separation between "life in God" and "life in the world" can be overcome in genuine, concrete unity. This is not to say, however, that God's position in man's life was diminished in the Chassidic worldview: "Chassidism preserves intact God's distance and superiority to the world in which He nevertheless dwells."[9]

Chassidic ideology, like that of the Geonic rabbis, transmitted largely through parables told orally by the pious rabbis to their eager followers, has emerged as pivotal in the organization of the Chassidic tales. The supporters of these rabbis who were relishing these didactic tales, were elaborating, and reproducing them with embellishments to avid masses of believers, as a homage to the greatness of their revered sage. Later, many of these tales were collected and written down for posterity.[10]

Chassidic tales, like the parables in the *Midrash*, continued to cling to God's law as an unquestionable guarantee for their authenticity and credibility, and aimed to instill faith in God in those who heard or read them. Yet the scaffolding upon which the eighteenth- and nineteenth-century rabbis have built their narratives is other than the primary text of the Scriptures, and the exegesis of the scriptural verses played only a secondary role to them.

In the rhetorical play with the pragmatics of didactics, the Chassidic rabbis positioned the receiver of the tale/parable at a lower level vis-à-vis an assumed discursive level. Unlike in earlier parables, their addressees were presumed unlearned and, more significantly, unbelievers. In telling the stories to the untutored, the rabbis were fulfilling their primary role: that of reinforcers of chassidic ideology aiming to bring the uninstructed to a higher spiritual level. By telling parabolic tales, the chassidic rabbis were bettering their people's lives and, at the same time, were improving their flock's relation with the divine. In short, the chassidic rabbis felt they were "turning Jews on" to God.

In promoting their tales, the East European rabbis were also revitalizing their communities, which were continually drained and depleted of their spirit by intense poverty, unrelenting deprivations, and harsh discriminatory laws.

Benno Heinemann says that Rabbi Kranz, known as the Maggid of Dubno, became famous particularly for his parables, which he called in Yiddish *mesholim*. His directness and classic simplicity with which he illustrated a lesson were known throughout the land.[11] "In addition to his great learning and eloquence," says Heinemann, "this rabbi was endowed with a rare talent of being able to treat commonplace subjects in an uncommon manner and finding a Scriptural verse or a parable to suit almost every aspect of day-to-day living and conduct."[12]

We analyze below one of Rabbi Kranz's well-known parables on the theme of mourning. He begins by setting the stage for his parable: "Every year," he would say, "for a period of three weeks beginning with the 17th day of Tammuz[13] and ending with the 9th of Ab,[14] the Jews go into deep mourning for the Holy Temple in Jerusalem. He would say to his listeners:

> We had two Temples, the first one destroyed by Nebuchadnezzar (Nabuchodonosor), the King of Babylonia, the second was razed by Titus and his Roman legions. Now we have no place that can be called the Sanctuary of God on earth. But our prophets have given us God's promise that in due time, we shall have a third Temple, which will remain for all eternity, and those who mourned the most bitterly for Israel's lost glory will have grief turned into great rejoicing."
>
> "The Prophet Isaiah said:
>
> שמחו את ירושלים וגילו בה בל אהביה
> שישו אתה משוש כל המתאבלים עליה ·
> (ישעיה סו')
>
> 'Rejoice with Jerusalem and be with her, all of you who love her; rejoice with her great rejoicing, all of you who mourn her.'"[15]

"In other words," the famous rabbi would continue, "those who genuinely keep the 'three weeks' of mourning for our Temple, who forgo all pleasure and entertainment in memory of Jerusalem, will be privileged in due time to rejoice in the rebuilding of our Holy City and the Sanctuary therein."

But why say "Rejoice . . . with her *great* rejoicing"?

The Maggid of Dubno had his answer ready in the form of a *moshol* (the singular of *mesholim*):

A man embarked on a long journey which was to take him to distant lands across the sea. After he had gone for some time, reports reached his home town that his ship had met with accident and that he had been drowned. His wife and children were prostrate with grief. His friends, too, were deeply shocked, and even those who barely knew him were momentarily stunned. As time went on, however, the memory of the man they had esteemed so highly grew dimmer in their hearts. But though the months passed, his immediate family never ceased to mourn for him.

Then, one day, the door of the man's house opened. Behold, there stood the man they had thought was dead, very much alive! The good news quickly spread through the town, and soon the house was crowded with friends who came to express their joy at his safe return. Those who had known him but slightly were pleased for him and his family. But his intimates, who had felt genuine sorrow when he had been presumed dead, were more than merely pleased; they were overjoyed that their friend was still among the living. And his family, of course, were beside themselves with happiness. Those who had mourned the most for the lost traveler were the happiest now that he had returned.

The same applies to our own mourning for the Temple and for Jerusalem, and to the happiness that will be ours when, in due time, both the City and the Sanctuary will rise again. Jeremiah said: "And I will turn their mourning into joy and I will comfort them, and make them rejoice from their sorrow" (Jeremiah 31:12). In other words: The exuberance of their rejoicing will be in direct proportion to the tears they shed when there was reason to mourn. All of Israel will rejoice when the Temple will rise again in Jerusalem, but the degree to which they will rejoice will depend upon the extent to which they wept before. And those of us who truly mourned for Jerusalem will then indeed *"rejoice with great rejoicing"* at its rebuilding.

Much the same idea is expressed in the *Shir Ha-Maaloth* which we sing on Sabbath and Holidays: *Hazorim beimah berinah yikzoru.* *"Those who sow in tears will accordingly reap in joy."*[16] The more genuine and heart-rending our tears for the lost Temple, the greater the joy and exultation that will be ours at its restoration.[17]

At first glance this *"moshol,"* or parable, seems to explain in the manner of ancient parables, the scriptural verse from Isaiah. The verse reads a bit differently: "Rejoice with Jerusalem with great joy." A closer scrutiny of the structure of the pre-parabolic text and the body of the parable, on the background of the history and socioeconomic conditions of the Jews in Eastern Europe, makes us realize that an actual reversal takes place in this early modern parable. The verses from Isaiah, Jeremiah,[18] and the Psalms,[19] were conjured up by the famous rabbi to validate and support his tale, aiming to encourage and bring solace to a despairing community that must have grown disheartened by the persistently adverse conditions in which it lived. In other words, the biblical verses have been invoked primarily to corroborate the Maggid's tale, which claims that better times are in store for the Jews in Diaspora, rather than to have the tale illuminate the meaning of the scriptural verse, as was the case with the *mashal*, or parable, in *Midrash*.

The body of the parable is preceded by the explanatory sentence: "The Maggid of Dubno gave his answer in the form of a *moshol*, or a parable." As in the introductory notes, or pre-parabolic text in ancient parables, the famous Chassidic rabbi alerts the listener to the fact that the narrative following is a parable. However, the discursive configuration of the parable deviates from the classic rabbinic pattern. The narrative begins with the verse from Isaiah followed by the "historic background," namely, "the mourning by the Jews for the Temple in Jerusalem" on each year after the destructions of the Temple. Next, the saying of the prophet Isaiah is invoked again, and the focal point of the parabolic narrative shifts immediately to the question of why does the prophet say to his people "rejoice with great rejoicing."

The intertwinement of the three scriptural statements, as well as the actual narrative, differ significantly from the classic form. Instead of the narrative fitting the scriptural verses, these verses are told to "express much the same idea" as the rabbi's narrative. Another noticeable change in this Chassidic parable is the fact that the protagonist is no longer a king, but a man, a traveler, who leaves his family and friends for a long time and who is presumed dead and mourned by all, especially by his close ones. Possibly, this change has been introduced so that the example can be made more graspable and closer conceptually to the poor and the uneducated, who no longer knew about kings or their lives.

All these transformations notwithstanding, the luminous mood, the happiness, and the exultation experienced in parable by the return of the departed man to the family who had the strongest of loves, were obviously meant to spill over to the audience of the Maggid, change its mood for a better one, and give it hope, as was the case in ancient parables.

To elaborate further on the character of Chassidic tales, and trace their narrative organization to classic rabbinic parables, we examine below a narrative labeled a "tale" by its Chassidic propounder. We submit that, despite important codic and structural differences manifest in this parabolic tale, its function, as much as its spirit, is akin to that of the classical rabbinic parable, therefore it may be inscribed in the helix of parabolic discourse that has come down to us since biblical times.

THE PARABLE OF THE TWO KINDS OF FAITH

Why do we say: "Our God and God of our fathers?" There are two kinds of people who believe in God. One believes because he has taken over the faith of his fathers, and his faith is strong. The other has arrived at faith through thinking and studying. The difference between them is this: The advantage of the first is that no matter what arguments may be brought against it, his faith cannot be shaken; his faith is firm because it was taken over from his fathers. But there is one flaw in it: he has faith only in response to the command of man, and he has acquired it without studying and thinking for himself. The advantage of the second is that, because he found God through much thinking, he has arrived at a faith of his own. But here too there is a flaw: it is easy to shake his faith by refuting it through evidence. But he who unites both kinds of faith is invincible. And so we say, "Our God," with reference to our studies, and "God of our fathers" with an eye to tradition.

The same interpretation has been given to our saying, "God of Abraham, God of Isaac, and God of Jacob," and not "God of Abraham, Isaac, and Jacob," for this indicates that Isaac and Jacob did not merely take over the tradition of Abraham; they themselves searched for God.[20]

This parabolic tale, attributed to Rabbi Nachman of Bratslav, was collected by Martin Buber, the tireless Jewish scholar of Chassidism.[21] In seeking to answer the tale's introductory question, Rabbi Nachman, like ancient parabolists, instead of focusing on the actual reasons why we say, in addressing the Lord: "Our God and God of our fathers," makes a shift and elaborates on why, by learning from others and studying for ourselves, we become "invincible." Here too, the tale's cause is the question. Just as the parables in the *Midrash*, this tale is a device, a didactic stratagem for teaching about a certain truth to the inquiring individual who ostensibly does not know the answer.

The ideological dimension of this parable comes within the scope of a semiotically oriented rhetoric. Semiotics, informed by rhetorical categories in its account of the labor performed to overcode, transform, or switch codes, seems most pertinent to reveal how Chassidic rabbis, as the ancient rhetoricians, used the art of persuasion.

This is not a pejorative comment upon the work of the ancient rabbis or their Chassidic followers. "Persuasion," Umberto Eco reminds us, "was not necessarily an underhanded device in antiquity, but rather a socially oriented form of reasoning that did not deal with the 'first principle' (such as those of formal logic, i.e., identity, non-contradiction, and the excluded middle principle) and could not therefore use apodictic syllogisms."[22] "Rhetoric," he argues further, "overtly dealt with *enthymems*, i.e., syllogisms which also moved *from* probable premises, but to 'emotionally' and 'pragmatically' influence the listener."[23]

In attempting to outline the chain of signifying systems by which the Chassidic rabbi persuaded his narratee in this Chassidic parable, it is useful to understand the textual mechanism of switching domains, of overcoding and undercoding. For example, the initial question "Why do we say . . . ?" vividly calls to mind the prefatory questions of the ancient sages: "Why is it [the thing] so?" or "what does this [thing] resemble?," because of the similarity in the semantic fields of the two expressions. With the initial question, this parabolic tale echoes the ancient tone and jolts the eighteenth-century listener and transposes him into a known and familiar, scriptural territory. The rhetorical deflection in the narrative and the new sequence, introduced by "There are two kinds of . . . ," is also suffused with the ancient lacemaker's handiwork. The subsequent narrative, imported rhetorically, with its own plot, parameters, and system of veridiction, functions here too *as* the explanation to the initial question of the rabbi/addressor.[24] The assumption here too is that the explanation and clarification of *this* parable entails the explanation and clarification of the original question, with which it is supposed to be analogical.

However, here again, the "equivalence" is only the effect of the rhetorical art and the persuasive skills of the parabolizer. As Umberto Eco asserts: "in the activity of rhetorical substitution, contextual and circumstantial selections are switched and overlapped, and short circuits of all sorts create sudden and unpredictable connections." The unexpectedness of these jumps and their suddenness has for the listener the effect of a revelation, or "illumination."[25]

As in classic rabbinic parables, the possessor of knowledge, the Chassidic rabbi, does not put into question the validity of each narrational segment presented to his listeners; like his predecessors, he assumes them self-evident.[26] His implied assumption, sustained by the tale's coding, is that the need for belief is unquestionable.

The rabbi stitches then together the epistemic and the alethic modalities, the modality of knowing with that of truth,[27] and convinces his addressee by playing on logic. The sage equates the act of "saying" with that of "believing" and with "becoming invincible" and proceeds to enunciate before his already lured listeners the rules for becoming invincible, rather than offering the reasons for saying "Our God and God of our fathers."

The Chassidic parabolizer encodes ideology by using the kind of reasoning found in ideological argumentation.[28] Enthymematic reasoning explicitly assumes that the premises from which it starts are probable (i.e., matter of opinion), the rules of the game are observed and straightforward persuasive intercourse results. To sway his addressee to act in the desired way, however, this chassidic rabbi makes a dramatic switch from the enthymematic to ideological reasoning. Specifically, he operates a rhetorical code-switching and turns the straightforwardly persuasive argument into an ideological one by erasing, or elegantly sliding, with a parabolic tale, over the threshold between what is considered an ideological argument and obvious persuasive discourse.

Through this process of "overcoding," the chassidic ideological message, which starts with a factual description, is being justified theoretically by the tale. In telling this parable, the rabbi is in actuality negotiating the acceptance of an ideology, and beyond that, an entire *Weltanschauung*. In this sense, the early modern parabolist's style is akin to the Marxist positive sense of ideology, where ideology is an intellectual and political weapon serving the social purpose of actively modifying the world.[29]

Indeed, interpreting the expression "Our God and God of our fathers" involves an ideological dimension that determines that interpretation. At the same time, this interpretation depends to a great extent on previous coding.[30] The ideological background upon which the listener has to rely in order to understand the string of words "Our God and God of our fathers" is reached through a complex coding system and through inference involving a series of presuppositions about the sender, Rabbi Nachman of Bratslav, and the object/subject of the sentence, "we."

The seduction and transposition of the listener from one sociocultural and linguistic domain to another by the sender, the Chassidic rabbi, who in reality wishes to teach him about belief, is organized and embedded in the narrative at the syntactic and semantic level of discourse. An investigation of the discursive syntax of the tale confirms that the narrator operates a conjunction of two divergent and separate narrative sequences, which he proceeds to present to the narratee side by side as analogical entities (figure 5.1).[31]

The question "Why do we . . . ," which has inspired the Chassidic rhetorician's answer dealing with the need for conjoining the two kinds of belief (A + B) in order to become invincible, is followed by the shifter "There are two." By switching modalities, the parabolic shifter functions here as a double marker: it introduces two operations in the narrative and, a new narrative that acts *as* the answer to the initial question.

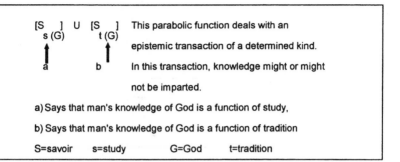

FIGURE 5.1
Conjunction of Two Divergent Narratives

Noteworthy is the first switch operated in the parable by the modal shift from the initial modality, related to "saying," to a new modality associated with "believing." This new modality is then assumed by the storyteller to be analogical to the first.

The answer of the narrator, beginning with the statement "One believes . . . ," produces the subsequent switch in reasoning. This produces in turn a kind of textual scission in the reply, a shift in gears, a "débrayage," which erases the enunciation markers and delegates to the actors/agents of the narrative all the expressional function.[32]

The discursive marker "two kinds of people" introduces new coded information about each of the two groups created by the first parabolic shifter. The parabolizer assumes that the marker *question* and the *answer* are equivalent and smoothed gently over the distortion created by that shift in the narrative.

We see that the entire tale is propelled forward by three types of parabolic shifters that operate several deflections in the narrative: *shifters of division* (S.D. generate differential gaps in the text), *shifters of information* (S.I. introduce new information such as, "but there is a flaw in it," "the advantage of the second," or "there too there is a flaw"), and finally, *shifters of analogy* (S.A. generate analogies such as, "the same interpretation has been given to").

If we mark knowledge (*savoir*) = S, S_s = man's savoir of study, S_t = man's savoir of tradition, and m = man in both instances $m_1 = m_2$; $m_1 = m_1$, we can express thus the makeup of the code *savoir*, or knowledge (figure 5.2).

S_s reads: man's knowledge of study is man's knowledge of God through that same man's knowledge = study/thinking of God.

S_t reads: man's knowledge of tradition is man's knowledge of God as function of another man's (antecedent) knowledge of God (figures 5.3 and 5.4).

$$S_s = S_{m_1}(G) \quad [\varphi \quad S_{m_1}{}_{(G)} \quad]$$

$$S_t = S_{m_1}{}_{(G)} \quad [S_{m_2}{}_{(G)} \quad]$$

FIGURE 5.2
The Formula for Supreme Knowledge

$$S_S = S - \rho \ (S_{m_2}) \quad \rightarrow$$

FIGURE 5.3
Knowledge of Tradition

$$S_t = S - [-\rho \ (S_{m_1})] \quad \rightarrow$$

FIGURE 5.4
Knowledge of Study

However, both S_s and S_t are said to be incomplete, namely the knowledge of study lacks knowledge through the other → where $\rho \ (S_{m_2})$ is a quantitative coefficient and the knowledge of tradition lacks knowledge through self → where $-\rho \ (S_{m_2})$ is also a quantitative coefficient, complementary with $\rho \ (S_{m_2})$

Therefore, $S = S_s + \rho$; $S = S_t + (-\rho)$

One can derive: $S = S_t \cup S_s =$

$$S_{m_1}(G) \cdot [\varphi S_{m_2 \ (G)}] - [-\rho (S_{m_1})] \cup S_{m_1 (G)} \quad [\varphi S_{m \ 1(G)}] - \rho (S_{m_2})$$

$$S = S_t \cup S_s = S - [-\rho] \cup S - \rho = S + \rho \cup S - \rho = S \ ^{33}$$

FIGURE 5.5
Supreme Knowledge

Rabbi Nachman of Bratslav needed to convince the poor and oppressed Eastern European Jew that he offered him not only the knowledge of the kinds of faith one needed to have in this world, but how to use each of them to become the invincible. In other words, the chassidic rabbi needed to persuade his listener that he was giving him a weapon with which to fight and win in this (here and now) world.

To bring the listener to see his worldview as logical, the rabbi had to use in his tale an augmentative kind of argumentation. Accordingly, each narrational sequence points the listener to a certain kind of power and makes him believe that each sequence in the narrative, if accepted as true, could give him additional insight into how to become invincible.

The rabbi had to put forth two kinds of knowledge: one transitive, the second reflexive. The subject of enunciation "we"—an intervention of the subject of enunciation in the narrative—like the instructor of the prince, in Machiavelli,[34] is cleverly showed first the advantages of each *valorized object* [each kind of faith]. He then proceeded to demonstrate the indisputable superiority of the believer who is capable of conjoining the two kinds of faith. This rhetoric move is translated syntactically by the narrator's unifying the two *acteurs*, or agents, to form an *acteur collectif*, namely, a collective actor/agent/subject.[35] This operation takes place with the aid of the conjunction "and," followed by expressions "the advantage of the first," and "the advantage of the second," "but here too," or "but."[36]

In surface structure, "faith," "obligation," and "transmission of faith" are signs circulated and recycled to produce new ones, proposed to the listener as better. This is accomplished in deep syntactico-semantic structure by a shift in temporality from the past to the present and, subsequently, to the future as in midrashic parables, where the parabolist also wished to orient his community to the "world to come," that is, to the future.

Abraham, the revered patriarch and originator of the faith, is invoked to bring the past swiftly into the present mood. The narratee is told that "Abraham had his faith and his God" in whom he believed and "he gave that faith" and "that belief in God to his son Isaac," who, in turn, "accepted" it and "verified" it. The listener is also told that "the following generations did likewise." A long lineage of illustrious predecessors—Abraham, Isaac, and Jacob, who have gained faith from their fathers and from their own study, in the act of "accepting" and "verifying"—is inaugurated by the addressor before his captivated listener whom he wishes to cast as well into "the loop" and entwine him into the generational thread of believers.

To accomplish this, Rabbi Nachman switches to a "now," a present, where one "ought to have the same need" for transitive *and* for reflexive knowledge, or *savoir*, and obtain this knowledge in the same fashion as the ancient Jewish people.

The transfer of knowledge is made in the first case, by father's believing (*croire*) in God, M (man) believes in God. In the second case, M (man) believes in God because M (man) studies about God.

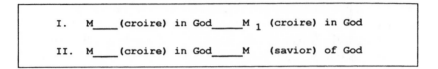

I.   M____(croire) in God____M $_1$ (croire) in God

II.   M____(croire) in God____M (savior) of God

FIGURE 5.6
Transfer of Knowledge

The "lack," or "the flaw," assumed in the first believers exists because their belief comes from other men's belief and the lack in the second type, because their belief comes from the self only. But the deficiency, as well as the "remedy" are construed *in* the parable, where the addressor plays also on the notions of "weakness," "power," and "invincibility." Each kind of belief is forceful, he claims, yet contains a flaw that transforms power into weakness. The parable-like tale clearly aims at inculcating the conviction that to conjoin the two kinds of belief is to eliminate weakness and become invincible.

Like the old sages, in parabolizing, the chassidic rabbi moves from one semantic category to another and equates vastly disparate domains. He persuades his listener that he is "decoding" the message of the two kinds of believers, when in reality, the addressee never finds out the answer to his initial question. Finding out "why" one should unite the two kinds of belief, is not finding out why are we saying: "Our God and God of our fathers."

The statement in the third sequence, "God of Abraham, God of Isaac, God of Jacob," is not at all the natural outgrowth, or logical consequence, of the sequence "God of Abraham, Isaac, and Jacob," but represents a significant rhetorical leap. This vigorous rhetorical maneuver, which ends with the marker "and so," has the addressee accept the entire reasoning and allows him to enter the narrative spiral set up in the parabolic tale.

If we mark knowledge and know how, respectively, *savoir* and *savoir faire* (in regard to a certain body of information X) and we note narrative with n, we can express how the transformations in modalities move the addressee to believe that knowing X = knowing X′ = knowing X″. The manipulation is achieved through φ P, a parable-like function and a deflective movement of the kind:

$$\varphi P = [FAIRE_{Ar} \, (FAIRE \; CROIRE)_{Ae}])$$

$$\begin{bmatrix} +\text{SAVOIR} \\ +\text{SAVOIR FAIRE} \end{bmatrix} \, _{Ar}{}^{(X)}$$

$[\text{VOULOIR FAIRE FAIRE}]_{Ar}\text{of (Ae)}:\varphi P_{Ar}\text{of (Ae)} \quad [\text{SAVOIR}]_{Ae}(X)=[\text{SAVIOR}]_{Ae}(X')$

FIGURE 5.7
Modalities Expressing Transfer of Knowledge

The Chassidic rabbi has never put into question a fundamental belief. He tells a parable to induce the listener to believe in God as his predecessors did and to that extent is purely dogmatic.

But the Chassidic parabolizer has to take one step beyond his predecessors because he is armed with new knowledge: that of diaspora conditions. In his despair over the modern Jew's circumstances, the Chassidic rabbi insists that believing only because one's ancestors did so is not enough, because this is, he shows, an opening to weakness. To learn about God on one's own, he attempts to persuade his listener, is an equal duty, and the conjunction of the two kinds of faith, a prerequisite to invincibility.

The scriptural verse upon which the *midrashic* parables were usually expanding has become marginal in this tale, even though their injunctions hover over the narrative and infuse it with a sense of immediacy and urgency. We suggest that the modern narrative moves the listener from "why we say" to "how we ought to believe," in a clearly opposite direction to the *midrashic* parables that moved the audience from a point of indisputable belief (in the Scriptures and in their absolute veracity), namely, from "we believe," to understanding what exactly the Scriptures "say." This dramatic change in parabolic discourse is quite telling of the changes in the semiosis of the Jewish community. In ancient times, the Jewish community, strongly bound by a common belief in God, was considering God and the God of its fathers, the only God. This is not so with Eastern European Jewry. Painfully fragmented by internal conflicts, disillusioned to a great extent by God (who has allowed the dismal and humiliating conditions of his "chosen people"), and continually agitated by the strong winds of modernity, this community had to be refocused and have its faith in God restored. The Chassidic rabbis' dilemma was not the lack of understanding what the holy texts said, precisely. They had a more urgent need to convince modern Jews to go on believing in God. And only after bringing them back to the ancient faith of their forefathers, by reminding them what all his ancestors were "saying," could the modern rabbi count on teaching them how to learn for themselves and, subsequently, concern themselves with what the Scriptures did actually say.

PART III

Imperial Messages

CHAPTER 6

Wisdom Lost:
Modern Parables

FRANZ KAFKA AND MODERN PARABLES

In this chapter, I deal with the last link in the parabolic chain. I chose to structure this chapter around Kafka, the man who has shaped modern parabolic discourse as well as our understanding of it. My hope is that this step will encourage future inquiries into modern parabolic discourse.

To illustrate the distinct turn taken in parables with the writings of Kafka, I highlight below the complex networks of codes in Kafka's parables, and trace his unique aesthetics—a new aesthetics of horror—together with the symbolism underlying Kafkan parabolic discourse. While it would be far beyond the scope of this study to embark on an exhaustive analysis of all the literature about Kafka and about modern parables, I offer here a limited assessment of Kafka's parabolic writing and his unique contribution to the genre, against the backdrop of major Kafka criticism. I also offer a sketch of the work of Jorges Luis Borges, Italo Calvino, and S. Y. Agnon, three other major modern parabolists who were influenced by Kafka.

To anchor my discussion of the transformations that occurred in modern parables, I examine first a number of new parameters that have become pivotal in Kafka's parabolic narratives. Next, to acquaint the reader with the flavor of modern parables, I look closely at one of Kafka's parables, side by side with representative parables by Borges, Calvino, and Agnon, three modern writers who have distinguished themselves in this stubborn yet resilient genre. Specifically, I analyze in detail Kafka's parable entitled "The Imperial Message," next to "Cervantes and *The Quixote*," a parable by Borges, and "Cities and Signs," by Calvino. Next, I add Agnon's "Before the Kaddish" to this sample of modern parabolic discourse, as an homage to his lifelong dedication to the revival of the ancient Jewish tradition. In this fashion, I show that the Kafkan parabolic system of codes is ubiquitous in parables written by authors who have followed him and have come to consider him their precursor. In doing so, I hope to indicate a number of innovations and unique features present in Kafka that prevail in the work of all those who wrote parables after him.

In choosing this order of presentation, I wish to evidence on the one hand Kafka's brilliant innovations, and on the other, his (and his followers') indebtedness to the ancient Jewish parabolic mode. In this fashion, Kafka and his followers can take their place as modern, pivotal links in a very long chain of skillful practitioners of parables who wrote or told parables since antiquity, and who have perennially transformed and adapted this recalcitrant genre and tuned it up to the needs of their time.

Revealing the prevalence of Kafkan parabolic features in a cross-section of modern parables brings further support to my overarching argument that the changes in the shape and use of parables have occurred as a result of radical religious and cultural transformations at the core of our being in the world and of our witnessing. That is to say, a careful scrutiny of the various changes in parables in a cross-cultural study allows the reader a glimpse of modern man's massive estrangement from his hermeneutic community and from tradition. Such insights enable the reader to understand the process by which modern man has learned to create stylistically more complex parables, but has lost the ability to understand what parables really mean. Indeed, by revisiting parabolic discourse since antiquity, the reader realizes that what parables meant to those for whom they were propounded in ancient times seems equally enigmatic and lost for us, post-Holocaustian inquirers, as for Kafka, the man who anticipated the Holocaust in his fragmentary writing. History has eroded the latent sense that originally was an integral part of the parable in its historical context. Modern parable "is born as a historical orphan," and "lacking any communalizing 'covenant,' the text refuses to disappear behind the interpretative commentary."[1] Finally, focusing on meaning, on patterns of change in the shape of parables, and on the cryptic messages reveals not only new information about this enduring genre, but helps us figure out the reasons for the dramatic changes in the configuration and purpose of parables in the course of time.

KAFKA'S AUTHORITY

With a large gesture, Harold Bloom claims that our understanding of Kabbalah is "Kafkan."[2] We wish to add that just as our modern understanding of Kabbalah seem to be Kafkan, our understanding of modern parabolic discourse is modeled upon a variety of ambitious interpretations and speculations about Kafka's parables. Richard Gray insight-

fully asserts that Kafka has shaped our very definition of modern parables, since we have come to understand the nature of modern parables
in the very act of interpreting Kafkan texts.[3] However, Gray fails to
point out that we have molded our understanding of modern parables
around those written by Kafka, because, despite his troubled relationship with Western classical writing and with Judaism, Kafka has become
its undisputable literary as well as spiritual leader.

By examining below Kafka's multifaceted literary and metaphysical
undertaking, we evidence the reasons for Kafka's prevalence as spiritual
and literary authority as well as his widespread influence on the Jewish
and non-Jewish world.

TENSIONS

Kafka's work dramatizes the tensions in his personal life as much as the
crises in the external world, which fueled his literary imagination. On a
personal level, Kafka had to contend with powerful outer forces and
inner struggles that pulled him incessantly in opposite directions. A profoundly unhappy man, Kafka was physically fragile and lacked the vigor
and robustness of his impressive father, whom he perpetually tried to
please. Despite the fact that Kafka had to fight all his life against his
father's powerful figure, Kafka admits that all of his writing intended to
explain himself to his father.[4]

Socioculturally, Kafka experienced great difficulties as well. As most
intellectual Jews of Central Europe, Kafka was brought up in the German culture and remained torn between his loyalty to his Jewish heritage and his deep fidelity to German enlightenment. His love for German, some say especially for high German, combined with a fierce
passion for language augmented his anxiety. For example, before allowing any of his writing to be published, Kafka took pains to adjust their
spelling, vocabulary, and punctuation to High German.[5] At the same
time, Kafka was strongly drawn to the Yiddish theater and to Jewish
mystical literature.

Some scholars, Gilles Deleuze and Félix Guattari among them,
maintain that Yiddish played a crucial role in Kafka's literary outlook.
According to them, Kafka viewed minor literature (Yiddish) as having a
predominant role in its society and as endowed with political significance to its people.[6] However, we agree chiefly with Ritchie Robertson,
who questions the validity of Deleuze and Guattari's claims about the
special place of Yiddish in Kafka's literary enterprise.[7] We doubt very
much that Yiddish was for Kafka a way of eluding his literary father,
Goethe, an escape from Goethe's overpowering masterful shadow. It is

not unusual that an artist's craft serves as an escape from his fears; therefore, we recognize that one of the many roles played by literature in Kafka's life must have been an escape. We find more plausible, however, Ritchie Robertson's assertion that "literature represented for Kafka a means of escaping from his actual father."[8]

Marthe Robert captures further tensions that characterized Kafka's life and work, which were shaped in an environment riddled with contradictions. Notably, she points to the tensions between Kafka, the Jewish writer in Central Europe, and Kafka, the German-educated man. Robert notes that Kafka's writing is so complex, it allowed the German critic Robert Müller to claim that "there is something profoundly German, smart, which does Kafka honor"; at the same time, Max Brod, Kafka's Jewish friend who refused to destroy his manuscripts as ordered by Kafka, could say that even though the word "Jewish" was never used in Kafka's texts, these texts are "among the most Jewish documents of our times."[9]

AT THE CROSSROADS OF CULTURES

Kafka's position at the crossroad of three cultures, German, Jewish, and Czech, allowed him to synthesize in his stories elements from all three cultures and offer his readers a devastating portrayal of the ills plaguing modern Jewish society, and Western culture as a whole. Kafka aimed at the core of modern predicament. With flawless craftsmanship, he made the most powerful statement in our century about the unsolvable paradox of human existence and inscribed it in the network of his parables as an indelible genetic specter haunting perennially their message.

Kafka's position vis-à-vis Judaism is reflected in many of his tales. Some of his parable-like stories, such as *Das Schloss (The Castle)*, the *Hundeschaft (On Being a Dog)*, *Beim Bau der chinesischen Mauer (The Great Wall of China)*, or *Josephine, the Mouse Artist*, contain, at one level, a veiled criticism of the Jews who have cut themselves off from history by surrounding themselves with the "impervious walls" of the Torah. At a deeper level, his parables hold subtle questions of the very principles upon which Judaism is founded. Kafka's stories are profound reflections about the sources of social cohesion and the basis for nationhood, from the position of an alienated hero, who remains at the margins of society. Kafka questions the very sources of leadership and a peoplehood—"Führerschaft" and "Volk"—and reaches the conclusion that the "bases of society are religious, perhaps mystical,[10] beyond the reach of the rational investigator."[11]

The essential conflict in Kafka was captured most vividly by another luminary of this century, Walter Benjamin. A brilliant early theorizer of Kafka's work, Benjamin made a number of important observations regarding Kafka's bipolar vantage point in his relation to traditional wisdom and modernity. In his essay entitled "Franz Kafka," he observes that "Kafka's work is an ellipse with foci that are far apart and are determined, on the one hand, by mystical experience, in particular the experience of tradition, and on the other, by the experience of modern big-city dweller."[12] Benjamin was the first in a series of prominent writers to understand Kafka's genius.[13] He asserted that Kafka was far from being the first to face this situation, and many had accommodated themselves to it by clinging to truth, or whatever they happened to regard as truth, and with a more or less heavy heart, forgoing its transmissibility. Kafka's real genius was that he tried something entirely new: He sacrificed truth for the sake of clinging to its transmissibility, its *Haggadaic* element.[14] In talking about Kafka's narrative *The Castle*, Benjamin asserts that

> we may, however, also recognize another village in it. It is the village in a Talmudic legend told by a rabbi in answer to the question why Jews prepare a festive evening meal on Fridays. The legend is about a princess languishing in exile, in a village whose language she does not understand, far from compatriots. One day this princess receives a letter saying that her fiancé has not forgotten her and he is on his way to her. The fiancé, so says the rabbi is the Messiah; the princess is the soul; the village in which she lives in exile is her body. She prepares a meal for him because this is the only way in which she can express her joy in a village whose language she does not know. This village of the Talmud is right in Kafka's world.[15]

If wisdom, defined by Benjamin as the "epic side of truth," is inherent in tradition, or what he calls "truth in its *Haggadaic* consistency," Kafka's work presents a "sickness of tradition," because the consistency of truth has been lost in modern times.[16]

In a clever comparison of Walter Benjamin's views of Kafka with those of Lionel Trilling's, Robert Alter most insistently agrees with Benjamin. He notes that, unlike Trilling, who argued Kafka's indifference and insensitivity to the relation between morality and spiritual life, Benjamin has correctly assessed Kafka's existential despair at the loss of legitimizing forces to morality "in the very intransigence" of his imagination. In tune with Walter Benjamin, who wrote that Kafka lived in a time when one could no longer speak of wisdom, only the products of its decay: "rumors about the true things, a sort of theological whispered intelligence . . . , and folly,"[17] Alter appropriately sees Kafka as "a story teller trapped in the era of the novel," for whom language remained the medium of wisdom, learning, and tradition at a point in time when the chain of tradition has broken, with no certain wisdom left to impart.[18]

KAFKA AND JUDAISM IN THE AGE OF CRISIS

Kafka lived in post-Haskalah (Enlightenment) Central Europe, in the midst of a crumbling Judaism. Enlightenment and modernity have exposed Judaism—already consumed internally by a loss of religious identity—to Christian and modern, secular ideas. This produced a radical scission at the very heart of the Jewish world, between those who embraced modernity and assimilated, and the stubborn "keepers of the faith" in the unyielding, orthodox world of the ghetto. The fatal blow to Judaism, further compounded and amplified by increasing anti-Semitism, provoked a deep sense of failure and an acute sense of exile in the Central European Jew.

This condition was felt with great intensity by a sensitive intellectual such as Kafka,[19] for whom, as Harold Bloom poignantly puts it, "the Jewish tradition was a message from an endless distance."[20] Indeed, we learn that Kafka, who wrote in his diaries "I am a memory come alive," was learning about Judaism from secondary sources, from books such as Friedländer's, *Die religiösen Bewegungen innerhalb des Judentums im Zeitalter Jesu,* which appeared in Berlin 1905, and from other noted scholars, mainly in translation.[21]

Cut off from normative Judaism and its positive embodiment in the Law, Kafka, like other Jewish intellectuals, had to forge for himself a "new" kind of Jewishness able to sustain him. Unlike his characters who remain suspended in anxiety-ridden regions "between the truth of the past, or Jewish memory, and Jewish messianism," a place where there is no transcendence, Kafka changed direction and invented a new kind of writing.[22] While the writing capable to satisfy Kafka's nostalgia for transcendence was apprehended by many as a "new Kabbalah," we suggest that he has found a new mode to reveal his principal conviction, that "truth" cannot be grasped and remains hidden to man.[23] More specifically, it may be said that Kafka, a modern *midrashist*, has incorporated in his parabolic tales commentary and interpretation. By choosing to speak in parables and aphorisms, he got closer than any other modern author to the spirit (of the letter) of Kabbalah without directly imitating it. In Kafka, Jewish mysticism figures side by side with various shades of Gnostic, Manichaen, Orthodox Jewish and Christian thought and are infused in his narratives, according to some scholars, mainly as vehicles that propel his stories.[24] Strauss claims that:

> Kafka's nostalgia for Kabbalah was not the result of an impulse toward hermeticism and esotericism but grew out of a conviction that the truth was, by definition, concealed and that in some ways this neg-

ative Kabbalah is not really a Kabbalah any longer, except in its root sense of "tradition . . ." because it has no key, or system—numerological or mystical—by means of which it can elucidate the cosmos and reopen the gates of paradise.[25]

Kafka penetrated the language of the prophets and the sayings of the wise men of antiquity and proceeded to invent a new artistic language, capable to express his despair about his powerlessness, his deep sense of guilt and absolute loss, and his sense of profound inadequacy as a Jew in modern times.[26] To that extent, in claiming that "to do justice to the figure of Kafka in its purity and its peculiar beauty one must never lose sight of one thing: it is the purity and beauty of a failure," Walter Benjamin was prefiguring Kafka's position in modernity.[27]

Other early commentators of Kafka were critical of him and saw in his work a failure in which they found no beauty. Hannah Arendt, for example, claimed that in creating images of submissive individuals as a sign of social and political failure of the European Jews, Kafka was acquiescing, at least in his fiction, to views that Jews have culturally assimilated as "pariahs."[28] While we feel that Arendt's political and literary claims have contributed greatly to Kafka studies, we essentially agree with Werckmeister that her claims are based only on Kafka's fiction and thus are in need of careful scrutiny. Our own view is that social conflict is far from absent in Kafka's literary work. And to uncover the extent to which social conflict is present in Kafka's work, we need to focus on the social aspects of Kafka's major narrative plots and the impact of his professional experience upon his literary imagination.[29]

Special attention must be given to Kafka's brilliant shift in metaphysical perspective as well. A Jew who lived before the Holocaust, Kafka has reached the "peculiar beauty" of which Benjamin talks, by going in his literary imagination beyond human suffering as it were and seeing man from the point of view of the divine who is impassive to human anguish and frustration. In some sense, in taking this position Kafka was hoping that his suffering might lead to redemption.[30] Whether Kafka was a religious figure of "the rank of a Jewish prophet who wrestled for his faith against a thousand temptations, essentially certain of heaven and of the transcendental," as Max Brod saw it, or "was writing from within a tradition of certainty of the unity of Israel, by virtue of which nothing whatsoever detracts from God's splendor," as Martin Buber saw it, one may be certain that these positions figure side by side in Kafka's work. They either negate each other and form a paradox, or coexist, thematize Jewish life and Jewish suffering in Diaspora and, no less, the suffering experienced in the act of writing.[31]

KAFKA CRITICISM

While grappling with the massive decline of Judaism, Kafka was also keenly aware of the erosion of modern man's place in the world and his estrangement from truth. To express his horror before man's tragic fate, Kafka needed to find a fitting mode of expression and a language capable to reach modern man, and send him his message.[32]

The literature dealing with Kafkan language and concern with modern man's fate is vast and interpretations of all political and critical shades have thrown contradictory light on his work. Without going into a comprehensive analysis of all Kafka criticism, an impossible task at any rate, I mention here a number of distinguished critics relevant to our discussion of parabolic discourse and move on to describe Kafka's innovations and changes in parables.

Prominent Kafka critics, such as Wilhelm Emrich and Heinz Politzer, have suggested that in pondering man's impasse in modernity, Kafka found him incapable to define himself. Any attempt to uncover the truth about man's being in the world and about his existence is expressed in language, therefore, is determined by, and obedient to the laws of language. Herein lies, according to Kafka, a most important dilemma. Language cannot offer a "truth" including the truth about man and his existence, because, it is a semiotic system and a network of arbitrary grammatical relations.

Emrich was among the first to appraise discerningly the apparatus at work in Kafka's representational system. He showed, quite convincingly, that "the gap between representation and its meaning is immense; hence, the more precise the representation, the more immense, the more inconceivable, indeed the more preposterous it must appear." As Emrich accurately states, "language cannot express what man or the world 'is'. Only in passing through all statements, in the 'chorus' of all falsehoods, might there be 'truth' of a kind."[33]

Henry Sussman commends Emrich for touching upon a very important element in Kafka, namely Kafka's awareness of "the tragic rift between transcendent (totality) and mutable (finiteness) worlds," but he criticizes him for stopping short of enunciating Kafka's uniqueness and for trying to "situate him on familiar grounds." A forceful critic of the deconstructionist school, Sussman deplores the fact that Emrich's analysis has risen at the moment of criticism at which it is possible to acknowledge "Kafka's assault upon the transcendental concept, but when 'structure' and 'form' of the concept still remain indispensable."[34]

Walter Soskel brought into the Kafkan equation the notion of tragedy,[35] long after Albert Camus had showed how the tragic operates in Kafka. Kafka, Camus claimed, arrives at the tragic by interfering in logic.

By pushing logic to its extremes, the absurd ceases to be absurd and becomes part of man's everyday life. In that sense, like the ancient sages, Kafka syncretizes in his work two worlds, the world of everyday life and the world of supernatural anxiety. . . . In this fashion, Camus tells us, "Kafka expresses tragedy by the everyday and the absurd by the logical."[36]

Soskel took these insights a step further. He argued that the notion and conventions of tragedy shed a particular light on the dilemmas plaguing the Kafkan hero. In the end, Kafkan heros, ironically, have no revelation because of their tragic self-alienation.

Some two decades later, Henry Sussman suggests that the self appears to be a construct applied retrospectively to a dynamic that operates primarily according to linguistic principles, and not as a preexisting entity.[37] He situates Kafka as a precursor of Derrida, who shows that the ideal, origin, or *presence,* and the self are all constructs, applied only retrospectively to a process whose operation is itself linguistic, for the sake of coherence.[38] Sussman hopes that he avoided the two pitfalls against which Walter Benjamin has cautioned future Kafka critics. Sussman maintains he succeeded because he has construed his analysis around *"how"* Kafka is "incomprehensible" and pinned his argument on how language is problematized in Kafka, how Kafkan texts dramatize textual activity and the elusive dynamic of language.

Sussman too reiterates Walter Bejamin's early insights that "there are two ways to miss the point of Kafka's work," Benjamin has cautioned. "One, to interpret them naturally, the other is the supernatural interpretation. Both the psychoanalytic and the theological interpretations, he warned, equally miss the essential points."[39]

Yet, by broaching his argument on Kafkan language and by observing where language appears as a theme in Kafka's fiction, Sussman has succeeded in taking Kafka interpretation one step further. Although others have identified Kafka as the initiator of modernity by the bizarre atmosphere pervading his works and, while they have acknowledged Kafka's concern for language, they have not escaped what Sussman calls "their deterministic operations . . . and thus have closed themselves before the wider system challenged by Kafka's fiction." Sussman limited his commentary to narrative structure, point-of-view, and specific rhetorical tropes, to claim authority, while avoiding to address unresolved philosophical arguments, or end up, like others, in a quest for "a term, which like a talisman, can account for *everything.*"[40] In investigating only one Kafkan site, Sussman shows that Kafka demonstrated the lack objectivity of space and time. Sussman says:

> He [Kafka] observes the violence wrought by linguistic and textual processes on logic and order. The relationship between the literary image

and the dramatic setting is a close one, but these images do not always involve dramatic interactions, or for that matter, even characters. And the movement set into play by the image ultimately describes not the characters or the thematic subject but the conditions that make the sense and the entire textual apparatus possible. . . . For Kafka, the metaphor does not transport significance from vehicle to tenor; it resides in the between-space linking yet separating the most incongruous pairs. . . . Rather than effect a transfer of meaning from one sign to the next, these mixtures halt the move precisely in the middle . . . the impact of these mixtures is uncanny.[41]

Sussman's insight further reinforces our own views that a semiotic approach, sensitive to Kafka's awareness of the deception embedded in language and to the elusive processes of codification, help us see the logic behind Kafka's choice of parables as a means of expressing the acute crisis in which he perceived modern man and Judaism.

The bewilderment before one's incapability to recover either the meaning of one's existence or the *halakhah* (the law) finds expression in Kafka's parables by ways of pointless quests that yield no revelation beyond the obvious, namely, that man cannot solve the riddle of his existence. As Kafka tells us in the parable "On Parables," "the incomprehensible is incomprehensible, and "this we know already."[42]

To conjure before his reader the image of abysmal despair before such impotence, Kafka leads him/her through an artful web of paradoxical, mirror-like images that bedazzle as they confuse. He creates a whole new mode of expression that, Politzer claims, in its paradoxical garb, "expresses the inexpressible without betraying it."[43]

Generally speaking, Kafka's parables center on their paradox. . . . Circling around this nucleus, they maintain a suspense originating in the never defined relation their actual plots maintain with their backgrounds. Only when the narrative stops to reveal its essentially fragmentary character will this background be thrown into bold relief. Otherwise it is reflected and refracted by an abundance of ambiguous word images. Thus imagery as well as background appear as expressions of the narrator's incapability of saying what these parables have been meant to say in the beginning. Franz Kafka's importance derives from the fact that he was probably the first and certainly the most radical writer to pronounce the insoluble paradox of human existence by using this paradox as the message of his parables.[44]

Politzer's claim is amply illustrated in Kafka's parable "An Imperial Message" where the dying Emperor sends out a messenger to tell the entire nation his last words. The message of the emperor never reaches his subjects, and for that matter any of Kafka's readers, because the emperor's messenger never reaches his destination. And so, Kafka's parable ends with the image of the man/subject dreaming the message for himself.

At the twilight of a philosophical and religious era, when man is left to imagine "the imperial message" for himself, Kafka understood that parables, an old instructional mode with an easily accessible surface meaning and another more profound, were a most suitable structure. Thus, Kafka stated his insights parabolically and required of his reader to go further and synthesize the meanings beyond the text's face value. As Camus noted, "the whole art of Kafka consists in forcing the reader to reread."[45]

To cross the boundaries between such diverse domains as psychology and mysticism, philosophy and divination of the future, childhood and his poetic vision, Kafka balanced on the tightrope of ambiguity. He put the reader in a double bind in narratives that stubbornly resist decoding. He launched his reader on a wild seesaw between figurative and literal interpretations without allowing him to rest on either. When trying to allegorize and arrive at the symbolic meaning of a narrative, the reader is forced to read the story literally and focus on its literality; when reading the text literally, he is compelled to determine its "other," indecipherable, yet perceived as very important, meaning. Kafka's reader alternates back and forth, without ever being able to determine what the Kafkan text ultimately signifies.[46]

KAFKA'S INNOVATION

Walter Benjamin had very early the insight "that Kafka has divested the human gesture of its traditional support and then had a subject for reflection without end."[47] To talk about Kafka, Benjamin used the beautiful image of "unfolding" for Kafka's parable "Before the Law," found in *The Country Doctor* and interpreted by K in *The Trial*. Walter Benjamin shows how an entire Kafkan novel may become the "unfolding" of one of his parables and stresses the double meaning of the word "unfolding." "A bud," he explains, "unfolds into a blossom, but the boat which one teaches children to make by unfolding paper unfold into flat paper. This second kind of 'unfolding' is really appropriate to the parable; it is the reader's pleasure to smooth it out so that he has the meaning on the palm of his hand. Kafka's parables, however, unfold in the first sense, the way a bud turns into a blossom."[48]

To get a picture of the extent to which we are indebted to Kafka's innovativeness for our modern understanding and definition of parables, we may wish to penetrate the paradoxical world that Kafka has invented through his skillful use of symbolism and fathom the mechanism that allowed his stories to "unfold" yet continue to remain enigmatic. In doing so, we hope to understand how Kafka came to dominate our perception of literary modernity, which is the reason we focus on his work to demonstrate transformations of codes in parables in the first place. At the same time, we may grasp how Kafka has become the yardstick for measuring everything that is not normative in Jewish cultural tradition.[49]

Conscious of the legacy left to him by ancient and medieval Judaism in the art of telling and writing parables, as well as of the work of modern parabolizers before him (Dostoevski, Nietzsche, and Heine), Kafka refined and adapted the genre, to make it suitable for telling the horror in the life of twentieth-century man, who realizes that the mind cannot overcome its own cognitive, or categorical, limitation in its quest to understand the world.

Interestingly, to communicate with modern man, Kafka experimented and expanded the ancient parabolic form, and clearly siphoned from the tradition from within which he has come, but from he was removed. However, in investigating his parables, we find them similar in many ways to those propounded by the early rabbis. This allows us to place Kafka in a long tradition, despite his immense originality.

Kafka's remoteness from normative Judaism was perhaps a sorrowful benefit that enabled him to create original parables for himself, unimpeded by the burden of a rather constricting tradition. A case in point is his emphasis on the communicative endeavor, the transferal of personal significance for the reader in the act of reception. Another, is the free blending of the natural and the supernatural, never explained, nor understood by most of the readers. A third example is the switch from the mysterious to the ordinary and back, without bridging the gap that yawns between them. Furthermore, the characters, walking ciphers Kafka has conceived in his stories, follow rules neither they nor the reader understand. They merely serve to state parabolically that he (Kafka) does not possess the knowledge of how to do such feats, nor can anyone acquire this knowledge. In his parable about "Prometheus," Kafka says:

> There are four legends concerning Prometheus:
>   According to the first, he was clamped to a rock in the Caucasus for betraying the secrets of the gods to men, and the gods sent eagles to feed on his liver, which was perpetually renewed.
>   According to the second, Prometheus, goaded by the pain of the tearing beaks, pressed himself deeper and deeper into the rock until became one with it.
>   According to the third, his treachery was forgotten in the course of thousand of years, the gods forgotten, the eagles, he himself forgotten.

According to the fourth, everyone grew weary of the meaningless affair. The gods grew weary, the eagles grew weary, the wound closed wearily.

There remained the inexplicable mass of rock.—The legend tried to explain the inexplicable. As it came out of a substratum of truth it had in turn to end in the inexplicable.[50]

Kafka seems to have understood, long before others, that in the modern aesthetic experience, the interpreter is aware that he is not discovering an external truth but that "he makes the encyclopedia work at its best."[51] In the space-time of his graceful narrational leaps, Kafka jumps between the mystical and the sensible world, deconstructs his writing as he invents it, and professes his ignorance, while, at the same time, admitting that, unlike others, he has made friends with his ignorance.[52] He seems to have anticipated by some fifty years Eco's remarks about what the modern symbol is. Long after Kafka, Eco states:

Modern poetic symbolism is a secularized symbolism where languages speak about their possibilities. In any case, behind every strategy of the symbolic mode, be it religious or aesthetic, there is a legitimating theology, even though it is the aesthetic theology of unlimited semeiosis or of hermeneutics as deconstruction. A positive way to approach every instance of the symbolic mode would be to ask: which theology legitimizes it? [53]

Kafka seemed to some a religious innovator and the potential founder of a future Judaism. Others maintained with equal passion that any such interpretations are mostly a blend of their wishful readings into Kafka's text, since Kafka, they claimed, seems to have taken every precaution against interpretation; therefore, his deliberate evasion of interpretation is what needs to be addressed first.[54] Finally, there are those who see theological dimensions in stories such as *The Castle*, which portray a man in search of grace and redemption. Kafka's real concern may not have been to offer theological views on Christianity or Judaism, yet he frequently invites his readers to think about the idea of redemptive suffering.

There is agreement that Kafkan text is supremely effective, and, perhaps, further investigations may evidence additional religious traces in Kafka's work. We suggest, however, that the impact of Kafkan texts on modern readers comes from his innovations in the areas of rhetoric and syntax and in the domain of logic, rather than religion. Kafka's forcefulness comes from the remarkable density of his text, achieved by compressing a multitude of rhetorico-poetic devices in the very limited textual space of a parable, or an aphorism.

Given Kafka's passion for language, on the one hand, and the distinct linguistic cleverness inlaid in the aphoristic genre, on the other, one can understand Kafka's attraction to this genre. Kafka has experimented extensively with the genre and has often chosen to express his ideas through aphorisms. Their succinctness, embedded metaphoricity, and engaging quality must have been very attractive to him, who wished to say a lot in a few words. Aphorisms, in which there is a "demand for completion or hermeneutic application in the act of reception,"[55] seemed uniquely appropriate to Kafka, who sensed that in the aphoristic mode, he could more readily provoke the reader to engage in a dialogue with the text that he offered to decode. At the same time, we like to note that Kafka has gone in his parables far beyond the aphorism's strict form and has extended the genre's boundaries. This, in Gray's term, he has done through a metaphorical process of extension, or what he calls a "metaphorism."[56]

Indeed, in his aphorisms as in his parables, Kafka's makes systematic use of an entire gamut of meaning producing parabolic and aphoristic apparatus, to subvert intentionally the reader's expectations. "For Kafka," claims Sussman, "the metaphor does not transport significance from vehicle to tenor; it resides in the between-space linking yet separating incongruous parts. Absolute metaphor, paradoxically, actually functions as neutralization of metaphor, i.e., as a refusal of metaphorical transferal and metaphorical trans-reference."[57]

Unlike his precursors, who embedded parables in larger texts to achieve a kind of symbiotic communicational interplay and, therefore, mutual communicational support, Kafka went on to write parables that he left to stand alone. His parables do not serve as mere ornamentation or supplements to other, larger texts. In evacuating the safe yet constricting surrounding text with its prefigured communication, Kafka has opened parables to a multiplicity of aleatory meanings, generated in the process of each new reading and enriched as well as extended their power of signification.

As seen in the preceding examples, ancient and medieval parables were propounded to teach their listeners and impart wisdom to them. These parables were pedagogical instruments in the hands of able rabbinic parabolizers, and their meaning was inextricably linked to a particular religious text or ideology. Kafka has radically altered the old rhetorico-poetic model of parable that instructed the addressees and offered new insights into a world that was likely to be understood and transformed. In a universe deemed incomprehensible and governed by an inaccessible God, who rules by unfathomable rules, Kafka created open, infinitely interpretable parables.[58]

Thus, unlike early parables, told to a privileged audience, to the members of a hermeneutic community, to enlighten them and them only, while keeping the "outsiders" outside, Kafka's modern parables reflect a barren world with no privileged addressee. Indeed, while Kafka's parables, with their multiple layers of interpretable meaning, can be compared to the scriptural parables because of their demand to be decoded, they remain equally enigmatic to us all. Furthermore, while ancient parables were interpreting a doctrine, a wisdom, Kafka's parables only allude to the doctrine that they presume to be interpreting. The reader of these parables gets only vague cues as to its existence.[59]

The "Kafkaesque," a term widely used now to designate a whole gamut of textual strategies and readers' responses, has been introduced to mean the new effect generated in Kafka's narratives. It is the use of logic and consistency to the point of excess. The Kafkan "effect" of the absurd was likened by Albert Camus to the existentialist's "hope," rather than to the mechanism at work in the Greek tragedy. In the Greek tragedy, explained Camus, the drama's whole effort is to show the logical system that, from deduction to deduction, will crown the hero's misfortune. This, merely to announce to us that uncommon fate is scarcely horrible, because it is improbable.

> But, if its necessity is demonstrated to us in the framework of everyday life, society, state, familiar emotion, then, the horror is hallowed. . . . In that revolt that shakes man and makes him say; "That is not possible," there is an element of desperate certainty that "that" is possible.[60]

To understand Kafka's position, we need to think of the reverse process. The textual activity by which the absurd is recognized, accepted, and man is resigned to it (and from then on knows that it has ceased to be the absurd) likens Kafka to the work of existential philosophers Kierkegaard, Chekhov, Dostoevski. Like them, Kafka goes in the direction of the absurd to the point where "it turns to hope." Like them, Kafka embraces the God that consumes him. The world Kafka creates in his parables is in truth an indescribable universe "in which man allows himself the tormenting luxury of fishing in a bathtub, knowing that nothing will come of it."[61] About the artistic mechanism by which Kafka achieves this effect, Camus says:

> If the nature of art is to bind the general to the particular, ephemeral eternity of a drop of water to the play of its lights, it is even truer to judge the greatness of the absurd writer by the distance he is able to introduce between these two worlds. His secret consists in being able to find the exact point where they meet in their greatest disproportion. And to tell the truth, this geometrical locus of man and the inhuman is seen everywhere by the pure in the heart. If Faust and Don Quixote are eminent creations of art, this is because of the immeasurable nobilities they point out to us with their earthly hands. Yet a moment always

comes when the mind negates the truth that those hands can touch. A moment comes when the creation ceases to be taken tragically; it is merely taken seriously. Then man is concerned with hope. But that is not his business. His business is to turn away from subterfuge. Yet this is just what I find at the conclusion of the vehement proceedings Kafka institutes against the whole universe. His unbelievable verdict is this hideous and upsetting world in which the very moles dare to hope.[62]

To state the mind's tragic realization of the void, Kafka was the first to translate it into paradox; to organize it linguistically, he played on logic and logical structures with the precision of a most accomplished master.[63]

WRITING TECHNIQUES

Kafka's writing, often referred to as "monolithic laconism," or "a palimpsest," evokes and suppresses meaning in the same gesture. What begins as pleasant, changes without any warning and becomes frightening and strange; what begins as natural, changes to nightmare and horror.[64]

In his fiction, Kafka uses distortion-displacement, deferral, and uncanny repetition. The "bugs," or distortions, spread over both coordinates: time and space. Spatially, Kafka transforms relations of remoteness into ones of contiguity, creates internalized spatial boundaries, uses "displacement," "misplacement," and "replacement" of objects and characters. Kafka does not restrain things to their customary spaces. The time element undergoes equally complicated distortions. Moreover, he fudges the fictive past with the future, mimes forgetting, uses anachronisms in the memories of the characters and repetitions at the basis of the narrative's inscription and continuity and finally, vastly differing velocities of activity seem to take place simultaneously.[65]

At the lexical level, Kafka changes a number of features and the number of times an item occurs, the semantic nuances. Likewise, he shifts from verb to noun, from intratextual to intertextual. This semantic ambiguity generates persuasive and rhetorical effect.[66]

The production of a highly analytical mind, Kafka's writing invariably turns and comments on itself and its own status. In his fiction, Kafka theorizes about fiction and about the act of writing, and puts into question the entire meaning producing machine activated in this process, by the inevitable use of allusive, tropological language.[67] For example, the perfectly contrived machine of Kafka's The Penal Colony, structured as a supreme punishing machine, is also the machine dealing with language and writing. It writes out the punishment of the prisoner on his body. To state his feelings of ambivalence toward the dynamics of language, Kafka stages the final, flawless, communication and enlightenment of the prisoner to coincide with that prisoner's moment of death. Thus, in Kafka, the "enlightened," but also "punished" body, is a "written" body, a body traversed (literally) by language. The double bind resulting from expressing oneself in language is such, Kafka tells us, that in the moment of its utmost clarity language communicates the least, and this becomes the sorrowful source of a writer's despair and destruction. This image is most vividly captured in the following lines from *The Penal Colony*:

> The Harrow is beginning to write; when it finishes the first draft of the inscription on the man's back, the layer of cotton wool begins to roll and slowly turns the body over, to give the Harrow fresh space for writing. . . .
> Enlightenment comes to the most dull-witted. It begins around the eyes. From there it radiates. A moment that might tempt one to get under the Harrow oneself. Nothing more happens than the man begins to understand the inscription, he purses his mouth as if he were listening. You have seen how difficult it is to decipher the script with one's eyes; but our man deciphers it with his wounds. To be sure, this is a hard task; he needs six hours to accomplish it. By that time the Harrow has pierced him quite through and casts him into the pit, where he pitches down upon the blood and water and the cotton wool. Then the judgment has been fulfilled, and we, the soldier and I, bury him.[68]

ART, MIMETIC IDEAL, THE POSITION
OF THE ARTIST IN SOCIETY

Kafka reflected quite extensively on the place of the artist in society and the value of mimetic art, for which he has opted (over self-exposure and self-denuding in journals, diaries, and in his autobiographical writing). In the story about Josephine, the mouse artist, Kafka considers the deception involved in the image an individual artist has about his importance to society and his autonomy, a deception, says Kafka, his people tolerate out of kindness and love. Kafka also suggests that, while the individual artist may deceive himself about his uniqueness and his importance (as artists usually do, because they seem to know less about art than the people for whom they create), the lasting contributions of that artist to his people ultimately resides in the fact that he is incorporated into the collective consciousness of his people, and thus, he ensures the survival of his people as a nation and participates in the communal spirit of their people.[69]

> She [Josephine] is a small episode in the eternal history of our people, and people will get over the loss of her. Not that it will be easy for us;

how can our gatherings take place in utter silence? Still, were they not silent even when Josephine was present? Was her actual piping notably louder and more alive than the memory of it will be? Was it even in her lifetime more than a simple memory? Was it not rather because Josephine's singing was already past losing it this way that our people in their wisdom prized it so highly?

So perhaps we shall not miss so very much after all, while Josephine, redeemed from the earthly sorrows which to her thinking lay in wait for all chosen spirits, will happily lose herself in the numberless throng of the heroes of our people, and soon, since we are no historians, will rise to the heights of redemption and be forgotten like all her brothers.[70]

As a mimetic artist, Kafka set out to present what he called *"die Welt ins Reine, Wahre, Unveränderliche [zu] heben,"* a purified version of the world, even though, as Marthe Robert pointed out, Kafka found this version flawed on two counts: first, the mimetic artist is more prone to vanity than the expressive artist, and secondly, the mimetic ideal of art seems to make art unnecessary.[71] Yet, despite his incisive criticism of art and artists, Kafka made his last statement a most powerful statement about himself, his beleaguered people, and the value of art. Robert correctly asserts that "In mentioning Josephine's disappearance he [Kafka] seems to be alluding to his own death. If so, the absence of self-pity, and the gentle, beautiful self-controlled mockery he directs against Josephine's claim to be indispensable, testify not only to his artistic integrity but to his rare fineness as a human being."[72]

About the process of reading, Kafka said that we are usually too easy on ourselves as readers. He encouraged his readers to read those books that ask of more of us than we normally are willing to give. He wrote that "we must have those books which come upon us like ill-fortune, and distress us deeply, like the death of one we love better than ourselves, like suicide. A book must be an ice-axe to break the sea frozen inside us." To that extent, even though Kafka was spared the abomination of the Holocaust, in demanding of his reader such radical reading, Kafka has anticipated the only reading possible for the post-Holocaustian man and has, thus, offered a modernist model for reading in addition to his model for writing.[73]

Kafka has contributed to what Martin Buber has called the "metaphysics of the 'door' [open to man]."[74] An example in point is his parable, "Before the Law," found in *The Trial.* Kafka's man never enters the door leading to the world of meaning, even though that door "was intended for him, and him alone." If there is a predominant philosophical statement in Kafka, that statement is that "the door" to access wisdom is still open to us; however, we no longer possess any the means of entering it. To that extent, in Kafka, the transcendental is also much like the mummy of the ancient king, whose shape survives but who is depleted of substance.

KAFKA'S PARABLES

Kafka's parables are narrative paradoxes, governed by an allusive meaning and form, therefore, any cogent analysis must look at both constraints. The meaning of Kafka's parables is dependent upon the form's constitutive parts. Likewise, it is highly dependent on the use of metaphors and other tropes, namely the clever conjunctions of phenomena or concepts not seen in relation to each other otherwise. The strict narrative structure of his parables restricts the writer from indulging in mimetic description. Kafka's parabolic discourse challenges our idea of meaning, and proves it to be illusory. In his parables, meaning is never available, only the conditions of possibility for it.[75]

An artistic high vaulting between an easily recognizable, precise form, and a meaning hoped for only when the parts have been decoded and constituted into a whole, Kafka's parables are "the productive interplay between contiguity and similarity, the confluence between horizontal structuring and vertical reference."[76] Kafka's modern parables are the bittersweet fruit of a comprehensive study of the aphoristic genre that has opened to him new vistas of textual interplay and enlightened him about the signifying power of the fragmentary text. Gray describes the majestic architecture of Kafkan parable in the following terms:

> Kafka's parable evokes a sense of formal simplicity primarily by means of the linearity of the syntax. Both paragraphs evolve in almost perfect syntactical parallelism to one another, each consisting of a single sentence composed of a series of paratactically arranged clauses which leads up to a hyphen; at this juncture each paragraph introduces the . . . and describes in a concluding remark his reaction to the narrated circumstances. This parallelism is set off by explicitly contrastive elements: one subjunctive, one indicative, radically different emotional moods one vicious, the other beautiful.[77]

Kafka took the parables of the ancient sages, adapted, and perfected them to disclose that he did not and could not know what they meant to communicate to the ancient sages and their hermeneutic communities. To these ends, he used an imagery leaden with ambiguity that alternately bares or smooth over the gap between his parables' background and their own narrational strategy.

In a truly theatrical gesture, Kafka engineered his parables to gyrate like dervishes around their vacuous core. Then, he re-articulated this void and made it visible when thematizing their interpretation. He played with textual ambiguity and fragmentariness to express, seamlessly, that the incomprehensible is incomprehensible, and claim, with the calm proper to an utmost despair, that "this we already know."

The simultaneous proclamation and concealment, that is, the promise to disclose, made side by side with the act of suppressing meaning, characteristic of all parables, rules at the heart of Kafka's paradoxical parables.[78] The parable "Couriers" is a good example of this double movement:

> There were offered the choice between becoming kings or the couriers of the kings. The way children would, they all wanted to be couriers. Therefore there are only couriers who hurry about the world, shouting to each other—since there are no kings—messages that have become meaningless. They would like to put an end to this miserable life of theirs but they dare not because of their oaths of service.[79]

Modern in their narrational strategy, Kafka's parables do not seek to convince nor dissuade; they aim mostly to disrupt our innermost regions of comfort and make us think and act. His parables obstinately maintain open the chasm between their two irreconcilable narrational planes, the plane of reality and that of illusion, and ask of the reader not to commit himself to any fixed model of them, or of the world, but to construct his, or her, own version of them.

Richard Gray and Jill Robbins, two dedicated Kafka scholars, point out that Kafka's parables are subversive of the expectations conditioned by cultural and religious tradition.[80] Robbins, for example, asks whether Kafka's discourse, marked by oscillations between fact and hypothesis, misunderstanding and understanding, and mutual interference between logic and rhetoric, could be accounted for by the "revelatory model," based upon the New Testament's relationship with the Old Testament, in favor of, or against which, some critics have argued.[81] To answer, Robbins shows that in Kafka's parables, the "new reading" has been "prefigured," by way of an incursion into Frank Kermode's elegantly construed analysis of Kafka's parable in *The Castle*. In interchanging fact and hypothesis to show that the "error" was not an error after all, but a lesson to a poor student, as it were, Kafka returns to the old law, the law of the Hebrew Bible. Kafka arrives there only after "a tour and a detour through Kierkegaard and the New Testament."[82]

This sophisticated reading of Kafka's deferred return to the old scriptural sources adds new information about Kafka's parables. At the same time, it supplies us with further evidence that, despite his innovations and recalcitrant style, Kafka inscribes himself in a long tradition, as its latest link.

KAFKA'S PARABLES AND DREAMS

Kafka's parables are being frequently likened to dreams. Like palimpsests, old inscriptions that are erased to make room for new ones, Kafka's parables hint at other layers of meaning beneath their surface. As in dreams, in Kafka's parables, sharply divergent elements are made to coexist. Radically different emotional moods are displayed side by side, the past and the present coexist, the good is next to the bad, the beautiful, next to the unsightly. This is most visible in the parable entitled, "The Sirens":

> There are the seductive voices of the night; the Sirens, too, sang that way. It would be doing them an injustice to think that they wanted to seduce; they knew they had claws and sterile wombs, and they lamented this aloud. They could not help it if their laments sounded so beautiful.[83]

Those particularly interested in investigating parables and dreams may wish to return to the analysis of this unique relationship I offer in Chapter 1, entitled "The Nature and Structure of Parables."

KAFKA AND THE ACT OF WRITING

Kafka left to us a devastating image of modernity as the locus of desolation and estrangement where the drama of modern man is played out, away from the possibility of knowledge and egosyntonia. He has endowed parabolic writing with new dimensions, called now "Kafkaesque," which open up to a multiple possible meanings capable of expressing man's modern concerns. As stated by Benjamin and reiterated later by Robert Alter:

> Kafka's parabolic fictions, are not, most essentially, dreams, or theological allegories, or enigmatic psychograms, or prophetic myths, but a body of Haggadah in search of a Halakhah, lore in quest of Law, yet so painfully estranged from what it seeks that the pursuit can end in a pounce of destruction, the fictional rending the doctrinal.[84]

The double image, of enlightenment and of torture, evoked by Kafka's parables tells also of his view that writing has a lethal quality. And while the pleasure of renouncing the greatest of happiness in favor of literature "traversed" all his muscles, Kafka thought that literature had a fatal side to it.[85] Kafka fended off modernity's spiritual emptiness by writing original stories, even though he was fully aware of writing's deadliness. Marthe Robert tellingly observes in *Seul, comme Franz Kafka*:

Literature is deadly in all is aspects and Kafka knows it, he is even one of the first in our history to grasp it in this easily ignored guise, where there is nothing ghastly, more a friend, a powerful theme to preserve in its adoration. [My translation].[86]

KAFKA AND CLASSIC PARABLES

Kafka's parables remain indebted to the ancient parabolic mode in many ways. Like the ancient parables, they allow for multiple shades of reading, all dependent to a great extent upon the addressee's background, interpreting capability, and the religio-cultural or social setting in which they are read.

In contrast to old parables that belonged to the didactic mode, taught the unlearned, and were eventually understood, Kafka's modern parables are open and indeterminate.[87] Moreover, Kafka's parables have no "insiders," or privileged addressees, distinguishable from the "outsiders," "the other" to the semiotic community to which they speak, the way the biblical parables had.[88] To Kafka's parables, we are all outsiders, ineluctably. Finally, unlike the ancient parabolizers, Kafka is not bound to the biblical text. He may choose to "reread and reverse," best/worst, first/last, and so on. In doing so Kafka is able to overcome the errors in previous interpretations.[89]

KAFKA AND RELIGIOUS BELIEF

Martin Buber, Max Brod, and other Jewish scholars wished to see in Kafka a new religious figure, an oracle of sorts, animated by a unique spirituality. By looking at his work, we can at best say with some certainty that Kafka inspired us to think about the notion of redemptive suffering. He did not seem concerned with new religious models or any particular interpretation in either Christianity of Judaism. If he aroused certain thoughts about the idea of redemptive suffering, it may quite possibly be that he was thinking of the possibility of his own suffering leading to redemption.

For example, Buber saw in Kafka a valiant defender of the Jewish faith, a modern mystic whose convictions were kindled by the fire of his ancient community, a community that conceived of God and His glory as impervious to human judgment and that could not be diminished by human pain, suffering, or human judgment. Likewise, Max Brod saw in Kafka's narratives, beneath their surface hopelessness, the recognition of a divine presence in the world. Bloom and Strauss even attribute to Kafka a new Kabbalah, which, they claim, is akin in spirit to traditional Kabbalah because of the dialectal interaction between text and metatext. Whether one chooses to see in Kafka the "religious hero" and "modern prophet" envisioned by Max Brod, Martin Buber, Bloom and Strauss, or see in him a man trapped between faith and temptation, as scholars like Ronald Gray see him, one most certainly becomes aware that a subtle irony is the troublesome lasting companion of Kafka's metaphysical yearnings and that this irony permeates his entire work.[90]

> In some ways this negative Kabbalah is not really a Kabbalah any longer, except in its root sense of "tradition" (its deepest wish to continue tradition, to pass on a heritage) because it has no key, or system—numerological, or mystical—by means of which it can elucidate the cosmos and re-open the gates of paradise.[91]

Kafka's affinity with the Kabbalah and other shades of mysticism resides to a great extent in the language of his parabolic stories. Thus to look for Kafka's mysticism one needs to look again at his language. But what does Kafka tell us in his cryptic language? He concedes that the doctrine that his parabolic narratives were meant to illuminate and interpret can only be alluded to. Kafka's parabolic stories are, thus, only pseudo-revelations, mirror-like images. As Kafka himself admitted in the moral of his parable "On Parables," the world is what it is: "incomprehensible." His parables are, therefore, "the pristine mirrors into which a mysterious world contemplates its incomprehensibility." There he affirms his ignorance with which, he later tells us, he has made peace.[92] Thus, while Kafka is celebrated in many circles as the creator of a new Kabbalah, by looking at the ironic stance of his baffling stories, one may claim that his attraction to mysticism does not indicate a particular predilection on his part toward esotericism. Rather, his narrative strategies mean to express his firm conviction that, "since the truth is hidden from us, writing, even the most powerful one, can only "reveal its hiddeness."[93]

KAFKA AND TRANSMISSIBILITY

Kafka's kind of explosive writing is the subject of Roland Barthes' cogent analysis in the classic essay "The Struggle with the Angel." In his essay, Barthes shows how the scriptural author creates an entire "metonymic montage" where the themes are not developed but "combined." This metonymic logic generates a reading that may lead to the text's "symbolic explosion," the text's "dissemination, not its truth." The symbolic explosion of the text insures that the readers would try not to reduce it to be a "signified," whether "historical, economic, folkloric or kerygmatic," but would manage, according to Barthes, "to hold its *significance* fully open."[94]

In the light of Barthes' reading of "The Struggle with the Angel," we may claim that Kafka followed, passionately, nostalgically, at least the vision of his scriptural predecessors, when he opted for transmissibility. To Kafka, for whom truth was hidden, this was a sensible strategy to adopt, a strategy that could hold the significance of the text fully open and still allow for that "symbolic explosion" of the text.

Unlike his scriptural predecessors for whom there was a stable universe of meaning, Kafka wrote from a sense of radical hopelessness, in an age of decline, loss of meaning, and erosion of tradition. Instead of being ventriloquial of the past tradition the way Agnon's fictional endeavor is, Kafka's literary answer seems to have acquired two interesting flavors, that of Kabbalah and that of irony. If Kafka glimpsed hope, he did so from the pit of despair, facing absolute absence. As Alter claims, in Kafka, "storytelling assumes its old Scheherezadean purpose of postponing the future, fending off death."[95]

KAFKA, HEALING AND RESTORATION

There is no real healing, nor cleansing in the Kafkan universe. Instead of obliterating the distortion involved in neurosis, thereby, mediating a psychic integration, Kafka's complex symbolic mechanism confirms and maintains it. His work does not provide a catharsis, nor a therapeutic cure, maintains Soskel. In fact, the opposite is true: "repression, ambivalence, and ego are so besieged and oppressed by the super-ego, that it can no longer maintain its unity."[96] In self-psychological terms, psychic fragmentation prevents the Kafkan subject from healing and so, in Kafkan narratives, the psyche remains forever a psyche in pain, an eternally tormented Odradek.

KAFKA'S HUMOR

Kafka's humor ranges from broad, Pantagruelian comic to most delicate shades of wit. The comic quality in Kafka's work arises from the way he treats the paradoxical nature of existence with its moral and cosmological duality. The perception of Kafka's humor includes a disparagement of the means that reveal it, a disparagement of the mind as a rational tool for analysis. In Kafka, the comic resides in the transparent error involved in any statement that can be made of the world. Such a world in which nothing can be said that cannot in the same breath be as plausibly contradicted, is a quintessential comic world. The only response it elicits is—ironic.[97] Kafka admits that no one would really research this topic were it not for the real existence of creatures like Odradek, the grotesque being suspended in hopeless immortality, who is doomed to lead an eternal existence at the margins of all human society with no real meaning or purpose. The feeling akin to pain evoked by the irony of Odradek's surviving its maker becomes a tragic reminder of Kafka himself, at work correcting feverishly by hand, samples of his latest stories, on the eve of his death, on June 2, 1924, despite his request that all his writings be destroyed.[98] Michel Dentan insightfully observes that, unlike in traditional humor where an author creates humor in relation to his characters and their individual circumstances, to deal with Kafka's humor, one has to look at the image of which the character is an integral part, namely the totality of the narrative as a means of self-awareness, ultimately, as an act of expression and of communication. Kafka's writing demands an extension of the notion of humor to encompass an *"intention ludique."* That is to say, Kafka adopts, by means of two temporalities, an unexpected point of view that puts into question the security and the order of the world as we know it and unveils it insufficiency. And Kafka proves it lacking. On the other hand, Kafka does it in such a way that his action is tolerable and is even the occasion of a pleasurable smile. This ironic simulation brings new insights into the world and makes unusual connections. Through dark humor, Kafka seems able to reconcile the quotidian and the dream-like world. In pushing universal truths to the absurd he succeeds to contest them, and ultimately, succeeds in taking the reader "away from the tranquility of certainty."[99]

KAFKA'S "FAILURE"

Benjamin talked at length about the tragic beauty of Kafka's work. Earlier in this chapter, I pointed out Kafka's philosophical insights and his keen awareness of the split in modern times between the here-and-now, subject to constant transformation, and the transcendental. The transcendental survives in Kafkan artistic vision only as a vestige, a structure whose substance, according to him, we can no longer retrieve. To that extent, Kafka is the melancholy messenger of the massive decline of a philosophical era, and, thus, as Benjamin so elegantly put it, "the beauty of his work is the beauty of failure." Kafka was painfully aware that the Divine Law is not within our reach. He chose to acknowledge the absolute absence of the divine and his incapability of beholding its truth, in the labyrinthal narratives through which he took his reader. To these ends, he proceeded to contrive his narratives as unassailable ciphers that convey unknowable messages, issued by an unknowable ruler.[100] Remarkably, "in Kafka, the image, the 'Haggadah' rises up before the senses, but it has lost forever its intimate unity with the supersensory totality, with 'Halakhah,' which is no longer retrievable."[101]

CHAPTER 7

Franz Kafka: An Imperial Message

As noted in our previous chapter, Kafka was among the first to protest man's loss of ability in modern times to gain access to wisdom and his radical estrangement from the divine. Painfully, Kafka also understood a fundamental human incapability of going back to its linguistic and conceptual origins. To facilitate his readers' understanding of the sense of despair and hopelessness before such insight, Kafka chose to communicate parabolically.

There are several good reasons why Kafka chose to express his pessimistic views of the world in parables. First, parables are short narratives that by definition demand interpretation and decoding, thus, are an efficient vehicle for someone who takes precautions not to be quickly understood. By suggesting a double meaning, one present in the text and one implied, parables are a uniquely fitting mode to articulate a covert attack on metaphysics. Moreover, because of the subversive network of rhetorical and discursive strategies present in parables, an astute thinker, such as Kafka, could successfully avoid the pitfall of settling for trivial answers. As we recall, in parables, a simulation of a return to "origins"—to the "source" and the "elsewhere" of the Holy Scriptures—commonly takes place as a result of a discursive ruse. Such simulation provided Kafka with an ideal medium to enlighten in some way his reader, in times when, as he claimed, true enlightenment was no longer possible. Finally, parables seemed more suitable to Kafka because of their powerful mechanism of seduction. As a result of a seductive ploy, parables instill in the reader a desire to stay longer "in" the text and acquire added competency of decoding, even though, in actuality, what the reader learns is to deduce one parabolic sequence from another and make inferences from each parabolic segment. The seduced reader is drawn in the spatiotemporality of the parabolic narrative. He is absorbed, as it were, in the text and is transformed into a disciple by an ever-present make-believe, and goes on reading, re-reading, and interpreting, in order to grasp the parable's "hidden" meaning/s.

Clearly, involving the reader in the time and space of a parabolic

149

narrative gave Kafka a chance to teach the reader about his own insights. Now, since the knowledge that Kafka disclosed was that of modern man's radical alienation in the world and of his growing remoteness from the divine wisdom (and toward fictionalized reference and auto-referentiality), Kafka imagined a way for his reader to "win in parable." Kafka figured out a way to teach his addressee parabolically that one can make "friends" with his failure and that, despite this awareness, he will always remain an outsider to the parables' original meaning, namely, will remain forever unenlightened.[1]

Many of Kafka's parables are independent narratives and stand alone, resplendent. However, to drive his point about modern man's estrangement from the divine home, he chose to embed the parable of "An Imperial Message" in a larger narrative, entitled *The Great Wall of China*. This is the story of the senseless, yet persistent, effort of a credulous people who, in a vain attempt to protect itself and to repel unwelcome hordes of invaders, has indefatigably built (for hundreds of years) an impenetrable wall all along its borders. *The Great Wall of China* provides a wonderful backdrop for Kafka's almost prophetic vision of the futility of modern man's desperate struggle to gain wisdom and, thereby, get closer to godliness.

The story of Kafka's own impossible quest for knowledge and his lamentable failure is forcefully expressed in this clever parable about the message of the distant, dying emperor. The message, intended for the emperor's subject, and for him alone, will remain purloined. The tireless messenger will be endlessly delayed by an infinite number of obstacles and prevented from delivering it to its intended addressee. Kafka's loyal, but infinitely remote, subject of the dying king will dream his king's message to himself, forever bereft of his king's special message.

AN IMPERIAL MESSAGE

The Emperor, so it runs, had sent a message to you, the humble subject, the insignificant shadow cowering in the remotest distance before the imperial sun; the Emperor from his deathbed has sent a message to you alone. He has commanded the messenger to kneel down by the bed, and has whispered the message to him; so much store did he lay on it that he ordered the messenger to whisper it back into his ear again. Then by a nod of the head he has confirmed that it is right. Yes, before the assembled spectators of his death—all the obstructing walls have been broken down, and on the spacious and loftily—mounting open staircases stand in a ring the great princes of the Empire—before all these he has delivered his message. The messenger immediately sets out on his journey; a powerful, indefatigable man; now pushing with his right arm, now with his left, he cleaves a way for himself through the throng; if he encounters resistance he points to his breast, where the symbol of the sun glitters; the way, too, is made easier for him than would be for any other man. But the multitudes are so vast; their numbers have no end. If he could reach the open fields how fast he would fly, and soon doubtless you would hear the welcome hammering of his fists on your door. But instead how vainly does he wear out his strength; still he is only making his way through the chambers of the innermost palace; never will he get to the end of them; and if he succeeded in that nothing would be gained; he must fight his way next down the stair; and if he succeeded in that nothing would be gained; the courts would still have to be crossed; and after the courts the second outer palace; and once more stairs and courts; and once more another palace; and so on for thousands of years; and if at last he should burst through the outermost gate—but never, never can that happen—the imperial capital would lie before him, the center of the world crammed to bursting with its own refuse. Nobody could fight his way through here, least of all one with a message from a dead man.—But you sit at your window when evening falls and dream it to yourself.[2]

When exploring Gospel parables, Alain Cohen claimed that to decipher codes in a parable implies making unexpected connections between its narrational sequences and allowing for their meta-communicational language to be glimpsed. "This is so," Cohen says, "because a parable is the topos of a meaning manifesting itself as an injunction to an addressee to decode, but offers itself only parabolically."[3] In other words, both the addressor and the addressees of parables are aware *a priori* that the codes in parables are narrational invitations that ask to be interpreted, their hidden meanings uncovered, to illuminate the reader, even when that hidden meaning and "truth" are never found.

As in classic parables, the parabolic event of "An Imperial Message" takes place in an infinitely vast land, between a humble and infinitely remote subject and his Emperor. Faithful to biblical parables' stereotypical story line, Kafka represents symbolically in this parable man's relation to God, by shifting to the relationship between a powerful king and his people. Kafka borrows this pattern from ancient parables and, in this respect, he belongs in a long tradition of Jewish parabolizers.

On the scaffolding of these ancient patterns, Kafka imposes, however, his innovations to the genre. Among the innovations observable in this parable are the departure from stereotypical interpersonal relationships between parabolic characters, abundant linguistic experimentation, and a clever replacement of the ancient moral lesson, with a meditation about the artificial nature of modern parabolic teaching—ultimately, a statement about the impossibility of real teaching or learning in modernity.

The characters in this parable, the Emperor, the messenger, and the humble subject of "the Emperor," are propelled into action by the Emperor's urgent desire/need to communicate with his most remote and humble subject. But, unlike in ancient parables, here, the ruler is ailing and cut off from his beloved servant. The Emperor, Kafka tells us, is still alive, but textually marked as a "dying" sovereign. Since the Emperor may pass away at any point in delivering his important message to his subject (via the "indefatigable messenger"), his action acquires a particular urgency. Interestingly, Kafka's dying Emperor is unusually eager to send his message to "you," his most faithful subject, but, unlike the royalty in ancient parables, cannot communicate with "you," his loyal servant.

The great master of modern parables is careful to mark the unique relation the Emperor has with the intended recipient of the message by an interesting linguistic gradation in intimacy and in confidentiality. From the initial neutral pronoun "you," there is a change to the noun phrase "humble subject," and "the insignificant shadow cowering in the remotest distance," which establishes the subserviency of the addressee to his Emperor. Later, Kafka returns to the original pronoun, but this time, he places it next to the intensifier "alone." By this latest strategy of augmentation and accumulation, Kafka establishes a clear note of unconventional intimacy between the "Emperor" and "his most humble and infinitely remote subject."

The confidentiality added to the uncommon familiarity with a servant and the utter urgency of the message increase the uncanniness of the situation and manifest Kafka's underlying injunction to his readers to begin to search in their memory for other cases where such a peculiar relation existed between a people and their supreme master. In pressing the reader to make immediately this connection, Kafka takes him/her another step in the direction of establishing that the relationship must be an extraordinary one, perhaps one between a man and the supreme Being.

A message from a dying king is usually regarded with respect and is considered very important. The paramount importance of the Emperor's present message (whose content, however, remains forever undisclosed) and the seriousness of the imperial messenger's mission are represented by Kafka with the help of unique linguistic and gestural exchanges. The "whispering[s]" and the "nod" establish an aura of great secrecy and confidentiality around the event; first, the Emperor proceeds to "whisper into the ear" (of the messenger), this is followed next by a "whisper into the ear" (of the emperor) and last, by "a nod of approval" (by the Emperor).

The Kafkan tactic of having the characters exchange secretive language and hinting gestures opens new vistas for interpretation and lends the dialogue in the parable an air of mystery that evokes/invokes in his reader a familiar, ancestral language and practice. Specifically, this echoes the mysterious language and signs used in the communications between ancient mystics, between kabbalists, or recipients of divine, secret knowledge. This discovery, in turn, prepares the reader to receive as well a very special kind of information.

To augment further the readers' curiosity about the secret intercourse between the powerful Emperor and his servant and make the reader wish to discover the hidden content of his important, secret message, Kafka offers further narrational cues. He tells the reader that "so much store did the Emperor lay on it" that, "in order to reassure the Emperor that he has perceived it correctly," the "messenger" had "to whisper it into the Emperor's ear again," and that "the Emperor confirms that it was right by a nod."

We are provoked in two ways by the new information. While the extreme caution that "the Emperor" takes to convey correctly his message further stimulates us to advance in the text, the interest exhibited by the "dying Emperor" toward one of his most humble subject titillates and puzzles us even more as to the content of that message.

We become increasingly suspicious that the powerful Emperor must have some important hidden motives that compel him to communicate and treat very fondly this subject who is most "remote" and "humble," and commonly ignored by royalty. Kafka makes us ask ourselves: Could this most "remote" and "insignificant" subject be in fact a favorite of the Emperor? Have the two been communicating before? By what means? What might have been the content of their previous communication? Finally, is the subject ever going to receive this most peculiar message? Are we ever going to find out the content of this dying Emperor's message?

By now, Kafka has turned his readers as well into "imperial subjects," who are curiously awaiting the message. At this point, we turn in fascination to Kafka's linguistic innovativeness at work to accomplish the transformation of his reader. Kafka anticipates his reader's response and absorbs him further in his parable. To answer the questions that he has provoked in his reader in the first place, Kafka creates a linguistic artifact, a labyrinthal parabolic narrative (with infinite obstacles) through which he sends the reader to wander together with "the messenger" of the Emperor on an impossible quest. And, even though Kafka describes the "messenger" as a very "powerful" and "indefatigable" man, he tells the reader at once that, despite all his unusual qualifications, "the messenger" will never reach his destination and never deliver the "Emperor's secret message" (and fulfill his obligation to the Emperor).

Kafka also lets his addressee know that this is not at all the messenger's fault, and thus prevents his readers from falling into faulty thinking (also from having false hope). He disabuses his readers of the idea that perhaps not all has been done to deliver the message by spelling out with painstaking precision the reasons for which "the Emperor's message" will never reach his "remote subject." He inscribes them augmentatively to overwhelm the readers who, by now, are made to identify themselves with the conscientious messenger and seek together with him a way out of this quandary.

In essence, Kafka creates a mathematical maze. At the same time, he feeds the bewilderment of his reader by relentlessly accruing the number and sets of infinite impediments: (1) "an infinite number of chambers," (2) "an infinite number of stairs," (3) number of courts posited as "without" number, (4) "an infinite number of palaces," (5) "an infinite number of people," (6) "the imperial capital, the center of the world," "bursting with its own refuse," (7) "nobody could fight his way through here," (8) "the messenger with a message from a dead king," and so on. Kafka mercilessly forces his reader together with "the Emperor's messenger," into this manufactured labyrinth of infinite obstacles. And, while he prevents the messenger from delivering his message, Kafka takes the opportunity to enlighten his reader about his lamentable position in the world.

Kafka teases his reader with a labyrinthal parable to make him/her realize that there is no possible way to extricate him/herself from this predicament. He does this by conceding in a narrational sequence of the parable that there is one way for "the dying Emperor's message" to reach the subject, "you." The precondition is that the "messenger" reaches the outermost gate (but there is an infinite number of gates) and that the "messenger" bypasses the last man.

Kafka, who appears to have masterminded also how to forewarn his naive reader at every turn in this labyrinth, comes back in the following narrational sequence and dismisses the illusion of possible success created in the cycle above. To dispel the reader's fleeting fantasy that the message may be delivered to its rightful addressee, Kafka introduces a final set of impediments with the statements "but there is an infinite multitude of men," and "even though he tries his utmost, the messenger cannot overcome either the courts, chambers and stairs, or the multitude."

With incredible rhetorical force, Kafka alternates acting as a mentor to his reader, with trapping him as well in the web of impediments facing the messenger who squanders his physical and intellectual energy by going over an infinite number of challenges impossible to overcome. In this fashion, he instills in his reader a feeling of hopelessness and helplessness akin to that of the lost messenger and the remote subject of the dying Emperor. We suggest that Kafka alludes parabolically to his own feeling of hopelessness and despair.

In an ingenious transposition of meaning and reference, Kafka draws his reader in the Kafkan hopeless world. In terms of Strawson's distinction between the meaning of an expression and referring, Kafka's modern parabolic ruse consists in expressing his existential pain by only "referring" to it, while offering (in its stead) a parable about the anguished, infinitely remote subject of the Emperor.[4]

To distract the reader from finding out his discursive stratagems and perhaps renounce further reading, Kafka, like ancient parabolizers, stages a spatial movement to an "elsewhere" and transports the reader, interiorizes him, so to speak, in the analogous world of the parable, to "another," original text/world. From the scene of the imperial deathbed, Kafka takes the reader, together with the messenger, through number-less courts, staircases, walls, doors, palaces, and multitudes.

His parabolic narrative—at first glance open to referentiality—closes upon itself, in other words, is auto-referential (refers to its own parabolicity), because Kafka's intention is to persuade his reader of the futility of all attempts to become enlightened (the message is undeliver-able). In this sense, Kafka's parable instantiates a growth in remoteness from the thing in itself, or, in Greimas' terms, has become "an interpre-tative instance—a fiction without reference representing the labor of dis-course on itself" (my translation).[5]

To achieve the eerie feeling of the *déjà vu*, a sense of neverending frustration and of uncanniness, or *unheimliche*, in Freud's sense, Kafka uses parallelism.[6] The narration of the impotent royal messenger, who cannot accomplish his delicate task despite his formidable efforts, is repeated in the portrayal of the sad and impotent royal subject. The statement "you sit despondent at your window when evening falls" is directed at all of Kafka's readers. By using the second person "you," which can mean both "you" the subject of the Emperor and "you" the reader of the parable, Kafka places all of the possible addressees of this parable in the position of the subject of the Emperor who remains remote, dejected, and forever dispossessed of the intimacy and the close-ness to his sovereign. Thus, Kafka indicates parabolically to all his potential readers, that, like the bereft subject of the Emperor, we, mod-ern men and women, are destined to remain forever "insignificant shad-ows cowering in the remotest distance before the imperial sun" and to "dream the message [from the Emperor] to yourself [ourselves]."

The moral lesson in Kafka's parable is a clear departure from the ancient parabolic mode. In Kafka's parable, there is no true recipient of the "symbol of the sun which glitters." The true meaning of the parable is not disclosed by the modern parabolizer—how could he, when he claims he will never know it either? Thus Kafka tells in his parable that, like the bereft subject, we modern readers will remain forever outsiders to the parable's meaning.

To those of us who, like Kafka, desire desperately to receive a message from our "Emperor," namely, wish to obtain knowledge closer to Godliness and to divine wisdom, Kafka tells that we are all destined to fail. All one can do in modern times is to dream the (His?) message to oneself.

Modernity's bleakness is further emphasized by the subject's having to "dream the message to himself," while at his window, "when evening falls," namely, alone in a world continuously darkening in the absence of the "imperial sun," which is Godliness.

Kafka's darkest message is that modern man will have to figure out the meaning of his being in the world, forever alone, in a dimming, silent universe. Absolute knowledge (of the "imperial message") is denied even to the one "chosen" among subjects, and the truth of the "imperial message" is kept from him eternally, like the desire of the ruler to communicate with him.

The modern parable "An Imperial Message" refuses its own secret message to the reader; it remains undeliverable and indecipherable, with no privileged reader, no Pharisee, and no disciple. Kafka's extraordinary mastery as a parabolizer consists in sending to his reader a veritable "imperial message": a parable; a promised secret communication of utter importance, forever expected, yet forever withheld. And, like the "imperial message," Kafka's parable will frustrate eternally those who enter its dejected world and are left to figure out its cryptic message for themselves.

Kafka tells us parabolically that "there is a fabulous yonder, something unknown to us," but, like the old "sages" of his parable, "On Parables," "he cannot designate [that fabulous yonder] more precisely, and therefore cannot help us in the least."

In figures 7.1 through 7.3 I show a schematic representation of Kafka's linguistic maze, construed with such precision that we are able to illustrate it mathematically.

$C = c_1 \quad c_n \quad c_\infty$ C = infinite crowd, c_n = person in the crowd
$W = w_1 \quad w_n \quad w_\infty$ w = infinite number of walls, courts,
w_n = one item
n: finite; ∞: infinite
= communication
$\neq$ non-communication
$C \times W$ = an infinite matrix.

IDEAL PARABOLICAL SPATIOTEMPORAL RELATIONSHIP

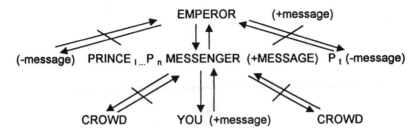

NOTE: non-communication, non-intelligibility
communication, intelligibility
+, -   having, or not having the message
I,n,t   finite natural numbers

FIGURE 7.1
Ideal Spatiotemporal Relationship

NARRATIONAL PARABOLICAL SPATIOTEMPORAL RELATIONSHIP

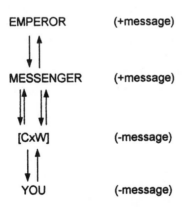

FIGURE 7.2
Narrational Spatiotemporal Relationship

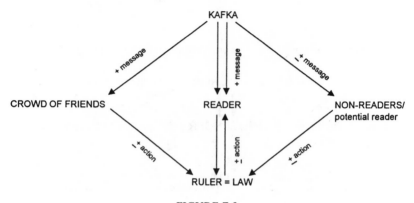

FIGURE 7.3
Structural of Communicational Path in the Parable

The parabolic situational relationship can be represented in two ways; the first, by means of an infinite set of two disjoined infinite subsets.

Subset 1: $C = c_1 \ldots C_n \ldots C_\infty$
Subset 2: $W = w_1 \ldots w_n \ldots W_\infty$
Compounded set: $[C] \times [W]$
$[C]$ and $[W]$ = disjunctive (walls and individuals are not interchangeable entities).

If we use the choice axiom that postulates that, given an infinite set of points, we can choose any one point of the set and there will still be left an infinite set of points to overcome. The second way of representing Kafka's mathematical ploy could be in terms of *Hilbert's Space*. The picture is the same; the message cannot be delivered to the subject "you." The messenger is always confronted with a "still permanently infinite set of X" to overcome, subsequently will be perpetually prevented from delivering his message to the one individual who is waiting for it.[7]

CHAPTER 8

Jorge Luis Borges:
The Parable of Cervantes
and The Quixote

"We read Kafka from something like a necessity; we read Borges for enjoyment, our own indifference taking pleasure in the frightful but robust spectacle of a disinherited cosmos," states John Ashbery[1] in trying to distinguish between the two literary giants of our time. Ashbery's efforts to illustrate the differences between Borges and Kafka seem to reinforce even more poignantly the intimate link between them.

Like Kafka, Borges was a most unhappy man. In "Remorse," Borges admits that "I have committed the worst sin that a man can commit. I have not been happy."[2] Borges's solitary strife to fathom the impenetrable permeates his fiction, just as Kafka's mirrors his personal inner struggle. In a way, Borges's writing became his histrionic performance. Borges concedes in an interview: "I shall not be happy, perhaps it does not matter/ . . . I am left with the pleasure of being sad."[3]

When faced with a painful historical reality, Borges too has withdrawn into his imagination and forged an amazing fictional world: a prodigious self-contained artifice, severed from historic reality. And as Kafka, Borges made friends with his sense of cosmic failure; therefore, the quest of his heroes is akin to the moving undertakings of Kafka's protagonists. Their futile quests are rich in significance, despite the fact they are the champions of exegesis in search of an archetypal significance that eludes them forever.

But how did Borges, this subversive epigone, connect at a deeper level with Kafka in his own work? How did Kafka become his literary precursor, and what is the nature of their literary kinship?

To answer questions about their affinities, we might wish to look at their reaction to the chaos of the outside world, rather than at their life experience. If, in his fecund imagination, Kafka anticipated a world of utter spiritual desolation where man is doomed to live his life like a mole, Borges saw the utmost human disfigurement become a historical reality. The great emulator of Kafka lived to witness the defacement of the world in the Holocaust and see his beloved Argentina crushed under the dictatorship of Peron, of whom, disappointingly, he approved.

Despite these radical differences and his belatedness, Borges, like Kafka, did not seek to confront the real world. Even advancing the study of philosophy seemed foolish to Borges, since he genuinely felt that those who had attempted this task before him "have travelled earnestly in circles, getting nowhere."[4] Borges fled in pain from the hard face of reality and renounced it. He then proceeded to invent a fiction where he could feel at home. Alfred Kazin made a most pertinent assessment of Borges's solipsistic writing. Kazin claimed that "Borges has built his work, and I [Kazin] suspect his life itself, out of the same effort to make himself at home in his own mind. . . . He certainly does not put us in close touch with his own country. His Argentina remains a place of dreams. Borges's mind is the realest thing in it."[5]

About Borges's interiorized life, Monegal, another scholar of Borges claims that "Borges's metaphysics is not only literature, it is first of all the experience of an anguish, dissimulated under a particularly lucid expression."[6]

To write about his profound existential angst and his consuming passions, Borges, too, frequently chose parables. For example, in a supremely crafted short narrative entitled "Borges and I," Borges acknowledges the bitter rift between Borges the man and Borges the writer: "I like hourglasses, maps, eighteen-century typography, the taste of coffee, and Stevenson's prose. The other one (I) shares these preferences with me, but in a vain way that converts them into the attributes of an actor."[7] Borges considered himself "a man who weaves hendeca-syllabics."[8] Jaime Alazraki, the author of *Borges and the Kabbalah*, recounts an interview not long before Borges's death, where Borges spoke of himself in similar terms: "I am the one who amidst the night counts the syllables."[9]

Statements such as these enlighten us not only about his deep inner struggle, they tell also of his singular dedication to his craft. For Borges, who, when confronted with the upheaval of the world, has chosen the safety and order of the library, or in his own terms, "the safety of a deci-pherable labyrinth," poetry and literature are not so much means of expressing experience, but well-crafted artifacts. This solitary Argen-tinean saw the act of writing, if not as an obligation, as something like a mission, and the library, a place he called home. The ambivalence about the power of his art, on the one hand, and the unyielding dedica-tion to it, on the other, bring Borges again close to Kafka.

In reading Borges's work, as in reading Kafka's, we also come to understand the preoccupations that animate modernism. Indeed, while Borges developed a pristine style of his own, typical modern philosophical questions traverse his work. For example, his belief that literature and intellectualization are apart from and above reality brings him close to modern philosophers and analysts such as Jung, Schopenhauer, and Berkeley. Love for antiquity, in particular for Jewish mysticism, figures prominently in his work as well.

Borges was immensely attracted to early Kabbalah and to the Talmud. And, like the Talmudic texts that have their roots in the interpretations of a (holy) book, Borges's books have their foundations in other books. His brilliant reflections indicate that he preferred "the lucid pleasure of thought and the secret adventures of order."[10]

Borges's tone compelled scholars like Myrna Solotarevsky to suggest that he considers literature a totality, "another witness" of the profound unity of the word, a unique analogous dissolution of individual authorship.[11] Her statement is very much in the spirit of Harold Bloom's claim that a single text has only part of a meaning; it is itself a synecdoche for a larger whole including other texts. A text is a relational event, and not a substance to be analyzed.[12]

His ideas regarding the creative process and the interpretative moment in literature remind us indeed of rabbinic writings, and their relationship to those early texts. Specifically, the interpretation tactics in Borges's work are akin to the spirit of the Midrash. Like the *Midrash*, which refers back to the totality of the Scriptures as the word of God, Borges's work compels us to look back at the totality of literature. Solotarevski suggests that it is comparable to *Midrash* in three particular ways: in its inherent metatextuality, in the infinite play of signifiers triggered in the act of decoding and decentering an arch-text, and in its intertextuality.[13]

The first similarity with *Midrash* is that for Borges literature is a multilayered text each writer reads, re-interprets, and rewrites. "Quotation with Borges," maintains John Sturrock, "stands for that necessary plagiarism of other men's writings without which no writer can survive."[14] In Borges's opinion, each author necessarily incorporates the writing of other authors, not so much to agree or disagree with them, but because whenever one writes, one necessarily engages with all other literary texts in a dialectical process of literary invention.

Borges's view that the task of literature is to find means of perceiving the old in a fresh new way, is most like the Kabbalah, which, as we recall, has created an entire new literature out of reading and interpreting the Holy Scriptures. As the early kabbalists, Borges used and reshaped in his fiction elements from existing myths, motifs, and tropes, because, according to him, the most fertile ground for the creative process is finding contradictions among old texts and reading them afresh. Borges's art and his innovation consist in seeing that revelation resides in the act of reading the new in an old text. The Borgesian universe is thus a new texture given to old texts, a polyphony of interpenetrated literary voices, all expressing themselves polysemically; in short, a modern Babel.[15] In that respect, Borges has anticipated current literary criticism that claims that "texts do not *have* meanings, except in their relations to other texts, so that there is something uneasily dialectical about literary meaning."[16]

When asked about his affinity with Kabbalah, Borges replied that "the idea that the whole world is a system of symbols, that the whole world including the stars, stood for God's secret writing that needs to be interpreted and understood. That idea is in the Kabbalah, and I think that may be my chief attraction to it."[17]

In "Pascal's Sphere," Borges claims that "perhaps universal history is the history of the diverse intonations of a few metaphors," and in "Circular Ruins," he proposes that the whole world is perhaps the dream of someone, or perhaps of no one. Thus, he alludes to the idealistic notion of the hallucinatory character of all reality.[18] In fact, Borges's dictum that each writer creates his own precursors is itself a "Sefirotic theosophy," claims Alazraki, and seems very much the point where Kabbalah begins.[19]

Another similarity with classic rabbinic writing is Borges's idea that interpreting texts activates an infinite play of signifiers in which signification and significance are by no means discarded. As in *Midrash*, "interpretative historiography functions as a source of symbolic expansion." This procedure, explains Solotarevsky, involves complementing and amplifying available facts by means of the addition of imaginary configurations such as stories, or parables, that have an explanatory and clarifying function, and exhibit a relation of equivalence to the primary subject of the moral lesson.[20]

The third affinity with the *Midrash* is that for Borges, as for the early sages, reading is not mere linearity, but a configuration of textual space, "the de-structuring of the text and the dis-integration of its very center [the word of God], as a condition of deciphering it, that is to say, totalizing interpretative functions."[21]

Borges, like his literary kinsman Kafka, has retreated into literature as a way of illuminating his imagination, when he deemed himself incapable of deciphering the nature of the real world. But, while Kafka used magic to perceive a magic world, Borges has renounced that possibility with respect to the world. He did not renounce it, however, with respect to the intellectual culture. Borges has given up "the labyrinth of the Gods but not the labyrinth of man"; in other words, Borges perceived this human labyrinth based on illustrious ideas that are no longer perceived as absolute truths, but as marvels, intuitions, and myths that stir the human imagination.[22] This has a definite Nietzschean flavor. It was Nietzsche after all who maintained that we know something about the things themselves, but we only possess metaphors of things. And these metaphors do not in the least correspond with the original essences; truth, the thing itself, is inaccessible and indefinable.[23]

Borges's lesson in writing is best captured by another eminent modernist, Julio Cortázar, who claims that "the great lesson Borges taught us was neither a lesson in themes nor in contents or techniques. It was a lesson in writing, an attitude."[24] Indeed, in telling a story, instead of tracing the line of the story, Borges indicates its possibilities, generally postponed or deferred. His critical essays are fictional even when they are about real works. This enlightens us also to the fact that his stories are told largely for the sake of the explicit self-criticism that they embody.[25]

Stories by Borges have a simple, mirror-like structure. They unfold in some way to add to their explicit or literal signification, or denotation, a supplementary power of connotation that enriches them with several secondary meanings. Borges's originality consists mostly in the clever linguistic and rhetorical devices he invents to tell his stories to his reader. His storytelling speaks of his insights about the nature of language and of his deep interest in its inherent powers of communication.

Borges's particular attention to the formalistic devices by means of which messages are conveyed in language, that is, to codes, comes from a view of literature according to which the performance and effectiveness of codes is intrinsically related to the importance and urgency of the message they convey. To create a good story, according to Borges, a writer has to encode his message with the signs that most effectively convey to the reader his intended message. More precisely, to create a story, a writer must transform ordinary language, that is, an arbitrary system of signs, into literary messages. This entails absorbing the linguistic sign and converting it into a new signifier whose own signifier transcends the orbit of language.

Because of his unique feat, the writer needs to choose most effectively his language. The forcefulness of a writer's stories, claims Borges, hinges directly on the effectiveness of the codes he uses.[26] According to Borges, an effective writer invents effective semiotic systems.[27]

True to his belief about the nature of language and literature, Borges concentrated in his stories mostly on their symbolism. Some of the symbols he used over and over have entered deeply into the metabolism of Borges's fiction. For example, the "labyrinth," the symbol of chaos and hopelessness, the "library," the symbol of the universe, and the "aleph," the symbol of symbols, the root of human discourse, occur frequently in Borges's stories, with similar semantic vigor and codic investment. The reader comes not only to recognize them but to expect them in Borges's fiction.

Hinting at abstract doctrines by means of symbols and allegories to be decoded by the reader seemed a most fitting mode for Borges. Asking his reader not to take his stories literally, but to seek and discover the hidden messages and truths they contain was for Borges the best way to engage his reader. In offering stories with a rich symbolism, he hoped to compel his reader to re-read, and to interpret them in order to find new meanings. And although no necessary contradiction exists between the realistic nature of a story and the possibility of its symbolic interpretation, of finding "another meaning," Borges made sure that the literal meaning of the story is not overshadowed by its symbolism. In essence, the reader is kept in infinite irresolution by what we call a "lie in the narrative," a discursive distortion, or a ruse.[28]

In a strict sense, Borges's narratives represent a new way of reading the systems of philosophy as well as the doctrines of theology. At the same time, they are a way of turning the author's "perplexities" into literature and of stating his existential disillusionment in a text.[29] The many parables and tales Borges wrote to express his bewilderment before an incomprehensible world demand interpretation, yet also contain a clear denial of decoding, consistent with the author's incapability to find a sound answer to his questions.

Borges learned from the ancient sage who made up parables to clarify a previous context that was partially unknown (or not understood properly) yet fully existent (the Scriptures) and he came up with his own brand of parables. His modern parables "communicate uncertainty as more radical or even terminal value, yet the process and the value of an interminable referentiality are not abridged."[30] And this, we claim, is the quality that lends to Borges's parables their "Kafkaesque," modern flair.

If a parable is a narrative that contains its transmitted message in its entirety, then a parable by Borges is a testimony to the impossibility of such a text. Borgesian parables are permanent deferrals pointing to the possibility of decoding, while generating their internal truth. The reader is made to turn in circles in a dreamlike world, in "Borgesian" labyrinths. And, like the messenger of Kafka's "An Imperial Message," he is absorbed in the narrative and never arrives at his destination.

Yet, despite the continuous process of referring, Borges's parables could potentially transmit a moral lesson that would finally determine their meaning.[31] To illustrate this point as well as show affinities between parables by Borges and those by Kafka, I analyze below "The Parable of Cervantes and *The Quixote*."

CERVANTES AND *THE QUIXOTE*

Tired of his Spanish land, an old soldier of the king sought solace in the vast geographies of Ariosto, in that valley of the moon where the time wasted by dreams is contained and in the golden idol of Mohammed stolen by Montalbàn.

In gentle mockery of himself, he imagined a credulous man, who perturbed by his reading of marvels, decided to seek prowess and enchantment in prosaic places called El Toboso or Montiel.

Vanquished by reality, by Spain, Don Quixote died in his native village in the year 1614. He was survived but a short time by Miguel de Cervantes.

For both of them, for the dreamer and the dreamed one, the whole scheme of the work consisted in the opposition of two worlds: the unreal world of the books of chivalry, the ordinary everyday world of the seventeenth century.

They did not suspect that the years would finally smooth away that discord; they did not suspect that La Mancha and Montiel and the knight's lean figure would be, for posterity, no less poetic than the episodes of Sinbad or the vast geographies of Ariosto.

For in the beginning of literature is the myth, and in the end as well.[32]

——

One cannot get to the origin of myth.

—Levi-Strauss

The more abstract the truth is that you would teach, the more you have to seduce the senses to it.

—Friedrich Nietzsche

"The Parable of Cervantes and *The Quixote*" has a mirror-like plot. Borges retells the deeds of Miguel de Cervantes, the "old soldier" who, "tired of his Spanish land," "sought solace" in marvelous fiction. The old soldier proceeded to "engender" a "credulous man" in "gentle mockery of himself," a fictional mirror image. Haplessly, the old soldier's invented man in Borges's tale also goes to "seek prowess and enchantment in prosaic places." Like his creator, "Cervantes," he dies defeated—his project defeated as well—in his native village.

In the "credulous man," the reproduction of the spectacular failure of his protagonist "Cervantes," fashioned after the Spanish author Miguel de Cervantes, Borges problematizes our understanding of fiction and of reality at the level of discourse. In duplicating the experiences of the "old soldier" in the soldier's reproduction of himself (the "dreamed up, credulous man"), Borges points to our misunderstanding of the multifaceted interplay between fiction and reality. He then proceeds to make a powerful statement about the interpenetration of myth and reality. In this fashion, he invites the reader to look anew at our understanding and definitions of the relationships between the two realms.

By proposing that "the beginning of literature is myth and the end as well" as the moral of his parable, Borges points to the deception involved in the perception of fiction and reality as distinct entities. He thereby brings into focus modern man's massive exile from a true understanding of the two worlds. With the aid of this parable, Borges summons the reader who believes in the impermeability of real life and myth to remain attuned to the work of temporality and to the eternal return in myths of our lived experience, not as identical to life, but as a difference stated aside from identity, pointing to the circularity of our endeavors.

To support his claim about man's labyrinthal and futile searches for the origins of myths about human experience and fiction, Borges builds the parable around the real author, Miguel de Cervantes, the creator of the fictional knight "Don Quixote," and enacts the process of mythization that will presumably take place. If the readers can be persuaded of the soundness of the parable's claim, Borges hopes they could accept his assertion about real life processes of mythization as well.

A firm believer that revelation resides in the act of re-reading old texts, Borges postures the old soldier to misreads other authors' works of "fiction" about the "real world," and sets up his imagined character to misunderstand the very aim of fiction. In this way, Borges inscribes in his parable not only the reasons for which the other author of fiction has failed; he explains also the reasons for failure of that author's "dreamed up credulous man," "Don Quixote."

To these ends, Borges proceeds to give us his own "reading" of "Don Quixote." The fictional character dies in his "native village," says Borges, "vanquished by reality" (and "by Spain"), even though the Spanish writer has created him as an opposition to reality. The conditions of possibility for the imagined man to function in the real world are eliminated a priori by his engenderer, Cervantes; he has set up an axiology by which reality and fiction are completely impermeable. The "old soldier" states Cervantes's premise: "the whole scheme of the work consists in the opposition of two worlds: the unreal world of the book of chivalry, and the ordinary everyday world of the seventeenth-century Spain."

Borges deconstructs the novel in another ingenious way. The drama takes place between the soldier and his imagined man. In the second narrative sequence, Borges alludes to the parable's "other text," and the "vast geographies of Ariosto." He places them side by side with the fictional *Orlando Furioso*,[33] which has inspired the real Miguel de Cervantes, and Cervantes's real life experience in seventeenth century Spain, and *Don Quixote*, the novel. Borges proceeds then to inlay the sequence about the work of time and temporality, to show to his reader that the presupposed rift between the two realms (reality and fiction) is being eliminated in time. He tells that: "They did not suspect that years would smooth away the difference."

This statement allows Borges to redirect his reader to a new vantage point from within which the latter can see the worlds of fiction and myths with new eyes.

In telling us that "He [Don Quixote] is survived but a short time by Miguel de Cervantes, the defeated soldier of the Spanish king," Borges underlines the uncanny similarity between reality and fiction. Borges underscores the similarity between the dreamt-up man and the defeated soldier at the level of "lack." The soldier of the king cannot go on living when his credulous knight dies vanquished by reality; the real world of the tired soldier crumbles when his myth dies. With this statement, Borges challenges Cervantes's premise that there is a radical distinction between the real world and the fictitious world he has created.

To persuade his readers, Borges immerses the "real world," or "Spain of the seventeenth century," in which Cervantes has dreamed up his "credulous man" together with Cervantes's book of chivalry, in a new topos, another "place," which is the space and time of Borges's own parabolic tale.

This rhetoric gesture atests to Borges's keen understanding of the mimetic power of parables as the locus of a perpetual reference and deferral, as a narrative pointing only to its internal reality and not to the real world. At the same time, he reapropriates in parable the two different and seemingly mutually exclusive worlds.

With an intuition remarkably Kafkan, Borges creates a vision of modern man exiled from myths, aspiring to them only as an outsider. To compensate his modern reader for this loss, Borges offers him a parable, a token: an "elsewhere," which may be "the elsewhere" toward which man strives as an outcast. Borges suggests that being in parable seems the only possible way for modern man to escape exile, because, in relation to a parable, which by definition siphons its discourse and its reader, one is never in exile.

Modern in structure, Borges's parable refers back to an "original text" without the power to disclose the means to end man's exile from wisdom. Nevertheless, it aspires to teach that the worlds of reality and of fiction are intermeshing in human myths and that, in relation to this process, sadly, man is postured as a pariah. While the gap between the two worlds, posited by "credulous" authors as irreconcilable and unsurmountable, will disappear in time, man partakes in this extraordinary adventure only in parable.

To illustrate his point, Borges sets up two parallel narrative paths: the narration of the death of the soldier, next to the narration of the demise of the fictional knight. The death of the real soldier, which reproduces that of his fictional replica, illustrates in a very powerful way how fiction is bleeding into reality, and puts into question our notion of literature as "unreal." This is to say that, in depicting the death of the author as miming the death of his invented character, Borges brings home the idea that in many respects real life simulates fiction.[34] This recognition, in turn, helps him question incisively the vitality and force of any fiction created with the presupposition that the world of fiction does not contaminate reality in the same way in which the real world provides fertile grounds for the proliferation of fiction.

The barrenness of the landscape of modern man, who is banished from the working of myths and of literature, is amplified in the following narrative sequence. In it, Borges throws onto the world his own fiction, "Cervantes," the old soldier, and Cervantes's mirror image, "The Quixote." The thematic repetition of a route already taken aims to show that their defeat is similar in many respects. The difference consists perhaps in the fact that in surviving, "by a short time," his myth, Cervantes transforms his defeat into a small success: he outlives the reinstantiation of his loss.

The option that Cervantes, "the real," and "Quixote," the fiction, can penetrate each other's realm is being dismissed at the beginning by an astute rhetorical move. Borges sets them up structurally with parallel yet opposite paths. Discursively the two characters can clearly never meet. Two parallel vectors, pointing in opposite directions, with trajectories aiming in opposite ways, they cannot travel even as parallel itinerants, at a distance from each other. Borges's protagonists, "Cervantes" and "Don Quixote," are bound to observe each other at a distance for just one fleeting moment, as if looking in a distorted mirror. This is a nightmarish moment during which the dreamer sees his dreamed-up man, the image of himself, "falling down into the same prosaic lands," the topos that has denied to him the prowess and the enchantment he was once seeking for himself. The old soldier "looks for solace" in (ascends to) "the vast geographies of Ariosto, in that valley of the moon where the time wasted by dreams is contained" (the fiction that has lulled Cervantes); the invented "credulous man," "perturbed by his reading of marvels," "descends into the real," "prosaic places" ("La Mancha," "El Toboso," and "Montiel") to act out the world of the fiction that has thrilled him when reading it.

Borges's mastery consists in containing (but enclosing at the same time) in his parable the "fictional," the "real," as well as the act of mythization. To accomplish this, he assigns to them two entwined narrative paths and functions. The fictional credulous man, moved by myths to seek the marvelous world of the "unreal books of chivalry" in "the prosaic reality of seventeenth-century Spain," is a fiction reacting to fiction, in the parable's narrative program. The dreamed-up man's self-exile into reality, into "the prosaic El Toboso, or Montiel" is posited in the parable as a "tale." In turn, Cervantes is presumed the "real," tired soldier who accedes to the world of the books. In this way, both the real life experience and the fiction, enter into the world of myths, and in Borges's world of parable.

To imbricate the separate projects into his parabolic narrative, the modern master deploys several spiraling rhetorical gestures. By depicting the irruption of fiction into the "real" world as an aborted enterprise, he indicates Cervantes's mistaken assumption about the process of mythization. By relating that the dreamed one, "vanquished by reality" and "by Spain," dies in his native village, deprived of prowess and enchantment, Borges insinuates that the dreamer, who retreated into fiction and "sought solace in the valley of the moon" and "in the vast geographies of Ariosto," dies when attempting to run from the real world, and from "his Spanish land." Borges directs us next to the "old soldier" who "seeks solace in the Valley where the time wasted by dreams is contained," and who enacts his quest for prowess and enchantment by generating a character "in gentle mockery." Finally, through a chain of rhetorical maneuvers, Borges transforms "The Quixote" into another "golden idol of Mohammed," "stolen," not by Montalbàn, but by Cervantes, and, this time, from fiction.

Borges's "Quixote" acquires a double status, that of *imago*, or image, belonging to the specular, and that of image, belonging to reproduction, representation, and, ultimately, to literary discourse. The old soldier, "imagining" the man, becomes God, in a disposition of gentle mockery of himself. The act of mimesis of self, in its very essence, prowess, and enchantment, could have provided solace, had he looked for it there. Thus, Borges alludes to the fact that the "old soldier" is in fact successful in a quest without realizing it. He is successful during the act of creating. Oblivious to this success, the "old soldier" fails. Having failed as a creator, his fiction dies of reality, so to speak, and the real dies of its fiction, neither capable of existing outside of its delineated narrow boundaries.

Borges adds next the element of time to the equation. Time, according to him, "remains in charge of smoothing away that discord" and, thus, of closing the circle of literary discourse, which tells of its inception, its being, and its end.

In stating that "in the beginning of literature is the myth and in the end as well," Borges reiterates parabolically his belief that reality and fiction are two interchangeable moments in the creation of myths, and that myths reappropriate the beginning and the end of literature, in a perpetual motion. For Borges, man's exile from the working of myths is ultimately his exile from a lasting existence and his only solace seems to be in parable.

To persuade his reader of the circularity of myths (they reappropriate their beginnings), Borges offers the story of the soldier who reappropriates his fictional image of himself after it has been made to replay the drama of his disillusionment and to "contain his own time wasted by dreams."

In claiming that "they did not suspect that the years would finally smooth away that discord" and that "La Mancha and Montiel and the knight's figure would be for posterity no less poetic than the episodes of Sinbad or the vast geographies of Ariosto," Borges takes over parabolically these projects into his own parable. The dreamer and the "dreamed one" are depicted by Borges as temporary failures only, because, according to him, time is at work, transforming them into myths, namely, incorporating them side by side into our lore. Time successfully erases the fictitious opposition established originally by Cervantes, and by Orlando, and so, Cervantes, his "credulous man," and Orlando's stories enter together the realm of myth (which, we are told, is generator of, and generated by, literary discourse).

Borges's parable finally turns upon itself to comment about the impossibility of retrieval of the origins of either literature or myth. The parable speaks of its own textuality and of its being a text of which the entire preceding literature is a metatext.

Like Kafka, he seduces the reader. He simulates concern with an old defeated soldier of the king who seeks solace by dreaming up an image of himself, but absorbs his reader in the world of his parable and persuades him to believe he will find new knowledge. The ruse in Borges's parable occurs with the shift from the predicator "for it is," to the parabolic claim "therefore," which, we are told, is not a valid inductive argument.[35] The premises

(a) the old soldier of the king seeks solace in the vast geographies of Ariosto and in dreams and dies when his dreams die

(b) the dreamed up man seeks prowess and enchantment in the "prosaic land of El Toboso or Montiel" and dies in his native village without prowess and enchantment

(c) time makes them both as poetic as "the episodes of Sinbad" and "the vast geographies of Ariosto,"

cannot logically yield the statement "in the beginning of literature is the myth and in the end as well."

A scrutiny of the parable discloses mathematical precision. A division into sequences according to topoi reveals fragmentation into: places belonging to the realm of fiction, and places belonging to the realm of reality. But the parable brings forth a third category; it "contaminates" fiction with elements of reality, which negates the assumption of the "dreamer."

1. The Spanish land—reality
2. The vast geographies of Ariosto—fiction
3. "[T]hat valley of the moon where the time wasted by dreams is contained"—fiction
4. The topos of "the golden idol stolen by Montalbàn—fiction
5. The topos of "the imagining of the credulous man"—fiction
6. The "prosaic place called El Toboso or Montiel"—reality
7. The native village of the "Quixote"—reality + fiction
8. Books of chivalry—fiction
9. The everyday world of the seventeenth century—reality
10. "La Mancha and Montiel"—fiction + reality
11. The "vast geographies of Ariosto"—fiction
12. The "land of the episodes of Sinbad"—fiction

The curve generated by the diagram in figure 8.1 shows how fiction and reality are imbricated. A portion of the realm of reality invades the realm of fiction, and thus it negates the proposition that there is a clear and unalterable distinction between the world of fiction and reality.

X_1, X_2–X_{12}, follow the twelve sights in the narrative; X_7 and X_{10} invade the realm of fiction and that the distinction is a function of time, since: "the years would finally smooth away that discord . . . for posterity, the knight's lean figure would be no less poetical than the episodes of Sinbad, or the vast geographies of Ariosto."

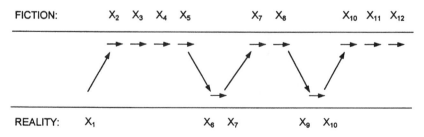

FICTION: X_2 X_3 X_4 X_5 X_7 X_8 X_{10} X_{11} X_{12}

REALITY: X_1 X_6 X_7 X_9 X_{10}

FIGURE 8.1
Entwined Fiction and Reality

The temporal, or chrononymic division follows closely the toponymic division of the text.

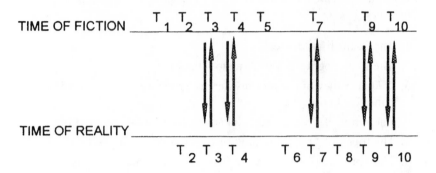

FIGURE 8.2
Fictional Time Entwined with Real Time

T_2 appears in both positions because as image of a self it also represents a real person. T_3 is a real time of death, but the death is of a fictional figure in literary discourse. T_4 is a real survival, but is also a survival narrated by a parable. T_9 and T_{10} are both presented by the parable as already contaminated, that is, as belonging to reality and to fiction at the same time.

In the spatiotemporal diagram combining the toponymic and the chrononymic segmentation, one notices the vectorlike motions of the two figures of the parable: the old soldier/Cervantes, and his "figure"/image, the knight/the credulous man/the Quixote (see both diagrams, figures 8.1 and 8.2, for reference).

TABLE 8.1
Narrative Trajectory

1. Time wasted by dreams—fictional

2. Time of imagining a man (in gentle mockery of himself)—fiction

3. Time of death of Quixote—fiction + reality

4. Time (short) of survival of Miguel de Cervantes—reality + fiction

5. Time of the book of chivalry—fiction

6. Seventeenth century—reality

7. "[Y]ears smoothing away that discord"—reality

8. "[P]osterity"—reality

9. Beginning of literature—fiction, reality (?)

10. End of literature—fiction, reality (?)

A series of topoi posited by the narrative as belonging to the world of fiction serve as points of ascension into the world of the dream. The subject operates a reflexive transformation, a transporting of the self into the world of the imaginary, "the unreal world of the books of chivalry," via engendering an image of self that mirrors the quest and the defeat suffered by the soldier.

At the anthroponymic level, we find an "operating subject" marked as "old soldier" of the king, as "tired" of his Spanish land. Cervantes and the dreamer wish to be conjoined with several valorized objects O_1–O_4 ("the vast geographies of Ariosto, the valley of the moon, the golden idol of Mohammed stolen by Montalbàn"). Finally, Cervantes wishes to be conjoined with his image posited as O_5, Quixote, the pale knight, the dreamed one, the credulous man.

```
Soldier————————————tired———————— seeks solace
Credulous man—————————perturbed————— seeks prowess and enchantment
Soldier——————————————vanquished———————\
                                         by reality, by Spain
Knight——————————————vanquished————————/
Soldier————————————————dies————————————\
                                         in native village
Knight——————————————dies——————————————/
```

If S_1 =   the soldier, and all the other textual demarcations
      S_2 =   the credulous man and all the other textual markers
      O_1 =   Ariosto, O_2 = valley of the moon, O_3 = golden idol
      O_4 =   books of marvels, O_6 = enchantment and prowess
      T_r1 =   reflexive transformation of S_1
      T_1 =   transitive transformation of S_1
      T_r2 =   reflexive transformation of S_2
      T_2 =   transitive transformation of $S2$

$$S_1 \xrightarrow{T_{r_1}} [S_1 \ (V_F \cap O_1) \cdot (S_1 \cap O_2 \cdot S_1 \cap O_3) \ v. \ (S_1 \cap O_4)] \dashrightarrow S_1 \xrightarrow{T_1} (S_1 \cap O_4)$$

EQUATION 8.1

$$S_2 \xrightarrow{T_2} (S_2 \cap O_5) \rightarrow S_2 \xrightarrow{T_{r_2}} [S_2 \cap O_6) \dashrightarrow (S_2 \cap O_7)]$$

EQUATION 8.2

However,

     $S_1 \cup O_5$——the soldier is disjoined from solace
     $S_2 \cup O_6$——the credulous man is not conjoined with prowess

W_r = dysphoric w_r real world: w_f world of fiction
W_f = euphoric

The two worlds are posited in opposition. We may modalize on the opposition between the dreamed-up man and the dreamer, and reality versus the books of chivalry, as in figure 8.3.

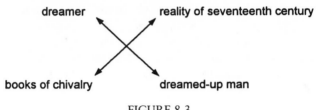

FIGURE 8.3
Subject Modalities

The other sets of opposition are illustrated in table 8.2.

TABLE 8.2
Sets of Oppositions

I. $\dfrac{\text{ARISTO + THE VALLEY OF THE MOON}}{\text{NATIVE LAND + MONTIEL+ EL TOBOSO}} = \dfrac{\text{ENCHANTING}}{\text{PROSAIC}}$

II. $\dfrac{\text{KNIGHT}}{\text{OLD SOLDIER}} = \dfrac{\text{PROWESS}}{\text{CREDULOUS MAN}}$

III. $\dfrac{\text{SEVENTEENTH CENTURY}}{\text{POSTERITY}} = \dfrac{\text{CREDULOUS MAN + DEFEATED SOLDIER}}{\text{KNIGHT} \quad + \text{ POETRY}}$

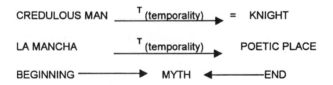

Additional oppositions are schematized in figures 8.4–8.6.

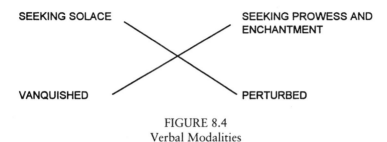

FIGURE 8.4
Verbal Modalities

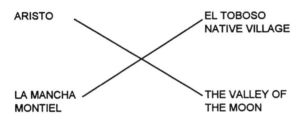

FIGURE 8.5
Real Places Modalities

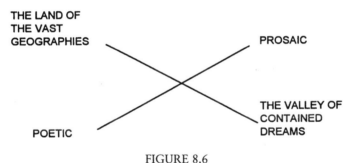

FIGURE 8.6
Fictional Places Modalities

The anthroponymic opposition is temporally and spatially bound. The syntactic expression of consequential actions is expressed in the following manner: (if actors A_1 and A_2) are the old soldier and Quixote, then:

TIRED ────────────> SEEKS SOLACE
PERTURBED ───────────> SEEKS PROWESS & ENCHANTMENT
VANQUISHED ──────────> DIES

The textual transformations can be shown in a schema as follows:

Myth—>Literature—>Cervantes—>Soldier—>Credulous Man—>
Cervantes—>Knight—>Literature—>Myth

    The verbs that move the narrative forward and the space-time dia-
gram follow in figures 8.7 and 8.8.

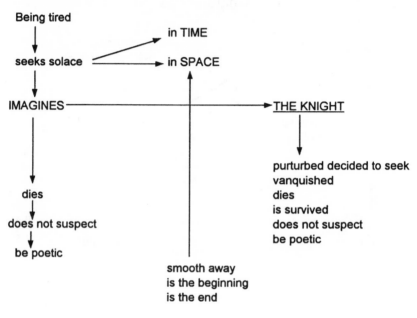

FIGURE 8.7
Verbal Propulsion of Narrative

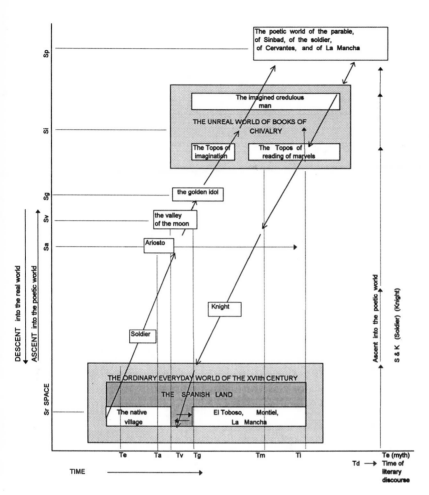

FIGURE 8.8
The Space-Time Diagram in "The Parable of Cervantes and *The Quixote*"

CHAPTER 9

Italo Calvino:
Cities and Signs

Unlike Kafka and Borges, who retreated into literature to escape from a world they could not confront, Italo Calvino experienced first hand the atrocities of World War II when his country fell prey to Fascism. After refusing to enlist in the Italian army as a defender of Fascism, he fought in Northern Italy with a brigade of partisans. At the end of the war, like many other of his compatriots, Calvino was inspired to write down his experiences.[1]

Exposed to an utter defacement of the world during World War II, Calvino became a firm believer that writing should lead to human action. He began by recounting his own story to bear witness to the recent past. His three short stories written in 1945, "The Same Things as Blood," "Waiting for Death at a Hotel," and "Anxiety in the Barracks," tell about his life during the last two years of the war. In his other stories, Calvino continued to transform his real life experience into "fables of estrangement in which the Resistance and its representation are redefined." Lucia Re claims that Calvino "tells tales that are memorable and can be repeated, retold, and disseminated, becoming the starting point of other stories and other symbolic reconfiguration of human experience and human action."[2]

A superior storyteller who collected and translated fairy tales and fables from dialect into modern Italian, Calvino, like his compatriots Eco, Sciascia, and Malerba, displays a predilection for children's literature and for fairy tales. Jo Ann Cannon suggests that, while Eco and Sciacia moved away from fairy tales and oriented their imagination mainly toward anti-detective stories, Calvino, more like the modern French writer Robbe-Grillet and the Latin American Luis Borges, focused on tales. He called into question in countless ways the image of the "well-made positivistic universe," projected by conventional detective stories. Calvino followed Elio Vittorini's injunction to create a "literature with a rational thrust." Calvino's writing points relentlessly to literature as a language game that, in essence, could offer various grammars for ordering the world of words and not as a mirror of the world.[3]

In the elaborate narratological paths of *Le città invisibili, Il castello dei destini incrociati,* or *Se una notte d'inverno un viaggiatore,* Calvino theorizes about the act of storytelling. He posits fabulating as endless dissemination of other stories.

In his stories, Calvino has adopted a style that can be easily committed to memory, where it may serve as a model for action. This trait of Calvino's fiction makes him very much a follower of Walter Benjamin. As we recall, Benjamin, whom Bertold Brecht considered one of the greatest minds lost in the Holocaust, viewed storytelling as designed to consolidate itself into the experience of the reader and to claim a place for itself in his memory.[4]

Calvino's narrative strategy is summarized by him early in his career in the prefatory note he wrote to *Gli amori.* In response to what he perceives as "una crisi della Ragione," or, a crisis of Reason, Calvino hopes to explore the question of indeterminacy plaguing modernity. The impossibility of absolute knowledge—acknowledged and explored already by Kafka—entails, according to Calvino, a lack of legitimacy to certain heuristic interpretative models. What matters most, according to Calvino, is to conceive of literature that displays an awareness of its own limitations, "as a game of language capable of ordering reality and of calling into question our philosophical assumptions."[5] Literature according to Calvino

> is a geometrical design, a *combinatoire,* a structure of symmetries and options, a chess-board on which the black squares and the white squares exchange places in accordance with a very simple mechanism. . . . For today's writer the story above is all a written page, a world in which only autonomous forces are at work?[6]

Like Kafka and Borges before him, Calvino had to come to grips with major dilemmas troubling modern writers. He realized quite early that the new individualism is approaching a complete loss of the individual in the sea of things, and a loss of the dialectic opposition between subject and object.

To express the complexity of modern human experience in crisis, the postmodern zeitgeist, Calvino introduced the notion of *labyrinth*: a densely coded reality that, to his mind, must be recognized, accepted, and finally interiorized by the modern artist.[7]

With Calvino, abstract conceptualization no longer corresponds to the reality for which it is supposed to account. His protagonists display a nostalgia for interpretative models to the point of obsession with form-giving structures. I. T. Olken, a reputable Calvino scholar, suggests that in Calvino's worldview only the acceptance of the challenges of the labyrinth promises to us survival as a viable intelligence.[8] Surrendering to it means capitulation and loss of any hope of understanding the inevitability of an ever-changing world. According to Calvino, today we need more than ever to confront the complexity of the real world.

But this can no longer be done in the usual ways. We must make a most detailed map of "the labyrinth," while, at the same time, resist the temptation of losing ourselves in it and in its representations of the absence of exits as the true condition of man.[9] "Today," argued Calvino in *Il Menabò*:

> we have begun asking from literature something more than a knowledge of the period or a mimesis of the external aspects of objects or the internal aspects of the human soul. We want a cosmic image from literature . . . that is, at the level of the stage of knowledge that historical development has put.[10]

Calvino asks his reader to substitute the passive dread of the labyrinth with a literature that reaffirms the distinction between consciousness and the sea of objectivity. He also defines the means by which man could escape from the labyrinth. The heroes of his stories adopt a "phenomenological" approach to the world, even in the casual encounter with rocks, clouds, lizards, statues.[11]

Kathryn Hume, another Calvino scholar, assesses that in his desire to find answers to his problems with meaning, Calvino often saw literature as a kind of web. The view of literature as a "mental spider's web bridging the chasm between fixed assumptions," or a "safety net between our acrobatics and the yawning void," is as dazzling as it is anxiety-inducing in Calvino.[12] While literature may indeed serve as a system for ordering experiences, as a web, literature is also haunted by nightmares and visions of the abyss from which it means to protect us but which nevertheless yawns threateningly. In this light, Calvino's statement about literature becomes even more relevant:

> Literature can seek and teach irreplaceable things: the manner in which one looks at one's fellow man and at oneself, the manner of relating personal and general facts, of attributing value to things small and large, of considering one's own limits and vices and those of others, of finding the proportions of life, and the role that love plays in it, and its force and its rhythm, and the role of death, the manner of thinking about it or not thinking about it; literature can teach harshness, compassion, sadness, irony, humor, and so many other necessary and difficult things. Go learn the rest from somewhere else, from science, from history, from life, as we all must constantly go to learn it.[13]

Believing that a writer has a moral responsibility toward his fellow men and that he must teach them how to overcome the many ills that befall society, Calvino chose action over inaction and assertion over resignation. In his fiction, he immerses his reader into meticulous analyses of contemporary society and its peculiar relation to industrial progress. His passionate involvement in social change reflects his conviction that, while literature may not find for us an exit from the labyrinth, it can put us in the frame of mind enabling us to find our own way out. Hume convincingly argues that "Calvino found a narrative stance that satisfies his desire for something more centrally active than mere bystander, but not just first-person protagonist, with the demands that would have made for more psychological depth."[14]

In his collection of short stories *Le città invisibili*, for example, Calvino explores the mysterious vistas of dreamlike ventures, where logic and chance act side by side, inexplicable to man, and unencumbered.[15] Yet, even though Calvino's city landscapes emerge as coded messages that reveal in some fashion only minute fragments of the laws that order human experience, Calvino teaches in his stories new ways of being in the world, and professes active change.

In Calvino's world vision, the underlying order of human nature is as precise as the logic of dreams, yet as elusive. The perpetual tensions between the characters of his magnificent tales and their environment, which they indefatigably attempt to know and to master, allow him to deploy a large-scale investigation of the ways in which texts call into question the concepts of identity, self, and ego, as unitary fictions.

An able innovator of tropes that transform factual reality into engaging imagery, Calvino is the heir to the revolutionary spirit of Cesare Pavese and Elio Vittorini.[16] However, in his firm belief that mythical revelation follows the fable and represents the end result of the fable's development, Calvino goes beyond his Italian compatriots and joins Kafka and Borges in his literary ventures.[17]

Teresa De Lauretis fittingly points to a dialectic process between "poiesis" and "praxis " at the foundation of Calvino's work. The extravagant artistic configuration of his fiction and his political message, to her mind, are not isolate impulses, but interconnect to express his vision of human activity.[18] This successful artistic integration of social concerns makes him, in De Lauretis's opinion, one of the most important writers today.

Like his precursors, Kafka and Borges, Calvino presents in his fiction a conception of the world that has been transformed by enchantment and magic. The worldview that each reader is able to see in Calvino's tales, suggests an important dimension of the process of reading: the reader finds his own image in the text that he/she reads but with the difference that "disrupts the comfort of an easy identification. Calvino's reader does not get a photograph of reality but a metaphor."[19]

We suggest that the reader learns something more from Calvino's work. Like in traditional fables, Calvino's imagery embodies a lesson that is meant to make his readers aware of how to face their own problematic realities. However pessimistic some of his work is, Calvino insists that there is no need for total despair. In *Le città invisibili,* for example, a fragile, invisible harmony between mankind and the external world can be glimpsed. Yet this harmony becomes possible, according to Calvino, only with man's moral, intellectual, and physical strength to deal with his surroundings. Man is summoned to learn from disorientation and bewilderment to become free.[20]

To study the universe that he deemed uncontrollable, Calvino used lists as a stylistic tool in his fiction. His attempts to make sense out of a chaotic world are reflected also in the way in which his protagonists ponder the universe and the possibility of isolating part of a seamless, infinite whole. The question Calvino's protagonists most frequently face is about the limitations involved in trying to frame reality. Calvino calls his project of imposing finite structures on an infinite universe "collezione di sabbia," or collections of knowledge. While our multiple frames of reference formulated in order to master the divisible but ultimately unmanageable universe will fail of necessity, Calvino tells us, we go on cataloging and enumerating out of sense of pleasure in the naming of things.[21] When lists come at the end of a story, they tend to create an acceleration into multiplicity, "a verbal vortex that mimics the loss of control and the breakdown of an ordering system."[22] The final passages of *Invisible Cities* offer a perplexing example of the vertigo experienced before the lists of today's cities which give way to utopias, dystopias, and the Infernal City underlying them all.

I investigate below Calvino's parable "Cities and Signs," one of the tales in the collection of stories *Invisible Cities.* I find it most telling of his use of parabolic stories to convey his insights about man and modernity.

CITIES AND SIGNS

You walk for days among trees and among stones. Rarely does the eye light on a thing, and then only when it has recognized that thing as the sign of another thing: a print in the sand indicates the tiger's passage; a marsh announces a vein of water; the hibiscus flower, the end of winter. All the rest is silent and interchangeable; trees and stones are only what they are. Finally the journey leads to the city of Tamara. You penetrate it along streets thick with signboards jutting from the walls. The eye does not see things but images of things that mean other things: pincers point out the toothdrawer's house; a tankard, the tavern; halberds, the barracks; scales, the grocer's. Statues and shield depict lions, dolphins, towers, stars: a sign that something—who knows what?—has as its sign a lion or a dolphin or a tower or a star. Other signals warn of what is forbidden in a given place (to enter the alley with wagons, to urinate behind the kiosk, to fish with your pole from the bridge) and what is allowed (watering zebras, playing bowls, burning relatives' corpses). From the doors of temples the god's statues are seen, each portrayed with his attributes—the cornucopia, the hourglass, the medusa—so that the worshiper can recognize them and address his prayers correctly. If a building has no signboard or figure, its very form or position it occupies in the city's order suffice to indicate its function: the palace, the prison, the mint, the Pythagorean school, the brothel. The wares, too, which the vendors display on their stalls are valuable not in themselves but as signs of other things: the embroidered headband stands for elegance; the gilded palanquin, power; the volumes of Averroes, learning; the ankle bracelet, voluptuousness. Your gaze scans the streets as if they were written pages: the city says everything you must think, makes you repeat her discourse, and while you believe you are visiting Tamara you are only recording the names with which she defines herself and all her parts.

However the city may really be, beneath this thick coating of signs, whatever it may contain or conceal, you leave Tamara without having discovered it. Outside, the land stretches, empty, to the horizon; the sky opens, with speeding clouds. In the shape that chance and wind give the clouds, you are already intent on recognizing figures: a sailing ship, a hand, an elephant.[23]

— —

In the end one loves one's desire and not what is desired.

—Friedrich Nietzsche

Invisible Cities foreshadows Calvino's misgivings regarding cognitive abstraction. The collection of stories depicts a fictional encounter between Marco Polo, the Italian traveler, and Kublai Khan, the mighty emperor, and can be viewed as a meditation on the possibility for humans to construct abstract models.

In an attempt to organize his vast chaotic empire, the Khan proceeds to construct a fantastic generative model from which all the empire's cities may be deduced. Calvino fabulates about the great emperor Kublai Khan's desire to create perfect order in his vast empire by engaging in fantastic chess games with Marco Polo. The Khan immerses himself in a fastidious work of measuring and calculating. In the end, however, his efforts prove to be reductive, and his extravagant models, of no real use. The Khan fails, because his empire is not controllable.

After failing in the endeavor to offer a picture of the imperial cities, namely, of the real world, Calvino's protagonists, unable to stifle their need to uncover the order of the universe, resort to cataloging "le forme visibili," namely, they resort to making lists of "the visible forms," a much more modest, yet more realistic and definitely more practical undertaking. Jo Ann Canon claims that Calvino, much like the French philosopher Merleau-Ponti, who favored the notion that the world is that which we perceive, argued in favor of cataloging. The modest merit of cataloging, according to Calvino, resides in the fact that it makes the perceived world intelligible.[24]

Classifying and making maps of places are favored in Calvino's fiction, because these activities make the universe more "padroneggiabili," or "governable." One notices that Calvino's parabolic cities are governed by an extraordinary logic, a humble way to protect man from the chaos governing the unmanageable, not masterable, and ultimately, unknowable universe. We suggest that in these tales, Calvino comes very close to Borges, the architect of the imaginary universe that man has no difficulty deciphering.

Even a cursory scrutiny of Calvino's parable "Cities and Signs" reveals its remarkable stylistic features. The depiction of Tamara, forever inviting yet destined to remain eternally unknown to its visitor because it lies beneath an impenetrable, thick coating of signs, exhibits a distinct likeness to Kafka's parable, "An Imperial Message," and to Borges's, "Cervantes and *The Quixote*." Like these other authors' parables, Calvino's tale narrativizes a return to a beginning and to some primeval origins, not as an actual return, rather as a detour, a deviation, or an *écart*. At the same time, it postpones perpetually the enlightenment of the would be visitor, and denies him the competence to decode its signs, by means of a complex rhetorico-poetic mechanism.

With a movement typical in modern parables, Calvino's tale engulfs the reader into its abysmal topos and alludes persistently that it is itself only a system of signs and a continual deferral, namely, it shows an explicit awareness of its own parabolicity.

The tale of the man who wishes to "visit" the "city of Tamara" is a parable about modern man who, in order to acquire knowledge, enters a web of signs and signification with no possibility of exiting it. In offering this parable, Calvino hopes to teaches his addressee that whenever man aspires to gain a more intimate understanding about things as they are, he inevitably finds himself incapable to know the laws governing the signs that replace the things and the laws codification.

Posited as an infinite semiotic net, the city of Tamara will thus elude continually a real visit, or desire to know. The visitor, as Calvino's reader, is destined to see/read forever mere formulas of "things" and not things:

Nous ne voyons les choses mêmes, le monde est cela que nous voyons: des formules de ce genre expriment une fois qui est commune à l'homme naturel et au philosophe dès qu'il ouvre les yeux, elles renvoient à une assise profonde 'd'opinions' muettes impliquées dans notre vie. Mais cette foi a ceci d'étrange que, si l'on cherche à l'articuler en thèse ou énoncé, si l'on se demande ce que c'est que *nous*, ce que c'est que *voir* et ce que c'est que *chose* ou *monde*, on entre dans un labyrinth de difficultés et de contradictions.[25]

The real "things" in the city of Tamara and the "signs of these things" are in discord as elements of discourse. In representing the city of Tamara *as* discourse, Calvino was able to comment about discourse as a world of dualities which cannot resolve themselves in an original, forever lost unity, as a world "without a *telos* or an *arché*," in Derrida's view. And, if we are to take seriously the metaphor of the labyrinth language in Calvino's portrayal, his parable tells about language and textuality, which provide a space whose beginning and end are lost, whose rationality escapes him who has the misfortune of being in it and who must submit to its meandering without the hope of ever unravelling it.

Calvino presents a subject, or *sujet opérateur*, who lacks the necessary competence to "visit" and "know" the city of Tamara. The discursive subject "you"/"man" needs therefore to enact a reflexive transformation and acquire the expertise needed to "really" discover it.

However, Calvino's parable points discursively to the impossibility for the man to acquire such competence. A visit of the city never quite takes place, despite the fact that "the man" finds himself at a certain point in time inside the place designated as "the city of Tamara." Calvino explicitly states that: "However the city may really be, beneath this thick coating of signs, whatever it may contain, or conceal, you leave Tamara without having discovered it."

The account begins with a subject designated "*uomo*" (man) who journeys through a desertlike space. His action is temporalized by the adverbial marker "for days," and amplified by a punctual temporal marker "only rarely." The itinerary of the "man," a well-ordered sequence of states and of transformations, begins with a shift in gears, or a *débrayage*, of the narrative.[26]

The bareness of the place visited by the protagonist is punctured by the inscription of objects "trees and stones," the components in the parabolic tale that are "the things which are only what they are." The verbal "walks" brings into focus a transformation of states, temporalized by another modal and adverbial marker "for days," "among trees and stones." The adverbial "for days" belongs to the durative, the cumulative, and the habitual. This marker is integrated further with a second temporal element, "only rarely," which is of the order of punctuality and discreteness. The image created by the modern parabolizer is of man wandering in a desolate place, a place with no deeper meaning: "stones and trees" are "only what they are." The gaze fixed on the ground obviously produces no illumination in the man. At this point, the invitation/injunction in Calvino's text is to enter the city and begin deciphering to find a deeper meaning to what is being seen.

To advance the plot, the next sequence produces a synecdochical switch in subjects. To the agent/subject "you," who "walks," "for days," the narrative adds the agent/subject "eye," which "lights on," "only rarely," only when it "recognizes a thing," *as* "the sign of another thing." The initial action of the subject "eye" takes place in the deserted place outside the city, among "tree and stones," those things designated as being "only what they are."

The middle section of the narrative takes place inside the city. There, the man/visitor moves among things that are individually "the sign of another thing," and "all the rest is silent and interchangeable." The eye lights on objects/things, but this event is contingent upon certain laws for recognition. Indeed, the condition of possibility for the "eye" to "light on" a particular thing is to know the codification, namely, to understand *a priori* the substitution laws according to which that object/thing is placed in a particular spot in the city. However, we were informed at the beginning that here everything is a sign of something else.

But as we recall, a sign according to Peirce, is something that stands for something else, rather than a thing itself.[27] Calvino offers here a practical application of semiotics. The man in his parable has to deal only with signs of things and not the things themselves. This is to say that in entering Calvino's parabolic city, man enters the universe of interpretation, which is potentially infinite. The enlightenment of the subject "eye" in the narrative is co-referential with the subject "man," and contingent upon the recognition of unique laws of substitution, in this city/web of signs/language. These laws are imposed *as* the only criterion for categorization of a thing/object, as a sign of another thing.

The following narrative sequence begins with scant moments of recognition, the acquisition of "a knowledge," by the visitor, an insight about some vague existing law of exchange of one concept for another. The text reads: "Rarely does the eye light on a thing, and then, only when it [the eye] recognizes that thing as the sign of another thing." Knowledge is being equated with deciphering a certain codic exchange in signification and it is narrationally restricted by the use of the adverb "only rarely."

Calvino restates, this time at the level of syntax, that the competence is obtained by a subject other than the initial subject, which was marked "you," even though "the eye" is co-referential with the subject "you" and the subject marked "eye."[28]

A new narrative segment begins with a shift to the temporal with the adverbial "finally" and the toponymic element "the city of Tamara." The moment in which the subject penetrates the city is made to coincide, not with the eye "seeing things," but with the eye who "does not see things," only "images of things." This apparent paradox is pointing to the discovery of the "eye" in the preceding sequence, namely, that the "eye" is presupposed not to see things as things, but as mimetic images of other things.

The basic relation between the eye, or I, and the cosmic flux is being explored here.[29] Until Louis Marin, one considered the image as a "lesser being," that is, a being without power, or a weaker and inferior being.[30] Calvino, the semiotician attuned to reinterpretations of the image as the powerful holder of the essence of the thing it represents, parabolized about the informed "eye" that does not spend time seeing things, but "recognizing" laws of representation, namely, viewing "things as images of other things." By portraying a visit of the city as a process of indexing symbolic representations, Calvino too reinstates the powers of the image. He shows in his parable that the recognition of the existence of such laws may facilitate only a limited familiarity with a restricted number of things, "as the signs of another thing": a print indicating the tiger's passage, a marsh announcing a vein of water, the hibiscus flower heralding the end of winter. But "the print," "the marsh," "the hibiscus flower," and so on, are all emptied of their original signification and invested with new meaning, a meaning semantically and pragmatically removed from the original one.

Beyond their new meaning, "the print," "the marsh," "the hibiscus flower," and so forth perform speech acts; they "announce," "indicate," "warn." Other things are precluded from performing such speech acts, by being defined as "silent," and "interchangeable." Finally, objects cannot become interchangeable; the laws governing the place preclude a reversal of signification.

The reader is led to think that the proliferation of data could serve as an instructional device to the visitor. However, this is not the case. Calvino comes back to show that the information offered is deceptive. An array of minimal units that might be used to make sense of flux become involved in this deception. And, while Calvino offers the reader an exceptionally ordered world, the abundance of elements embodies no values of beauty or taste. The city is fragmented and categorized in ways that elude our normal sense of order. The movement through space does not produce an advancement in the visitor's understanding of the place; it represents only a displacement away from the city's real objects and from the things contained in it, a displacement occasioned by the complex semiotic web of representations governing the parabolic city.

Just as in Borges's "Cervantes and *The Quixote*," where the old soldier encounters his mimetic image, Don Quixote, falling into prosaic lands, the visitor and the city are made to follow opposite narrative trajectories, according to opposite action plans. More precisely, as the visitor advances toward the city, the city withdraws by veiling itself with an encrypted texture, perpetually alluding to a text other than itself, in a continual process of deferral. By definition, all its "things" are "images" representing "things," representing, in turn, "other things."

Calvino offers no longer "imperial messages" to be decoded. The city he envisions demands to be read as a page of text, an unknown and unknowable text, absconding the laws of its legibility to the "eye"/"I" that reads it. In this parable, the subject, invisible and unattainable, imposes its will and its power on the visitor, by telling him how "it" must be read/cognized. In essence, for the subject to "visit" the city is to understand "visiting" *as* other actions: reading and interpreting.

With this adroit rhetorical transformation, Calvino thematizes man's encounter with the world of things, as a perplexing encounter with language and its laws of symbolization. His parable speaks of man's loss of power to "name," and stages the drama of his incapability to understand the being of things communicated through language. While Walter Benjamin could still claim that "man is the name giver, and all nature, insofar as it communicates itself, communicates itself in language, and so finally in man, hence, he is bound to the language of things,"[31] Calvino can tell parabolically only about a radical loss of man's ability to comprehend the being of things.

To interpret properly the text/texture of things in the parabolic city, "the visitor" of Tamara must know *a priori* what are the things whose "images" and "signs" are the things his "eye" lights on. He thus becomes a reader and a decoder of the riddles of language sprawled before him. He is continually kept thinking, interpreting, and repeating an imposed discourse, with an enigmatic order.

The translation of the nameless into the named is no longer at man's disposal; through his gaze things do not grow more perfect, as was the case in the Scriptures. In Calvino's tale, the city/text, with its thick encodings, becomes the acting subject, as soon as the visit begins. The city keeps the visitor in its mesmerizing grip, by prescribing its rules and by imposing them *as* the only possible actualization of a visit. In Calvino's modern parable, the city/text has the power to act autonomously, a power of which the visitor was stripped and which, we are told, he will never regain.

By becoming a visitor of the city/text, the "man" ceases to be an agent of change; he is turned into a "subject in a state of," a *sujet d'état,* impotence, subjected to the power of the city/text. The man in this modern parable cannot become a *connoisseur* of the text that is the city; he remains subjected to unknown laws and transformations imposed on him. In a sense, he is like K, the man of Kafka's *Trial.* The visitor must "read" an ankle bracelet as voluptuousness, a gilded palanquin as power, an embroidered headband as elegance, the volumes of Averroes as learning, and so on. Therefore, while he believes that he visits the city, he only records the names by "which the city defines itself and its parts," that is to say, he only reiterates the laws of the city, which are also the laws of discourse.

Subjected to a "heavy coating of signs," the man remains trapped in language, in the interplay of signs, between hyperinterpretation and the impossibility of interpreting them. This relation to signs has been discussed at length by Derrida. Signs are generated as a passage between two moments, explains Derrida, only a notion of presence, a presence always already lost (*toujours-déjà perdue*). The sign operates a motion of interiorization without attempting to retrieve the thing itself. Yet, "by the mere fact that the sign is subjected to the work of negativity within the dialectics of interiorization and exteriorization, it will reappropriate, not the thing, not the signifier, but the signified." In reading signs, we lose the thing, but we gain meaning. This supplement of signification generates in turn a "thickening" of the literary sign, and a reduplication of the "auto-referential" in literature.[32] Similarly, Louis Marin suggested that a sign does not fulfill its signification except through a process of substitution and representation. For a sign to act as a sign, there needs to be a complete substitution of the represented by that which represents "C'est une substitution totale et complète du représenté au représentant qui définit la propriété du mot, par une sorte de catachrèse originaire qui serait la version rhétorique du contrat logothétique."[33]

Accordingly, the visitor of Tamara, trapped in the interplay of signs and signification, does not, cannot discover/uncover the city, and, as a consequence, has to leave "without having discovered it." He comes away instead with a different system of valorization, and will attempt to enact it outside the boundaries of the city.

What, then, constitutes a visit of the city of Tamara? Perhaps the recognition of the existence of laws of exchange among signs and perfect obedience to them. But this is also to say that visiting the city means, in Calvino's worldview, entering a labyrinthal world, fashioned upon the laws of discourse. A visit is then a decoding of the laws of discourse and, therefore, the "actual" visit is perpetually deferred and, in actuality, never takes place. In short, a visit to Calvino's city, which is itself a text, can take place only mimetically.[34]

But a "literary," rather than a literal, visit means also that the subject "man" is seduced and moved to an impassioned state, despite (or because of) the ruse. The parabolic city tempts its visitor to go on repeating its discourse, and to acknowledge his defeat, namely to recognize that he is fundamentally incapable to construe a personal narrative about it.

Contrary to the expectations evoked by the idea of "visiting," namely, a sequence of actions with multiple discoveries, the sojourn through Tamara is construed upon an impossibility of initiative and produces no real discovery of the place. Just as Borges created *"The Quixote"* to repeat the failure of the old soldier Cervantes and, therefore, destined him to failure, the visitor is made to reproduce the city's discourse, and, therefore, Calvino fated him to disillusionment.

Astonishingly, when the visit comes to an end, "the visitor," expelled from the city without a clue, continues to reiterate its discourse outside its boundaries. In the last narrative sequence, introduced by the temporal adverb "outside," the subject "man"/"you" has his eyes uplifted and observes "the sky," which "opens, with speeding clouds." The banished visitor, now an "outsider" of the city, is conditioned by the parable to "see" in the motion of clouds "shapes," even though these shapes are given by "chance" and the "wind." He goes on interpreting long after his failed visit. He who was incapable of visiting the city because he did not know how to decode its symbolism, continues compulsively to practice the rules of Tamara and attempts to decipher the shapes given this time by chance. Amazingly, like Freud's neurotic, he remains a reader/visitor and obsessively reproduces incomprehensible laws.[35]

"Outside," the neurotic visitor gazes upon the sky. His "eye" moves away from the "land," "which stretches, empty, to the horizon" and looks up toward the heavens, to read and decode their signs. And even though the rules of Tamara remain unknown to him, he continues to read things as signs of other things. He has acquired a certain competence, but more amazingly, an ambitious aspiration: to decipher the heavenly images/text.

An interesting message begins to take shape. The symbolization of the heavenly topos, compulsively explored by the neurotic, is governed, ironically, by "chance" and the "wind." The man who could not "really" visit the city of Tamara, a human creation, thus easier to interpret, attempts foolishly now to "visit"/"read" the sky and the domain of the divine, impenetrable and above human understanding.

To underscore the senselessness of the visitor's behavior, Calvino submits him to further ridicule and failure. Whereas in the early narrative sequences, the city of Tamara, covered "with a thick coating of signs," offered the man at least the illusion of possibility to discover, or uncover it, the sky, despite being "open," remains radically forbidden to this faltering man. The "speeding clouds" and their shapes are being continually reshaped and changed by accident. This aleatory motion, contingent upon luck, is unpredictable, thus the prospect that this man gains any knowledge about the sky vanishes as the speeding clouds.[36]

At the discursive level, Calvino stages an ordered passage from an initial state to a final one, through a succession of actions containing verbs of the type "do." These actions induce shifts from states of conjunction with the valorized object (the visit of the city) to states of disjunction from it (impossibility to visit the city). Yet the parable decontextualizes its primary narrative, and displaces itself away from an actual "visit."

Like ancient parables, "Cities and Signs" has a well-defined beginning, a series of transformations, and an ending. But, in the end, Calvino does not interpret his parable; in fact, we suggest that the labyrinth he has created cannot be decoded/"uncovered." A continual displacement occurs in the narrative, which revolves around a lack, an impossibility. The man looking for enlightenment is trapped in this modern parable as in a black hole, and revolves like a dervish between hypersignification and meaninglessness. On the one hand, a proliferation of signs and a "coating with signs," with no "openness" to knowledge, becomes man's lot. On the other, the paranoid fear of emptiness compels the "visitor," turned compulsive reader, to inscribe perpetually the non-inscribed and the non-systematized space.

The linguistic deep structure of Calvino's parable evidences kinships and dissimilitude not expressed openly in the text.

The actor "city of Tamara" has an actual role: preventing the subject from uncovering it.[37]

if A is acteur

A_1 = The visitor, is conjoined with V_{f_1} (will to do/*vouloir faire*) a visit and discovery of A_2.
A_2 = The city of Tamara
A_2 is conjoined with V_{f_2} (will to prevent the visitor from discovering it).
A_2 causes A_1 to reiterate its discourse
$\Rightarrow$ transformational action by A_2
$\rightarrow$ passage from one state to another state = faire transformateur/transformational doing
$\cup$ conjunction with the valorized object (A_2 makes A_1 do what it dictates/A learns the laws of exchange of signs)
$\cap$ disjunction from the valorized object = leaves the city without discovering it.

$$A_1 \cap V_{F_1}$$
$$A_2 \cap V_{F_2}$$

EQUATION 9.1

$$A_2 \Rightarrow [A_1 \cdot \cap V_{F_1} \rightarrow \cap V_{F_2}]$$

EQUATION 9.2

In deep syntactic structure we distinguish a fragmentation in the organization of the spatial domain relative to a place/topos designated "the city of Tamara." The space is organized as follows:

BEGINNING	*TAKES PLACE*	*ENDS*
Outside——————>	inside——————>	outside

The actions are organized as follows:

OUTSIDE	You	walk	for days
	the eye	lights	only rarely
	the eye	recognizes	Law X* of symbolization

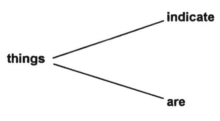

FIGURE 9.1
Things Becoming Signs

Things		
a print	——————>	tiger's passage
a marsh	——————>	a vein of water
the hibiscus flower	——————>	the end of winter
all the rest	——————>	"silent"
all the rest	——————>	"interchangeable"
trees and stones	——————>	are only what they are

A new sequence begins with a shift in temporality: "Finally the journey leads to the city of Tamara."

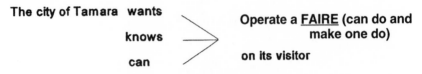

The city of Tamara   wants

knows

can

Operate a **FAIRE** (can do and make one do)

on its visitor

FIGURE 9.2
The City of Tamara as Agent of Action

The city defines "herself"; the visitor does not. This is visible at the level of "being" (*être*) and "doing" (*faire*) modality structure. While the visitor thinks he acts, he is actually made to re-act, "made to do" (*on lui fait faire*); he is made to record the names with which "she defines herself and her parts."

statues . . . . are seen
statues . . . . are portrayed
worshipers . . . . can recognize
worshipers . . . . can address their prayers
buildings . . . . occupy positions

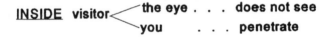

INSIDE visitor   the eye . . . **does not see**

you   . . . **penetrate**

FIGURE 9.3
The Position of the Visitor

all other . . . are pointing, depicting, warning

of what is forbidden

of what is allowed

FIGURE 9.4
Signs in the City of Tamara

A new shift returns us to the initial definition of "things," which are not valuable in themselves, but as "signs of other things."

Headbands . . . . stand for . . . . elegance
gilded palanquin . . . . stands for . . . . power

Averroès . . . . stands for . . . . learning
ankle bracelet . . . . . . stands for . . . . voluptuousness

For the "inside" of the city there are two deep structural trajectories: that of the "man," and that of the "eye." This is reinforced linguistically though a shift in narrational gears. With this shift the city becomes operating subject/agent, while the visitor is reduced to passivity and to reacting.

*INSIDE*₁

your	*gaze*	scans
you	*believe*	you visit
you	*are recording*	the names (by which she)

*INSIDE*₂

The city of Tamara	*says*	what you must think
The city of Tamara	*makes*	you repeat her discourse
The city of Tamara	*defines*	herself and her parts

*INSIDE'*₁

You leave the city of Tamara
You have not discovered the city of Tamara

*INSIDE'*₂

The city of Tamara may really be
The city of Tamara may really contain
The city of Tamara may conceal

*OUTSIDE*₂

the land stretches empty to
the horizon
the sky opens
the clouds are speeding

$$\frac{\text{INSIDE}}{\text{OUTSIDE}} : \frac{\text{CITY COVERED}}{\text{LAND STRETCHES}}$$

There is also a structural opposition between the "city covered with codes" and the "empty stretched-out land." Likewise, a syntactic parallel between "law" and "lawlessness," or chance.

INSIDE = a perfectly functioning law established and reinforced by the city of Tamara

OUTSIDE = lawlessness, of clouds shaped by "chance" and the "wind."

We note different treatments of the subject "you":

You / outside₁ . . . dim understanding of a law of symbolization
you / inside . . . . . reduced to a recognition of the law of the city
you / outside₂ . . . "intent on recognizing" the law of the city

The seduction of the visitor/reader is expressed as follows:

If A_1 = actor₁ → you/the eye/the visitor
and A_2 = actor₂ → the city of Tamara
V = Vouloir = Wanting to Do
F = Faire = Do = Operate a transformation/a state of being, an *état*
O = valorized object/*object of desire*, then we have an equation of the type:

$$A_1 \rightarrow [V_{F_1} \rightarrow (A_1 \cap O_1) \cdot V_{F_2}(A_1 \cap O_2)]$$
$$A_2 \rightarrow [V_{F_3} \rightarrow (A_1 \cap O_3) \cdot (A_1 \cap O_4) \ldots (A_1 \cap O_n)]$$

EQUATION 9.3

O_1 = visit the city of Tamara
O_2 = discover the city of Tamara
V_{F1} = Want to visit/performative
V_{F2} = Want to discover the city of Tamara

The "want to do" of actor number one is the linguistic negative of the "want to do" of the second actor.

$$A_2 \cdot V_{F_3} = \sim A_1 \cdot V_{F_1}$$
$$A_2 \cdot V_{F_4} = \sim A_1 \cdot V_{F_2}$$

EQUATION 9.4

O_3 = See things as images of other things
O_4 = Repeat the discourse dictated by the city
O_5 = Read the city as a written page
O_6 = Think what the city wants him to think
O_n = Obey all the city's injunctions

The "dysphoric" and the "euphoric" components of the narrative are presented as alternate moments. The parable's *phoric*, or emotional program, is unknowable to the reader, because the city's narrative program is an antiprogram to that of the visitor.

$$A_2 \Rightarrow F_{(F)_{A_1}} \cdot \zeta \ F \ (C_r) \ A_1$$

EQUATION 9.5

The subversive aspect of the visit is ascribed in deep linguistic structure to the city. The city "textualizes" the visitor as well; he becomes a part of "her written text." The movement of the marker "you" is unidirectional:

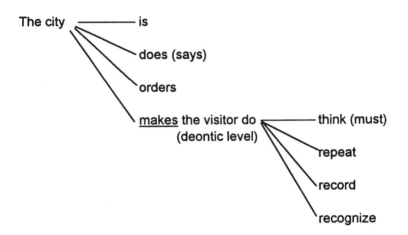

FIGURE 9.5
Textualization of the Visitor

OUTSIDE of the city of Tamara —-> *INSIDE* the city of Tamara —->
OUTSIDE of the city of Tamara.

We can observe yet another discursive movement:

OUTSIDE the city of Tamara
OUTSIDE the city of Tamara
INSIDE the city of Tamara

FIGURE 9.6
Discursive Movement Inside-Outside

A_1 outside of T (city of Tamara)
A_1 inside of T
The OUTSIDE inside of T (mediated by A_1 instructed by Tamara)

Syntactic parallelism in this sequence insures that A_1, the subject man, transforms the outside A_2 into another inside, namely, he converts the "empty," "stretched-out land" and the "open sky," into a topos covered by "a thick coating of signs." Calvino shows parabolically that after his encounter with the "city"/"language"/"textuality" man is fated to reproduce it as a human habit—the habit of textualizing. If, as Peirce claims, the belief in a rule is a habit, promoting the habit formed in the city of Tamara can be equated with promoting textuality and language.[38]

INSIDE A_2 acts A_1 reacts
OUTSIDE A_1 incorporates, ingests, assimilates the empty OUTSIDE into the city A2

The laws of the city, and the corresponding occurrences of indexed things:

1. "that thing as the sign of another thing"
   print . . . . the tiger's passage
   marsh . . . . the vein of water
   hibiscus flower . . . . end of winter

2. "the eye does not see things but images of things that mean other things"
   (the eye needs to de-code according to a prescribed law of decoding)
   Pincers. . . . . pointing out . . . tooth drawer's house
   Tankards . . . pointing out . . . tavern
   Halberds . . . pointing out . . . barracks
   Scales. . . . . . pointing out . . . grocer's
   Statues. . . . . depicting . . . . . lions
   Shield . . . . . .depicting . . . . . dolphins towers stars

3. A sign that something—who knows what?—has as its sign X
   (sign T_{h_a})   is   Image (T_{h_b})
   the palace . . . . . is positioned . . . to be understood as P
   the prison . . . . . is positioned . . . to be understood as P
   the mint . . . . . . is positioned . . . to be understood as P
   Pythagorean . . . is positioned . . . to be understood as P school

4. Wares that the vendors display in their windows are valuable not in themselves but as signs of other things:

Embroidered headband. . . . stands for . . . elegance
Gilded palanquin . . . . stands for . . . power
the volumes of Averroès . . . stand for. . . . learning
the ankle bracelet . . . . stands for . . . voluptuousness

INSIDE the things are petrified, impregnated, and immobilized in signification.
OUTSIDE the land opens, the land stretches out, the land is empty to
the horizon, the sky opens, the clouds are speeding.

The juxtaposition of "outside" and "inside" acquires yet another
linguistic expression. Outside the city, there is a mobility and a flexibility characteristic of the things "shaped by chance and by [the] wind," a
lightness due to the void, and to the lack of signification. To the bur-
dened multitude of precisely shaped representations of things, shapeless
speeding clouds are the reply of emptiness. The choice of clouds seems
poignant. The visitor, lacking all competence, is free in a way like the
clouds. He ends up losing his autonomy to the city/language/text by
assigning "figures" to the clouds, to be understood both as shapes of
things and as images, as figurative speech and as symbolization: a "sailing ship, a hand, figures an elephant."

In assigning meaning to shapeless and meaningless clouds, man
enlarges the boundaries of the city/language/text. In the end, his
acquired desire to obey the order of the city/text allows him to remain
in the space and time of the parable, absorbed in the fictional space generated by the narrative. In other words, the visitor/reader who could not
get back to the things themselves, becomes himself a law of the city,
namely, of textuality (figures 9.7 and 9.8).

The parabolic city has incorporated the non-city, and covered up
this movement with new signs. Calvino's own "circular ruin" does not
allow exiting either. "Leaving" the city is only a simulation and a further drawing in of the outside.

As the city of Tamara, Calvino's parable retreats into auto-referentiality, underneath a "thick coating of signs," leaving us outside, with
the calm platitude of speeding clouds and land stretching out, empty.
Calvino has taken us for a circular ride and expelled us, desirous to "recognize, to see ships, and hands, and elephants in the speeding clouds."

In reiterating the impossibility of escaping the moment of representation and of capturing the "thing itself," Calvino captures in parable
our absolute lack of power to uncover/discover things for what they
really are, because we are in the grip of language and its processes of
symbolization. In doing so, Calvino also theorizes about the act of
parabolizing. His parable becomes an isotopic world with illusory referentiality. It is a device capable of moving us through a series of trans-

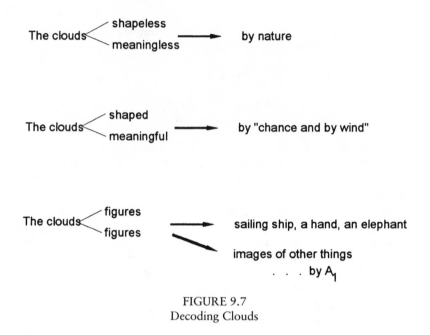

FIGURE 9.7
Decoding Clouds

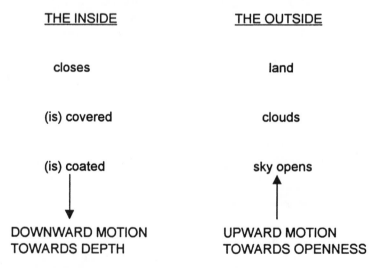

FIGURE 9.8
Discursive Movement Outside-Inside

formations, simulations, and displacements, and causing us to have "an intention to recognize . . . ," and "a volition to perform," namely, to remain in the quest for what it (the parable) might be underneath *its* "thick coating of signs." Rather than resolving the original tension, the parable passes before our own "gaze" as "a speeding cloud" and leaves us too "intent to recognize. . . ." In the purest sense the work of discourse, Calvino's parable "stretches over the empty land."

Calvino's "inventive fancifulness" is an effective means of drawing the reader toward moral and social concerns: "Beneath Calvino's tireless shimmer of fancy, his concern over how men live together has carried into our minds. . . . Led to read on . . . we find the civic ideal unfolding within us."[39] John Updike sums it up well when he claims about *Le città invisibili* that:

> the gift of space that this book ends by calling for, then, is just what the book itself bestows; amid the crowded, confused, consuming "infernal city" that is "already here, the inferno where we live every day," art and imagination, creating inner space, are offered as amelioration.[40]

CHAPTER 10

S. Y. Agnon:
An Opening to Kaddish

When considering modern parables, one cannot fail to pay tribute to S. Y. Agnon, the Israeli Nobel Prize laureate of 1966, whose great achievements in the field of fiction and language have been the subject of numerous studies.

Since the publication in 1968 of *Nostalgia and Nightmare: A Study of the Fiction of S. Y. Agnon*, Arnold Band's comprehensive study of Agnon's work, many scholars have recognized that Agnon's contribution to fiction is compelling.[1]

Most scholars seem to agree that to adequately understand S. Y. Agnon's monumental work, the reader must engage in decoding its manifold encrypted messages and immerse himself/herself in over three thousand years of literary activity. He/she must trace Agnon's multifaceted dialogue with a massive network of intertextual commentaries and references.

Agnon's interest in parabolizing is the feature relevant to our present study. While Agnon wrote few parables per se, and the parables he wrote do not fall under the category of "modern imperial messages" (by Kafka, Borges, and Calvino), there is an interesting way in which, when read parabolically, many of his short narratives harken back to the verses of the Bible and evoke with great vigor the parables by early parabolizers.

In a unique way, with S. Y. Agnon, parables come full circle. By that, I mean not only a return to the cradle of their beginnings, the land of the old sages, but also a revival of their function. Agnon uses parables as a means to explicate the sacred Scriptures and to teach them to the masses. In fact, he was called a "ventriloquist of the past," because he uses the sacred texts to point to a lack of belief in present times.[2]

Agnon's parables differ from those of other modern parabolizers because of their hybrid status. In Agnonian universe, parabolic tales are "quotations of the past"[3] that serve to echo it and to bring the ancient Scriptures to life in the present for his modern readers who have lost their faith. As in early parables, in Agnon's tales, the *midrash*, or the interpretation, contains authentic Scriptural material that provides a solid religious context. In contrast, his own interpretations are pulsating with life and with modern impetus. Agnon's lacework becomes a perplexing embroidery of real sacred phrases with imagined ones.[4] The motive for which Agnon wrote parables is also vastly different from that of his contemporaries. The interweaving of secular and sacred in Agnon's fiction blurs the boundaries between them and, therefore, claims Stern, "one never knows if the sacred sanctifies the secular, or the secular sanctifies the sacred in his work."[5] In a similar vein, Anne Golomb Hoffman convincingly argues that

> to enter Agnon's fictive universe, one must acknowledge the very central place occupied by the Torah as the fabric of the word that both contains Creation and binds God to Israel. As the mythic center of Agnon's fictive universe, Torah constitutes a text of presence where word and thing join. . . . Mystical and rabbinic approaches to language and writing constitute an attractive source for Agnon, insofar as they retrieve a relationship to the letter of a holy alphabet out of which the world was formed.[6]

Hoffman further suggests that in commenting on its own textuality, "Agnon's writing may activate in the reader a nostalgia for the imaginary coalescence of signifier with signified, as well as a sense of their inevitable separation and dislocation in discourse." To her mind, Agnon's fiction may also provide a unique access to processes of subjectivity, in other words, the reader's engagement with the texts in the illusory safety of the act of reading it.[7]

This modern intellectual of Eastern European origin creates a majestic intertextual web of connected and contradictory layers of language, and, ultimately, demands to be inscribed as the heir of "the poets of the Temple." At the same time, his thematic imbrications become the backdrop for voicing modern concerns. Appropriately, David Stern claims that traditional Jewish language and themes appear in Agnon's fiction almost as purely formal channels or media for expressing "messages concerned with the doubtful presence of faith, if not its actual absence. In Agnon, the parabolic tale becomes its message, which is a lesson of emptiness."[8]

We suggest that this particular feature of Agnon's parabolic tales places him close to Kafka, Borges, and Calvino, the modern parabolizers discussed in this study. Fabulating to express the void is a modern and postmodern predilection, and Agnon shares it with his contemporaries. However, Agnon's parabolic tales encourage us in a unique way to go back to the old, "to save" the present. As Hoffman and Alan Mintz state in their introduction to the volume commemorating Agnon's fifty years of publishing, Agnon has taken his readers on a monumental journey back to the "baffling ritual practices of the ancient Hebrews," while continually fashioning and refashioning the myth of himself as a writer.[9]

While intelligently self-conscious, Agnon's work strives to overcome the temporal gap to a yearned for past when the world was deemed knowable, rather than to restate dispassionately the unknowability of the universe. Indeed, while many critics tended to attribute Faulknerian or Joycean qualities to his writing, Agnon downplayed the similarities. In his famous acceptance speech for the Nobel Prize for literature, Agnon stated that the true sources of his inspiration "were first and foremost, the sacred Scriptures and, after that, the teachings of the medieval Jewish sages, the spectacle of nature, and the animals of the earth."[10]

Agnon loved to reminisce about his own life as much as he loved to recount the tales of the old Jewish sages. Some say even more. Concerned with the accuracy of Agnon's recollections and with the practical obstacles encountered in the writing of biographies, Arnold Band encourages investigators of Agnon to "sift carefully his personal testimony" (and that of the others) when attempting to reconstitute Agnon's biographical facts. He insists that Agnon's imagination is extraordinarily fecund and at his advanced age he should not be expected to recall facts with accuracy.[11]

While we understand Band's concern, we suggest that one should perhaps go directly to Agnon's fiction to get the most satisfying answers. In our opinion, his fiction provides us with a most powerful statement both about his life and the lost world of the Jews he so painstakingly brought to life.

Born in the Eastern European city of Buczacz in Galicia, in 1888, Shmuel Yosef Agnon became the chronicler of a people threatened with total annihilation and, later, reborn with the creation of the State of Israel. After claiming that his birthday coincided with the date of the destruction of the first and second Temples, and after inventing a new name for himself, Agnon proceeded to entwine deliberately and systematically his own life story with some of the dates considered since antiquity pivotal in Jewish life. In so doing, suggest Hoffman and Mintz, Agnon sought to fit his public image to a simpler notion of membership in a community unified by its history.[12]

The son of a pious rabbi, and a passionate student of the Jewish Scriptures in his own right, Agnon wrote from the point of view of belatedness and exile.[13] After the destruction of the Second Temple, when all the priests have perished, the Jewish writer, claimed Agnon, is reduced "to starving himself over the words of the (our) sages" and to lament this irremediable loss. He stated his position as a modern Jewish writer thus:

> When I [Agnon] look at their [the old sages'] words and see that of all
> the delights we possessed in ancient times there remains only this mem-
> ory, my heart fills with grief. That grief makes my heart tremble, and
> it is out of that trembling that I write stories, like one exiled from his
> father's palace who makes himself a little hut and sits there telling of
> the glory of his father's house.[14]

In the Agnonian worldview, the modern Jewish writer is, alas, a
latecomer compelled to erect literary shrines to the precious world that
animated his youth, and that has been ruthlessly destroyed. As part of
this self-imposed mission to preserve in imagination the treasures of
ancient Jewish life and the centuries old accumulated wisdom by Eastern European Jewry, Agnon has recreated artistically the Jewish experience and the places Jews lived in Eastern Europe, and memorialized
them in many of his stories. A good example is *The Book of Buczacz*. In
it Agnon depicts his hometown, which was destroyed in the Holocaust.

Gershom Scholem, the luminary who brought Jewish mysticism to
modern man, recalls Agnon as a passionate reader of Hebrew texts, a
young man who spent endless hours in the library of the Community
Council looking for texts "he has not read yet" and who, according to
Scholem, inhabited the unique world that he tirelessly invented. In
Scholem's view, Agnon was a man with a visceral understanding of the
devastating consequences of the Holocaust, who appropriated in his
imaginative world traditional Jewish customs and storytelling techniques to mythologize his relationship to his people, to God, and to the
Holy Land.[15]

The dilemmas displayed in Agnon's luxuriant fiction transcend
parochial issues of an epic world. His work projects a vision of the
human condition that is universally valid for our times. In *Masot 'al
sipure Shai Agnon* (*Commentaries to S. Y. Agnon's Stories*), Baruch
Kurzweil, another passionate reader of Agnon, suggests that Agnon's
work was epic in conception and meant to encompass all aspects of traditional Jewish life. Arnold Band, who produced the most comprehensive study of Agnon to date, saw him as a neoromantic writer and intimates that his work, Kafkaesque in some of its subtle comic impulses,
revolves, nonetheless, around a lyric center. In arguing in favor of a
dialectic between two antithetical thrusts in Agnon's fiction, Band
claimed that:

> Common to Agnon and many neoromantic writers is the sensation
> often impressed upon the reader that much of what happened in the
> story actually takes place in the hero's psyche—and it makes little dif-
> ference whether the hero is described in the third or first-person nar-
> rator. If the empirical world seems to represent a realm of cosmic
> implications, this is because the writer has bridged the gap between

him and the empirical world by internalization that is otherwise rarely so successful or nearly complete. The failure to achieve complete internalization might result in nightmare, but more often it evokes from highly literate writers [and Agnon was highly literate] relentless irony and parody. Paradoxically, the most poignant expressions of the tragic absurdities of life in the past century and of the disinherited mind are often subtly comic, and Agnon, too is essentially a comic writer as is Kafka.[16]

Band has also noted that even though Agnon's tales have a Kafkan flavor, and even though he seems to have undergone a serious spiritual crisis during the early thirties, it is erroneous to attribute to Agnon's stories (in particular the early ones) a Kafkaesque provenance simply because some of these stories (the Yiddish story entitled "Toiten-Tans" is his specific example) were written before Kafka began to publish his stories.[17]

Yet, despite the awareness that some of Agnon's stories are antecedent to Kafka's, Agnon has been deemed "Kafkaesque." In particular, scholars who engage in comparative studies have gone to great lengths to show the similarities that exist between Agnon and Kafka, and for good reasons. Agnon moved away from the univocal fiction predominant in Hebrew literature and proceeded to build into his work multiple strategies of indeterminacy. He compelled his reader to act. In Agnon's fiction the reader needs to infer, evaluate, reevaluate and accept apparently contradictory information. This brings about new and surprising discoveries.

In reflecting on the "Drama of Signification" in her study of Agnon, Hoffman also places Kafka together with Agnon. When discussing the notion of "hunger," she claims that, in reading Kafka and Agnon, "the reader responds to resonances of language, the articulation of a vocabulary that is open-ended." She further observes that "in both Kafka and Agnon, 'hunger' is an overwrought or overdetermined verb that leads to the open-ended question of its subject: *hunger* for what? In both, 'hunger' defies the capacity of language to name the object of desire. The Hunger Artist cannot name the food he wants, while Agnon's narrator insists on having a 'whole loaf' that not only opens up a yearning for wholeness, but also opens up a universe of citations . . . a sampling of intertexts."[18]

Understanding how Agnon opens up "a universe of citations" is of special interest, because it uncovers affinities between Agnon and other modern parabolizers. We find that, beyond exploring the void in his parabolic tales, Agnon engages with a multitude of sacred texts and creates a polyphony of voices very much like Kafka or Borges. Beyond that, the lavish use of a plethora of old texts, side by side with linguistic innovations, lends a purely modernist vigor to Agnon, the iconoclast, who dares to suggest that traditional religious and moral values can no longer adequately sustain modern man.[19]

In comparing Agnon to other Eastern European authors, Baruch Hochman sees Agnon alone amidst writers "who were busy excoriating the lassitude and corruption they saw in East European Jewry."[20] To Hochman's mind, Agnon was the only one "busy evoking the felicities and bereavements of the 'community of the faithful,' wherever it might be."[21] We suggest that this claim can easily be substantiated by looking at Agnon's fiction. For instance, one could support this assertion by choosing Agnon's *Oreah nata lalun (A Guest for the Night)*.[22] In this story, Agnon bemoans the erosion of the culture of a village and the waning of its people. As their tradition is vanishing, the "The Song of the Alphabet" is no longer sung; the people can no longer speak their language. In fact, tellingly, the language and its alphabet have become inaccessible to the people of the village. All that is left of their tradition are the vision of it and the consciousness of people such as the hapless guest. In that same story, Samuel confesses that he would like to live by the Torah, "but the vessels of our souls are broken and cannot hold them. The Torah is whole but the ark in which it its kept is broken" (4:254). Agnon's allusion to the kabbalistic notion of "broken vessels" is most obvious.

As in many other of his stories, the images of fragmentation, division, or of being torn to shreds are quite frequent and explicit. These images in Agnon hint at emotional unwholeness. Numerous examples heighten our awareness that Agnon's longing for wholeness permeates his entire work. Objectionable in Aberbach's opinion is that "Agnon made the choice to attain wholeness ultimately through art, and this seems somewhat artificial and evanescent."[23]

Agnon's most successful attempt to transcend unwholeness, through art and a spiritual unification with Jewish tradition, is the story "At the Outset of the Day," published in 1951. The daughter's clothes are on fire, the father's home is destroyed. Both father and daughter escape to the courtyard of the House of Study. Standing outside, at the door of the House of Study, the old author of one of the scrolls has a transformation. According to Aberbach, Agnon's art is not to clothe the naked girl, the soul, but to show father and daughter transformed on the Day of Atonement by the vision of Jews praying passionately in the House of Study, with sweet melodies no ear has ever heard, from delicately ornate Torah scrolls, visible from the door of the open ark.[24] In this fashion, the masterful storyteller narrativized his own position in regard to tradition and to the artistic recreation of this tradition.

To express imaginatively his sadness and his profound sense of loss when realizing the utter misfortune of his people, Agnon favored the notion of *aginut*, or bereavement, as his central theme. In addition to writing a major story by the name of "Agunot," the man named Shmuel Yosef Czaczkes, adopted "Agnon" as his pseudonym.

This pseudonym became the only name by which the author is known. He called himself Agnon because he too felt bereft. Like the "Guest" of his story, who lived outside the pale of the old culture but craved the religious communion, Agnon saw his own people live in the present estranged from their cultural roots and the tradition that infused vitality into their lives. At the same time, he perceived them incapable of belonging to any other culture.

A solitary, sad man, Agnon expressed his personal feelings in his stories. "The scrolls of the Law stand silent in the Ark," Agnon says in *A Guest for the Night*. "All love and mercy and compassion are enclosed and enfolded in them."[25] Back in Israel, Agnon felt at home, yet he continued to yearn, like his protagonist in *A Guest for the Night*, for the lost tradition and the old pre-exilic golden age.

Agnon made retrieving this ancestral tradition a lifetime quest. Yet there is more to Agnon's genius than the lyrical remembrance of a bygone era. In addition to revitalizing the Jewish past, he relentlessly questioned about man's place in the world. The images of the ancestral world Agnon supplied to his readers are very rich and have a graspable, real-life quality, yet they represent an escape from a desolate present: a modern writer's retreat from the abyss.

Agnon carefully probed the limits of the alternative way of life that he offered to his readers. Quite bravely, he thematized a sense of futility that underlies all human endeavors.[26] While the protagonist, Reb Alter, mimics ancient spirituality to perfection, present circumstances render him no less than foolish. Perhaps, in this sad story, where going back to spirituality seems not a true option, Agnon attempts, in a gentle way, to give his bitter answer to his struggling "guest."

However, unlike Kafka or Borges, who had the boldness to confront the void and make peace with it, Agnon pointed to the abysmal quality of existence in ways that provoke us to say that he has refused to fathom its depths. Agnon told stories in which he glorified a marvelous past with eloquence and passion, in the false hope that, like Scheherazade, he could fend off the future.

His perpetual struggle to understand the meaning of life led him to obsess over death and dying. Many of his protagonists are facing the deaths of loved ones, or empty lives, lacking meaning, or wholeness. Though, unlike his precursor Kafka, who confronted the void, Agnon hopelessly tried to avert it. This is perhaps the point where Agnon, and his famous precursor stand farthest apart. Baruch Hochman says the following in *The Fiction of S. Y. Agnon*:

Much as [his protagonist] Yitzhak averts his eyes from the terror in himself, Agnon, struggles to fill the void of his terror and unbelief with lovely evocations. . . . While, in *Yesteryear,* Agnon confronts nullity and negation in their most extreme forms, one feels disappointed that Agnon failed to take hold of those implications sooner and to press them relentlessly to the end.[27]

In the hope to overcome life's futility, Agnon relentlessly cultivated his pessimism. The dejected condition of Eastern European Jewry, the crisis of faith, and the unprecedented losses during the Holocaust may explain in part the acute pessimism pervading Agnon's major works. His unconcern with the world around him, and the interest in death and deathliness may have their basis in an extreme preoccupation with inner reality.

There are those who, like Aberbach, even claim a biological basis to such pessimism.[28] To support his assertion, interestingly, Aberbach had to go to Kafka, who attempted to explain to his father his cold indifference as a means of survival "against destruction of a child's nerves by fear and a sense of guilt."[29] Aberbach concludes that in Agnonian *Weltanschauung,* side by side with art go faith, Torah, the land of Israel, and Jerusalem:

The fundamentally schizoid character of Agnon's art—his creating a radically new Hebrew style while preserving the posture of a naive ultra-conservative—can be understood to satisfy the need to confront the unacceptably harsh and unpleasant, and make it acceptable, even deceptively familiar, by fitting it into a traditional Jewish framework.[30]

Agnon is not commonly read by the English-speaking world, despite the fact that he is considered by many the greatest modern Hebrew writer and one of the ten most important writers of the twentieth century.[31] The reasons given by critics are very specific. Yehuda Friedlander claims that "it is difficult to have a substantial knowledge of Agnon's writing without a profound knowledge of the Jewish sources, both in the written Torah and the oral Torah, and in the various Responsa literature."[32] Indeed, the writings of Agnon are saturated with reminiscences from the wells of Judaism throughout the generations. Halkin, another noted Agnon critic, appropriately claims that what makes Agnon so difficult to translate is his continual alluding in his work to the classic texts of Judaism, in other words, intertextuality, which he brings into play with the subtle biblical references that may escape the casual reader's attention.[33] Other critics, among them Cynthia Ozick, insist that the English public's indifference to Agnon is to be attributed not to his "intranslateability" as some have suggested, but to some of the critics who claimed that it is no use in trying to get at Agnon in any language other than the original, and also to poor translations.[34] Nitza Ben-Dov asserts that, despite all difficulties we might have in grasping Agnon,

> through the use of paradox, the fusion of antinomies, the breaking down of logically marked categories, the revelation of chaos in the belief systems of apparently naive legends whose heroes appear to be models of mental and spiritual integrity, and the subtle reversal of readings that he himself has constructed, Agnon places himself firmly within the circles of the most profound twentieth-century writers in molding his art to resemble the indistinctness of the reality it attempts to engage.[35]

To get the full impact of Agnonian distinct handling of scriptural material in order to make statements about the present and connect to an ancestral past, we investigate below his parabolic opening to the recitation of the *Kaddish* for those who were killed in the Land of Israel.

BEFORE THE KADDISH: AT THE FUNERAL OF THOSE WHO WERE KILLED IN THE LAND OF ISRAEL

When a king of flesh and blood goes forth to war against his enemies, he leads out his soldiers to slay and to be slain. It is hard to say, does he love his soldiers, doesn't he love his soldiers, do they matter to him, don't they matter to him. But even if they do matter to him, they are as good as dead, for the Angel of Death is close upon the heels of everyone who goes off to war, and accompanies him only to slay him. When the soldier is hit, by arrow or sword or saber or any of the other kinds of destructive weapons, and slain, they put another man in his place, and the king hardly knows that someone is missing—for the population of the nations of the world is big and their troops are many. If one man is slain, the king has many others to make up for him.

But our king, the King of kings of kings, the Holy One blessed be He, is a king who delights in life, who loves peace and pursues peace, and loves His people Israel, and He chose us from among all the nations: not because we are a numerous folk did He set His love upon us, for we are the fewest of all people. But because of the love He loves us with and we are so few, each and every one of us matters as much before Him as a whole legion, for He hasn't many to put in our place. When from Israel one is missing, God forbid, a minnishing takes place in the King's legions, and in His kingdom, blessed be He, there is a decline is strength, as it were, for His kingdom now lacks one of its legions, and His grandeur, blessed be He, has been diminished, God forbid.

That is why for each dead person in Israel we recite the prayer "Magnified and sanctified be His great Name." Magnified be the power of the Name so that before Him, blessed be He, there be no decline in strength; and sanctified be He in all the worlds which He created according to His will, and not for ourselves let us have fear but for the superlative splendor of His exalted holiness. May He establish His sovereignty so that His kingdom be perfectly revealed and visible, and may it suffer no diminishing, God forbid. In our lifetime and in your days and in the lifetime of the whole house of Israel speedily and soon—for if His sovereignty is manifest in the world, there is peace in the world and blessing in the world and song in the world and a multitude of praises in the world and great consolation in the world, and the holy ones, Israel, are beloved in the world and His grandeur continues to grow and increase and never diminishes.

If this is what we recite in prayer over any who die, how much the more over our beloved and sweet brothers and sisters, the dear children of Zion, those killed in the Land of Israel, whose blood was shed for the glory of His blessed Name and for His people and His land and His heritage. And what is more, everyone who dwells in the Land of Israel belongs to the legion of the King of kings of kings, the Holy One, blessed be He, whom the King appointed watchman of His palace. When one of His legion is slain, He has no others as it were to put in his place.

Therefore, brethren of the whole house of Israel, all you who mourn in this mourning, let us fix our hearts on our Father in heaven, Israel's king and redeemer, and let us pray for ourselves and for Him too as it were: Magnified and sanctified be His Great Name in the world which He created as He willed. May He establish His kingdom, may He make His deliverance to sprout forth, may He bring nigh His messiah, and so to the end of the whole prayer. May we be found worthy still to be in life when with our own eyes we may behold Him who makes peace in His high place, in His compassion making peace for us and for all Israel, Amen.[36]

In a manner comparable to ancient sages, Agnon offers this parabolic tale as a *petiḥah*, an "opening" presentation to another activity which is about to take place. This other activity is the recitation of the mourners' prayer, or *Kaddish,* for those killed in the Land of Israel.

The gesture of affixing the parabolic tale to an ancient Jewish communal religious ritual offers important cues about Agnon's intention to revive an age-old Jewish tradition: the legacy of telling parables to elucidate difficult scriptural passages and, ultimately, to enlighten the listener about certain customs or the meaning of a verse in the holy texts. Likewise, this parabolic tale provides a good illustration of the techniques Agnon has used repeatedly to revive other traditional practices, while engaging his readers in his fiction.

The genius of Agnon affords him to teach brilliantly a modern lesson in how to tell parables and in how to bring to life in the present the

Jewish past. The strategy Agnon adopts to accomplish this difficult task is to graft every part of his own discourse onto the content and form of scriptural classic texts. With a mastery unmatched in modern times, Agnon proceeds to engage in each line with scores of biblical verses and classic Jewish prayer pieces.[37] He imbricates cleverly the parable's narrational segments, or *isotopies*, in multiple layers of traditional Jewish texts, to the point where the listener stops distinguishing the old texts from this new one, and the voice of Agnon, the modern author, becomes undistinguishable to him from that of the ancient sages. At that point, the single voice of the modern Jewish writer, resonating vibrantly with ancestral chords, acquires the register of the ancient choirs he wishes to bring back to life.

In using this astute rhetorical ploy, Agnon, an ambitious man despite his mild-mannered appearance, accomplishes two important tasks: he unearths a precious Jewish tradition before the eyes of the modern Jew/reader/listener and, at the same time, enshrines his own writing next to those of the great sages.

Even a cursory reading of Agnon's parable reveals that its structure follows very closely that of the parables in the *Midrash*. Like many of the 'king' parables in the *Midrash* or in the Gospel parables, the first narrational segment of Agnon's parabolic tale brings to the foreground the endeavors of a "king." To teach his present lesson, Agnon, like the ancient parabolizers, generates two parallel narrative paths, connected, as they were in the past, by the disjunctive conjunction "*aval*," "but": the first one, about "*meleḥ bassar vedam*," a "king of flesh and blood" and the second, about "*malkenu meleḥ malchei hamelachim, hakaddosh baruch hu*," "our (God) king, the King of kings of kings, the Holy One, blessed be He." In each of the two segments, Agnon uses abundantly biblical verses and stereotypical phrases from the Jewish prayerbooks, where the Lord is designated indeed as "*malkheneu meleḥ malkei hamlaḥim, hakaddosh baruch hu*," "our king, the King of kings of kings, the Holy One blessed be He."

With a typical rabbinic formulaic structure, *lefikah*, "In accordance with this," Agnon cleverly introduces an additional shift, and the parable's third narrational segment. Here, he moves the reader from glorifying God, who has chosen Israel as his people and loves Israel despite its scant numbers, to the domain of "*ahar kol met*" "(mourning) after one person." At this point, Agnon encourages the listener to pause and remember the Holy Scriptures where God declares that the Hebrews are His people.[38] At the same time, he gives his reader a taste of the elegant sophistication with which the ancient sages were reasoning and propounding their parables.

Agnon proceeds to a new narrational level with the formulaic expression "*kal va homer*," "how much more," and imports in his narrative, as an integral part, another favorite rabbinic approach: the *a minori ad majus* argumentation. The use of inference, a typical rabbinic form of reasoning, is bound to resonate very strongly in the hearts of the assembled mourners. This new narrational segment is inlaid as well with allusions to traditional texts and rabbinic and biblical descriptions of the unique relations between God and the men and women living in the Holy Land.[39] Numerous syncretic religiocultural elements are being cleverly entwined and brought together in the last narrative segment, where Agnon also introduces the classical "*nimshal*," or moral lesson of the parable, "*leficah*," "therefore."

Just as his parable is an "opening," or prelude, to the important Jewish custom of mourning, his dialogue with the classic genre seems a prelude for Agnon to initiate a polylogue with tradition. The lesson Agnon wishes to teach is in truth not about mourning—he knows well that Jews have had ample opportunity to learn how to mourn—but about the need to bring Jews back, after the Holocaust, to a proper posture vis-à-vis God and Judaism.

A man who saw his native town turned into ashes and his people annihilated because of an unfounded anti-Semitism, Agnon takes advantage of another tragic event in the lives of the Jews living in Israel. He wishes to inculcate in his fellow countrymen the belief that they must regain faith in God and go back to their old tradition, to find solace.

To bring his readers back to God even in such moments of deep sorrow, Agnon chooses to speak in parable. And even though mourning over the men and women who died for Israel was the event that occasioned his parable, Agnon built it around the need to glorify the greatness of God, reflected in the ancient tradition, and not around glorifying only the dearly departed. Thus, Agnon adroitly shifts the focus from mourning for the departed, to the reason for which Jews must exalt God and pray for His power, during the recitation of the *Kaddish*. This covert shift in the center of gravity of the parable is a common discursive ploy, and Agnon uses it flawlessly.

But Agnon was intent on presenting his parabolic argument in a classical manner. To these ends, in the first narrational segment he told of the "king of flesh and blood" and his relation to his "soldiers." The "king of flesh and blood" is depicted as insensitive and, in essence, indifferent to his people. To impress this upon his listeners, Agnon used several parallel (positive and negative) structures that lend an air of doubt and ambiguity about the qualities of a king of flesh and blood: do they matter, don't they matter; does he love them, doesn't he love them. His love, if it exists, is compared to that of "the Angel of Death," since he sends his people to die for him. Here, Agnon uses the augmentative structure to show how little the people count in that king's life. This clever parabolizer adds next two qualifying statements: "the king hardly notices that one was slain" and "the king hardly knows that someone is missing." In preparation of a comparison with God in the next narrational segment, he proceeds to explain the reason for such indifference on the part of that king and suggests a different kind of king to the listener: "the population of the nations of the world is big and their troops are many."

With the classical disjunctive conjunction "but," Agnon juxtaposes in the next segment of the narrative God with the "king of flesh and blood." To each of the ambiguous statements in the previous narrational segment he opposes a statement meant to exalt God's kindness and love of His people. First, Agnon opposes the greatness of God to the blunt materiality of the king's "flesh and blood." He gives "Our king" the titles God has been given since antiquity in the Bible and that persist to this day in prayers: "King of king of kings," and "the Holy One, blessed be He." Following the names, come God's many attributes—also repeated perennially during prayers, and, therefore, undoubtedly known by the mourners as well[40]—"a king who delights in life," "who loves peace and pursues peace, and loves His people Israel."[41]

After enumerating the glorious attributes of the Lord, Agnon brings to the foreground the notion of "chosenness of the Jews" and the "covenant" that God made with His people Israel. He reminds the audience of the reason: God's "love" of the people of Israel. Agnon inscribes this concept textually by saying "[God] loves his people," and "He chose us from among all the nations," "because of the love He loves us with."

Agnon's next strategic move is to shift from the love of God to the limited numbers of the people of Israel. Thus, the choice God has made is connected not to "numerous folks," but to being "so few." Agnon can proceed now to claim that "we matter as much before Him as a whole legion, for He hasn't many to put in our place."[42] In this fashion Agnon shrewdly reconnects the very power of God to the numbers of the people of Israel.

In evoking God's love for His people and the importance they have to Him, Agnon creates a parabolic displacement to connect linguistically the survival of each of the Jewish people to the greatness of God Himself. This major discursive shift enables Agnon to talk finally about the pain experienced by the loss of "one" of the fellow Jews. This pain, however, is experienced now by the present mourners not as mere human loss; it has been elevated by Agnon's talent to the status of a divine loss, which must now be prevented by God Himself, since, as one understands it from Agnon's parable, a loss of Jewish life is a loss in

God's own dominion and a "decline in strength [in the divine], as it were, for His kingdom now lacks one of its legions and His grandeur, blessed be He, has been diminished."

Agnon's penultimate parabolic shift is to extrapolate from the statement made about "one" fallen Jew, to "all" inhabitants of Israel. He introduces this narrational sequence with another stereotypical parabolic phrase, "*Im kah anu*," "that is why . . . we," which allows him a new incursion into the *Kaddish*'s lines he reinscribes systematically in the story and intersperses them with his own commentary. Thus, Agnon restates and reinscribes in his parable the entire *Kaddish*, while deconstructing all its lines in order to elucidate their deeper meaning to his listeners/readers.

Agnon ends his parable with yet another stereotypical parabolic phrase, "*leficah*," "therefore." The parable's "*nimshal*," or lesson, becomes an appeal to his countrymen to pray for God when praying for the dearly departed. The connection Agnon has established in the antecedent sequences of the parable enable him to make a rhetorical pirouette and beseech the people of Israel who mourn their beloved, to pray for God and to go back to loving God, as He loves them. Only by loving in return a God who loved them will the people of Israel be able to finally return to a more happy way of living in the world.[43]

To bring his readers/addressee to a higher level of understanding of the word of God, Agnon takes them for a circular ride in the manner of the ancient parabolists. His use of traditional methods and traditional texts places him next to the ancient sages. His use of linguistic innovation and his questions about the possibility of divine knowledge, which he ponders in his narrative, make his endeavor a modern one.

Agnon's fiction represents an ironic rethinking of the past and a brilliant return to fictional forms of coherent storytelling. Agnon's position as a writer vis-à-vis the Jewish tradition was best captured by Umberto Eco's example:

> I think of the postmodern attitude as that of a man who loves a very cultivated woman and knows he cannot say to her, "I love you madly," because he knows that she knows (and that she knows that he knows) that these words have been written by Barbara Cartland. Still, there is a solution. He can say, "As Barbara Cartland would put it, I love you madly." At this point, having avoided false innocence, having said clearly that it is no longer possible to speak innocently, he will nevertheless have said what he wanted to say to the woman: that he loves her, but he loves her *in an age of lost innocence*. If the woman goes along with this, she will have received a declaration of love all the same. Neither of the two speakers will feel innocent, both will have accepted the challenge of the past, of the already said, which cannot be

eliminated, both will consciously and with pleasure play the game of irony. . . . But both will have succeeded, once again, in speaking of love.[44]

Of Agnon's parables, one may indeed say that he succeeded to speak of an old and almost forgotten love, in an almost forgotten style. With him, parables come to life and, hopefully, teach both the modern teacher and the student about the Jewish tradition of speaking in parables.

TOWARD A
CONCLUSION:
"SOME FABULOUS
YONDER"

In ending my incursion into the domain of parables, I return to Kafka, the author who stimulated my curiosity about them in the first place. We read in "On Parable" that:

> When the sage says: "Go over," he does not mean that we should cross to some actual place, which we could do anyhow if the labor were worth it; he means some fabulous yonder, something unknown to us, something too that he cannot designate more precisely, and therefore cannot help us in the very least.[1]

The plea with which I conclude is in keeping up with both the methodology of this study and the elusive art of parables, this recalcitrant type of discourse that has endured for over two millennia.

Have I sent the reader to "go over" to that unknown "fabulous yonder" that the sage cannot designate more precisely?

Biblical Parables and Their Modern Recreations: From "Apples of Gold in Silver Settings" to "Imperial Messages" suggests the tensions in a discourse of amazing resiliency and flexibility that moves in a universe defined by continual change, playing out the double gestures of convention and innovation, indicating age-old practices and unsettling them. The required context for my study has been the sociohistorical change in our ritualistic core, that is, the dramatic shifts in human thinking in modernity echoed in the transformations that occur in parables.

With that context constantly made available, it has been possible to investigate parables, which originated in the sacred texts and moved away from them and were transformed, as a result of extreme events that shaped modernity and postmodernity.

A critical reading of texts is an endeavor to extract the secrets harbored by those texts. The attempt made in these pages to trace the transformational chain in parables from the scriptural parabolic narratives, the "apples of gold in silver settings" upon which the philosopher Maimonides theorized, to the Kafkaesque, undecipherable parables I call

219

"imperial messages," ends best on a note of uncertainty because the layers of meaning hidden beneath the surface of a text are by definition speculations about the interactive processes at work. In this sense, literary criticism modifies the old sense of the text as autonomous artifact and the reader as invisible interrogator. Part of the value of criticism, Walter Benjamin taught us, is to give access to the working of the process by which a text is received, assimilated, and reformulated in readers' statements about it. Benjamin states poetically:

> Suppose you make the acquaintance of a young person who is handsome and attractive, but who seems to be harboring a secret. It would be tactless and reprehensible to try to penetrate this secret and wrest it from him. But it is doubtless permissible to inquire whether he has any siblings, to see whether their nature could not perhaps explain somewhat the enigmatic character of the stranger. This is exactly how the true critic inquires into the siblings of the work of art. And every great work has its sibling (brother or sister) in the realm of philosophy. Just as philosophy makes use of symbolic concepts to draw ethics and language into the realm of theory, in the same way it is possible for theory (logic) to be incorporated into ethics and language in symbolic form. Thus the emergence of ethical and aesthetic critique.[2]

Transformations prompted by sociocultural and historical change, as I have demonstrated throughout this book, have radically changed the shape, the function, and the dissemination modes of parabolic discourse. These parallel shifts surface most clearly by focusing on scriptural and synoptic parables. Against this backdrop, I inscribed the rabbinic, Chassidic, and modern parables that display structures that go back to the prototypical parables of antiquity.

I showed that at the core of the discursive makeup of parables exists a double signal. On the one hand, parables, a primitive communicatory force, invoke elementary passions and short-circuit the path to understanding by putting the addressee in touch immediately with a primeval "ought," or "must do," an early deontic mode, and, on the other hand, parables baffle the mind because their messages are allusive and their means indirect. This doubleness is made possible in parables by a specific tropologico-rhetorical system, as well as a system of modifications. A displacement in the parabolic text generates pseudo-analogies. As a result, in addition to the regular transitions from one narrative sequence to another, parabolic narratives stage a return to one or more metatexts.

I demonstrated in this study that, because of their inherent doubleness and allusiveness, parables have been a most efficient tool in the service of ideology. I showed also that ideology can be inculcated, because parables propose a "likeness" between two dissimilar elements and disguise with linguistic craft the "seam" in their discursive texture. That a particular parable means something specific to someone is largely the work of auto-reflexivity, that is to say, the meaning of a parable is essentially the by-product of that parable's internal cohesion, and its cohesion is ultimately the veiled artifact of a skilled parabolizer/storyteller.

Parables, most vividly in the *Midrash*, assume that the addressee knows *a priori* the literal text upon which they build their system of tropes and intricate systems of transformations. To that extent, parables are subversive. A tension is generated between the text and the context, between the demand to decode or understand, and an impossibility in modern times to decode.

The movement of displacement from one time-space frame to another generates an isotopic or analogical world/space into which they draw the addressee and keep him occupied with attempts at decoding. This movement is a regression that absorbs the reader, like the city of Tamara in Calvino's parable. The receiver of a parable is taken from one point to another, and from one narrational segment to another, in a chain of textual substitutions with the false understanding that all the segments are logically derived from one another. In reality, the propulsory force in the parabolic game, where a parabolist explains a text by offering a parable, is the receiver's own desire. And the syntax of that desire manifested in language as moving energy is made visible at the level of discourse. In other words, it is the passion aroused in the addressee in the process of parabolizing that causes him to believe the truth of the parable and to perform as a believer.

I have shown that parables shift constantly between the text and a metatext, in a dialectical motion that contributes to a dreamlike effect. As a result of the similarity between dream-texts and parabolic discourse, one may draw some interesting parallels. Like the truths the dreams describe, which are complex and often not fully accessible to consciousness because they undergo processes of transformations and condensation, the internal cohesion in parables comes from transformations and syncretizing. Furthermore, parables allude to real events in our daily lives in an oblique, cryptic fashion, and, just as dreams are the "royal road" to the unconscious, parables are the "royal road" to the other texts, or metatexts. The more divergent the elements encoded in dreams and in parables, the more puzzling they become. In other words, the message received in dreams, or obtained parabolically, always points covertly and "lackingly," to our intersubjective relations. Likewise, as in dreams, the *latent* meaning of the parabolic text is supplied by the lacunae in it, namely, by "lacks" and absences. A dialectic is generated also between the injunction to interpret the lack and fill in "the blank" in the text, and the need to keep the gap open as a reminder of that "other" text to which the parable alludes.

The texts I have chosen and analyzed in this study demonstrate that parables were used as an effective teaching tool. Early parabolizers meant to teach about the Holy Scriptures and God. Those diaphanous parables were understood by the semiotic community for which they were propounded, because their metatext, although deemed divine, was accessible to man. But, like their modern counterparts, they embodied cunning sophistry.

I have shown that the sophistical teaching of parables results from the fact that parables proceed to generate their own "truth," during the space and time of the narrative, and point reflexively to their internal cohesion. Parables never really answer the parabolic question being asked at the beginning of the narrative; they point the addressee in the direction they want him/her to go. In essence, parables decontextualize their primary narrative and generates an internal gap. To that extent, a parable writer undertakes an enterprise akin to that of Henry Michaux's "student of magic":

> Walking on the two banks of a stream is a laborious exercise. Frequently, you see a man (a student of magic) going upstream that way, walking on the one bank and the other at the same time: being very preoccupied, he does not see you. For what he is performing is delicate and tolerates no inattention. He would very soon find himself on one bank, and how disgraceful that would be![3]

To men and women, uncertain, as Kafka was, about the possibility of accessing knowledge, modern parables have become unfathomable labyrinthal structures, elaborate, yet opaque, expressed in a language that can only point to "some fabulous yonder," and whose undeliverable messages compel the addressee to "dream the message to himself as the evening falls." These modern parables are called "Kafkaesque," to signal the nightmarish effect they create, the eerie sensation of hopelessness before an incomprehensible universe whose wisdom is enshrouded in silence.

Kafka, Kierkegaard, Dostoyevsky, Gogol, Borges, Calvino, Agnon, and Schopenhauer are but a few of the modern parabolizers who tell us in their parables that to know the truth in modernity is to know the nature of the void. Lacking the support of the divine myth expressed in the old days with the invocation of a verse of the Holy Scriptures, modern parables generate their own fictional grounds by imploding into self-referentiality and self-canceling, "Kafkaesque" messages. Instead of bridging the gap between the signifier and the signified, the thing and the artistic representation of that thing, modern parables offer a kind of subterranean "point of flight," a punctual moment of illumination akin to that of the enlightenment of the man in Kafka's *Penal Colony*, who is also killed by the machine that inscribes (literally) knowledge. In essence, modern man learns about the impossibility of knowing.

In parabolizing, Kafka brought into sharp focus this crisis experienced by modern man. Modernity, it seems, has irrevocably barred man's access to that "fabulous yonder" of which Kafka spoke; even the magisterially gifted, like Borges, Calvino, Cortazàr, Garcia Marques, or Agnon, can only decry their predicament.

Incapable to attain true wisdom, modern parabolists concentrate on the refinement of their craft, to the point of a consuming preoccupation with "the word." The word, the representational image, has become the only law and the ultimate authority to which the modern artist has recourse.

As artifacts, parables are unique, because they mimic an entire epic chain of search and of findings, a journey into an isotopic world of reward and discovery. Yet the reward is a competence in the parabolic game; the discovery: an appalling realization of the fundamental human inability to go back to its linguistic and conceptual origins. Kafka's statement that "parables are meant to remain parables," shows that in parables we remain always torn between allegory and literality.

Ancient parabolic efforts were more successful because they postulated that the divine world is immutable and that the divine intercedes in man's world. In modernity, unable to get to our ontological truths, we are bound to shout meaningless messages, or reiterate old messages, without the benefit of understanding them. As Umberto Eco claims,

> in modern aesthetic experience the possible contents are suggested by the co-text and by the intertextual tradition: the interpreter knows that he is not discovering an external truth but that, rather, he makes the encyclopedia work at its best. Modern poetic symbolism is a secularized symbolism where languages speak about their possibilities. Behind every strategy of the symbolic mode, religious or aesthetic, there is a legitimating theology, even though it is the aesthetic theology of unlimited semiosis or of hermeneutics as deconstruction.[4]

Faced with modern multifarious and enigmatic parables, we, like Edmond Jabès's Rabbi Mendel, are bound to say to our reader, "True knowledge is our daily awareness that, in the end, one learns nothing . . . the nothing is also knowledge, being the reverse of the all as the air is the reverse of the wing. Our hope is the wing of despair. For how would we progress otherwise? Only our hope to be right is real."[5]

Why then go on writing and studying parables?

I showed that their attraction provokes the highest expectations and seduces us. Their beauty motivates us to make the most extravagant demands of ourselves. The pleasure the work offers compensates for the many drawbacks: the vast range of very difficult material, the many skills and languages one needs to have or acquire quickly, the intimidating temporal stretch. These drawbacks seem to fade away before a Borgesian parable with astonishing architectonics and exquisite language. As the disciple of Machiavelli,[6] or the analysand who is "impelled to submit himself" and rid himself of repression because of his desire for recovery,[7] we ask of our parabolist: "Master, tell us more."

NOTES

INTRODUCTION

1. Louis Marin, "La syntaxe du désire," in *Semiology and Parables*, ed. Daniel Patte (Pittsburgh, Penn.: The Pickwick Press, 1976), 215–226, and Jonathan Culler, *Structuralist Poetics* (Ithaca, N.Y.: Cornell University Press, 1975), 98–120. Both claim that parables make obvious the production of ideology by reproducing reality in the form of a sign (semēion) that becomes the only reality.

2. Rolland Barthes, *Le degré zéro de l'écriture* (Paris: Éditions du Seuil, 1953); Émile Benveniste, *Problèmes de linguistique générale* (Paris: Gallimard, 1966); Juliet and Dean MacCannall, *The Time of the Sign* (Bloomington: Indiana University Press, 1982).

3. C. H. Dodd, *The Parables of the Kingdom* (Glasgow: William Collins, 1961); J. Petuchovsky, "The Theological Significance of the Parables in Rabbinic Literature and the New Testament," *Christian News from Israel* 23.10 (1972): 76–86, 144; David Flusser, *Yahadut Umekorot Hanatsrut* (Tel Aviv: Shamgar Sifriat Hapoalim, 1979); J. Jeremias, *The Parables of Jesus* (London: SCM Press Ltd., 1981), in German, *Die Gleichnisse Jesu.* (Göttingen, 1962); *Dan Via, The Parables: Their Literary and Existential Dimension* (Philadelphia: Fortress Press, 1980); Davis Stern, "Moses-cide: Midrash and Contemporary Literary Criticism," *Prooftexts* 4.2 (1984): 193–204; Daniel Boyarin, "Rhetoric and Interpretation: The Case of the Nimshal," *Prooftexts* 5 (1985): 260–270; Geoffrey Hartman and Sanford Budick, eds., *Midrash and Literature* (New Haven: Yale University Press, 1986), 19–37.

4. Michel Riffaterre, "The Intertextual Unconscious," *Critical Inquiry* 13.2 (1987): 373. He defines intertextuality as the "double action of the sign . . . the perception of our reading of a text or textual component is completely satisfactory only if it constrains us to refer to or to cancel out its homologue in the intertext." And see Mikhail Bakhtin, *Problems of Dostoyevsky's Poetics*, trans. M. Holquist (Austin: University of Texas Press, 1984), 198. "Intertextuality is a dialogue in the text."

5. Jeremias, *The Parables of Jesus*, 70–77, 79–85, 86–88, and Adolph Jülicher, *Die Gleichnisreden Jesus* (Tübingen: J.C.B. Mohr, 1886–1910; reprinted Darmstadt: Wissenschaftliche Buchgesellschaft, 1963); Dodd, *The Parables of the Kingdom*; David Flusser, *Yahadut Umekorot Hanatsrut* [Judaism and the Sources of Christianity] (Hebrew) (Tel Aviv: Shamgar Sifriat Hapoalim, 1979). Flusser shows conclusively the affinities between the parables by Jesus and the rabbinic parables.

6. Umberto Eco, *A Theory of Semiotics* (Bloomington: Indiana University Press, 1976), 34–97; MacCannall, *The Time of the Sign*, 68–98, and 106–120; Culler, *Structuralist Poetics*, 11–54; C. S. Pierce, "Elements of Logic," in *Collected Papers* (Cambridge: Harvard University Press, 1960).

7. Hartman and Buddick, *Midrash and Literature*, 3–18. Hartman claims that writing is a fusion of heterogeneous stories or types of discourse, layered or even "macaronic," seeking the appearance of unity.

8. Emanuel Levinas, *Quatre lectures Talmudiques* (Paris: Les Éditions de Minuit, 1968), 122–126.

9. In Sun Tzu's *The Art of War*, when the disciple asks the Zen Master about truth, he raises his stick and threatens him with it. The disciple must decode by himself the master's koan.

CHAPTER 1. THE NATURE AND STRUCTURE OF PARABLES

1. Ecclesiastes 12:9; 1 Kings 5:12–13. There is a sense in which *dugma* is synonymous with *mashal* (parable). See "Royal Wisdom," in *Wisdom in Israel and in Ancient Near East*, ed. M. Noth and D. W. Thomas (Leiden: E. J. Brill, 1969), 3:262–270; *Dugma* (Hebrew) comes from the Greek *deigma* (specimen, example), the stem of which is *deikuynai* (to show) with the derivatives *degem, degam, dugma*.

2. Proverbs 1:6.

3. Cf. Midrash to Song of Songs 1:1.

4. Moses Maimonides, *The Guide for the Perplexed*, trans. Shlomo Pines (Chicago: Chicago University Press, 1963), 11.

5. Proverbs 25:11.

6. Genesis 26:8.

7. Maimonides, *The Guide for the Perplexed*, 11.

8. Ibid., 14.

9. Ibid., 14–15.

10. Matthew 13:1–14.

11. *Buddhist Birth Stories, or the Jātāka Tales*, trans. Rhys Davids (London: Trubner, 1880); *The Path of Purification* (*Visuddhimagga*), vol. 2 (Berkeley, Calif.: Shambala, 1976), 690–691; G. F. Moore, *Judaism in the First Centuries of the Christian Era*, vol. 1 (Cambridge: Harvard University Press, 1927–30), 487. The author intimates that an Indian story might be the source of several versions of a parable in the Talmud.

12. Aristotle, *Poetics*, trans. Gerald F. Else (Ann Arbor: The University of Michigan Press, 1976), 51–52, and Aristotle, 23 *The Poetics*, trans. Hamilton Fyfe (Cambridge: Harvard University Press, 1927), 23:3, 91. "The story [in a parable] must be constructed as a tragedy, dramatically, round a single piece of action, whole and complete in itself with a beginning, middle and end, so that like a living organism *it may produce its own peculiar form of pleasure*" [my emphasis].

13. Bradford Young, *Jesus and His Jewish Parables* (Mahwah, N.J.: Paulist Press, 1989), 245; David Stern, *Parables in Midrash* (Cambridge: Harvard University Press, 1991), 35.

14. Jean-François Lyotard, *The Differend*, trans. George van Den Abbeele (Minneapolis: University of Minnesota Press, 1988), 3–49. Lyotard shows that communicational chains are formed in a culture and that citizens become "subjects" by "being interpellated."

15. Vladimir Propp, *Morphology of Folktales*, trans. L. Scott and L. A. Wagnes (Austin: University of Texas Press, 1983), 14–35; J. Heinemann and Dov Noy, eds., "Studies in Aggadah and Folk-Literature," in *Scripta Hierosolymitana* (Jerusalem: Ktav, 1971), vol. 22; Barbara Kirshenblatt-Gimblett, "A Parable in Context: A Social Interactional Analysis of Storytelling Performance," in *Folklore: Performance and Communication*, ed. D. Ben-Amos and K. Goldstein (The Hague: Mouton de Cruyter, 1975).

16. Proverbs 25:11.

17. Franz Kafka, "The Parable of the Imperial Message," in *Parables and Paradoxes*, trans. Clement Greenbaum et al. (New York: Schocken Books, 1974), 34.

18. Edward Synan, *Thomas Aquinas, Propositions and Parables* (Toronto: Pontifical Inst. of Med. Studies, 1979), 17–18. He quotes Aquinas: *"Per hunjus modi parabolas absconduntur sacra ab infidelibus ne blasphement"* (parables hide so that the infidels won't commit blasphemy). *Parabola, in qua ponitur impedimentum de audienda doctrina* (parables possess an obstacle to understanding).

19. David Stern, *Parables in Midrash* (Cambridge: Harvard University Press, 1991), 15.

20. David Flusser, *Yahadut Umekorot Hanatsrut*, 15–149.

21. Ibid., 150–155; Daniel Boyarin, "Rhetoric and Interpretation: The Case of the Nimshal," *Prooftexts* 5 (1985): 270–280.

22. See also translation by W. Braude and I. Kapstein, *Pesikta de-Rab Kahana*, 40. Transformations and abbreviations seem to appear where the parable is attributed to R. Levi. See also note 34 on p. 253, Braude and Kapstein's version in the Parma manuscript version.

23. The Spoiled Son, *Pesikta de-Rab Kahana* 3:1; parallels, 86, 179.

24. *Midrash* must be understood as the sum total and the activity of Scripture interpretation that was formulated by the fourth century C.E.

25. E. L. Koeler and W. Baumgartner, *Lexicon in Veteris Testamenti Libros* (Leiden: E. J. Brill, 1958), 575. The double reference: mašal/matla "kann ja neben Gleichnis den spruch, das sprichwort die metaphor, den vergleich und eine hermeneutische Regel bedeuten." Ben Yehuda, *Milon Halashon Haivrit Hayashanah Vehachadashah* (The Dictionary for the Old and Modern Hebrew) (Jerusalem: Hotzaah leOr, 1959), 7:3386–91; M. Noth and D. W. Thomas, eds., *Wisdom in Israel and in the Ancient Near East* (Leiden: Brill Studiam Vetus Testamentuum, 1955), vol. 3, 162–169. And see Psalms 49:13, Isaiah 14:10.

26. Numbers 23:7, Ezekiel 24:3, Jeremiah 24:1, Proverbs 1:1. In Ezekiel 17:2, the narrative is being referred to as both riddle and parable and could even mean a fable, *mashal* or *chidah* (riddle).

27. L. Finkelstein, "Midrash, Halachot, Vehagadot," in *Yizhak F. Baer Jubilee Volume*, ed. S. Baron, B. Dinur, S. Ettinger, and I. Halperin (Jerusalem: Historical Society, 1960), 28–45; A. Heschel, *Between God and Man* (New

York: The Free Press, 1960), 138–150 and 214–222; J. Fraenkel, *Eyunim Bao-lam Haruchani Shel Sipor Haagadah* (Tel Aviv: Hakibbutz Hameuchad, 1981), 187–194.

28. F. Talmage, *Sefer Habrit* (The Book of the Covenant) (Jerusalem: Bialik Institute, 1974), 32; Bradford Young, *Jesus and His Jewish Parables*, 34–48.

29. Adolph Jülicher, *Die Gleichnisreden Jesus* (Tübingen: J. C. B. Mohr, 1886–1910; reprinted Darmstadt: Wissenschaftliche Buchgesellschaft, 1963); Joachim Jeremias, *The Parables of Jesus*, trans. W. Wells (London: SCM Press Ltd., 1981). The relation between the parabolic narrative and the external world, the connection between the *mashal* and the *nimshal* (the story and the lesson), and the primacy of one over the other has been the source of much scholarly debate.

30. "The Parable of the Vineyard" (Isaiah 5:1–7), "The Tree and Its Roots" (Avot 3:17), of "The Tekoite Woman" (2 Samuel 14:2–21), "The Trees and the Bramble" (Judges 9:7–21), "The Parable of Oholah and Oholibah" (Ezekiel 23:1–36), "The Parable of the Ewe-Lamb" (2 Samuel 11:1–14). And see Jeremiah 3:1–5 and 1 Kings 20:35–43.

31. "The Parable of the King's Banquet" (b. Sabbath 153 a, R. Johanan ben Zakkai), "The Lame and the Blind" (*The Apocryphon of Ezekiel*), "The Spoiled Son" (Pesikta de-Rab Kahana 3:1 & parallels). David Flusser, *Yahadut Umekorot Hanatsrut*, 203–204. Says Flusser: "That Jesus was such a craftsman is itself evidence for the great tradition from within which he came."

32. Ezek. 10:19, 11:23.

33. *A History of the Land of Israel until 1880*, Israel Pocket Library (Tel Aviv: Keter, 1973); Lester L. Grabbe, *Judaism from Cyrus to Hadrian: The Persian and Greek Periods*, vol.1 (Minneapolis: University of Minnesota Press, 1992), 270–311; Max Radin, *The Jews among the Greeks and Romans* (Philadelphia: The Jewish Publication Society of America, 1915), 118–267.

34. H. Schwartbaum, "Talmudic-Midrashic Affinities of Some Aesopic Fables," *IVth International Congress for Folk-Narrative Research* (Athens: Athenaeum, 1965), 466–483, in David Stern, *Parables in Midrash*, 289. Stern brings the example of R. Joshua b. Hananiyah (90–130 C.E.), who told the parable to convince the Jews not to rise up against the Romans.

35. Michael Fishbane, "Inner Biblical Exegesis," in *Midrash and Literature*, ed. J. Hartman and S. Budick (New Haven: Yale University Press, 1991), 19–37.

36. Saul Liberman, *Hellenism in Jewish Palestine* (New York: The Jewish Theological Studies, 1962), 83–88; David Flusser, *Yahadut Umekorot Hanatzrut*, 150–208.

37. Ezra (whose lineage goes back, it seems, to Aaron), has brought to Jerusalem a new attitude. The group founded the "Great Assembly," which is mentioned under the name of the "Tradition of the Elders," Matthew 15:2 and Mark 7:3–5. The Assembly, *Sanhedrin*, had an Upper House; the Sadducees, and a Lower, the Pharisees. The infiltration of heretics was quite heavy, and this necessitated a cryptic language.

38. Yehezkel Kaufman, *The Religion of Israel*, trans. Moshe Greenberg (Chicago: University of Chicago Press, 1960), 427–445.

39. Jeremiah 24:7, 31:33.

40. J. Jeremias, *The Parables of Jesus*, 103; David Flusser, *Yahadut Umekorot Hanatzrut*, 211.

41. A. J. Saldarini, "Reconstructions of Rabbinic Judaism," in *Early Judaism and Its Modern Interpreters* (Atlanta: Emory University Press, 1986), 437–477; Louis Finkelshtein, "The Transmission of the Early Rabbinic Traditions," in *Exploring the Talmud*, ed. H. Dimitrovsky (New York: Ktab Publ. House, 1976), 241–262; R. M. Johnston, "Parables among the Pharisees and Early Rabbis," *History of the Mishnaic Law of Purities*, ed. Jacob Neusner (Leiden: E. J. Brill, 1976), 224–230; William G. Braude and Israel J. Kapstein, *Tanna De Bei Eliyahu* (Philadelphia: The Jewish Press, 1981), 3–15.

42. These parables were collected late in the seventh century C.E. in the volume of *Semachot Derabbi Hiyyah* 2.1 and 4.1 and attributed to the sage Yohanan ben Zakkai, the founder of Yavneh, who lived during the late first century.

43. Deuteronomy 33:21.

44. Numbers 20:12; "Ye" referring to Moses and Aaron.

45. Numbers R. 19. 13 et cet. loc.

46. Umberto Eco, "On Symbols" in *Frontiers in Semiotics*, ed. John Deely et al. (Bloomington: Indiana University Press, 1986), 153–179; Umberto Eco, *A Theory of Semiotics* (Bloomington: Indiana University Press, 1976), 217–261. Eco demonstrates that a symbol is a *textual modality*, a way of producing and interpreting the aspects of a text, as a mere *replica*, but also a process of recognition: the *projection*, by *ratio difficilis* of a content nebula.

47. Louis Marin, "La syntaxe du désire," in *Critique du discours* (Paris: Les Éditions de Minuit, 1975), 303–323.

48. Aristotle, *The Art of Rhetoric*, trans. John Henry Fresse (London: William Heinemann, 1926), vol. 21, and 1.2.3–14, 15–24.

Rhetoric resembles dialectics, and Politics, by its being *indifferent to the truth of its conclusions*, so far as it is considered as an *art*, and the speaker as an *artist* [emphasis already in text]: both argue indifferently on either side of a question and may prove the affirmative or the negative according as either of these happen to suit the reasoner's immediate purpose. . . . Rhetoric deals with human actions, characters' motives and feelings; and so it becomes closely connected with the study of Politics; The object of Rhetoric is the *probable*; "Such is the aim of our science (rhetoric) which is a kind of politics" (οὐθεὶς δὲ βουλεύεται περὶ τῶν μὴ ἐνδεχομένων ἄλλως ἔχειν).

49. Friedreich Nietzsche, "Truth and Falsity in an Ultramoral Sense," in *The Philosophy of Nietzsche*, trans. G. Clive (New York: Mentor Books, 1965), 503–504.

50. Eugenio Donato, "Seminar on Deconstruction," University of California, San Diego, fall 1976. "Such is the law of representation or of re-presentation that here, more than ever, *Vorstellung and Derstellung* are indissociable: only that which is not present can be represented, that is to say, we represent only what was always representable" (my translation).

51. Edmond Jabès, *The Book of Questions*, trans. Rosmarie Waldrop (Middletown, Conn.: Wesleyan University Press, 1966), 12–14. "What will we get out of these questions? . . . The promise of a new question . . . truth is the void."

52. Exodus 32:14, 33:17.

53. Jacques Derrida *L'écriture et la différence* (Paris: Édition du Seuil, 1966), 103; idem, *Writing and Difference*, trans. Alan Bass (Chicago: Chicago University Press, 1978), 133.

54. Jean Baudrillard, "De la séduction," seminar, University of California, San Diego, fall 1979. We use here the notion of "seduction" differently. While for him seduction is opposite to production, parabolic discourse is "productive" because it generates a "desire to do" and action: interpretation.

55. Jacques Derrida, "La mythologie blanche," in *Marge de la philosophie* (Paris: Éditions de Minuit, 1972), 132–144.

56. Louis Marin, "La syntaxe du désire," in *Critique du discours* (Paris: Les Éditions de Minuit, 1975), 323.

57. Proverbs 22:6.

58. In *The Codex Assemeni 66, Torat Kohanim*. At least two similar parables appear in this manuscript of *Sifra*.

59. Aristotle, *The Art of Rhetoric*, 2.20.1389–1395; cf. M. H. McCall Jr., *Ancient Rhetorical Theories of Simile and Comparison* (Cambridge: Harvard University Press, 1969), 25–30.

60. Sifre Numbers 131; M. Friedmann 47a; P. Levertoff, *Midrash Sifre on Numbers* (New York: The Society for Promoting Christian Knowledge, 1926), 133–135; S. Safrai, *Rabbi Akkiva Ben-Yosef Hayyav Umishnato* (Jerusalem: Bialik, 1970), 250.

61. The King's Banquet, b Sabbath 153a, R. Johanan b. Zakkai, 13 n. 13; and Semachot Derabbi Chiyah 2:1 and Ecclesiastes Rabbah 9:7.

62. Monroe Beardsley, *Aesthetics: Problems in the Philosophy of Criticism* (New York: Harcourt, Brace, and World, 1958), 403.

63. Vladimir Propp, *Morphology of the Folktale*, trans. Lawrence Scott and Louis A. Wagnes (Austin: University of Texas Press, 1968), 12–45; J. Lottman, *The Structure of the Artistic Text*, trans. Ronald Vroon (Ann Arbor: University of Michigan Press, 1971), 130–146.

64. *Midrashim*, in *Semachot Derabbi Chiya* 3:3, 178; 187 n. 41.

65. "The Parable of the Blind and the Lame," in *The Babylonian Talmud*. Cf. Mekhilta Derabbi bar Yochai, Sanhedrin 91a–b (*Talmud Bavli, The Babylonian Talmud*, Wilna Edition, reprint, Tel Aviv, 1970). The lame and the blind in the king's orchard try to eat of the fruit of the king. One cannot see, the other cannot walk; only together can they eat the fruit.

66. Mark 4:11–12.

67. Stern, *Parables in Midrash*, 203. Stern calls this speech a "hermeneutical conceit."

68. A. J. Greimas, *Sémantique structurale* (Paris: Librairie Larousse, 1966); A. Greimas, *Maupassant: La sémiotique du texte, éxercises pratiques* (Paris: Éditions du Seuil, 1976), 83–97; Umberto Eco, *A Theory of Semiotics*, 1976, 67–78. The modality of *faire, pouvoir, vouloir, savoir,* and *devoir* (do, can do,

want, know, must do) and *croire* (believe) combine in modal logic to create new, more complex textual modalities, such as *faire croire* = make believe, pretend, *faire faire* = cause one to do/make one do, etc. (The Greimasian theory of modalities is based on modal logic.)

69. Matthew 13:1–9; W. S. Kissinger, *The Parables of Jesus: A History of Interpretation and Bibliography* (Metuchen, N.J.: Scarecrow Press, 1979), 67–71; C. H. Dodd, *The Parables of the Kingdom* (Glasgow: William Collins, 1961), 13–40; Jülicher, *Die Gleichnisreden Jesus*, 112–119; Jonathan Culler, *Structuralist Poetics* (Ithaca: Cornell University Press and London: Kegan Paul, 1975; Louis Marin, *Le récit parabolique*, 134–199; Christian Metz, ed., *Signes et paraboles: Sémiotique et texte Évangélique* (Paris: Éditions du Seuil, 1977), 213–246.

70. Vladimir Propp, *Morphology of the Folktale*, 20ff.; J. M. Foley, *The Theory of Oral Composition* (Bloomington: Indiana University Press, 1988); J. M. Foley, ed., *Oral Tradition in Literature* (Columbia, Mo.: University of Missouri Press, 1986), 103–135.

71. Rabbinic parables were used for ideological purposes. First, to preserve the rabbis' authority, and second, for theodicy.

72. Joseph B. Heinemann, *Derashot Betzibur Betekufat Hatalmud* [Public Sermons of the Talmud Period] (Jerusalem: Keter, 1974), 11ff., and "The Proem in the Aggadaic Midrashim—A Form Critical Study," in *Scripta Hierosolymitana* (Jerusalem: Magnes Press, 1971), 22:100f.

73. Daniel Boyarin, "Rhetoric and Interpretation: The Case of the Nimshal," *Prooftexts* 5 (1985): 260–270; David Stern, "Midrash and Indeterminacy," in *Critical Inquiry* 15.1 (1988): 132–161.

74. David Stern, *Parables in Midrash*, 187.

75. *Mechilta Derabbi Ishmael* on Ex. 13: 2; parallels 63; 112 n. 17.

76. Geoffrey Hartman and Sanford Budick, eds., *Midrash and Literature* (New Heaven: Yale University Press, 1986), xi.

77. E. P. Sanders, *Jesus and Judaism* (London: SCM Press, 1985), 39–40; Bradford Young, *Jesus and His Jewish Parables*, 109; David Flusser, *Yahadut Umekorot Hanatsrut*, 30–56.

78. Heinemann, "The Proem in the Aggadaic Midrashim," 21ff. and idem, "The Nature of Aggadah," in *Midrash and Literature*, 41–55.

79. Daniel Boyarin, "Rhetoric and Interpretation: The Case of the Nimshal," *Prooftexts* 5 (1985): 260–270; Geoffrey Hartman, "The Struggle for the Text," in *Midrash and Literature*, 4–17; David Stern, "Moses-cide: Midrash and Contemporary Literary Criticism." *Prooftexts* 4.2 (1984): 193–204, and "Midrash and Indeterminacy," *Critical Inquiry* 15.1 (1988): 132–161.

80. Geoffrey Hartman, "The Struggle for the Text," *Midrash and Literature*, 12; Stern, *Parables in Midrash*, 146–147.

81. Daniel Patte, "Structural Analysis of the Parable of the Prodigal Son," *Semiology and Parables* (Pittsburgh, Penn.: The Pickwick Press, 1976), 71–150; Metz, ed., *Signes et paraboles: Sémiotique et texte Évangélique*; Marin, *Semiology and Parables*, 189–221.

82. Ronald Williams, "The Fables in the Near East," in *A Stubborn Faith*, ed. E. C. Hobbs (Dallas: Southern Methodist University Press, 1956), 3–26;

Uriel Simon, "The Mashal of Yotham—The Fable, Its Application, and Its Narrative Framework" (in Hebrew), *Tarbiz* 34 (1964): 1–34; H. J. Blackman, *The Fable as Literature* (London: Althone Press, 1985), 81–122.

83. Williams, "The Fables in the Ancient Near East," 7–9.

84. Ibid., 5.

85. Culler, *Structuralist Poetics*, 115–128, Louis Marin, *Le récit parabolique* (Aubier Montaigne, France: Éditions du Cerf, 1974), 216–256; George Lakoff, *Metaphors We Live By* (Chicago: University of Chicago Press, 1980), 13–69.

86. Frank Kermode, *The Genesis of Secrecy: On the Interpretation of Narrative* (Cambridge: Harvard University Press, 1979); Gerald Prince, "Introduction to the Study of the Narratee," in *Reader-Response Criticism*, ed. Jane P. Tompkins (Baltimore: John Hopkins University Press, 1980), 7–25; Wolfgang Iser, *The Implied Reader* (Baltimore: John Hopkins University Press, 1974); Naomi Shor "Fiction as Interpretation/Interpretation as Fiction," in *The Reader in the Text*, ed. Susan Rubin Suleiman and I. Crosman (Princeton: Princeton University Press, 1980), 165–181.

87. Stern, *Parables in Midrash*, 5.

88. Rabbinic anthropomorphic efforts tend to be mainly toward "humanization" of God.

89. Hesiod, "Nightingale and the Hawk," in *The Poems of Hesiod*, trans. R. M. Frazer (Norman: Oklahoma University Press, 1983), 105. This earliest fable appears in a larger text and is vastly distinct from a parable. We may use it to illustrate the distinction between a fable and parable.

90. John Whitman, *Allegory: The Dynamic of an Ancient and Medieval Technology* (Oxford: Clarendon Press, 1987), 2–10 and 265–267.

91. James C. Little, and B. D. Glasgow, "Parable Research in the Twentieth Century," *The Expository Times* 87 (1976): 356–360, and 88 (1977): 40–44, 71–75; David Flusser, *Yahadut Umekorot Hanatsrut*, 157. Flusser agrees with Jülicher, Jeremias, and Dodd, who claim that parables are not allegorical stories even though they contain allegorization.

92. This idea originated with Paul Fiebig and Jülicher who use the categorization according to Aristotle. See Aristotle's *Rhetoric*, 2.20–3.4.

93. Paul Ricoeur, *La métaphore vive* (Paris: Éditions du Seuil, 1975), 9. Ricoeaur calls it a "dédoublement" (doubling).

94. Paul de Man, "The Rhetoric of Temporality," in *Interpretation Theory and Practice* (Baltimore: The John Hopkins Press, 1969), 190–191; Jaques Lacan, *The Language of the Self: The Function of Language in Psychoanalysis*, trans. Anthony Wilden (Baltimore: The John Hopkins University Press, 1968), 189–234.

95. Claude Chabrol, "Question sur la parabole," in *Le récit évangelique: Pour une théorie du texte parabolique*, ed. Louis Marin (Paris: Édition du Cerf, 1967), 165–192; also see Noam Chomsky, *Aspects of the Theory of Syntax* (Cambridge: Harvard University Press, 1965), 89–136.

96. Cf. Strawson, "On Referring," *Mind* 59.235 (1950): 326–327. "To give the meaning of an expression is to give general directions for its use in making true or false assertions."

97. Marin, *Le récit parabolique*, 216. Marin argues that a reader filters through the parable's codic net, and defines his position in relation to it.

98. Sigmund Freud, "The Unconscious," in *Traumdeutung*, in *The Standard Edition of the Complete Psychological Works*, trans. and eds. James Strachey and A. Tyson (London: Hogarth, 1974), 14:167, and Sigmund Freud, *The Interpretation of Dreams*, in *The Complete Works*, 4:134–162, and 5:175–180 and 350–382.

99. Freud, *The Interpretation of Dreams*, in *The Complete Works*, 4:350–383.

100. Freud, "Die Traumenstellung," *The Complete Works*, 4:152 n. 1.

101. Jacques Lacan, *Écrits* (Paris: Éditions du Seuil, 1966), 94–99.

102. Ibid., 301.

103. This is a notion of "wound" different from the "wound of femininity," suggestive of the female body or "feminization" and implied in castration. See Sigmund Freud, *Medusa's Head*, in *The Complete Works*, vols. 27–28 (1922); Anne Golomb-Hoffman, *Between Exile and Return* (Albany: State University of New York Press, 1991), 158–159.

104. Jacques Lacan, *Écrits*, 201–217. He claims that the *foreclosure (Verwerfung)* of the signifier, at the calling of the Name-of-the-Father, leaves a void in the place of the phallic signification in the Other.

105. Ibid., 219.

106. Ferdinand de Saussure, *Course in General Linguistics*, ed. C. Bally, A. Sechehaye, and A. Reidlinger, trans. Wade Baskin (New York: McGraw-Hill, 1966), 156–167; Charles S. Pierce, *The Collected Papers* (Cambridge: Harvard University Press, 1960).

107. Aristotle, *The Poetics*, trans. Hamilton Fyfe (Cambridge, Mass: Harvard University Press, 1927), 23:49–58.

108. Michel Foucault, *Madness and Civilization: A History of Insanity in the Age of Reason*, trans. Richard Howard (New York: Vintage, 1965), 126–127. "Language may refer to nothing in nature."

109. Cynthia Ozick, "S. Y. Agnon and the First Religion," in *Metaphor and Memory* (New York: Knopf, 1989), 265 and 285. In equating the equal with the unequal, metaphor interprets memory.

110. Friedreich Nietzsche, *The Birth of Tragedy and the Genealogy of Morals*, trans. F. Golffing (New York: Doubleday, 1987), 67–89; see also trans. and ed. Geoffrey Clive (New York: New American Library, 1965), 501–511.

111. A *Tanna* (pl. *Tanna'im*) is a teacher, the Aramaic equivalent to the Hebrew *Shannah*, "to repeat." The Tannaic period ends with Rabbi Judah the Prince and the codification of the Mishnah, at about 200 C.E.

112. *Mishnah, Ḳiddushin* 40b.

113. Ludwig Wittgenstein, *Tractatus Logico-Philosophicus*, trans. G. E. M. Anscombe (Oxford: Basil Blackwell, 1963), 5–61. "That which expresses *itself* in language, *we* cannot express *by* language, one must 'climb out' beyond the explicit language, to the non-explicit language, beyond the limits of the world, the horizon."

114. Edmond Jabès, *Le livre des questions* (Paris: Gallimard, 1963), 12; *The Book of Questions*, trans. Rosmarie Waldrop (Middletown, Conn.: Wesleyan University Press), 16.

115. E. Levinas, *Quatre lectures Talmudiques* (Paris: Les Éditions de Minuit, 1968), 74, 94, and 116. "The temptation of temptations is the temptation for knowledge, which leaves us pure."

116. Moshe Idel, *Kabbalah: New Perspectives* (New Haven: Yale University Press, 1988), 226–230; Gershom Scholem, *Major Trends in Jewish Mysticism* (New York: Schocken Books, 1954), 163–170, and *Kabbalah* (New York: Schocken Books, 1974), 212–230.

117. Maimonides, *The Guide of the Perplexed (Dalalat al-ha'irin)*, trans. Shlomo Pines, introd. Leo Strauss (Chicago: University of Chicago Press, 1963); Bahya Ibn Pequdah, *The Duties of the Heart* (my trans. from the Arabic title), ca. 1180.

118. Maimonides, *The Guide for the Perplexed*, part III, ch. 51.

119. Gershon Shaked, *Hasipporet ha'ivrit 1880–1970*, vol. 1 (Tel Aviv: Ktav, 1977), 283–303; Gershon Shaked, "Midrash and Narrative: Agnon's Agunot," in *Midrash and Literature*, 285–303. Shaked claims that Agnon, the self-proclaimed heir to the "poets of the Temple, writes works that extend the continuum of sacred literature, even while these new works stand in direct contradiction to it." Agnon's intertextuality is of *aginut* (he who lost the rightful partner and place). By actualizing "the holy paradigm," he creates a story of frustrated love *which profanes the sacred and sanctifies the profane* (my emphasis).

120. Myrna Solotoravsky, "The Model of Midrash and Borges's Interpretative Tales and Essays," in *Midrash and Literature*, 262–268. Borges's work is "possessed by a strange demon of rapprochement"; his parables are "the denial of the possibility of such text that includes the last word of the message since it designates the incessant reference from one word to another."

121. Gershom Scholem, *Major Trends in Jewish Mysticism* (New York: Schocken Books, 1954), 123. Scholem tells the story of the chassid who in old days knew the words, the tune, and the melody of the transmitted song and the place where it could be learned. The next generation knew only the tune, the place, and the melody. And so, until in modern times they just hum to themselves a melody. The point of connection is that of ancient parables we now have only the form and the transmissibility.

122. Gila Safran Naveh, "Semiotic Considerations of 'The Imperial Message': Truth and Chronotopicity in Kafka's Parable," *Semiotics* 8.1 (1987): 165–175.

123. Jonathan Culler, *Structuralist Poetics* (Ithaca: Cornell University Press, and London: Kegan Paul, 1975), 227; S. Sandbank, "Parable and Theme: Kafka and American Fiction," in *Comparative Literature*, 37.3 (1985): 252–268.

124. Gila Safran Naveh, unpublished thesis, "Semiotic of Parable: Implosive Rhetoric and Pseudo-Displacement" (University of California, San Diego, 1981), 121. I call the infatuation with form the malaise of the end of the millennium.

125. Walter Benjamin, "Some Reflections on Kafka," in *Illuminations*, ed. Hannah Arendt, trans. H. Zohn (New York: Schocken Books, 1969), 143–144; Shimon Sandbank, "Parable and Theme: Kafka and American Fiction," *Com-*

parative Literature 37.3 (1985): 252–268; "Structures of Paradox in Kafka," *Modern Language Quarterly* (1967): 462–472.

126. Joseph Dan, *Hasippur hahasidi* [The Hasidic Tale] (Jerusalem: Keter, 1969); "Midrash and the Dawn of Kabbalah." In *Midrash and Literature,* 127–141; Gershom Scholem, *Origins of the Kabbalah*, trans. Allan Arkush, ed. R. J. Z. Werblowsky (Princeton: Princeton University Press, 1987), 49–198. Scholem explains how the early kabbalistic text uses the rabbinic parable to express gnostic doctrines.

127. Genesis 6:9–11:32, *Zohar*, vol. I, 64a.

128. Numbers 24:35. The Hebrew for "gathering" is *Atsereth* and indicates the gathering of all blessings, from which no other nation draws sustenance save Israel.

129. Jacques Derrida, "La mythologie blanche," in *Marge de la philosophie* (Paris: Éditions de Minuit, 1972), 249–277. He indicates that the theory of metaphor remains a theory of meaning (*une théorie du sense*), and presupposes that a certain original naturalness (*naturalité originnaire*) belongs to the trope. He cautions us not to forget that the original gesture of metaphorization was of "effacing the element" and replacing it with a "coined metaphor."

130. Stern, *Parables in Midrash*, 129.

131. Robert Funk, *Jesus as Precursor* (Philadelphia: Fortress Press, and Missoula, Montana: Scholars Press, 1975), 4; see also idem, "The Parable as Metaphor," in *Language, Hermeneutic, and Words of God* (New York: Harper & Row, 1966).

132. Shimon Sandbank, "Parable and Theme: Kafka and American Fiction," *Comparative Literature* 37.3 (1985): 255; Max Brod, *Franz Kafka: A Biography*, trans. G. H. Humphreys and R. Winston (New York: Schocken Books, 1963); Kafka, *The Diaries 1914–1923*, ed. Max Brod (New York: Schocken Books, 1949), entry for January 19, 1915, 109.

133. Umberto Eco, "On Symbol," in *Frontiers in Semiotics*, ed. J. Deely et al., with a foreword by Thomas Sebeok (Bloomington: Indiana University Press, 1982), 180.

134. Edmond Jabès, *Le livre des questions*, 53; *The Book of Questions*, trans. Rosmarie Waldrop (Middletown, Conn.: Wesleyan University Press, 1977), 33.

135. See note 108.

CHAPTER 2. BIBLICAL PARABLES

1. Jacques Derrida, *La dissémination*, trans. Barbara Johnson (Chicago: University of Chicago Press, 1981), 128.

2. Joshua Guttmann, "The Ewe Lamb," *Beth Mikra* 18–19. 3/4 (1964): 4–20; Uriel Simon, "The Poor Man's Ewe-Lamb: An Example of Juridical Parable," *Biblica* 48 (1967): 207–242.

3. 1 Samuel 16, 18.

4. 2 Samuel 5.

5. 1 Samuel 16:12.

6. Vladimir Propp, *The Morphology of the Folktale*, 12–45.

7. 2 Samuel 11:1.

8. 2 Samuel 11:1.

9. 2 Samuel 15:4.

10. Simon, "The Poor Man's Ewe-Lamb," 207–242; Joshua Guttmann, "The Ewe Lamb," *Beth Mikva* 18–19.7 (1964): 211. Guttmann compares Batsheva with the Susannah (Apocrypha). She took great pain to be seen by the man she wanted.

11. We do not know whether her father's name is in fact Israelite or not. Conversation with Professor Steven Bowman, at the University of Cincinnati, 12 October 1994. Bowman suggested that the name is not Hebrew; Batsheva, or Batshua, could have been a Jebusite, or a Western Semitic name.

12. 2 Samuel 11:2.

13. Joshua Guttmann, "The Ewe Lamb," 211. He suggests that David takes Batsheva during her menses; see Joseph Caro, "Niddah," in *Shulkhan Arukh*, vol. 4, trans. Hyman Goldin (New York: Hebrew Publ. Co, 1961), 21–24 and 31b.

14. Deuteronomy 24:6, 15.

15. 1 Samuel 11:4.

16. Gesenius, *Gesenius Hebrew Grammar*, trans. T. J. Conant (New York: Appleton & Co, 1853), 121, 141.

17. 2 Samuel 11:1.

18. 2 Samuel 11:8.

19. J. Pedersen, *Israel: Its Life and Culture* (London: Oxford University Press, 1959), 8–11; Gerhard Von Rad, *Old Testament Theology*, trans. D. Stalker (New York: Harper, 1962), 11–18.

20. 2 Samuel 11:12.

21. 1 Samuel 21:4–5. Abstinence was required of soldiers by religious sanctions.

22. 2 Samuel: 3:17. "The Lord promised David saying, 'By the hand of my servant David I will save my people Israel from the hands of the Philistines, and from the hand of all other enemies.'" Yehoshua Guttmann, "The Ewe Lamb," in *The Bulletin of the Israel Society for Biblical Studies* and *The World Jewish Bible Society* 18–19.3/4 (1964): 4–20.

23. 2 Samuel 11:15. "In the morning David wrote a letter to Jo'ab, and sent it by hand of Uri'ah. In this letter he wrote, 'Set Uri'ah in the forefront of the hardest fighting, and then draw back from him, that he may be struck down and die'."

24. Guttmann, "The Ewe Lamb," 14–16; Simon, "The Poor Man's Ewe-Lamb: An Example of Juridical Parable," 227–242.

25. Simon, "The Poor Man's Ewe Lamb," 220–222; Josephus, *Antiquities*, ed. and trans. H. J. Thackeray (Oxford: Oxford University Press, 1959), 7.6.1.

26. 2 Samuel 11:21. "Your servant Uri'ah is dead also."

27. David has sons from six other wives, so one needs to read further in the text of 1 Kings to understand the intricate palace fights and intrigues that force him to opt for Batsheva's son.

28. Susan Rubin Suleiman, "Writing and Motherhood," *The (M)Other Tongue: Essays in Feminist Psychoanalytic Interpretation*, ed. Shirley Nelson

Garner and Claire Kahane (Ithaca: Cornell University Pres, 1976), 367. And see Ita Sheres, *Dinah's Rebellion: A Biblical Parable for Our Times* (New York: Crossroad, 1990), 12–70; Alice Jardine, *Gynesis: Configuration of Woman and Modernity* (Ithaca: Cornell University Press, 1985).

29. David Biale, *Power and Powerlessness in Jewish History* (New York: Schocken, 1987); Louis Ginsberg, *The Legends of the Jews*, 7 vols. (Philadelphia: The Jewish Publication Society, 1968).

30. 1 Kings 1:17–31.

31. 2 Samuel 28:29.

32. 2 Samuel 17.

33. Luce Irigaray, *Ce sexe qui n'en est pas un* [This Sex Which Is Not One] (Paris: Editions de Minuit, 1976); Jardine, *Gynesis*; Ita Sheres, *Dinah's Rebellion: A Parable for our Times*. These authors show that women have been defined as the "alien" and the "other" that must be dominated.

34. Josephus, *Antiquities*, 7.6.1–8.

35. Genesis 22:6.

36. M. Zucker, "Towards the Solution of the Problem of the 32 Middot (about the Logical, the Poetic, and Rhetorical Devices): 'The Mishnat R. Eliezer,'" *The Proceedings of the American Academy for Jewish Research* 21–23 (1954): 5–39.

37. Deuteronomy 24:6, 15.

38. Simon, "The Poor Man's Ewe Lamb," 221; see Isaiah 5:1–7, Jeremiah 3:1–5, 1 Kings 20:35–43.

39. 2 Samuel 11:27.

40. 2 Samuel 12:1.

41. 1 Samuel 12:7.

42. 1 Samuel 10:1–3.

43. 1 Samuel 16:1–14.

44. 2 Samuel 12:13.

45. Jacques Lacan, "Les écrits techniques," in *Les séminaires livre I* (Paris: Éditions du Seuil, 1975), 255–256. "Truth, lie and other registers enter language through the word, in ambiguous back-planes, which go "beyond the literal is found in its *mimicry, its cramps, and agitations* [my emphasis], in all the emotional correlations of the word."

46. 2 Samuel 12:10–14.

47. Exodus 21:23–25; Leviticus 24:23–25; Deuteronomy 19:21. When evil is done, the same kind of evil will come to the evil doer.

48. 2 Samuel 12:17.

49. 2 Samuel 12:22.

50. 1 Samuel 18:23.

51. Simon, "The Poor Man's Ewe Lamb," 239. Simon claims that King David humiliates himself; humbling himself is a form of lowering oneself beyond resignation.

52. Sigmund Freud, *Traumdeutung*, trans. James Strachey (New York: Basic Books, 1955), 46.

53. Jacques Lacan, *The Function of Language in Psychoanalysis*, trans. Anthony Wilden (Baltimore: John Hopkins University Press, 1968), 46–78.

54. Jacques Lacan, "Subversion du sujet et dialectique du désir dans l'inconscient freudien," in *Écrits* (Paris: Éditions du Seuil, 1966), 793–827; idem, *The Language of the Self*, 31–38; Shoshana Feldman, *Jacques Lacan and the Adventure of Insight* (Cambridge: Harvard University Press, 1987), 112; Shoshana Felman, *Literature and Psychoanalysis: The Question of Reading Otherwise* (Baltimore: John Hopkins University Press, 1982), 418. "The unconscious memory trace, or signifier in Lacan's terminology, is inscribed only *with* the loss of the real object. The object that causes desire is primarily lost, and the signifier, connected in that way to the body, marks its disappearance. Desire arises from this pure loss and is what traverses the gap or space that separates the metonymically linked signifiers in the unconscious."

55. Jacques Lacan, "Seminaire á propos du *désir*," École Freudienne de Paris, Paris, 1966.

56. Luce Irigaray, "Commodities among Themselves," in *Ce sexe qui n'en est pas un* [This Sex Which Is Not One], 31 and 192–197. Irigaray claims that women are marked phallically by their fathers, husbands, procurers; Fredric Jameson, "Postmodernism: The Cultural Logic of Late Capitalism," *New Left Review* 146 (1984): 53–93.

57. Luce Irigaray, *The Speculum of the Other Woman*, trans. Gillian Gill (Ithaca: Cornell University Press, 1985), 177–180; Luce Irigaray, "Towards the Hysterical Body: J. Lacan and His Others," in *Gynesis: Configuration of Woman and Modernity*, 159–177.

58. Yael Feldman, "Biblical Gender Roles and Freud's Jewishness," lecture, the University of Cincinnati, 16 October 1992. Feldman contends that the Bible narrativizes androcentrically its characters.

59. Jacques Lacan, "Seminar on the 'Purloined Letter'," in *The Purloined Poe: Lacan, Derrida and Psychoanalysis*, trans. Jeffrey Mehlman, ed. J. Muller and W. Richardson (Baltimore: John Hopkins University Press, 1988), 34–78. In a phallocentric economy, the "phallus" symbolizes to a larger extent and in the first place the penis.

60. Susan Rubin Sulleiman, "Writing and Motherhood," in *The (M)Other Tongue*, 353.

61. 2 Samuel 11:2–6.

62. Lacan, *Le séminaire*, 256–264.

63. Gila Safran Naveh, "Ideological Aesthetics and Meta-Modalization: Semiotics of Descartes's *Passions of the Soul*," *The American Journal of Semiotics* 5.3–4 (1987): 479–491, and "Semiotic Considerations of an Imperial Message: Truth and Chronotopicity in Kafka's Parable," *Semiotics* 8 (1989): 165–175.

64. Algirdas Greimas, *Sémiotique des passions* (Paris: Editions du Seuil, 1991), 21–45; idem, *Du sense* (Paris: Éditions du Seuil, 1970); idem, *Maupassant: La sémiotique du texte, éxercices pratiques* (Paris: Éditions du Seuil, 1976); idem, "Pour une théorie des modalités," *Language* 43.2 (1978): 37–49.

65. Umberto Eco, "'Latratus Canis' or: The Dog's Barking," in *Frontier in Semiotics*, ed. John Deely (Bloomington: Indiana University Press, 1982), 63–73.

66. The notation ATT = attribute, ERG = ergative, ACC = accusative, DAT = dative, LOC = locative, BEN = benefactive, RES = resultative, FIN = final, INS = instrumental. Modalizations affect the cognitive and the pragmatic

dimensions of discourse. These are further projected on the *thymic* (*thymos* = soul mind) dimension, which is posited outside of narrative syntax, pragmatics or cognitive narrative, and defined by the vacillation of the subject between states of euphoria and dysphoria as a result of pathemic processes, or the subject's pathemic role.

67. Judges 19:9.

68. François Rastiers, "Systématique des isotopies," in *Essays de sémiotique poétique*, ed. A. J. Greimas (Paris: Larousse, 1972), 149; idem, *Sens et textualité* (Paris: Hachette, 1989), 103; Ferdinand de Saussure, *Course in General Linguistics*, ed. C. Bally, A. Sechehaye, and A. Reidlinger, trans. Wade Baskin (New York: McGraw-Hill, 1966).

69. Rastier, *Sens et textualité*, 103.

70. Araf-el-Aref, *The Bedouin Tribes in the District of Beersheva*, trans. M. Kapeliuk (Tel Aviv: Keter, 1958), 66–67. The information about the Zerkha and the special treatment of some animals in the herd, cf. G.W. Murray, *Sons of Ishmael: A Study of the Egyptian Bedouin* (New York: Humanities Press, 1950), 60; and see Emmanuel Marx, *Bedouins of the Negev* (Manchester: Manchester University Press, 1967).

71. 2 Samuel 1:6.

72. C. J. Filmore, "Pragmatics and the Description of Discourse," in *Radical Pragmatics*, ed. Cole (New York: Academic Press, 1981), 143–166; G. Gazdar, *Pragmatics: Implicature Presupposition and Logical Form* (New York: Academic Press, 1979), 56–80; H. P. Grice, "Logic and Conversation," in *Pragmatics*, ed. Cole and Morgan (New York: Academic Press, 1975), 41–58; R. Montague, "Pragmatics," in *Contemporary Philosophy*, ed. R. Klibansky (Florence: La Nova Italia, 1968), 102–121; P. Werth, *Conversation and Discourse* (New York: St. Martin's Press, 1981); L. Karttunen, "Presuppositions of Compound Sentences," *Linguistic Inquiry* 4 (1973): 169–193.

73. Gila Safran Naveh, "Although Thou Speakest in My Tongue, I Understand Thee Not: The Pragmatics of Communication in Eminescu's 'Luceafarul,'" paper presented at the Modern Language Association, December 1985.

74. Edmond Jabès, *Le livre des questions*, 24.

CHAPTER 3. SYNOPTIC GOSPEL PARABLES

1. Dan O. Via, *The Parables: Their Literary and Existential Dimension* (Philadelphia: Fortress Press, 1967), 70.

2. Wittgenstein, *Tractatus Logico-Philosophicus*, trans. G. E. M. Anscombe (Oxford: Basil Blackwell, 1963), 60–61: "The limits of language are the limits of the world but this *cannot be demonstrated* [my emphasis]. To understand the logic of explicit language we must go beyond it, to non-explicit language." Robert Funk, *Parables and Presence* (Philadelphia: Fortress Press, 1982), 67–79.

3. Asher Feldman, *The Parables and the Similes of the Rabbis* (Cambridge: Cambridge University Press, 1924), 227–230.

4. The consolidation of Christianity takes place against the backdrop of brutal Roman ruling and fierce fighting among Jewish religious factions.

5. Northrop Frye, *Anatomy of Criticism: Theory of Genre* (Princeton: Princeton University Press, 1973), 79–116 and 152–155. Frye categorizes narratives into high and low mimetic modes (*mimesis,* imitation of life and action); Aristotle's *Poetics* 1.4.6.

6. Eric Auerbach, *Mimesis* (Princeton: Princeton University Press, 1974), 29 and 131–136.

7. Jeremias, *The Parables of Jesus,* 20–23. He agrees with Cadoux, and claims that we owe to Jülicher the final discarding of the allegorical method of interpretation. D. H. Dodd, *The Parables of the Kingdom* (Glasgow: William Collins Sons and Company, 1961), 40–51; Dan Via, *The Parables: Their Literary and Existential Dimension,* 14–35; Northop Frye, *Anatomy of Criticism,* 116–154; René Wellek, *Theory of Literature* (New York: Harcourt, Brace and World, 1956), 14–15 and 206–207.

8. James Little, "Parable Research in the Twentieth Century," in *The Expository Times* 87 (1976): 356–360, and 88 (1977): 40–44 and 71–75; C. H. Dodd, *The Parables of the Kingdom,* 23–45; Joachim Jeremias, *The Parables of Jesus,* 18–35; Adolph Jülicher, *Die Gleichnisreden Jesus,* 23–29; David Flusser, *Yahadut Umekorot Hanatsrut,* 136–147; T. Guttmann, *Hamashal Bitkufat Hatannaim* [The Parable in the Time of the Tannaim] (Jerusalem: Magden, 1949), 13–24.

9. K. Y. Kutscher, *Hebrew and Aramaic Studies* (Jerusalem: Israel Exploration Society, 1975), 27–65; E. A. Abott, *The Corrections of St. Mark* (London: Adam and Clark Black, 1901), 307–325; Haim Rabin, "Hebrew and Aramaic in the First Century," *The Jewish People in the First Century,* 1007–1139; G. Dalman, *The Words of Jesus* (Edinburgh: T. and T. Clark, 1902); idem, *Jesus Joshua* (New York: Ktav reprint, 1971).

10. Jeremias, *The Parables of Jesus,* 40–68.

11. Flusser, *Yahadut Umekorot Hanatsrut,* 67–80. He indicates a Semitic "Urevagelicum," this verifies what we call a "hebraiadi dialekto" proposed by Eusebius, *Ecclesiastical History,* 3.39 (Loeb vol. 1, 296).

12. Jeremias, *The Parables of Jesus,* 94–95. He suggests fusions of two parables into one: The Parable of the Great Supper (Matthew 22:1–14), of uninvited guests must have fused with a Parable of the Wedding Garment.

13. David Flusser, *Hamekorot . . .* [Jewish Sources in Early Christianity], 150; Jakob Petuchovsky, "The Theological Significance of the Parables in Rabbinic Literature and in the New Testament," in *Christian News from Israel* 2.10 (1972): 76–86.

14. Jehoshua Grinz, "Hebrew as the Spoken Language of the Second Temple," in *The Journal of Biblical Literature* 79 (1960): 32–47; Emil Schürer, *The History of the Jewish People in the Age of Jesus Christ,* rev. and ed. Geza Vermes, F. Miller, and Matthew Black (Edinburgh: T. and T. Clark, 1974–79), 2:20–28; David Flusser, *Judaism and the Origins of Christianity* (Jerusalem: Magnes, 1989), cf. Bradford Young, *Jesus and His Jewish Parables,* 163 n. 67: "It was highly doubtful that the words of Jesus, considered sacred to his disciples, would have been preserved in Aramaic rather than Hebrew."

15. Eusebius, *Ecclesiastical History;* A. Huck, *Synopsis of the First Three Gospels* (Oxford: Oxford Univesity Press, 1968), vii.

16. Matthew 22:1, Mark 4:1.

17. Matthew 7:3–5, Luke 6:43–45, Matthew 13:31–33, Mark 4:30–32, Matthew 18:21–35.

18. L. Langer, *The Holocaust and the Literary Imagination* (New Haven: Yale University Press, 1975), 287; Alvin Rosenfeld, *A Double Dying: Reflections on Holocaust Literature* (Bloomington: Indiana University Press, 1980). Survivors of the Holocaust are seized by a desire to retell the events that have changed their lives and all the accounts, even conflicting ones, are kept side by side. A paradoxical situation is created between the need to keep alive the voices and the memory of those who fell victims and faltering memory and the need to shroud the unspeakable in silence. Refer also to Elie Wiesel, *Night* (New York: Bantam Press, 1982); Jerzy Kosinski, *The Painted Bird* (New York: Bantam Press, 1965); Primo Levi, *Survival in Auschwitz* (New York: Collier Press, 1958).

19. Claude Lévi-Strauss, *Tristes tropiques* (Paris: Plon, 1955); Sigmund Freud, *Civilization and Its Discontents, Moses and Monotheism* in *The Standard Edition of the Complete Psychological Works*, trans. and ed. James Strachey, with A. Freud, A. Strachey, and A. Tyson (London: Hogarth, 1928–29), vols. 21–22.

20. Gershom Scholem, *The Messianic Idea in Judaism and Other Essays on Jewish Spirituality* (New York: Schocken Books, 1971), 285–290. To Scholem, tradition itself is a revisional process in which any claims of fidelity to prior texts are made for interpretations of great originality.

21. Golomb Hoffman, *Between Exile and Return*, 106.

22. J. Derrida, *Of Grammatology*, trans. Gayatri Spivak (Baltimore: John Hopkins University Press, 1976), 136.

23. L. Lindsey, *A Hebrew Translation of the Gospel of Mark* (Jerusalem: Dugith Press, 1973), xiv and 19–25, 30–35. B. H. Streecher, *The Four Gospels a Study of Origins* (London: Macmillan Press, 1953), 145–156; T. Stephenson, "The Overlapping of Sources in Matthew and Luke," *The Journal of Theological Studies* 21 (1920): 128–32; Birger Gerhardson, *Memory and Manuscript: Oral Tradition and Written Transmission in Rabbinic Judaism and Early Christianity* (Lund, Sweden: G. W. K. Gleerap, 1964). And see Luke 4:16–30, Mark 6:1–6, Matthew 13:53–58 or Mark 7:24–30, Matthew 15:21–28.

24. Stern, *Parables in the Midrash*, 205. Stern says that they meant just a "nod to the disciples, to tell them that they are among the elect."

25. Matthew 13:35.

26. Compare Isaiah 42:1–25 with Isaiah 35:5–6:

> Then the eyes of the blind shall be opened,
> And the ears of the deaf shall be unstopped.
> Then shall the lame man leap as a hart,
> And the tongue of the dumb shall sing:
> For in the wilderness shall water break out in the desert.

27. Mark 4:11–14.

28. Friedreich Nietzsche, *The Joyful Wisdom*, trans. Thomas Common (Edinburgh: Foulis, 1910), 134; Jacques Derrida, "La mythologie blanche," in *Marge de la philosophie* (Paris: Éditions de Minuit, 1972), 249–251.

29. J. L. Austin, *How to Do Things with Words* (Cambridge: Harvard University Press, 1961), 68–97. Austin claims that the signified supersedes the statement in the case of the utterance "I promise." The "sui-referential" property of the "enoncé performatif" is a trap because it produces the illusion of referentiality by statements that are auto-referential by definition. See also John Searle, *Speech Acts* (Cambridge: Harvard University Press, 1969).

30. Friedrich Nietzsche, *The Birth of Tragedy and the Genealogy of Morals*, trans. F. Golffing (New York: Doubleday, 1987), 508.

31. Friedrich Nietzsche, "Truth and Falsity in an Ultramoral Sense," in *The Philosopy of Nietzsche*, trans. and intro. G. Clive (New York: Mentor Books, 1965), 503, 508.

32. Jacques Derrida, *La mytologie blanche*, 253–260. "Une mythologie blanche inscrite à l'encre blanche invisible et recouvrant dans le palimseste." Since metaphor is defined as the trope of resemblance between a signified and a signifier, and between two signs, one designating the other, metaphor should be placed next to fables, myth, and analogies.

33. F. Nietzsche, *The Birth of Tragedy and the Genealogy of Morals*, 509–515.

34. "The Parable of the Mustard Seed," and "The Leaven" (Matthew 13:31–33, Mark 4:30–32, Luke 13:18–21) illustrate the theme of gradual growth of the kingdom. See also "The Hidden Treasure," and "The Pearl of Great Price" (Matthew 13:44–46 and in Thomas, Logion 109, and 76), which introduce the Kingdom of Heaven.

Compare with the story the Amora Rabbi Johanan tells Aba bar Hiyya, *Pesikta de-Rab Kahana* 27:1, ed. B. Mandelbaum (New York: The Academic Press, 1962), 402–403.

35. Matthew 22:1–14.

36. G. Dalman, *The Words of Jesus* (Edinburgh: T. and T. Clark, 1902), 92–94; Bradford Young, *Jesus and His Jewish Parables*, 196. He claims that "in contrast to Jewish apocalyptic, the term kingdom of heaven occurs quite frequently in the synoptic gospels and expresses a well-defined concept."

37. Luke 14:24.

38. Matthew 22:9–10.

39. Luke 14:7–8.

40. Luke 14:19.

41. Luke 14:20.

42. Luke 14:21.

43. Conversations with Prof. Ben Zion Wacholder, the scholar of *The Dead Sea Scrolls*. He pointed out that the priesthood in the Qumran remorselessly excluded the maimed, the lame, and other physically handicapped.

44. 2 Samuel 5:8.

45. Matthew 22:7.

46. N. Avigad, *Discovering Jerusalem* (Jerusalem: Exploration Society, 1980), 120–123; Thomas Idinopulos, *Jerusalem Blessed, Jerusalem Cursed: Jews Christians and Muslims in the City* (Chicago: University of Chicago Press, 1991); John A. T. Robinson (*Redating the New Testament* (London: SCM Press, 1978), 19–22; see Bradford Young, *Jesus and His Jewish Parables*, 185 n. 24.

47. Matthew 22:10.

48. Luke 16:10–12; *Exodus Rabbah* 2:324, ed. Shenan, vol. 1, 106–107; A. Harnack *The Sayings of Jesus* (New York: Williams and Norgate, 1908); M. Dibelius, *From Tradition to Gospel* (New York: Scribner's, 1934).

49. Moshe Davis, "Palestinian Judaism in the First Century," in *Israel: Its Role in Civilization,* ed. Moshe Davis (New York: The Jewish Theological Seminary of America, 1956), 67–81.

50. V = Vouloir/Want to do; F = Faire/Do. The Gremasian taxonomy is also used in modal logic. See also Alan White, *Modal Thinking* (Ithaca: Cornell University Press, 1975), 34–50; Georg von Wright, *An Essay in Modal Logic* (Amsterdam: North Holland Publishing, 1951), 43–78.

51. The code of dress and cleanliness had to be obeyed. See b. Shabbat 153a, Ecclesiastes Rabbah 9:7 and *Semachot Derabbi Hiyyah* 2:1, Higger 216f.

52. Matthew 11:16, 20:13, 22:12.

53. Dan Via, *The Parables of Jesus,* 130–131.

54. Gerald Prince, "Introduction to the Study of the Narratee," in *Reader-Response Criticism,* ed. Jane Tompkins (Baltimore: John Hopkins University Press, 1980), 5–25; Iser, *The Implied Reader.*

55. Propp, *The Morphology of the Folktale,* 12–47.

56. Lacan, *The Language of the Self,* 35–36.

57. Martin Heidegger, *Being and Time,* trans. J. Macquarrie and E. Robinson (London: SCM Press, 1962), 211–213.

58. Funk, *Parable and Presence,* 176.

CHAPTER 4. RABBINICAL PARABLES

1. The legal and homiletic midrashim are called respectively *midrash halakhah* and *midrash aggadah.*

2. José Faur, *Golden Doves with Silver Dots* (Bloomington: Indiana University Press, 1986), 121. Faur claims that "by excluding the vowels from the text of Scriptures, Hebrew tradition was in fact excluding one semiotic reading."

3. Ibid., 120–123.

4. Ibid., 121.

5. Ibid., 123.

6. Susan Handelman, *The Slayers of Moses: The Emergence of Rabbinic Interpretation in Modern Literary Theory* (Albany: State University of New York Press, 1982), 78–96.

7. Refer to Hartman and Budick, eds., *Midrash and Literature.*

8. Faur, *Golden Doves with Silver Dots,* 120–121.

9. Hartman and Budick, *Midrash and Literature,* 229.

10. Harold Bloom, *The Anxiety of Influence: A Theory of Poetry* (New York: Oxford University Press, 1973), 56–90.

11. Hartman and Budick, eds., *Midrash and Literature,* 232–233.

12. Robert Alter, *Modern Hebrew Literature* (New York: Behrman, 1975); idem, *Defenses of the Imagination: Jewish Writers and Modern Historical Crisis* (Philadelphia: The Jewish Publication Society of America, 1977); idem, *The*

Art of Biblical Narrative (New York: Basic Books, 1981); idem, *The Art of Biblical Poetry* (New York: Basic Books, 1985).

13. Robert Alter, "Old Rabbis, New Critics," in *The New Republic* 5 (12 January 1987): 30.

14. James Klugel, "Two Introductions to Midrash," in *Midrash and Literature*, 92.

15. Robert Alter's "Old Rabbis, New Critics," 27–33. Alter claims that "the Midrash operates on a paradox: its reading habits are atomistic, but what enables it is a conception of the Bible as an endlessly complex comminatory unity. He claims that in finding similarities, the Midrash harmonizes contradictions, easing tensions, seeking to make bright but distant narrative ends explicitly present in the darkest beginnings."

16. Hartman and Budick, *Midrash and Literature*, 15. "The truth claim of the Bible is so imperious that reality in its sensuous or charming aspect is not dwelt upon; the spotlight effect, which isolates major persons or happenings is due to the same anagogical demand that excludes all other places and concerns."

17. J. Heinemann, *Agadot Vetoldotehen* (Jerusalem: Keter, 1974), 1–15; J. Heinemann, *Darche Haagadah* (Jerusalem: Massada, 1970), 1–12; J. Fraenkel, *Eyunim Baolam Haruchani Shel Sipour Ha'aggadah* (Tel Aviv: HaKibbutz Hameuchad, 1971), 1–13, and 65–82.

18. Raphael Rabinovicz, *Ma'amar 'al Hadpasat ha-Talmud* [An Essay on the Printing of the Talmud] (Hebrew) (Jerusalem: Mossad Harav Kook, 1952), 14–90.

19. Heinrich Graetz, *The Structure of Jewish History and Other Essays* (New York: The Jewish Theological Seminary of America Press, 1975); Jakob J. Petuchowski, "Judaism as 'Mystery'—the Hidden Agenda?" *The Hebrew Union College Annual* 52 (1981); Thorleif Boman, *Hebrew Thought Compared with Greek* (New York: W. W. Norton, 1970); Dan Otto Via Jr., *The Parables of Jesus;* C. H. Dodd, *The Parables of the Kingdom.*

20. David Stern, *Parables in Midrash*, chapter 1 and passim.

21. I. Ziegler, *Die Königsgleichnisse des Midrasch* (Breslau: Schlesische Verlags-Anstalt, 1903), xxii–xxvi. Cf. Stern, *Parables in Midrash*, 7–24; and see Young, *Jesus and His Jewish Parables*, 27–58.

22. *Ecclesiastes Rabbah* 3.9, on 3.9, f.10a. The fragment of the verse is taken from Isaiah 50:11.

23. Isaiah 50:11.

24. George Lakoff, *Women, Fire, and Dangerous Things* (Chicago: University of Chicago Press, 1987), "Family resemblance," 12–13 and 68–90; Eleanor Rosch, "Prototype Classification and Logical Categorization: The Two Systems," in *New Trends in Cognitive Representation: Challenges to Piaget's Theory*, ed. E. Scholnick (Hillsdale, N.J.: Lawrence Erlbaum, 1989), 73–86; and see Gerald Gazdar, Ewan Klein, Geoffrey Pullman, and Ivan Sag, *Generalized Phrase-Structure Grammar* (Cambridge: Harvard University Press, 1985).

25. Julia Kristeva, *Sémiotiké, recherches pour une sémanalyse* (Paris: Éditions du Seuil, 1969), 14, 25. She first used the term "classème" to designate a morpheme with a particular semiotic function.

26. David Stern, "Midrash and the Language of Exegesis," in *Midrash and Literature*, 115.

27. A. J. Greimas, *Sémantique structurale* (Paris: Larousse, 1966), 210–241; idem, *Sémiotique des passions* (Paris: Seuil, 1991), 157–160. Greimas views the sign as a complex structural network and intermeshing of sociocultural factors and states (of affairs) at a specific historical moment, a function of change over time. Discursive transformations from one state or modality to another may cause that subject's transformation from a "passive subject" into an "acting subject." As a result of minute transformations in either of the layers of narrative, the subject may become a *sujet passioné*, an "impassioned subject," propelled into action that moves the narrative ahead. A narrative trajectory is a complex system of micro-actions and states that are themselves functions of modalization, aspectualization, and pathemization.

28. A. J. Greimas, *Sémiotique des passions*, 157. "Pathemization" or sensibilization also belongs to discursive semantics: "La patémisation peut être conçue comme une opération appartenant à la syntaxe discursive, conçue comme une instance culturelle."

29. Isaiah 50:11.

30. Georg H. von Wright, *An Essay in Modal Logic* (Amsterdam: North Holland Publishing, 1951), 1–41; Alan White, *Modal Thinking* (Ithaca: Cornell University Press, 1975), 5–189. In modal thinking, when the first sequence A is offered and accepted as true by the addressee, sequence B can also be accepted as true, because it is analogous to A. The same goes for C and D, because they are supposedly analogous to sequence A. The semantic markers establish pseudo-analogies enabling the addressor to make the textual transition from sequence A to sequence B, to sequence C.

31. Joseph Heinemann, "The Proem of the Aggadaic Midrash—Their Origin and Function" (Hebrew), in *Papers of the Fourth World Congress of Jewish Studies* (Jerusalem: World Union for Jewish Studies, 1965), 43–47; Stern, "Midrash and the Language of Exegesis," in *Midrash and Literature*, 107–109.

32. "Decree" is the modal "able to do," "able to make one do," and "want to do" (*pouvoir faire*). Semantically opposed is "should bring," which points to the deontic modality, or "having to do, act" (*devoir faire*).

33. Yuki Kuroda, "Syntactic Structures," seminar, University of California at San Diego, fall, 1976.

34.　　　　+ DO NOT WANT TO DO

I. Ae. (brings X) <————————————————> Ae.　(sleeps on X)
　　　Agent (X)　　　　　　　　　　　　　　　　Patient (X)

THEN	ALWAYS	Ar.	KING/I
THERE	EVERYWHERE	Ae.	GUESTS/THEY/YOU/SUBJECTS

　　　　　　　　　Ø
Ae (lights Y) ————————>　　　　Ae.　(walks in the light
　Agent of　　　　　　　　　　　　　of Y Patient of (Y)
　(Y)

35. 1 Samuel 2:30, Isaiah 43:7.
36. 1 Samuel 2:30.

37. Cf. *Mishnah, Seder Nezikim, Massehet Avot 4, Aleph.* See also R. Shimshom Raphael Hersh, chap. 4, *Ethics of the Fathers,* 473. In the *Ethics of the Fathers,* chap. 4:2, R. Ben Azzai says that שְׂכר מצוה מצוה שְׂכר עברה עברה, "the reward of a good deed is a good deed, and the reward of sin is sin [virtue has its own reward and sin its own penalty]," and in chap. 4:5, R. Yohanan ben Berokah commented: "Whoever profanes the name of God secretly is punished publically, whether the profanation is committed intentionally or unintentionally."

38. Isaiah 43:7.

39. Cf. *Mishnah, Seder Nezikim, Massehet Avot 6, 11.*

40. See Yuki Kuroda, *Syntactic Structures,* (Cambridge: MIT Press, 1976), 14–36; J. L. Austin, *How to Do Things with Words,* ed. F. O. Ursmsom (Cambridge: Harvard University Press, 1965), John Searle, *Speech Acts* (Cambridge: Harvard University Press, 1969); George Lakoff, *Metaphors We Live By* (Chicago: University of Chicago Press, 1980).

41. Stern, *Parables in the Midrash,* 46; Daniel Boyarin, "Rhetoric and Interpretation: The Case of the Nimshal," *Prooftexts* 5 (1985): 260–270; Peter Brooks, "Fiction of the Wolfman," *Diacritics* 9 (1979): 75–81.

42. The *nimshal,* the moral lesson, shifts from this world to the Kingdom of God. The conjoining of "lie down" with the dysphoric "in pain" is without a syntactic antecedent.

43. Paul de Man, "Semiology and Rhetoric," *Diacritics* (1975), 51, reprinted in *Allegories of Reading: Figural Language in Rousseau, Nietzsche, Rilke, Proust* (New Haven: Yale University Press, 1979); cf. D. Richter, ed., *The Critical Tradition* (New York: St. Martin's Press, 1989), 1019.

44. Noam Chomsky, *Aspects of Theory of Syntax* (Cambridge: MIT Press, 1965); François Rastier, *Interpretative Semantics* (Paris: Édition du Seuil, 1986).

45. Note the sequence of the action of the law: *he said* comes after *they said,* and *God will say* is subsequent to *they will say.*

46. De Man, "Semiology and Rhetoric," 51; cf. D. Richter, *The Critical Tradition,* 1019–1023.

47. De Man, "Semiology and Rhetoric," 51.

48. Jacques Lacan, "Seminar on the Purloined Letter," *Yale French Studies* 48 (1972), 30–32.

49. Meir Sternberg, *The Poetics of Biblical Narrative, Ideological Literature and the Drama of Reading* (Bloomington: Indiana University Press, 1985), 1–55: Jonathan Culler, *The Pursuit of Signs: Semiotics, Literature, Deconstruction* (Ithaca: Cornell University Press, 1981), 169–187. See analysis of Lacan, "Seminar of the Purloined Letter"; Derrida, "The Purloined Letter," in *The Purveyor of Truth.*

50. De Man, "Semiology and Rhetoric," 1015.

51. (A) w (B) w (C̃) ≠ D
(A) w (B) w (C̃) = D'

This is a faulty syllogism, where the propostion would lead to a conclusion other than the one which the parabolizer would like us to reach.

52. Isaiah 50:11.

CHAPTER 5. CHASSIDIC PARABLES

1. *Geonim* were distinguished pious rabbis of the eighteenth and early nineteenth centuries, whose teachings and sayings have been recorded for posterity.

2. Frank Talmage, "Apples of Gold: The Inner Meaning of the Sacred Texts in Medieval Judaism," in *Jewish Spirituality: From the Bible through the Middle Ages*, ed. Arthur Green (New York: Schoken, 1986), 311–350.

3. Samuel H. Dresner, *The Zaddik* (New York: Schocken Books, 1974), 150–225; *Shivhei Habesht* (Hebrew, 1814), in English, *In Praise of the Ba'al Shem Tov*, ed. and trans. Dan Ben Amos and Jerome R. Mintz (Bloomington: Indiana University Press, 1970); *Toledot Yaakov Yosef* [The Story of Yaakov Yosef of Polnoy] (Hebrew, 1780).

4. Jacob Kranz, *The Maggid of Dubno and His Parables*, ed. Benno Heinemann (New York: P. Feldheim, 1967), 187–206. The famous *maggid*, whose actual name was Yaakov ben Ze'ev Kranz, lived from 1741 to 1804. A *maggid* was an itinerant preacher who traveled from town to town and delivered messages of instruction and exhortation to his fellow Jews.

5. Arnold J. Band, "Folklore and Literature," in *Studies in Jewish Folklore*, ed. F. Talmage (Cambridge: Harvard University Press, 1980), 1–45; Stern, *The Parable in the Midrash*, 231–232.

6. Umberto Eco, *Theory of Semiotics*, 8. "Something actually presented to the perception of the addressee *stands for* something else, there is *signification.* . . . [C]odes are systems of signification, insofar as they couple present entities with absent units."

7. Martin Buber, *The Origins of Hasidism* (New York: Horizon Press, 1960), 12–67.

8. Ibid., 27–99.

9. Ibid., 23–45.

10. Ibid., 27–99; Arnold J. Band, "Folklore and Literature," in *Studies in Jewish Folklore*, ed. F. Talmage (Cambridge: Harvard University Press, 1980), 1–45; Heinemann, *The Maggid of Dubno*, 190–200.

11. Ibid., 3.

12. Heinemann, "Biographical Sketch," in *The Maggid of Dubno*, 3–7.

13. July and part of the month of August.

14. A part of the month of August.

15. Isaiah 66:10.

16. Psalms 126:5.

17. Heinemann, *The Maggid of Dubno*, 14–16.

18. Jeremiah 31:12.

19. Psalms 126:5.

20. Martin Buber, *Two Kinds of Faith*, trans. Norman P. Goldhawk (New York: Harper Torchbook, 1961), 12.

21. Martin Buber, *The Origin and the Meaning of Hasidism* (New York: Horizon Press, 1960), 12; idem, *The Tales of Rabbi Nachman* (New York: Horizon Press), 1956; idem, *Two Types of Faith*.

22. Eco, *A Theory of Semiotics*, 277.

23. Ibid., 278. Eco summarizes the rhetorical divisions into *inventio, dispositio* (where the entymemes appear), and *elocutio*. If rhetorical discourse includes all discourses (the theological, the philosophical, the political) but the axiomatical ones, then rhetoric is one of the most complex manifestations of sign production, involving the choice of given probable premises, the disposition of rhetorical syllogisms, and the necessary "clothing" of expressions with rhetorical figures.

24. Eco, *A Theory of Semiotics*, 284. "The tracing of underlying connections in the semantic field has revealed fertile contradictions. By establishing further connections, rhetorical substitution has to take place between branches of the *sememes* and runs the gamut of the global semantic field, revealing its 'topological' structure."

25. Ibid.

26. A. J. Greimas, "Pour une théory des modalités," *Langage* 43 (1978): 2–16. The modalities of can, believe, do, want (pouvoir, croire, faire, vouloir) are concatenated with savoir and être. The epistemic model is of the form

Certain	Excluded
Probable	Improbable

with a large **X** between the columns.

The alethic modalities are obtained by homologating couples of modal categories such as *devoir être* (having to be) with *pouvoir être* (being able to be) to obtain compatibility, conformity, contrariety, or contradiction.

27. Greimas, "Pour une théory des modalités," 2–16.

28. Umberto Eco, *A Theory of Semiotics*, 278. Eco ascertains that ideological discourse is a mode of argumentation that uses probable premises and only a partial section of a given semantic field. However, it pretends to develop a "true" argument, covers up the contradictory nature of the global semantic system, and presents its own point of view as the only possible conclusion.

29. Ibid. "The speaker's *Weltanschauung* depends on a process of interpretation and on previous codes. What has to be presupposed (since it is not assured by any previously established code) is that the sender subscribes to a given ideology, whereas the ideology itself, the object of the presupposition, is an organized world-vision which must be subjected to a semiotic analysis."

30. We discern here a conscious code-switching that has ideological "effects." Ideology seen as unconscious code-switching and the complexity of thoughts and representations appearing as an Absolute Truth to the thinking subject for the interpretation of the world produces a self-deception.

31. Jean Baudrillard, *De la séduction* (Paris: Seuil, 1984), 135–148; Herman Paret, "La pragmatique des modalités," prepublication, 1–21.

32. Greimas, "Theory of modalities," 1–21; Paret, "La pragmatique des modalités," 1–20.

33. von Wright, *An Essay in Modal Logic*, 34–40; White, *Modal Thinking*, 56–61.

34. Nicolo Machiavelli, *The Art of War: Book V,* trans. Neal Wood (New York: The Library of Liberal Arts, 1965), 130–149.

35. Ronald Langacker, "The Interaction of Grammar and Grammatical Change," *An Overview of Uto-Aztecan Historical Linguistics* (Dallas, TX, 1977). Langacker explains that syntactic differences generate the entire semantic change. While morphology is "below" the word level, syntax, nothing more than patterns of symbolization above the word level, where the integration of complex phonological space of their symbolization, e.g., by the grounding of words into phrases.

36. A. J. Greimas, *Maupassant, la sémiotique du texte* (Paris: Éditions du Seuil, 1976); idem, *Du sens* (Paris: Seuil, 1983); idem, *Sémantique structurale* (Paris: Larousse, 1966).

CHAPTER 6. WISDOM LOST

1. Richard Gray, *Constructive Deconstruction: Kafka's Aphorisms, Literary Tradition and Literary Transformation* (Tübingen: Max Niemeyer Verlang, 1987), 275: "Modern parables consciously and automatically refuse, or relativize all attempts to derive a latent sense from the manifest text." See Klaus-Peter Philippi, "Parabolisches Erzählen," *Deutche Vierteljahrsscharfte* 43 (1969): 309.

2. Harold Bloom, *Franz Kafka: "The Metamorphosis"* (New York: Chelsea House Publications, 1988), 2. Bloom argues that since "Kafka has profoundly influenced Gershom Scholem, and no one will go beyond Scholem's creative or strong misreading of Kabbalah for decades to come, . . . we read Kabbalah via Scholem, from a Kafkan perspective . . . a Kafkan facticity or contingency now governs our awareness of whatever in Jewish cultural tradition is other than normative."

3. Gray, *Constructive Deconstruction*, 273. According to Gray, we are indebted to Kafka for arriving at a definition of modern parable that distinguishes between the ancient, didactic mode and the "open," "indeterminate," new parables; and see Norbert Miller, "Modern Parabel," *Akzente* 6 (1959): 211; Kermode, *The Genesis of Secrecy* (Cambridge: Harvard University Press, 1979).

4. Franz Kafka, *Dearest Father* (New York: Schocken Books, 1954), 161–174 and 381–386; A. P. Foukles, *The Reluctant Pessimist: A Study of Franz Kafka* (Paris: Mouton de Gruyter, 1967), 33. Kafka claims a lack of "Lebenskraft," or "life power." He ascribed his misery and lack of "lebenskraft" to art. Kafka sees the writer as the "Sündenbock der Menschheit," whose function is to allow mankind to enjoy its sins guiltlessly.

5. Marthe Robert, *Seul, comme Franz Kafka* (Paris: Calmann-Levi, 1979), 22–23.

6. Gilles Deleuze and Félix Guattari, *Kafka: Pour une littérature mineure* (Paris: Éditions de Minuit, 1975), 12–14; idem, *Kafka: Towards a Minor Literature*, trans. Dana Polan (Minneapolis: University of Minnesota Press, 1986).

7. Ritchie Robertson, *Kafka: Judaism, Politics, and Literature* (Oxford: Clarendon Press, 1985), 45.

8. Ritchie Robertson, *Kafka, Judaism, and Politics*, 22–23. He claims that "it is more likely that Yiddish offered him a refuge from literary and family pres-

sures." Gilles Deleuze and Félix Guattari, *Kafka*, 15, 23–28, 32–33, 40–41, and note 94; Franz Kafka, *Diaries*, 33–34 (15 December 1910), and 61–62 (20 August 1911).

9. Marthe Robert, *Seul, comme Franz Kafka*, 37–38: "Le récit étant construit de tell sorte qu'aucune formule n'en puisse résumer le contenu, la question juive n'est donc *littéralement* tranché nulle part; traitée chaque fois partiellement, et chaque fois par un hero partial, elle ne peut être approchée que par un inventaire minutieux de toutes les images de Kafka." And Robets Müller, "Phantasies," *Der Jude* 1 (7 Oct. 1916): 457.

10. Heinz Politzer, *Franz Kafka: Parable and Paradox* (Ithaca: Cornell University Press, 1962), 17. "Kafka is close to Ludwig Wittgenstein who says that 'the inexpressible, this shows itself, it is mystical'."

11. Ritchie Robertson, *Kafka, Judaism, and Politics,* 164–175, 279–285. Robertson talks about *Das Schloss*, the *Hundeschaft*, and about the 'Volk der Mäuse' and Josephine's ambiguous position. He claims that Kafka subscribed to the ideal of a *Gemeinschaft* founded on religion; 'Führerschaft' may have been suggested to him by the Jewish view of the Lord as an architect of the Torah.

12. Walter Benjamin, "Some Reflections on Kafka," *Illuminations*, ed. Hannah Arendt, trans. H. Zohn (New York: Schocken Books, 1969), 144–145.

13. Robert Alter, *Defenses of the Imagination: Jewish Writers and Modern Historical Crisis* (Philadelphia: The Jewish Publication Society of America, 1977), 60–65; Heinz Politzer, *Franz Kafka Parable and Paradox*, 280–281; Simon Sandbank, "Parable and Theme: Kafka and American Fiction," *Comparative Literature* 37.3 (1985): 252–268; idem, "Structures of Paradox in Kafka," *Modern Language Quarterly* 28 (1967): 462–471; Henry Sussman, *Franz Kafka: Geometrician of Metaphor* (Madison: University of Wisconsin Press, 1979), 21–34.

14. Benjamin, "Some Reflection on Kafka," *Illuminations*, 144–145.

15. Ibid., 126.

16. Ibid., 146.

17. Ibid., 144.

18. Alter, *Defenses of the Imagination: Jewish Writers and Modern Historical Crisis*, 56–60; Walter Strauss, *On the Threshold of a New Kabbalah* (New York: Peter Lang, 1988), 212: "Kafka's combat . . . was the despair of all those who, unlike Kierkegaard, cannot 'leap' into faith, and who cannot become 'knights of infinite resignation,' either; all those in whom the temptation of reason subverts a commitment to faith, because it is necessary for faith to be at least consistent with reason, even if faith *per se* is not reasonable."

19. Walter Strauss, *On the Threshold of a New Kabbalah: Kafka's Later Tales*, 205: "Kafka more than any other Jew including Buber, Levinas, Scholem, lived and suffered these contradictions at the deepest level"; see similar statement, Robertson, *Kafka, Judaism, and Literature*, 36–37.

20. Bloom, *Franz Kafka: "The Metamorphosis,"* 7–8.

21. Ibid., 15. "Whether or not he intended it, he was always Jewish memory come alive."

22. Ibid., 11. Bloom agrees with Gershom Scholem that "we sense a Jewish element in Kafka's apparent Gnosticism."

23. Ibid., 10–17; and see Ernest Pawel, *The Nightmare of Reason: A Life of Franz Kafka* (New York: Schocken Books, 1984), 148–152; Hartmut Binder, *Kafka: Ein Leben in Prag* (Munich, 1982); Klaus Wagenbach, *Franz Kafka: Eine Biographie seiner Jugend, 1883–1912* (Bern, 1958); and Klaus Hermsdorf, *Kafka: Weltbild und Roman* (Berlin, 1961).

24. Strauss, *On the Threshold of a New Kabbalah: Kafka's Later Tales*, 2 and 211–212. He observes that Kafka's writing is a construction that deconstructs itself; its strength derives from the dialectical interaction of these two forces; Ronald Gray, *Franz Kafka* (Cambridge: Cambridge University Press, 1973), 7.

25. Strauss, *On the Threshold of a New Kabbalah*, 212.

26. Robertson, *Kafka, Judaism, and Literature*, 36–37, 82–87, and 164–169.

27. Benjamin, "Some Reflections on Kafka," 148.

28. Hannah Arendt, "Franz Kafka: A Revaluation," *Partisan Review* (1944): 412–422; idem, "The Jew as Pariah: A Hidden Tradition," *Jewish Social Studies* 6 (April 1944): 99–122; O. K. Werckmeister, "Kafka 007," *Critical Inquiry* 21.2 (1995): 491.

29. Werckmeister, "Kafka 007," 482. According to Werckmeister, Kafka has anticipated the political self-critique of literature to the point that he did not publish the material containing criticism about the social upheaval; Malcom Paisley, ed., *Nachgelassene Schriften und Fragmente*, vol. 2 (New York, 1992–93), 1–171.

30. Gray, *Franz Kafka*, 96. "An absence of humanity so complete in Kafka's *Penal Colony*, that it can only be explained in terms of the position beyond humanity which Kafka sometimes fancied himself to have reached."

31. Max Hymitis, *Franz Kafka: A Biography* (New York: Schocken Books, 1947) 10–16; Martin Buber, "Kafka and Judaism," in *Two Types of Faith* (London & New York: Macmillan, 1951), 162–169; idem, in *The Germanic Review* (New York: Columbia University Press, 1952), 157–162. Also Hannah Arendt, "The Jew as Pariah: A Hidden Tradition," *Jewish Social Studies*, 99–122. Cf. Werckmeister, "Kafka 007," 468–495.

32. Benjamin, "Some Reflections on Kafka," 116: "Kafka said: 'men are nihilistic thoughts, suicidal thoughts that came into God's head.'" Heinz Politzer, *Franz Kafka Parable and Paradox*, 19: "Kafka has anticipated the waste land as the landscape of modern man. There he sits unsheltered and totally exposed to a region fraught with horror and imbued with nonsense."

33. Wilhelm Emrich, *Franz Kafka: A Critical Study of His Writings* (Bonn: Athenäum, 1958), trans. Shema Zeben Buehne (New York: Ungar, 1968), 91.

34. Sussman, *Franz Kafka: The Geometrician of Metaphor*, 7–9; and see Wilhelm Emrich, *Franz Kafka: A Critical Study of His Writings* (Bonn: Atheneuum, 1958), 44–46, and 90–91, trans. Shema Zeben Buehene (New York: Ungar, 1968), 76–98.

35. Walter H. Soskel, "Kafka's 'Metamorphosis': Rebellion and Punishment," *Monatshefte* 48.4 (1956): 203–214; idem, *Franz Kafka: Tragik und Ironie*, trans. Henry Sussman (Munich: Langen-Müller, 1964); idem, "Franz Kafka as a Jew," *Leo Baeck Institute Yearbook* 18 (1973): 223–228.

36. Albert Camus, "L'espoir et l'absurde dans l'oeuvre de Kafka," in *Le Myth de Sisyphe* (Paris: Gallimard, 1948), 169, and 170–189. English translation: "Hope and the Absurd in the Work of Franz Kafka," *Kafka,* ed. Ronald Gray (Englewood Cliffs, N.J.: Prentice Hall, 1962), 148–149.

37. Emrich, *Franz Kafka: A Critical Study of His Writings,* 44–45. He claims that in Kafka one can find a transcendental concept whose *substance* withers but whose *structure* endures; "a fossil, the hulk emptied of metaphysical presuppositions as 'true universal'." Cf. Soskel, "Kafka's 'Metamorphosis': Rebellion and Punishment," 203–214; idem, *Franz Kafka: Tragik und Ironie,* 11; Sussman, *Franz Kafka: Geometrician of Metaphor,* 9; Samuel Webber, "The Side Shows, or Remarks on a Canny Moment," *Modern Language Notes,* 88 (1973): 1102–33; Robertson, *Kafka, Judaism, and Politics,* 22–23, 36–37.

38. Sussman, *Franz Kafka: Geometrician of Metaphor,* 3.

39. Benjamin, "Some Reflections," 127.

40. Sussman, *Franz Kafka: Geometrician of Metaphor,* 6–7.

41. Sussman, *Franz Kafka: Geometrician of Metaphor,* 30–31.

42. Shimon Sandbank, "Parable and Theme: Kafka and American Fiction," *Comparative Literature* 37.3 (1985): 254; Politzer, *Franz Kafka Parable and Paradox,* 21. Politzer offers his interpretation of Kafka's statement.

43. Politzer, *Franz Kafka: Parable and Paradox,* 84.

44. Ibid., 22.

45. Camus, "Hope and the Absurd in the Work of Franz Kafka," 147.

46. Strauss, *On the Threshold of a New Kabbalah: Kafka's Later Tales,* 2–3: "The reader is in a quandary. And that is clearly where he is meant to be . . . : everything [in Kafka] must be read literally, and yet nothing can be taken at face value"; and Benjamin, "Some Reflections," 124: "Kafka's parables are never exhausted by what is explainable; on the contrary, he took all conceivable precautions against the interpretation of his writings." See also Simon Sandbank, "Parable and Theme: Kafka and American Fiction," 252–268, 1985; idem, "Structures of Paradox in Kafka," 462–472.

47. Benjamin, "Some Reflections," 122.

48. Ibid., 124.

49. Harold Bloom, ed., *Kafka's "The Metamorphosis,"* 2; Politzer, *Franz Kafka,* 19 and 84.

50. Franz Kafka, "Prometheus," in *Parables and Paradoxes: Kafka,* trans. Willa and Edwin Muir (New York: Schocken Books, 1974), 83.

51. Eco, "On Symbols," *Frontiers in Semiotics,* 176.

52. Gustav Janouch, *Conversations with Kafka,* trans. Goronway Rees (New York: Frederick A. Praeger, 1953), 93: "Kafka's parables are not the fruit of wisdom but the profession of his ignorance." Simon Sandbank, "Parable and Theme: Kafka and American Fiction," 252–268. Sandbank claims that "Benjamin points to a radically new conception, in Kafka, of the status of fiction. His stories present themselves as interpretations, point to a text beyond themselves, but are deprived of the doctrine they interpret . . . a secret code whose secret is irrevocable."

53. Eco, "On Symbol," *Frontiers in Semiotics,* 180.

54. Strauss, *On the Threshold of a New Kabbalah: Kafka's Later Tales,* 211; Bloom, *Kafka's "The Metamorphosis,"* 4.

55. Ronald Gray, *Constructive Deconstruction* (Cambridge: Cambridge University Press, 1973), 61: "The primary virtue of the aphorism is precisely that it cannot be read casually and requires of its reader a 'kunst der Ausslegung' [an art of interpreting]; Strauss, *On the Threshold of a New Kabbalah*, 2: "Kafka gravitates toward parable ["pure" narrative] and phorism ["pure" wisdom]—the arts of the prophet or the sage. His writing is a construction that deconstructs itself; its strength derives from the dialectical interaction of these two forces."

56. Gray, *Constructive Deconstruction*, 252 and 267–269. According to Gray, Kafka uses devices commonly associated with rhetoric: parallelism, antithesis, antimetabole. He also coins the term *met-aphorism* to explain what Kafka did to the aphorism.

57. Sussman, *Kafka: Geometrician of Metaphor*, 278–279. Cf. Roamn Karst, "Kafka und die Metapher," *Literatur und Kritik* 180 (1983): 472–480.

58. Norbert Miller, "Modern Parabel?," *Akzente* 6 (1959): 211. Ancient parables are *Lehrparabel* and modern, *Vorgangsparabel*; Ulrich Fülleborn, "Zum Verhältnis von Perspectivismus und Parabolik in der Dichtung Kafkas," *Wissenschaft als Dialog*, ed. R von Heydebrand and A. G. Just (Stuttgart: Meltzer, 1969), 308–310 ("Kafka's aphorism are *gleichnisse*" [parables]); Gray, *Constructive Deconstruction*, 264 and 269: "Kafka's suggestive metaphoric aphorisms prove that the aphoric brevity and the parabolic portrayal are wholly reconcilable"; Kermode, *The Genesis of Secrecy*, 46–47.

59. Kermode, *The Genesis of Secrecy*, 46; Gray, *Constructive Deconstruction*, 275: "The modern parable can be distinguished from its traditional counterpart by the fact that it knows no 'insiders'"; Politzer, *Franz Kafka*, 21: "Like literary Rorschach tests, Kafka's parables reveal the characters of the interpreters rather than their own."

60. Camus, "Hope and the Absurd in the Work of Franz Kafka," *Kafka*, 149.

61. Ibid., 150.

62. Ibid., 155.

63. Sandbank, "Structure and Paradox in Kafka," 462–472.

64. Politzer, *Franz Kafka*, 19–21; Anthony Thorlby, *Kafka: A Study* (London: Heinemann, 1972), 3.

65. Camus, "Hope and the Absurd in the Work of Franz Kafka," 157–159; Buber, "Kafka and Judaism," 157–162; Buber calls it "a kind of Paulism of the unredeemed, one from which the abode of grace is missing."

66. Sussman, *Franz Kafka*, 2 and 134; Gray, *Constructive Deconstruction*, 237.

67. Roamn Karst, "Kafka und die Metapher," *Literatur und Kritik* 180 (1983): 472–480. "Absolute metaphor, paradoxically functions as neutralization of metaphor."

68. Franz Kafka, *The Penal Colony*, trans. Willa and Edwin Muir (New York: Schocken Books, 1976), 203–204.

69. Robertson, *Kafka, Judaism, and Literature*, 279–285; cf. Politzer, *Franz Kafka*, 215.

70. Franz Kafka, "Josephine the Singer, or the Mouse Folk," in *Selected Stories of Franz Kafka*, 328.

71. Robert, *Seul, comme Franz Kafka*, 279.

72. Ibid., 35–36;

73. James Young, *Reading and Writing after the Holocaust* (Bloomington: Indian University Press, 1993), 18 n. 7.

74. Buber, "Kafka and Judaism," 157–162; William G. Dotty, "The Parables of Jesus, Kafka, Borges, and Others," *Seminar Papers*, ed. George MacRae (Cambridge, Mass: Society of Biblical Literature, 1973), 2:119–141; Benjamin Fondane, "Kafka et la rationalité absolue," *Deucalion* (Paris) 2 (1947): 125–140.

75. Patte, *Semiology of Parables*, 320–321; Marin, *Semiology of Parables*, 194.

76. Gray, *Franz Kafka*, 282; Doty, "The Parables of Jesus, Kafka, Borges, and Others," in *Seminar Papers*, 138–141.

77. Gray, *Constructive Deconstruction*, 288.

78. Kermode, *The Genesis of Secrecy*, 47.

79. Franz Kafka, "Couriers," *Parables and Paradoxes*, ed. Nachum N. Glatzer, trans. Clement Greenberg (New York: Schocken Books, 1974), 175.

80. Gray, *Constructive Deconstruction*, 276: "Modern parable seeks 'a-suasion,' namely the undermining and abandoning of any and all dogmatically fixed points, the overthrowing of systems of secure beliefs and knowledge interests, the destablizing of the static in the name of productive dynamism." See Jill Robins, "Kafka's Parables," *Midrash and Literature*, 265–284.

81. Walter Benjamin, "Franz Kafka: On the Tenth Anniversary of His Death," *Illuminations*, 1969; M. Blanchot, "Kafka et l'éxigence de l'oeuvre," *L'espace littéraire*, 1955; Martin Buber, *Two Types of Faith*, 1961; Politzer, *Franz Kafka*.

82. Robbins, "Kafka's Parables," 265–284.

83. Franz Kafka, "The Sirens," *Parables and Paradoxes*, 93.

84. Alter, *Defense of the Imagination*, 60.

85. Marthe Robert, *Seul, comme Franz Kafka*, 174–175.

86. Ibid.

87. David Stern, "Midrash and Indeterminacy," *Critical Inquiry* 15.1 (1988): 132–161; Daniel Boyarin, *Intertextuality and the Reading of Midrash* (Bloomington: Indiana University Press, 1990).

88. Gray, *Constructive Deconstruction*, 273; Kermode, *The Genesis of Secrecy*, 31; Ulrich Fülleborn, "Zum Verhältnis von Perspektivismus und Parabolik in der Dichtung Kafkas," *Wissenschaft als Dialog* 8 (1969), 310; Norbert Miller, "Modern Parabel?," 211.

89. Robbins, "Kafka's Parables," 265–281.

90. Max Brod, *Franz Kafka: A Biography* (New York: Schocken Books, 1960), 12; Buber, "Kafka and Judaism," 162–169; idem, "Kafka and Judaism," 157–162; Strauss, *On the Threshold of a New Kabbalah: Kafka's Later Tales*, 2–34.

91. Strauss, *On the Threshold of a New Kabbalah*, 211.

92. Janouch, *Conversations with Kafka*, 93. Kafka noted, "I have made friends with my ignorance."

93. Strauss, *On the Threshold of a New Kabbalah*, 212.

94. Hartman, *Midrash and Literature*, 14 n. 14; Roland Barthes, "The Struggle with the Angel," in *Image Music Text*, trans. Stephen Heath (London: Fontana Collins, 1977), 125–141.

95. Alter, *Defenses of the Imagination*, 64–65.

96. Walter Soskel, *Franz Kafka: Tragik und Ironie*, 19.

97. Gray, *Franz Kafka*, 144; Felix Weltsch, *Religion und Humor im Leben und Werk Franz Kafkas* (Berlin: Grunewald, 1957).

98. Robert, *Seul, comme Franz Kafka*, 254 and 256–257: "Il [Odradek] est attendu par une imortalité sans espoir, aussi vide, aussi morne que l'existence qu'il a menée inutilement en marge de toute humanité."

99. Michael Dentan, *Humour et création littéraire dans l'oeuvre de Kafka* (Geneve and Paris: Librairie Droz et Librairie Minard, 1961), 38, 42, and 143.

100. Benjamin, "Some Reflections," 148.

101. Sandbank, "Parable and Theme," 263.

CHAPTER 7. FRANZ KAFKA

1. Franz Kafka, "On Parables," in *Parables and Paradoxes*, trans. Clement Greenbaum et al. (New York: Schocken Books, 1974), 12. To the man who complains that he was wrong in parable, Kafka replies through his character: "no, you were right only in parable, in reality you have lost."

2. Franz Kafka, "An Imperial Message," in *Parables and Paradoxes*, 4–5.

3. Alain J. J. Cohen, "Le spectacle du sens dans le récit parabolique chez Matthieu," *Le récit Évangélique* (Paris: Editions du Cerf, 1974), 14–26.

4. P. F. Strawson, "On Referring," *Mind* 49.235 (1950): 326–313. Strawson claims that in "mentioning" or "referring" (also truth or falsity), "meaning is a function of the sentence or expression . . . the rules, habits, conventions governing its correct use in all occasions, to refer or to assert."

5. Algiras J. Greimas, "Signes et paraboles," in *Sématique structurale* (Paris: Librarie Larousse, 1966), 181.

6. Sigmund Freud, "The Uncanny," in *On Creativity and the Unconscious* (New York: Harper & Row, 1958), 123–124. The 'uncanny' created by Kafka belongs to the third kind of 'uncanny' in Freud's analysis, namely, the literary/fictional uncanny, where a writer creates the "uncanny effect, which is an "effect of discourse," and it is "the writer's playing, pretending, irony."

7. Because of the infinite matrix, an integral is used instead of a determinant (reference is made to a function instead of discrete points, finite in number). In the *Great Wall of China* (in pre-parabolic datum), the addressor delivers a message: The highly sophisticated bureaucracy surrounding the 'Emperor' is permanently eroding his power and slowly destroys his accomplishments. However, we, the subjects and the addressees, are forever ignorant of the carnage, this perpetual bloodshed, because of our existence "at the end of some densely thronged side street peacefully munching our food . . . while far away in front, in the market's square, at the heart of the city, the execution of one ruler is proceeding."

CHAPTER 8. JORGE LUIS BORGES

1. John Ashbery, "A Game with Shifting Mirrors," in *Critical Essays*, ed. Jaime Alazraki (Boston: G. K. Hall, 1987), 96.

2. Jorge Luis Borges, "El remordimiento," in *Memoria Historica* (Buenos Aires: Emecé, 1976), 89.

3. Jaime Alazraki, *Critical Essays on J. L. Borges* (Boston: G. K. Hall, 1987), 14.

4. John Sturrock, *Paper Tigers: The Ideal Fiction of J. L. Borges* (Oxford: Clarendon Press, 1977), 21–40.

5. Alfred Kazin, "Meeting Borges," in *Contemporaries: Critical Essays* (Boston: Little, Brown, 1962), 120.

6. Rodriguez E. Monegal, *Borgès par lui même* (Paris: Écrivains de toujour, 1970), 42.

7. Jorge Luis Borges, "Borges and I," in *Fictions (Ficciones)*, trans. Emecé Editores (New York: Grove Press, 1962), 18.

8. Jorge Luis Borges "La moneda de hierro," in *Obras Completas* (Buenos Aires: Emecé, 1974), 42.

9. Jaime Alazraki, *Borges and the Kabbalah* (Cambridge: Cambridge University Press, 1988), 180. Alazraki recounts his interview with the poet, only a short while before the poet's death.

10. Jorge Luis Borges, *Other Inquisitions*, trans. Ruth Simmons (Austin: University of Texas Press, 1964), 78.

11. Myrna Solotoravsky, "The Model of Midrash and Borges's Interpretative Tales and Essays," in *Midrash and Literature*, ed. Geoffrey Hartman and Sanford Budick (New Haven: Yale University Press, 1986), 251–252.

12. Harold Bloom, *Kabbalah and Criticism* (New York: The Seabury Press, 1975), 106.

13. Solotoravsky, "The Model of Midrash," 254.

14. Sturrock, *Paper Tigers*, 162.

15. Jorge Luis Borges, *Other Inquisitions*, 111. "Once I planned to make a survey of Kafka's precursors. At first I thought he was as singular as the fabulous Phoenix; when I knew him better I thought I recognized his voice, or his habits, in the texts of various literatures and various ages."

16. Bloom, *Kabbalah and Criticism*, 106.

17. W. Barnstone, ed., *Borges at Eighty* (Bloomington: Indiana University Press, 1982), 82; Kathy Acker, "In the Tradition of Cervantes, Sort of," *The New York Times Book Review*, 30 November 1986, 10.

18. Jaime Alazraki, *Kabbalah and Borges*, 10–32. Examples cited are "The Circular Ruins," "Golem," "Chess."

19. Borges quotes Paul Valéry's "Letter about Mallarmé," 1927, trans. Malcolm Cowley. In this letter, Valéry states that "we say that an author is original when we cannot trace the hidden transformations that others underwent in his mind; we mean to say that the dependence of what he does on what others have done is excessively complex and irregular."

20. Solotarevsky, "The Model of Midrash," 261.

21. Ibid., 254–259; Jean Genette, *Figures* (Paris: Seuil, 1966), 123.

22. Alazraki, *Borges and the Kabbalah*, 146; idem, *La prosa narrativa de L. J. Borges* (Madrid: Gredos, 1984), 128, and 189–195. First Alazraki claims that Borges sees reality "sub specie aeternitatis." Then, he states that in Kafka and in myths Borges sees a magic world by which man attempts to understand "that other reality," by painstaking endeavors of the human mind.

23. Geoffrey Clive, ed., *The Philosophy of Nietzsche: Truth and Illusions* (Chicago: Mentor Press, 1965), 501–511.

24. Ernesto Gonzáles Bermejo, *Conversationes con Cortázar* (Barcelona: Edhasa, 1978), 21.

25. Pierre Macherey, "Borges and the Fictive Narrative," in *Borges and the Kabbalah*, 80.

26. Roman Jakobson, "Linguistics and Poetics," in *Style and Language*, ed. Thomas A. Sebeok (Cambridge: MIT Press, 1960), 351. Jakobson offers a clear explanation of the process.

27. Roland Barthes, *Essayes critiques* (Paris: Éditions du Seuil, 1964), 306. Barthes has a very insightful analysis of how Borges's narratives signify.

28. Solotarevsky, "The Model of Midrash," in *Midrash and Literature*, 261.

29. Jorge Luis Borges, "Foreword" to Ronald Christ, *The Narrow Act: Borges's Art of Allusion* (New York: New York University Press, 1969), 9.

30. Jaime Alazraki, *La Prosa Narrativa*, 128.

31. Solotarevsky, "The Model of Midrash," 262.

32. Jorge Luis Borges, *Labyrinths* (New York: New Directions Books, 1964), 19.

33. Ariosto dedicated his work *Orlando Furioso* to Cardinal Ippoloto d'Este, who said in response, "Where did you find so many stories?"

34. Sigmund Freud, "Creative Writers and Daydreaming," *The Complete Works*, 10:34. "The motive forces of fantasies are unsatisfied wishes, and every single fantasy is the fulfillment of a wish, a correction of unsatisfying reality." Borges too insists on the confluence of the realm of reality with that of fantasy.

35. Charles Sanders Peirce, "Elements of Logic," in *Collected Papers* (Cambridge: Harvard University Press, 1960), 174–213 and 495–497.

CHAPTER 9. ITALO CALVINO

1. Italo Calvino, *Il sentiero dei nidi di ragno* (Turin: Einaudi Press, 1946); idem, *Ultimo viene il corvo* (Turin: Einaudi Press, 1949).

2. Lucia Re, *Calvino and the Age of Neorealism: Fables of Estrangement* (Stanford: Stanford University Press, 1990), 159.

3. Jo Ann Cannon, *Postmodern Italian Fiction: The Crisis of Reason in Calvino, Eco, Sciascia, Malerba* (London: Fairleigh Dickenson University Press, 1989), 10. She argues that Calvino followed Elio Vittorini's projected alternative view of a literature nourished by the firm belief in the "conoscibilità del mondo," the possibility of knowing the world.

4. Re, *Postmodern Italian Fiction*, 157–159.

5. Italo Calvino, *Gli amori*, trans. W. Weaver et al. as *Our Loves* (San Diego: Harcourt, 1984), x–xi.

6. Cannon, *Postmodern Italian Fiction*, 13.

7. Italo Calvino, "Il mare dell'oggettività," in *Il Menabò* 2 (1960): 9.

8. I. T. Olken, *With Pleated Eye and Garnet Wing: Symmetries of Italo Calvino* (Ann Arbor: University of Michigan Press, 1984), 19–20.

9. Italo Calvino, "La sfida al labirinto," *Il Menabò* 4 (1959): 96.

10. Ibid., 99.

11. Italo Calvino, Mr. *Palomar* (Turin: Einaudi, 1983); idem, *Le città invisibili* (Turin: Einaudi, 1972).

12. Kathryn Hume, *Calvino's Fictions: Cogito and Cosmos* (Oxford: Clarendon Press, 1992), 105–106.

13. Italo Calvino, "Il midollo del leone," in *Paragone* 62 (February 1955): 27.

14. Hume, *Calvino's Fictions*, 56.

15. Calvino, *Le città invisibili*, trans. William Weaver as *Invisible Cities* (San Diego: Harcourt Brace Jovanovich, 1974).

16. Sara Maria Adler, *Calvino, The Writer as Fabulator* (Potomac, Md.: Porrua Turanzas, North American Division, 1979), 13. And see Giuliano Manacorda, *La letteratura italiana contemporanea (1940–1965)* (Rome: Riuniti, 1967); Giorgio Pullini, *Il romanzo italiano del dopoguerra (1940–1960)* (Vicenza: Marsilio, 1965); Leonardo Sciascia, "Il barone rampante," *Il ponte* 13 (1957); Italo Calvino, "Progettazione e letterature," introduction to *La ragione conoscitiva*, ed. Italo Calvino reprinted in *Il menabò della letteratura* 10 (1967): 48–58.

17. Italo Calvino, "Cibernetica e fantasmi," *Le conferenze* 21 (1967–68): 18–20. Calvino says "The fable unravels from phrase to phrase, where does it lead? To the point in which something yet unsaid, something only obscurely intuited is revealed."

18. Teresa De Lauretis, "Narrative Discourse in Calvino: Praxis or Poiesis," *Publications of Modern Language Association* 90.3 (1975): 414–425; idem, "Semiotic Models, *Invisible Cities*," *Yale Studies* 2.1 (1978): 13–37.

19. Sara Maria Adler, *Calvino, the Writer as Fablemaker*, 121–122.

20. Calvino, "Cibernetica e fantasmi," 22.

21. Teresa De Lauretis, "Narrative Discourse in Calvino," 414–425.

22. Hume, *Calvino's Fictions*, 49–56; Detlev W. Schumann, "Enumerative Style and Its Significance in Whitman, Rilke, Werfel," *Modern Language Quarterly* 32 (1976): 171–204.

23. Italo Calvino, "Cities and Signs," in *Invisible Cities* (*Le città invisibili*), 5.

24. Cf. Cannon, *Postmodern Italian Fiction*, 101–103, and 106–108. Cannon claims that Calvino's work had been conceived as a "diagram for praxis," where "praxis is defined as the potential and the will to change." And see Richard Andrews, *Writers in Society in Contemporary Italy*, ed. Michael Caesar and Peter Hainsworth (New York: St. Martin's Press, 1984).

25. Eugenio Donato, "Merleau-Ponti, *Le visible et l'invisible*," *Modern Language Notes* 85 (1970): 804–805.

26. A. Greimas, "Paraboles," in *Signes et paraboles*, ed. Christian Metz (Paris: Du Seuil, 1977), 182.

27. Charles S. Pierce, "Elements of Logic," in *Collected Papers* (Cambridge: Harvard University Press, 1960), 34–35.

28. $S_1 \neq S_2$ but co-referential; S = subject; S2 $\cap$ O (not with the discovery of the city but of a formula, an image of S); O = knowledge that Th_a S (Th_b). The subject S is conjoined with the object of desire of another subject N_1, i.e., the city of Tamara. The valorized object is, therefore, the knowledge that a thing Th_a is the "sign of another thing," Th_b, where $Ta_a \neq Th_b$, or that Th_a means Th_b. The acting subject "eye" discerns that a thing X has as its sign a thing Y, and Y is the image of another thing Z, and not the original subject "man/you," who, supposedly, visits a place called in Calvino's parable "the city of Tamara." See explanation about the shift in subject.

29. Hume, *Calvino's Fictions*, 133. "The two novels *Invisible Cities* and *Mr. Palomar* explore Calvino's basic dialectic between the eye or I and cosmic flux, as well as the schemes for ordering that flux which the mind generates."

30. Jacques Derrida, "By Force of Morning," in *Critical Inquiry* 22.2 (1996): 175; cf. Louis Marin, *Des pouvoirs de l'image: Gloses* (Paris: De Seuil, 1993), 16–17. He reclaims the power(s) of the image.

31. Walter Benjamin, *Selected Writings 1913–1926*, ed. Marcus Bullock and Michael W. Jennings (Cambridge: Harvard University Press, 1996), 64.

32. Jacques Derrida, *Le puit et la pyramide*, 82; idem, analysis in *La dissémination*, 288–301 and 275–276.

33. Louis Marin, "La Syntaxe du désir," in *La critique du discours*, 237.

34. A. J. Greimas, "Pour une théorie des modalités, *Language* 43.2 (1977): 17–18.

35. Sigmund Freud, "Obsessive Actions and Religious Practices," in *The Complete Works by Sigmund Freud*, vol. 9 (1907): 117–127. Freud shows that the neurotic goes on repeating compulsively the gesture of the original trauma, with no possibility to extricate himself from his predicament (outside of psychoanalytic treatment).

36. A. J. Greimas, "Pour une théorie des modalités," in *Language* 43 (1978): 2–16. An epistemic model is of the form

$$
\begin{array}{ccc}
\text{Certain} & & \text{Excluded} \\
 & \text{X} & \\
\text{Probable} & & \text{Improbable}
\end{array}
$$

Alethic (chance) modalities are obtained by homologating couples of modal categories with the above.

37. Functions of the verbal "do": cognitive, persuasive, and interpretative. The epistemic system and the system of veridiction are:

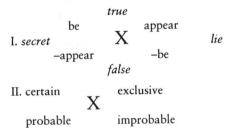

38. Charles Sanders Peirce, "Elements of Logic," *Collected Papers*, 176–211.

39. John Updike, "'The Invisible Cities' by Italo Calvino," *The New Yorker*, 24 February 1975, 138.

40. Updike, "The Invisible Cities," 140.

CHAPTER 10. S. Y. AGNON

1. Arnold J. Band, *Nostalgia and Nightmare: A Study in the Fiction of S. Y. Agnon* (Berkeley and Los Angeles: University of California Press, 1968); Robert Alter, "The Genius of S. Y. Agnon," *Commentary*, August 1961; Edmond Wilson, "The Fiction of S. Y. Agnon," *New Yorker*, 12 December 1954, 186–193; idem, *Red, Black, Blond and Olive* (New York: Oxford University Press, 1956), 443–452; Esther Fuchs, *Omanut hahitmamut: Al ha'ironia shel Shai Agnon* [Cunning Innocence: On S. Y. Agnon's Irony] (Tel Aviv: Makhon Katz, 1985); Anna Golomb Hoffman, *Between Exile and Return: S. Y. Agnon and the Drama of Writing* (Albany: State University of New York Press, 1991); Gershon Shaked, "Midrash and Narrative: Agnon's 'Agunot,'" in *Midrash and Literature*, 283–303; Yair Mazor, *HaDinamika shel Motivim biTzrat S. Y. Agnon* [The Dynamics of Motifs in Agnon's Works] (Tel Aviv: Dekel, 1979); Warren Bargad, "Agnon and German Neoromanticism," *Prooftexts* 1 (1981); Yael Feldman, "The Latent and Manifest: Freudianism in *A Guest for the Night*," *Prooftexts* 7 (1987).

2. Stern, *Parables in Midrash*, 233. "The literary form of the parable becomes in this way a guarantee of meaning and stability that also lies behind the story's ideal equation between Torah scroll and child, or art and life."

3. Stern, *Parables in Midrash*, 234.

4. Gershon Shaked, "Midrash and Narrative: Agnon's 'Agunot'," in *Midrash and Literature*, 283–303.

5. Stern, *Parables in Midrash*, 235.

6. Golomb Hoffman, *Between Exile and Return*, 5.

7. Ibid., 11–12.

8. Abraham Holtz, "The Open Parable as a Key to S. Y. Agnon's 'Sefer Hama'asim,'" (Hebrew), *Hasifrut* 4 (1973): 298–333.

9. S. Y. Agnon, *A Book That Was Lost* (New York: Schocken Books, 1995), 5. Golomb Hoffman and Mintz claim that Agnon "told the story of his upbringing in Galicia, his journey to the Land of Israel, his extended sojourn in Germany, and his return to Jerusalem in many different versions, placing the persona of the writer at times in the center of the story and at times at the margins as a kind of ironic scaffolding."

10. S. Y. Agnon's Nobel Prize acceptance speech, reprinted in *The New York Times*, 11 December 1966.

11. Arnold Band, *Nostalgia and Nightmare*, 2.

12. S. Y. Agnon, *A Book That Was Lost, and Other Stories*, ed. and introduction, Alan Mintz and Anne Golomb Hoffman (New York: Schocken Books, 1995), 12.

13. Band, *Nostalgia and Nightmare*, 12; Golomb Hoffman, *Between Exile and Return*, 12–16.

14. Cf. Alan Mintz and Anne Golomb Hoffman, eds., *S. Y. Agnon, A Book that Was Lost*, 138; S. Y. Agnon, *Eilu Ve'eilu* [These and Those], in *Collected Stories*, vol. 2 (Jerusalem and Tel-Aviv: Schocken, 1968); And see S. Y. Agnon, "Hush hare'ah," ["A Sense of Smell"], *Collected Works*, trans. Arthur Green.

15. Gershom Scholem, *From Berlin to Jerusalem*, trans. Harry Zohn (New York: Schocken Books, 1980), 91–94.

16. Band, *Nostalgia and Nightmare*, 449–450.

17. Ibid., 27.

18. Golomb Hoffman, *Between Exile and Return*, 51–53.

19. Nitza Ben-Dov, *Agnon's Art of Indirection* (Leiden, New York, Köln: E. J. Brill, 1993), 5. Ben-Dov sees a connection between Agnon's modernism and his use of sacred texts. Agnon's "elusiveness and equivocation are derived from his use of Hebrew sacred texts." Cf. S. Y. Agnon *Shivkhei 'Adi'el 'Amzeh* [The Praises of Adiel Amzeh: "Forevermore" and "Edo and Enam"] (Tel Aviv and New York: Schocken Books, 1989), 15.

20. Baruch Hochman, *The Fiction of S. Y. Agnon* (Ithaca and London: Cornell University Press, 1970), 149.

21. Agnon, "Agunot," published in 1908; in the first *Works*, vol. 3, 1908, 233–251; in the second *Works*, vol. 2, 405–416.

22. S. Y. Agnon, *Oreah nata lalun*, appeared in 1939 as vol. 7 of the first *Works*; vol. 4 of the second *Works*, trans., Misha Louvish, in 1968.

23. David Aberbach, *At the Handles of the Lock: Themes in the Fiction of S. Y. Agnon* (Oxford: Oxford University Press, 1984), 167–168.

24. S. Y. Agnon, *A Guest for the Night*, trans. Segal Glatzer, ed., 259–60, in first *Works*; cf. Aberbach, *At the Handle of the Lock*, 174–175.

25. Agnon, *A Guest for the Night*, 165.

26. S.Y. Agnon, *Temol Shilshom* [Yesteryear], 1945, in first *Works*, vol. 9, in second *Works*, vol. 5.

27. Hochman, *The Fiction of S. Y. Agnon*, 188–189.

28. Aberbach, *At the Handle of the Lock*, 146–161. Aberbach argues in favor of a schizoid personality.

29. Franz Kafka, "Letter to My Father," in *Wedding Preparations in the Country and Other Stories*, 61.

30. Aberbach, *At the Handle of the Lock*, 161.

31. Cf. Gabriel Moked, *Shivhei 'Adi'el 'Amzeh* [The Praises of Adiel Amzeh: "Forevermore" and "Edo and Enam"] (Tel Aviv: Ktav, 1989), 15. Gabriel Moked, the Agnon critic who also worked on Kafka, Mann, and Borges, places Agnon among the ten best twentieth-century writers.

32. Yehuda Friedlander, forward to Israel Rosenberg, *Shay Agnon's World of Mystery and Allegory: An Analysis of "'Ido and 'Aynam"* [Edo and Enam] (Philadelphia and Ardmore: Dorrance and Copany, 1978), 2–9.

33. Hillel Halkin, "Sexual Perversity in Jerusalem," *New Republic*, 20 November 1989.

34. Cynthia Ozick, "Agnon's Antagonisms," *Commentary*, December 1988, incorporated in "S. Y. Agnon and the First Religion," *Metaphor and*

Memory (New York: Alfred A. Knopf, 1989), 209–223; and see Robert Alter's afterword to S. Y. Agnon's *Shira*, trans. Zeva Shapiro, in *The American Jewish Congress Monthly*, 1991, 18–20.

35. Nitza Ben-Dov, *Agnon's Art of Indirection*, 15.

36. "Petihah le-Kaddish," in *The Works of S. Y. Agnon*, vol. 10, 5th edition (Tel Aviv: Shocken Books, 1959), trans. Judah Goldin, *The Jewish Expression*, ed. Judah Goldin (Tel Aviv: Schocken Books, 1976), 15–17. Another good translation, S. Dresner, in *National Jewish Monthly* (Oak Park) 70.1 (September 1965): 14–16; idem, *Conservative Judaism* (New York) 19.2 Winter (1965): 32–34.

37. Isaiah 10:20, "the Lord, the Holy One of Israel, in truth"; Isaiah 4:3, "And he who is left in Zion will be called holy"; Isaiah 5:7, "For the vineyard of the Lord of hosts is the house of Israel and the house of Judah are his pleasant planting"; Isaiah 10:24, "Therefore thus says the Lord, the Lord of hosts: 'O my people, who dwell in Zion'"; Isaiah 14:3, 5, 7, "When the Lord has given you rest . . . and 'The Lord has broken the staff of the wicked' . . . the whole earth is at rest and quiet; they break forth into singing"; Jeremiah 23:3, 31:7, "The people of Israel, God will bring back and make great."

38. Isaiah 5:7, "For the vineyard of the Lord of hosts is the house of Israel and the house of Judah are his pleasant planting"; Isaiah 10:24, "again, the Lord calls the Jews his people: 'Therefore thus says the Lord, the Lord of hosts: "O my people, who dwell in Zion."'

39. Isaiah 4:3, "And he who is left in Zion will be called holy"; Isaiah 5:7, "For the vineyard of the Lord of hosts is the house of Israel and the house of Judah are his pleasant planting."

40. The expression "*Malkenu meleh malkei hamelaḥim*," "our King the King of kings," is recited during the Rosh Hashanah (New Year) prayer, or "*baḥar banu mikol ha'amim*," "He chose us from among all other people," is recited during the "*alyah laTorah*," or coming up to the Torah, or "*ahav Israel 'amo*," is recited during *tefilat ma'ariv*, the afternoon prayer, just before the "*Shema*" ("Hear O Israel").

41. Isaiah 5:7.

42. The Lord promises (to Abraham) to make the Jewish people into a "*goy gadol*," a great nation; Jeremiah 23:3, 31:7, "The people of Israel, God will bring back and make great."

43. Isaiah 14:3, 5, 7, "When the Lord has given you rest . . ." and "The Lord has broken the staff of the wicked . . . the whole earth is at rest and quiet; they break forth into singing." See also Jeremiah 31:12–14, "They shall come and sing aloud on the height of Zion, and they shall be radiant over the goodness of the Lord. . . . I will turn their mourning into joy, I will comfort them, and give them gladness for sorrow . . . and my people shall be satisfied with my goodness, says the Lord.

Psalms 33:6–12, "Blessed is the nation whose God is the Lord, the people whom He has chosen as his heritage!"; Psalms 105:43, "So he led his people with joy, his chosen ones with singing"; Psalms 106:1, "Praised be the Lord! give thanks to the Lord for He is good; for His steadfast love endures forever!"

44. Umberto Eco, *Travels in Hyperreality* (Bloomington: Indiana University Press, 1985), 67.

CONCLUSION

1. Franz Kafka's parable, "On Parables," 14.

2. Benjamin, "The Theory of Criticism," 217.

3. Michaux, "In the Land of Magic," 46.

4. Umberto Eco, "On Symbol," in *Frontiers in Semiotics*, ed. John Deely et al. (Bloomington: Indiana University Press, 1982), 180.

5. Edmond Jabès, *The Book of Questions*, trans. Rosmarie Waldrop (Middletown, Conn.: Wesleyan University Press, 1977), 31.

6. Nicolo Machiavelli, *The Art of War: Book V*, trans. Ellis Farneworth (New York: The Library of Liberal Arts Press, 1965), 130–149.

7. Sigmund Freud, *A General Introduction to Psychoanalysis*, trans. J. Strachey (New York: Liveright Publishing Co., 1963), 438–439 and 455–456. "How is a repression to be removed? First, the discovery of the repression, and then the removal of the resistance which maintains it. How do we get rid of resistance? We interpret, identify, and inform the patient: First, the patient's desire for recovery which impels him to submit himself to work with us, and secondly, his intelligence which reinforces our interpretation."

BIBLIOGRAPHY

Aberbach, David. 1984. *At the Handles of the Lock*. Oxford: Oxford University Press.

Abrahams, D. Roger. 1983. "Open and Closed Forms in Moral Tales." In *Studies in Aggadah and Jewish Folklore*, vol. 7, pp. 19–33. Ed. I. Ben-Ami and J. Dan. Jerusalem: The Magnes Press, The Hebrew University.

Adler, Sara Maria. 1979. *Calvino, the Writer as Fablemaker*. Potomac, Md.: Porrua Turanzas North American Division.

Agnon, S. Y. 1968. *Kol sipurav shel Sh. Y. 'Agnon* [The Collected Stories of S. Y. Agnon]. 8 vols. Jerusalem and Tel-Aviv: Schocken Books.

———. 1968. *Kol sipurav* [The Collected Stories]. Vol. 2: *Elu ve'elu* [These and Those]. Jerusalem and Tel Aviv: Schocken Books.

———. 1968. *Kol sipurav* [The Collected Stories]. Vol. 4, *Oreah natah lalun* [A Guest for the Night]. Jerusalem and Tel Aviv: Schocken Books.

———. 1970. *Twenty-One Stories*. Ed. Nahum Glatzer. New York: Schocken Books.

———. 1976. *Me'atsmi le'atsmi* [Book, Writer, and Story]. Jerusalem and Tel Aviv: Schocken Books.

———. 1995. *A Book That Was Lost, and Other Stories*. Ed. and intro., Alan Mintz and Anne Golomb Hoffman. New York: Schocken Books.

Alazraki, Jaime. 1968. *La prosa narrativa de Jorge Luis Borges*. Madrid: Gredos.

———. *Jorge Luis Borges*. New York and London: Columbia University Press, 1971.

———, ed. 1987. *Critical Essays on J. L. Borges*. Boston: G. K. Hall.

———. 1988. *Borges and the Kabbalah*. Cambridge: Cambridge University Press.

Alter, Robert. 1961. "The Genius of S. Y. Agnon." *Commentary*, August.

———. 1970. "On Lea Goldberg and S. Y. Agnon." *Commentary*, May.

———. 1971. "Agnon's Last Word." *Commentary* 51.6: 74–81.

———, ed. 1975. Modern Hebrew Literature. New York: Behrman.

———. 1977. *Defenses of the Imagination: Jewish Writers and Modern Historical Crisis*. Philadelphia: The Jewish Publication Society of America.

———. 1981. *The Art of Biblical Narrative*. New York: Basic Books.

———. 1985. *The Art of Biblical Poetry*. New York: Basic Books.

Alter, Robert and Frank Kermode, eds. 1987. *The Literary Guide to the Bible*. Cambridge: The Belknap of Harvard University Press.

Andrew, Richard. 1984. *Writing and Society in Contemporary Italy*. Ed. Michale Caesar and Peter Hainswordth, New York: St. Martin's Press.

Arendt, Hannah. 1944. "Franz Kafka: A Revaluation." *Partizan Review*, 412–422.
———. 1944. "The Jew as Pariah: A Hidden Tradition." *Jewish Social Studies* 6: 99–122.
———. 1945. "The as Pariah." *Times Literary Supplement*, 16 June.
———. 1947. "Essay of Kafka." *Times Literary Supplement*, 27 May.
Aristotle. 1927. 23 vols. Vol. 23: *The Poetics*. Trans. Hamilton Fyfe. Cambridge: Harvard University Press.
———. 1926. 23 vols. Vol. 21: *The Art of Rhetoric*. Trans. John Henry Fresse. London: William Heinemann.
———. 1967. *Poetics*. Trans. Gerald F. Else. Ann Arbor: The University of Michigan Press (pp. 25–52).
Auerbach, Erich. 1974. *Mimesis: The Representation of Reality on Western Literature*. Trans. William Trask. Princeton: Princeton University Press.
Austin, J. L. 1961. *How to Do Things with Words*. Ed. A. Ursmsom. Cambridge: Harvard University Press.
Babylonian Talmud. 1938. Ed. I. Epstein. London: Soncino.
Bakhtin, Mikhail. 1987. *The Dialogic Imagination: Four Essays*. Ed. Michael Holquist. Trans. Michael Holquist and C. Emerson. Austin: University of Texas Press.
Band, J. Arnold. 1968. *Nostalgia and Nightmare: A Study in the Fiction of S. Y. Agnon*. Berkeley and Los Angeles: University of California Press.
Banks, Robert. 1975. *Jesus and the Law in the Synoptic Tradition*. Cambridge: Cambridge University Press.
Bar-Adon, Aharon. 1977. *Sh. Y. Agnon uthiyyat halashon ha'ivrit* [S. Y. Agnon and the Revival of the Hebrew Language]. Jerusalem: Bialik.
Bargad, Warren. 1981. "Agnon and German Neoromanticism." *Prooftexts* 1.
Baron, Naomi. 1987. "When Seeing's Not Believing: Language, Magic, and AI." *The American Journal of Semiotics* 5.3/4: 321–341.
Barthes, Roland. 1953. *Le degré zéro de l'écriture*. Paris: Éditions du Seuil.
———. 1963. "Littérature et Signification." *Tel Quel*.
———. *Essays Critiques*. 1964. Paris: Éditions du Seuil, 138–142. English translation: *Critical Essays*. Trans. R. Howard. Evanston: Northwestern University Press. 1972.
———. 1971. "L'Ancienne rhétorique: Aide-mémoire." *Communications* 16.1: 172–229.
———. 1974. *S/Z*. Trans. Richard Miller. New York: Hill and Wang.
———. 1975. *The Pleasure of the Text*. Trans. Richards Miller. New York: Hill and Wang.
Barzel, Hillel. 1973. *Bein Agnon le Kafka* [Agnon and Kafka: A Comparative Study]. Ramat Gan: Bar Ilan University Press.
Baudrillard, Jean. 1977. *L'Effet Beaubourg: Implosion et dissuasion*. Paris: Galilée.
———. 1979. *De la séduction*. Paris: Galilée.
Barwise Jon and John Perry. 1983. *Situation and Attitudes*. Cambridge: MIT Press.
Beck, Evelyn T. 1971. *Kafka, and the Yiddish Theater: Its Impact on His Work*. Madison: University of Wisconsin Press.

Ben-Dov, Nitza. 1993. *Agnon's Art of Indirection: Uncovering Latent Content in the Fiction of S. Y. Agnon*. Leiden: E. J. Brill.

Benjamin, Walter. 1969. "Some Reflections on Kafka." *Illuminations*, ed. Hannah Arendt. Trans. H. Zohn. New York: Shocken Books.

Benveniste, Émile. 1966. *Problèmes de linguistique générale*. Paris: Gallimard.

Biale, David. 1979. *Gershom Scholem: Kabbalah and Counter-History*. Cambridge: Harvard University Press.

———. 1987. *Power and Powerlessness in Jewish History*. New York: Schocken Books.

———. 1992. *Eros and the Jews: From Biblical Israel to Contemporary America*. New York: Basic Books.

Bialik, Ch. and J. Rabnitzki. 1973. *Sefer Haagadah*. Tel Aviv: Dvir.

Blanco, Mercedes. 1985. "La parabole et les paradoxes." *Poétique 55*: 28a.

Block, René. 1978. "Midrash." Trans. M. H. Callaway. In *Approaches to Ancient Judaism*. Vol. 1: *Theory and Practice*. Ed. William Scott Green. Missoula, Mont.: 29–50.

Bloom, Harold, ed. 1988. Trans. *Kafka: "The Metamorphosis."* New York: Chelsea House.

———. 1973. *The Anxiety of Influence: A Theory of Poetry*. New York: Oxford University Press.

———. 1975. *Kabbalah and Criticism*. New York: The Seabury Press.

Bokes, B. Z. 1951. *Wisdom of the Talmud*. New York: Harcourt Brace World.

Borges, Jorge Luis. 1962. "Kafka and his Precursors." In *Labyrinths*. Ed. Donald A. Yates and James E. Irby. New York: New Directions, 126–128.

———. *Ficciones*. 1962. Edited and with introduction by Anthony Kerrigan. New York: Grove Press.

———. 1964. *Labyrinths*. New York: New Directions.

———. 1964. *Other Inquisitions*. Trans. Ruth Simmons. Austin: University of Texas Press.

———. 1974. *Obras Completas*. Buenos Aires: Emecé Editores.

Booth, Wayne. 1961. *The Rhetoric of Fiction*. Chicago: University of Chicago Press.

Boyarin, Daniel. 1985. "Rhetoric and Interpretation: The Case of the Nimshal." *Prooftexts 5*: 260–270.

———. 1990. *Intertextuality and the Reading of Midrash*. Bloomington: Indiana University Press.

Bremond, Claude. 1973. *Logique du récit*. Paris: Seuil.

Breton, André. 1966. "Kafka." In *Anthologie de l'humour noir*. Paris: J. J. Pauvert, 439–60.

Brod, Max. 1963. *Franz Kafka: A Biography*. Trans. G. H. Humphreys and R. Winston. New York: Shocken Books.

Brooks, Peter. 1982. "Freud's Masterplot." In *Literature and Psychoanalysis: The Question of Reading Otherwise*. Ed. Shoshana Felman. Baltimore: Johns Hopkins University Press.

———. 1984. *Reading for the Plot: Design and Intention in Narrative*. New York: Knopf.

Bruns, L. Gerald. 1987. "Midrash and Allegory: The Beginnings of Scriptural Interpretation." In *The Literary Guide to the Bible*. Ed. Robert Alter and Frank Kermode. Cambridge: The Belknap Press of Harvard University Press.

Buber, Martin. 1948. *Tales of the Hasidim: Later Masters*. New York: Schocken Books.

———. 1951. "Kafka and Judaism." In *Two Kinds of Faith*. London and New York: Macmillan, 162–169.

———. 1952. "Kafka and Judaism." In *The Germanic Review*. New York: Columbia University Press, 157–162.

———. 1956. *The Tales of Rabbi Nachman*. New York: Horizon Press.

———. 1960. *The Origin and the Meaning of Hasidism*. New York: Horizon Press.

———. 1961. "Two Kinds of Faith." In *Ten Rungs*. Trans. Norman P. Goldhawk. New York: Harper Torchbook.

———. 1976. Trans. *"Or haganuz: sippurei hasidim."* [*The Hidden Light: Chassidic Stories*.] Jerusalem and Tel Aviv: Schocken Books.

Calvino, Italo. 1955. "Il midollo del leone." In *Paragone* 62 (February): 27.

———. 1960. "Il mare dell'oggettività." *Il Menabò* 2: 9.

———. 1972. *Le città invisibile*. Turin: Einaudi Press.

———. 1983. *Mr. Palomar*. Turin: Einaudi.

Camus, Albert. 1948. "L'espoir et l'absurde dans l'oeuvre de Kafka." In *Le myth de Sisyphe*. Paris: Gallimard, 1948, 169–189. English translation: "Hope and the Absurd in the Work of Franz Kafka." In *Kafka*. Ed. Ronald Gray. Englewood Cliffs, N.J.: Prentice Hall, 1962.

Cannon, Jo Ann. 1989. *Postmodern Italian Fiction: The Crisis of Reason in Calvino, Eco, Sciascia, Malerba*. Rutherford, N.J.: Fairleigh Dickinson University Press.

Carrouges, Michel. 1968. *Kafka contre Kafka*. Trans. Emmet Parker. English translation: *Kafka versus Kafka*. Tuscaloosa: University of Alabama Press, 1968.

Casey, Edward S. and J. Melvin Woody. 1983. "Hegel, Heideger, Lacan: The Dialectic of Desire." In *Interpreting Lacan*. Ed. Joseph Smith and William Kerrigan. New Haven: Yale University Press.

Cassirer, Ernst. 1944. *Language and Myth*. Trans. Suzanne K. Langer. New York: Harper and Brothers.

de Certeau, Michel. 1980. *L'Invention du quotidien*. Paris: Union Générale.

———. 1982. *La fable mystique*. Paris: Gallimard.

———. 1984. *L'art de faire*. Berkeley: University of California Press.

Chabrol, Claude. 1973. *Sémiotique narrative textuelle*. Paris: Larousse.

———. 1974. "Question sur la parabole." In *Le récit Évangélique*. Paris: Édition du Cerf.

Chatman, Seymour. 1978. *Story and Discourse*. Ithaca: Cornell University Press.

Chomsky, Noam. 1965. *Aspects of the Theory of Syntax*. Cambridge: MIT Press.

———. 1975. *Reflections on Language*. New York: Pantheon Books.

Christ, Ronald J. 1969. *The Narrow Act: Borges's Art of Allusion*. New York: New York University Press.

Cixous, Hélène and Catherine Clément. 1986. *The Newly Born Woman*. Trans. Betsy Wing. Minneapolis: University of Minnesota Press.

Clive, Geoffrey, ed. 1965. *The Philosophy of Nietzsche*. New York: New American Library.

Cohen, J. Alain. 1974. "Le spectacle du sens dans le récit parabolique chez Mathieu." In *Le récit Évangélique*. Paris: Édition du Cerf.

Cope, E. M. 1867. *An Introduction to Aristotle's Rhetoric*. London and Cambridge: Macmillan.

Coquet, Claude. 1972. *Sémiotique littéraire*. Paris: Librairie Larousse.

Cortàzar, Julio. 1968. *The End of Game and Other Stories*. Trans. Paul Blackburn. New York: Random House.

Cortinez, C. 1982. Ed. "Outside and Inside the Mirror in Borges's Poetry." In *Simply a Man of Letters*. Orono: University of Maine Press.

Crossan, John D. 1976. "Parable, Allegory, and Paradox." In *Semiology and Parables: An Exploration of the Possibilities offered by Structuralism for Exegesis*. Ed. Daniel Patte. Pittsburgh Theological Monograph Series 9. Pittsburgh: Pickwick Press, 247–281.

Culler, Jonathan. 1975. *Structuralist Poetics*. Ithaca: Cornell University Press and London: Kegan Paul.

———. 1981. *The Pursuit of Signs: Semiotics, Literature, Deconstruction*. Ithaca: Cornell University Press.

Dan, Yosef. 1969. *Hasippur hahasidi* [The Hasidic Tale]. Jerusalem: Keter.

———. 1986. "Midrash and the Dawn of Kabbalah." In *Midrash and Literature*. Ed. G. Hartman and S. Budick. New Haven: Yale University Press.

Davis, Robert Con, ed. 1983. *Lacan and Narration: The Psychoanalytic Difference in Narrative Theory*. Baltimore: John Hopkins University Press.

Deely, John. 1982. *Introducing Semiotic*. Bloomington: Indiana University Press.

Deleuze, Gilles, and Félix Guattari. 1975. *Kafka: Pour une littérature mineure*. Paris: Éditions de Minuit, 1986. English translation: *Kafka: Towards a Minor Literature*. Trans. Dana Polan. Minneapolis: University of Minnesota Press.

De Man, Paul. 1969. "The Rhetoric of Temporality." In *Interpretation Theory and Practice*. Baltimore: The John Hopkins University Press.

———. 1971. *Blindness and Insight: Essays in the Rhetoric of Contemporary Criticism*. New York: Oxford University Press.

———. 1979. *Allegories of Reading: Figural Language in Rousseau, Nietzsche, and Proust*. New Haven: Yale University Press.

Dentan, Michael. 1961. *Humour et création littéraire dans l'oeuvre de Kafka*. Geneva: Droz.

Derrida, Jacques. 1966. *L'écriture et la différence*. Paris: Éditions du Seuil. Trans. Alan Bass. 1978. English translation: *Writing and Difference*. Chicago: Chicago University Press.

———. 1972. "La mythologie blanche." In *Marge de la philosophie*. Paris: Éditions de Minuit.

———. 1973. *Speech and Phenomena*. Trans. and introd. David B. Allison. Evanston: Northwestern University Press.

———. 1977. "La retraite de la métaphore." *Seminar*. (University of California, Irvine, 10/23/77).

———. 1978. *Writing and Difference*. Trans. Alan Bass. Chicago: University of Chicago Press.

———. 1981. *Dissemination*. Ed. and trans. Barbara Johnson. Chicago: University of Chicago Press.

———. 1990. *Limited Inc*. Paris: Galilée.

———. 1996. "By Force of Morning," in *Critical Inquiry*. Vol 22, # 2, 175.

Dodd, C.H. 1961. *The Parables of the Kingdom*. Glasgow: William Collins.

Donato, Eugenio. 1970. "Merleau-Ponti, a Text in Case." *Modern Language Notes* 85: 803–814.

———. 1977. "The Idioms of the Text: Notes on the Language of Philosophy and the Fiction of Literature." *Glyph* 2, Baltimore: Johns Hopkins University Press.

Doty, Wiliam G. 1973. "The Parables of Jesus, Kafka, Borges, and Others." In *1973 Seminar Papers: Society of Biblical Literature*. Ed. George MacRae. 2 vols. Cambridge, Mass.: Society of Biblical Literature, 2:119–141.

Dunham, Lowell, and Ivar Ivask, eds. 1971. *The Cardinal Points of Borges*. Norman: University of Oklahoma Press.

Eastman, Richard M. 1960–61. "The Open Parable: Demonstration and Definition." *College English* 22.

Eco, Umberto. 1976. *A Theory of Semiotics*. Bloomington: Indiana University Press.

———. 1979. *The Role of the Reader: Explorations in the Semiotics of Texts*. Bloomington: Indiana University Press.

———. 1982. "On Symbol." In *Frontiers in Semiotics*. eds. J. Deely et al. Foreword by Professor Thomas Sebeok. Bloomington: Indiana University Press.

Emrich, Wilhelm. [1958] 1968. *Franz Kafka: A Critical Study of His Writings*. Trans. Shema Zeben Buehne. New York: Ungar.

Faur, José. 1986. *Golden Doves with Silver Dots: Semiotics and Textuality in Rabbinic Tradition*. Bloomington: Indiana University Press.

Feldman, A. 1924. *The Parables and the Similes of the Rabbis*. Cambridge: Cambridge University Press.

Feldman, Yael. 1987. "The Latent and Manifest: Freudianism in *A Guest for the Night*." *Prooftexts* 7: 29–39.

Felman, Shoshana. 1980. *Le scandale du corps parlant*. Paris: Éditions du Seuil.

Fiebig, Paul. 1904. *Altjüdische Gleichnisse und die Gleichnisse Jesu*. Tübingen: J. C. B. Mohr.

Fishbane, Michael. 1991. "Inner Biblical Exegesis." In *Midrash and Literature*. Ed. J. Hartman and S. Budick.

Flores, Angel and Homer Swander, eds. 1964. *Franz Kafka Today*. Madison: The University of Wisconsin Press.

Flores, Angel, ed. 1976. *A Kafka Bibliography, 1908–1976*. New York: Gordian Press.

———, ed. 1977. *The Problem of "The Judgment": Eleven Approaches to Kafka's Story*. New York: Gordian Press.

Flusser, David. 1979. *Yahadut Umekorot Hanatsrut*. Tel Aviv: Shamgar Sifriat Hapoalim.

Fondane, Bejamin. 1947. "Kafka et la rationalité absolue." *In Deucalion* (Paris) 2: 125–140.

Fontanier, Pierre. 1977. *Les figures du discours*. Paris: Flamarion.

Forster, E. M. 1927. *Aspects of the Novel*. London: Arnold.

Foucault, Michel. 1965. *Madness and Civilization: A History of Insanity in the Age of Reason*. Trans. Richard Howard. New York: Vintage.

Foulkes, A. P. 1967. *The Reluctant Pessimist: A Study of Franz Kafka*. Paris: Mouton.

Fraiberg, Selma. 1957. "Kafka and the Dream." In *Art and Psychoanalysis*. Ed. William Phillip. New York: Criterion Books.

Freeman, H. and Moris Simon, eds. 1961. *The Midrash*. 9 vols. London: The Soncino Press.

Freud, Sigmund. 1963. *A General Introduction to Psychoanalysis*. Trans. J. Strachey. New York: Liveright Publishing Co.

———. 1974. *The Standard Edition of the Complete Psychological Works*. Trans. and ed. James Strachey, with A. Freud, A. Strachey, and A. Tyson. 24 vols.

———. "The Uncanny." In *On Creativity and the Unconscious*. New York: Harper & Row, 1958, 123–124.

———. [1900] Vols. 4–5: *The Interpretation of Dreams*.

———. [1907] Vol. 9: "Obsessive Actions and Religious Practices."

———. [1912–13] Vol. 13: *Totem and Taboo*.

———. [1915–17] Vols. 15–16: *The Introductory Lectures to Psychoanalysis*.

———. [1922] Vol. 17–18: "Medusa's Head."

———. [1925] Vol. 19: "Note on a Mystic Writing-Pad."

———. [1929] Vol. 21: *Civilization and Its Discontents*.

———. [1931] Vol. 21: "Female Sexuality."

Friedman, Maurice. 1963. "The Modern Job: On Melville, Dostoyevsky, and Kafka." In *Judaism* (NY) 12: 436–455.

———. 1963. *Problematic Rebel: Melville, Dostoyevsky, Kafka, Camus*. New York: Random House. Revised edition: Chicago: University of Chicago Press, 1970.

Friedman, Richard. 1977. "The Biblical Expression of Mastir Panim." *Hebrew Annual Review* 1: 19–33.

———. 1981. *The Creation of Sacred Literature: Composition and Redaction of Biblical Text*. Berkeley: University of California Press.

Fromm, Erich. 1952. *The Forgotten Language*. London: Gonzales.

Frye, Northrop. 1973. *Anatomy of Criticism: Theory of Genre*. Princeton: Princeton University Press.

Fuchs, Esther. 1985. *Omanut hahimamut: Al ha'ironia shel Shai Agnon* [Cunning Innocence: On S. Y. Agnon's Irony]. Gefen: Jerusalem.

Funk, Robert. 1966. "Saying and Seeing: Phenomenology of Language and The New Testament." *The Journal of Bible and Religion* 34.3: 196–213.

———. 1966. "The Parable as Metaphor." In *Languge, Hermeneutic, and Words of God*. New York: Harper & Row.

———. 1966. *Language, Hermeneutics and Words of God*. New York: Harper and Row.

———. 1975. *Jesus as Precursor*. Philadelphia: Fortress and Missoula, Montana: Scholars Press.

Gay, Peter. 1968. *Weimar Culture: The Outsider as Insider*. New York: Harper & Row.

Genette, Gerard. 1964. "Frontières du récit." *Communications* 8.

———. 1966. *Figures I*. Paris: Éditions du Seuil.

———. 1969. *Figures II*. Paris: Éditions du Seuil.

———. 1972. *Figures III*. Paris: Éditions du Seuil.

Germana, Pescio Bottino. 1970. *Calvino*. Florence: La Nuova Italia.

Gilman, Sander. 1986. *Jewish Self Hatred: Anti-Semitism and the Hidden Language of the Jews*. Baltimore: Johns Hopkins University Press.

Ginsberg, L. 1968. *Legends of the Jews*. 7 vols. Philadelphia: Jewish Publication Society.

———. [1968]. *The Gaon R. Elijah of Vilna*. Vol. 4. Philadelphia: Jewish Publication Society.

Glatzer, Nahum. 1969. *The Judaic Tradition*. Boston: Beacon Press.

———. ed. 1974. *I Am a Memory Come Alive: Autobiographical Writings by F.K.* New York: Schocken Books.

Goethe, J. Wolfgang. 1963. *The Parable*. Trans. John Resnin. New York: Harcourt, Brace and World.

Goldin, Judah. 1976. *The Jewish Expression*. New Haven and London: Yale University Press.

Golomb Hoffman, Anne. 1991. *Between Exile and Return: S. Y. Agnon and the Drama of Writing*. Albany: State University of New York Press.

Gore, Vidal. 1974. "Fabulous Calvino." *The New York Review of Books* (30 May): 13–21.

Grabbe, L. Lester. 1992. *Judaism from Cyrus to Hadrian: The Persian and Greek Periods*. Vol. 1. Minneapolis: Fortress Press.

Gray, Richard T. 1987. *Constructive Deconstruction: Kafka's Aphorism: Literary Tradition and Literary Transformation*. Tübingen: Max Niemeyer Verlag.

Gray, Ronald. 1973. *Franz Kafka*. Cambridge: Cambridge University Press.

Green, Arthur. 1981. *Tormented Master: A Life of Rabbi Nahman of Bratslav*. New York: Schocken Books.

Greenberg, Clement. 1964. "At the Building of the Great Wall of China." In *Franz Kafka Today*. Ed. Angel Flores and Homer Swander. Madison: The University of Wisconsin Press.

Greimas, A. J. 1966. *Sémantique structurale*. Paris: Librairie Larousse.

———. 1970. *Du sense*. Paris: Éditions du Seuil.

———. 1976. *Maupassant: La sémiotique du texte, éxercises pratiques*. Paris: Éditions du Seuil.

———. 1978. "Pour une théorie des modalités." In *Language* 43.2: 37–49, 2–16.

———and Jacques Fontanille. 1990. *Sémiotique des passions*. Paris: Éditions du Seuil.

Grice, Paul. 1957. "Meaning." In *Philosophical Review* 66: 377–388.

Gross, J. 1966. "The Art of Agnon." In *New York Review of Books* 3.11.

Guglielmi, Angelo. 1959. "La realtà truccata di Calvino." *Approdo letterario* 7 (April–July): 74–82.

Gunvaldsen, Kaare. 1963. "Franz Kafka and Psychoanalysis." *University of Toronto Quarterly* 23: 266–281.

Guttman, T. 1949. *Hamashal Bitkufat Hatannaim*. [The Parable in the Time of the Tannaim]. Jerusalem: Abir Yaakov, 13–24.

Guttman, Yehoshua. 1964. "The Ewe Lamb." The Israel Society for Biblical Research and the World Jewish Bible Society. *Beth Mikra* 18–19:3/4: 4–20.

Halkin, Shimon. 1964. "Al *Oreah natah lalun*." In *Le Agnon Shai: Devarim al hasofer usefarav* [To S. Y. Agnon: Words on the Writer and His Books]. Ed. Dov Sadan and Ephraim Urbach. Jerusalem: The Jewish Agency.

Handelman, Susan. 1982. *The Slayers of Moses: The Emergence of Rabbinic Interpretation in Modern Literary Theory*. Albany: State University of New York Press.

Hartman, Geoffrey. 1985. "On the Jewish Imagination." *Prooftexts* 5.3: 201–220.

—— and Sanford Budick, eds. 1986. *Midrash and Literature*. New Haven: Yale University Press.

Hayman, Ronald. 1981. *K: A Biography of Kafka*. London: Weidenfeld and Nicolson.

Hegel, G. 1975. *Aesthetics*. Trans. T. M. Knox. Oxford: Clarendon Press.

Heinemann, J. 1974. *Agadot Vetoldetehen* [Tales and Their History]. Jerusalem: Keter.

Heinemann, J. and Dov Noy, eds. 1971. "Studies in Aggadah and Folk-Literature." In *Scripta Hierosolymitana*, vol. 22. Jerusalem: Magnes Press.

Hengel, Martin. 1974. *Judaism and Hellenism*. Trans. John Bowden. Philadelphia: Fortress Press.

Hertz, J. H. 1959. *The Authorized Daily Prayer Book*. New York: Block Publishing.

Hharm, Daniil. 1971. *Russia's Lost Literature of the Absurd*. Ed. George Gibian. Ithaca: Cornell University Press.

Hintikka, Jaakko. 1962. *Knowledge and Belief: An Introduction to the Logic of the Two Notions*. Ithaca: Cornell University Press.

Hirshman, Albert. 1977. *The Passions and the Interests*. Princeton: Princeton University Press.

Hochman, Baruch. 1970. *The Fiction of S. Y. Agnon*. Ithaca: Cornell University Press.

Holtz, Avraham. 1973. "*Hamashal hapatuaḥ kemafteaḥ le'sefer hama'asim shel Shai 'Agnon*" [The Open Parable as Key to Agnon's "The Book of Deeds"]. *Hasifrut* 4: 298–333.

Horodetzky, S. A., ed. 1975. *Sefer shivḥe habesht* [The Book of Praises of the Baal Shem Tov]. Tel Aviv: Sifriat Hapoalim.

Hume, Kathryn. 1992. *Calvino's Fictions: Cogito and Cosmos*. Oxford: Clarendon Press.

Husserl, Edmund. 1913. *Logische Untersuchungen*. Halle, Germany: Niemyer.

Idel, Moshe. 1988. *Kabbalah: New Perspectives*. New Haven: Yale University Press.

Illiano, Antonio. 1972. "Per una definizione della vena cosmogonica di Calvino: appunti su *Le cosmicomiche e Ti con zero*." *Italica* 49.3 (Autumn): 291–301.

Iser, Wolfgang. 1974. *The Implied Reader*. Baltimore: John Hopkins University Press.

Jabès, Edmond. 1963. *Le livre des questions*. Paris: Gallimard.

———. 1977. *The Book of Questions*. Trans. Rosmarie Waldrop. Middletown, Conn.: Wesleyan University Press.

———. 1964. *Le livre de Yukel*. Paris: Gallimard.

———. 1976a. *Le livre des ressemblances*. Paris: Gallimard.

Jacobson, C. David. 1987. *Modern Midrash*. Albany: State University of New York Press.

Jakobson, Roman. 1961a. "Linguistique et théorie de la communication." In *Proceedings of Symposia in Applied Mathematics* XII (American Mathematical Society).

———. 1973. *Questions de poétique*. Paris: Éditions du Seuil.

Jakobson, Roman and Morris Halle. 1956. *Fundamentals of Language*. The Hague: Mouton.

James, Henry. 1947. *The Art of the Novel*. New York: Scribner.

Janouch, Gustav. 1953. *Conversations with Kafka: Notes and Reminiscences*. Trans. Boronwy Rees. London: D. Verschoyle.

Jardine, Alice. 1985. *Gynesis: Configuration of Woman and Modernity*. Ithaca: Cornell University Press.

Jenny, Laurent. 1982. "The Strategy of From." In *French Literary Theory Today*. Ed. Tzvetan Todorov. Cambridge: Cambridge University Press.

Jeremias, Joachim. 1981. Trans. *The Parables of Jesus*. London: SCM Press. German original: *Die Gleichnisse Jesu*. Göttingen, 1962.

Jones, G. V. 1964. *The Art and Truth of the Parables*. London: Society for Promoting Christian Knowledge.

Josephus Flavius. *Antiquities*. 1959. Ed. and trans. H. J. Thackeray. 9 vols. Oxford: Oxford University Press.

Jülicher, Adolph. 1963. *Die Gleichnisreden Jesus*. Tübingen: J.C.B. Mohr, 1886–1910. Reprinted, Darmstadt: Wissenschaftliche Buchgesellschaft.

Kafka, Franz.1946. *Das Urteil und andere erzählungen*. New York: Schocken Books.

———. 1954. *Beschreibung eines Kampfes: Novellen, Skizzen, Aphorismen aus dem Nachlass*. Ed. Max Brod. Frankfurt.

———. 1971. *The Complete Stories*. Ed. Nahum Glatzer. New York: Schocken Books.

———. 1974. *Parables and Paradoxes*. Trans. Clement Greenbaum et al. New York: Schocken Books.

———. 1977. *Letters to Friends, Family and Editors*. Trans. Richard Winston and Clara Winston. New York: Schocken Books.

Kasher, Chana. 1989. "The Parable of the Royal Palace in the *Guide of the Perplexed* as Instruction for a Student." *American Jewish Studies Review* 14: 1–19.

Kaufman, Yehezkel. 1960. *The Religion of Israel*. Trans. Moshe Greenberg. Chicago: University of Chicago Press.

Kermode, Frank. 1967. *The Sense of an Ending*. New York: Oxford University Press.

———. 1979. *The Genesis of Secrecy: On the Interpretation of Narrative.* Cambridge: Harvard University Press.

———. 1987. "Introduction to the New Testament." In *The Literary Guide to the Bible.* Ed. Robert Alter and Frank Kermode. Cambridge: The Belknap Press of Harvard University Press.

Kirshenblatt-Gimblett, Barbara. 1975. "A Parable in Context: A Social Interactional Analysis of Storytelling Performance." In *Folklore: Performance and Communication.* Ed. D. Ben-Amos and K. Goldstein. Paris and The Hague: Mouton de Gruyter.

Koelb, Clayton. 1989. *Kafka's Rhetoric: The Passion of Reading.* Ithaca: Cornell University Press.

Kranz, Jacob. 1967. *The Magid of Dubnow and His Parables.* Ed. Benno Heinemann. New York: P. Feldheim.

Kristeva, Julia. 1968b. "La productivité du dite texte." *Communications* 11.

———. 1969. *Sémiotiké, recherches pour une sémanalyse.* Paris: Éditions du Seuil.

———. 1970. *Le texte du roman.* Paris and The Hague: Mouton de Gruyter.

———. 1972. *Essais de sémiotique poétique.* Paris: Larousse.

———. 1986. *The Kristeva Reader.* Ed. Toril Moi. New York: Columbia University Press.

Kuepper, Karl J. 1970. "Gesture and Posture as Elemental Symbolism in Kafka's *The Trial.*" *Mosaic* 3.4 (Summer): 143–152.

Kurzweil, B. 1970. *Massot al Sippure S. Y. Agnon* [Essays on Agnon's Stories]. Jerusalem and Tel Aviv: Schocken Books.

Lacan, Jacques. 1966. *Écrits.* Paris: Éditions du Seuil.

———. 1975. *The Language of the Self: The Function of Language in Psychoanalysis.* Trans. and notes Anthony Wilden. New York: Dell.

———. 1978. *The Four Fundamental Concepts of Psychoanalysis.* Trans. Alan Sheridan. New York: Norton.

———. 1982. "Desire and the Interpretation of Desire in *Hamlet.*" In *Literature and Psychoanalysis: The Question of Reading Otherwise.* Ed. Shoshana Felman. Baltimore: John Hopkins University Press.

———. 1988. "Seminar on 'The Purloined Letter'." Trans. Jeffrey Mehlman. In *The Purloined Poe: Lacan, Derrida and Psychoanalytic Reading.* Ed. John P. Muller and William J. Richardson. Baltimore: John Hopkins University Press.

Lakoff, George. 1980. *Metaphors We Live by.* Chicago: University of Chicago Press.

———. 1987. *Women, Fire, and Dangerous Things.* Chicago: The University of Chicago Press.

Langacker, Ronald W. 1977. *An Overview of Uto-Aztecan Grammar.* Dallas, TX. Summer Institute of Linguistics.

———. 1986. *Foundations of Cognitive Grammar,* vol. 1. Stanford: Stanford University Press.

Lanigan, Richard L. 1977. *Speech Act Phenomenology.* The Hague: Martinus Nijhoff.

Laplanche, Jean and J. B. Pontalis. 1973. *The Language of Psychoanalysis.* Trans. Daniel Lagache. London: Hogarth.

Laswell, Harold. 1968. *Language of Politics*. Cambridge: MIT Press.

Levinas, Emmanuel. 1968. *Quatre lectures Talmudiques*. Paris: Les Éditions de Minuit.

———. 1977. *Du sacré au saint: Cinq nouvelles lectures Talmudiques*. Paris: Les Éditions de Minuit.

Linton, Olof. 1980. "Coordinated Sayings and Parables in the Synoptic Gospels." *New Testament Studies* 26: 139–163.

Little, C. James. 1976. "Parable Research in the Twentieth Century." *The Expository Times* 87: 356–360; 88 (1977): 40–44, 71–75.

Lotman, Juriy M. 1977. *The Structure of the Artistic Text*. Trans. Ronald Vroon. Ann Arbor: University of Michigan Press.

———. 1971. "Problema 'obuchenija kul'ture kak ee tipologichskaia charakteristika." *Trudy po znakovym sistemam* V. Tartu: Acta et Commentationes Universitatis Tartuensis.

Lotman, Juriy M. and B. A. Uspenskij. 1971. "O semioticheskom mechanizm kul'tury." *Trudy po znakovym sistemam* V. Tartu: Acta et Commentationes Universitatis Tartuensis.

Lubock, Percy. 1921. *The Craft of Fiction*. London: Cape.

Lukács, Georg. 1960. *La signification présente du réalisme critique*, Paris: Gallimard. J. and N. Mander. English translation: "Franz Kafka or Thomas Mann?" Trans. J. and N. Mander. In *The Meaning of Contemporary Realism*. London: Merlin Press, 1962, retitled *Realism in Our Time*, New York: Harper & Row, 1964.

Lyotard, Jean-François. 1979. *Au juste*. Paris: Christian Bourgeois.

———. 1988. *The Différend*. Trans. Georges Van Den Abbeele. Minneapolis: University of Minnesota Press.

MacCannall, Dean and Juliet MacCannall. 1982. *The Time of the Sign*. Bloomington: Indiana University Press.

Machiavelli, N. 1965. *The Art of War*. Trans. Ellis Farneworth. New York: The Library of Liberal Arts Press.

Maimonides, Moses. 1963. *The Guide of the Perplexed (Dalalat al-ha'irin)*. Trans. Shlomo Pines. Intro. Leo Strauss. Chicago: The University of Chicago Press.

Manacorda, Giuliano. 1967. *La letteratura italiana contemporanea (1940–1965)*. Rome: Riuniti.

Marin, Louis. 1971. *Utopique: jeux d'espace*. Paris: Les Éditions de Minuit.

———. 1974. *Le récit parabolique*. Aubier Montaigne: Éditions du Cerf.

———. 1975. "La syntaxe du désire." In *Critique du discours*. Paris: Les Éditions de Minuit.

———. 1993. *Des pouvoirs de l'image: Gloses*. Paris: Éditions du Seuil.

Mazor, Y. 1979. *HaDinamika shel Motivim biTzrat S. Y. Agnon* [The Dynamics of Motifs in Agnon's Works]. Tel Aviv: Dekel.

Mekilta Derabbi Shimeon Bar Yochai. 1980. [From the Teachings of Rabbi Bar Yochai]. Ed. Y. N. Epstein and E. Z. Melamed. Jerusalem: Hillel Press.

Metz, Christian, ed. 1977. *Signes et paraboles: Sémiotique et texte Évangélique*. Paris: Éditions du Seuil.

———. 1977. *Essais sémiotiques*. Paris: Edition Klincksieck.

Meyer, Michael. 1967. *The Origins of the Modern Jew: Jewish Identity and European Culture in Germany, 1749–1842.* Detroit: Wayne State University Press.

Midrash Hagadol. 1975. [The Big Midrash]. 5 vols. Jerusalem: Mosad Harav Kook.

Midrash Rabbah. 1983. Ed. H. Freedman and Maurice Simon. 10 vols. London: Soncino.

Midrash Shemuel. 1893. Ed. S. Buber. Krakau.

Mintz, Alan. 1981. "Agnon in Jaffa: The Myth of the Artist as a Young Man." *Prooftexts* 1.

———. 1984. *Hurban: Responses to Catastrophe in Hebrew Literature.* New York: Columbia University Press.

———. 1989. *Banished from Their Father's Table: Loss of Faith and Hebrew Autobiography.* Bloomington: Indiana University Press.

Miron, Dan. 1961. "Hasifrut ha'ivrit bereshit hameah ha'esrim: Perakim mitoh massah." In *Me'asef ledivrei sifrut, bikkoret, vehagut* 2: 436–464. ["Hebrew Literature at the Beginning of the Twentieth Century: Chapters in the Journey." In a *Collection of Literature, Criticism, and Conceptualization*].

Mitchell, W. J. T, ed. 1982. *The Politics of Interpretation.* Chicago: The University of Chicago Press.

Moked, Gabriel. 1989. *Shivḥei 'Adi'el 'Amzeh* [The Praises of Adiel Amzeh: "Forevermore" and Edo and Enam"]. Tel Aviv: Schocken Books.

Monegal, E. Rodriguez. 1970. *Borgès par lui même.* Paris: Écrivains de toujour.

———. 1982. "Borges: The Reader as Writer." *TriQuarterly* 25 (Fall): 102–143.

Montefiore, G. C. and H. Loewe. 1960. *A Rabbinic Anthology.* Philadelphia: The Jewish Publication Society of America.

Mosse, George. 1985. "Jewish Emancipation: Between *Bildung* and Respectability." In *Jew Jewish Response to German Culture.* Ed. J. Reinhartz and W. Schatzberg. Hanover, N.H.: University Press of New England.

Nahman of Bratslav. 1978. *The Tales.* Trans. and ed. Arnold Band. Mahwak, N.J.: Paulist Press.

———. 1983. *The Captive Soul of the Messiah: New Tales about Reb Nachman.* Trans. Howard Schwartz. New York: Schocken Books.

Neusner, Jacob. 1981. *Judaism: The Evidence of the Mishnah.* Chicago: University of Chicago Press.

Nietzsche, Friedreich. 1910. *The Joyful Wisdom.* Trans. Thomas Common. Edinburgh: Foulis.

———. 1965. *Truth and Faulsity in an Ultramoral Sense.* Trans. G. Clive. New York: Mentor Books.

———. 1987. *The Birth of Tragedy and the Genealogy of Morals.* Trans. F. Golffing. New York: Doubleday.

Noy, Dov. 1961. "Mishle Melakim Shel Rashbi." *Machanayim* 53–54, 73–87.

Ogden, K. C. and I. A. Richards. 1946. *The Meaning of Meaning.* New York: Harcourt, Brace and World.

Olken, I. T. 1984. *With Pleated Eye and Garnet Wing: Symmetry of Italo Calvino.* Ann Arbor: University of Michigan Press.

Ozick, Cynthia. 1950. "*Parable in Henry James.*" Master thesis, Ohio State University.

———. 1983. *Art and Ardor*. New York: Knopf.

———. 1989. "S. Y. Agnon and the First Religion." In *Metaphor and Memory*. New York: Knopf. First appeared as "Agnon's Antagonisms." In *Commentary*, December 1988.

———. 1989. *Metaphor and Memory*. New York: Knopf.

Parret, Herman. 1978. "La pragmatique des modalités." University of California, San Diego. Seminar, fall 1978.

Patte, Daniel, ed. 1976. *Semiology and Parables*. Pittsburgh, Penn.: The Pickwick Press.

Perrin, Norman. 1979. *Jesus and the Language of the Kingdom*. London: SCM Ltd. Press.

Pesikta Rabbati: Discourse for Feasts, Fasts, and Special Sabbaths. Trans. William Braude. 2 vols. New Haven: Yale University Press, 1968.

Petuchovsky, Jakob. 1972. "The Theological Significance of the Parables in Rabbinic Literature and the New Testament." *Christian News from Israel* 23.10: 76–86, 144.

Pierce, Charles S. 1960. "Elements of Logic." In *Collected Papers*. Cambridge: Harvard University Press.

Plato. 1871. "The Sophist." In *The Collected Dialogues of Plato*. Trans. Benjamin Jowett. Intro. Raphael Demos. Oxford: Clarendon Press.

———. 1928. *The Republic*. Third edition of the B. Jowett translation. Intro. Charles M. Bakewell. New York, Chicago: Scribner's.

Politzer, Heinz. 1962. *Franz Kafka: Parable and Paradox*. Ithaca: Cornell University Press.

Prince, Gerald. 1973. *A Grammar of Stories*. Paris and The Hague: Mouton de Gruyter.

Propp, Vladimir. 1968. *Morphology of the Folktale*. Trans. Lawrence Scott and Louis A. Wagnes. Austin: University of Texas Press.

Pullini, Giorgio. 1965. *Il romanzo italiano del dopoguerra (1940–1960)*. Vicenza: Marsilio.

Putnam, Hilary. 1984. "The Craving for Objectivity." *New Literary History* 15.2, 229–39.

Quilligan, Maureen. 1979. *The Language of Allegory*. Ithaca: Cornell University Press.

Rabbinovicz, Raphael N. N. 1952 (5712). *Ma'amar 'al ha-Talmud* [An Essay about the Talmud]. Jerusalem: Mossad Harav Kook.

Radin, Max. 1915. *The Jews among the Greeks and Romans*. Philadelphia: The Jewish Publication Society of America.

Rastiers, François. 1972. "Systématique des isotopies." In *Essays de sémiotique poétique*. Ed. A. J. Greimas. Paris: Larousse.

———. 1989. *Sens et textualité*. Paris: Hachette.

Rawidowicz, Simon. 1974. *Studies in Jewish Thought*. Ed. Nahum Glatzer. Philadelphia: Jewish Publication Society.

Re, Lucia. 1990. *Calvino and the Age of Neorealism: Fables of Estrangement*. Stanford: Stanford University Press.

Reeder, Harry. 1978. "Cogito Ergo Sum: Inference and Performance." *Eidos* 1: 30–49.

Ricoeur, Paul. 1975. *La métaphore vive*. Paris: Éditions du Seuil.

Riffaterre, Michael. 1987. "The Intertextual Unconscious." *Critical Inquiry* 13.2: 371–385.

Robert, Marthe. 1979. *Seul, comme Franz Kafka*. Paris: Calmann-Levi.

———. 1979a. *D'Oedipe à Moïse: Freud et la concience juive*. Paris: Calmann-Levi.

Robertson, Ritchie. 1985. *Kafka: Judaism, Politics, and Literature*. Oxford: Clarendon Press.

Romily, Jacqueline de. 1975. *Magic and Rhetoric in Ancient Greece*. Cambridge: Harvard University Press.

Rousell, Raymond. 1963. *Comment j'ai écrit certains de mes livres*. Paris: Pauvert.

Russell, D. S. 1967. *The Jews from Alexander to Herod*. London: Oxford University Press.

Sadan, Dov. [1959] 1973. *On S. Y. Agnon*. Tel Aviv: Hakibbutz Hameuhad.

Safran-Naveh, Gila. 1987. "Ideological Aesthetics and Meta-Modalization: Semiotics of Descartes's *Passions of the Soul*." *The American Journal of Semiotics* 5.3–4: 479–491.

———. 1988. "Semiotic Considerations of an Imperial Message: Truth and Chronotopicity in Kafka's Parable." *Semiotics* 8: 165–175.

———. 1994. "To Know Women: Ethics and Politics of Sexual Difference Reflected in Contemporary Israeli Literature." *Cincinnati Judaica Review* 4 (Spring): 57–70.

Sandbank, Simon. 1985. "Parable and Theme: Kafka and American Fiction." *Comparative Literature* 37.3: 252–268.

———. 1967. "Structures of Paradox in Kafka." *Modern Language Quarterly* 28: 462–472.

Sanders, E. P. 1985. *Jesus and Judaism*. London: SCM Ltd. Press.

Sanders, Frank, K. 1928. *History of the Hebrews*. New York: Scribner's.

Sartre, Jean-Paul. 1947. "*Aminadab* ou le fantastique consideré comme un language." In *Situations I*. Paris: Gallimard, 12–142. English translation: "*Aminadab* or the Fantastic Considered as a Language." Trans. Annette Michelson. In *Literary Essays*. New York: Philosophical Library, 1957, 56–72.

de Saussure, Ferdinand. 1966. *Course in General Linguistics*. Ed. C. Bally, A. Sechehaye, and A. Reidlinger. Trans. Wade Baskin. New York: McGraw-Hill.

Scholem, G. Gershom. 1954. *Major Trends in Jewish Mysticism*. New York: Schocken Books.

———. 1967. "Reflections on S. Y. Agnon." *Commentary*, December.

———. 1969. *On the Kabbalah and Its Symbolism*. Trans. Ralph Mannheim. New York: Schocken Books.

———, ed. [1970]. 1994. *The Correspondence with Walter Benjamin, 1910–1940*. Trans. Manfred R. Jacobson and Evelyn M. Jacobson. Chicago: The University of Chicago Press.

———. 1971. *The Messianic Idea in Judaism and Other Essays on Jewish Spirituality*. New York: Schocken Books.

Schumann, W. Detlev. "Enumerative Style and Its Significance in Whitman, Rilke, Werfel." *Modern Language Quarterly* 32: 171–204.

Schürer, Emil. 1961. *A History of The Jewish People in the Time of Jesus*. New York: Schocken Books.

Schwartz, Howard. 1982. "Rabbi Nachman of Bratslav: Forerunner of Modern Jewish Literature." *Judaism: A Quarterly Journal* 31.2: 211–228.

Schwartzbaum, Haim. 1979. *The Mishle Shu'alim (Fox Fables) of Rabbi Berechiah Ha-Nakdan*. Kiron, Israel: Institute for Jewish and Arab Folklore Research.

Searle, John. 1969. *Speech Acts*. Cambridge: Harvard University Press.

Sebeok, Thomas. 1960. Ed. "Linguistics and Poetics." In *Style and Language*. Cambridge: MIT Press.

———. 1979. "Looking in the Direction for What Should Have Been Sought in the Source." In *The Sign and Its Masters*. Austin: University of Texas Press. 84–106.

———. 1986. "The Doctrine of Signs." In *Frontiers in Semiotics*. Ed. John Deely, Brooke Williams, and Felicia Kruse. Bloomington: Indiana University Press.

Sebeok, Thomas and Jean Umiker-Sebeok. 1979. "'You Know my Method': A Juxtaposition of Charles S. Peirce and Sherlock Holmes." *Semiotica* 26: 203–250. Reprinted in 1980, in an enhanced monograph. Bloomington: Indiana University Press.

Shaked, Gershon. 1973. *Omanut haSippur shel S. Y. Agnon*. (Hebrew) [The Narrative Art of Agnon]. Tel Aviv: Sifriat Poalim.

———. 1977. *Hasipporet ha'ivrit 1880–1970* [Hebrew Literature 1800–1970]. Vol 1. Tel Aviv: Hakibbutz Hameuchad and Keter.

———. 1986. "Midrash and Narrative: Agnon's Agunot." In *Midrash and Literature*. Ed. Geoffrey Hartman and Sanford Budick. New Haven: Yale University Press.

———. 1989. *Shmuel Yosef Agnon: A Revolutionary Traditionalist*. New York: New York University Press.

Sheres, Ita. 1990. *Dinah's Rebellion: A Biblical Parable for Our Times*. New York: Crossroad.

Silverman, Kaja. 1983. *The Subject of Semiotics*. New York: Oxford University Press.

Simon, Uriel. 1967. "The Poor Man's Ewe-Lamb: An Example of Juridical Parable." *Biblica* 48: 207–242.

Sokoloff, Naomi. 1984. "Metaphor and Metonymy in Agnon's *A Guest for the Night*." *American Jewish Studies Review* 9.1.

Solotoravsky, Myrna. 1986. "The Model of Midrash and Borges's Interpretative Tales and Essays." In *Midrash and Literature*. Ed. Geoffrey Hartman and Sanford Budick. New Haven: Yale University Press.

Soskel, Walter H. 1956. "Kafka's 'Metamorphosis': Rebellion and Punishment." *Monatshefte* 48.4 (April–May): 203–214.

———. 1964. *Franz Kafka: Tragik und Ironie*. Trans. Henry Sussman. Munich: Langen-Müller.

———. 1973. "Franz Kafka as a Jew." *Leo Baeck Institute Yearbook* 18: 223–228.

Steinberg, Yehuda. 1904. *Sihot hasidim*. Warsaw: Tushiyyah.

Stern, David. 1984. "Moses-cide: Midrash and Contemporary Literary Criticism." *Prooftexts* 4.2: 193–204.

———. 1988. "Midrash and Indeterminacy." *Critical Inquiry* 15.1: 132–161.

———. 1989. "Jesus' Parables from Rabbinic Perspective: The Case of the Wicked Husbandmen." In *Parable and Story in Judaism and Christianity.* Ed. C. Thoma and M. Wyschogrod. Mahwah, N.J.: Paulist Press. 42–80.

———. 1991. *Parables in Midrash.* Cambridge: Harvard University Press.

Stern, J.P. 1965. "Franz Kafka: The Labyrinth of Guilt." *Critical Quarterly* 7: 35–47.

Strack, Hermann L. [1920] 1978. *Introduction to the Talmud and Midrash.* New York: Meridian Books.

Strauss, Walter A. 1988. *On the Threshold of a New Kabbalah: Kafka's Later Tales.* New York: Peter Lang.

Strawson, P. F. 1950. "On Referring." *Mind* 59.235: 320–344.

Sturrock, John. 1977. *Paper Tigers: The Ideal Fiction of J. L. Borges.* Oxford: Clarendon Press.

Suleiman Rubin, Susan. 1983. *Authoritarian Fiction: The Ideological Novel as a Literary Genre.* New York: Columbia University Press.

Sussman, Henry. 1979. *Franz Kafka: Geometrician of Metaphor.* Madison: University of Wisconsin Press.

Synan, Edward. 1979. *Thomas Aquinas: Propositions and Parables.* Toronto: Pontifical Institute of Medieval Studies.

Talmage, Frank. 1986. "Apples of Gold: The Inner Meaning of Sacred Texts in Medieval Judaism." In *Jewish Spirituality: From the Bible though the Middle Ages.* Ed. Arthur Green. New York: Crossroad, 313–355.

Talmud Babli. 1880–86. [The Babylonian Talmud]. Wilna edition. Romm Press, 1970. Bnei Berziek, Is.: T. Rubenstein Press. Reprint.

Talmud Yerushalmi. 1971. [The Jerusalem Talmud]. 4 vols. (Based upon the Leiden Manuscript, Scal. 3, from 1334). Jerusalem: Kedem.

Tcherikover, Victor. 1974. *Hellenistic Civilization and the Jews.* New York: Athenaeum.

The Holy Bible. Ed. Herbert G. May and Bruce Metzger. Oxford: Oxford University Press. Translated from the Original, 1611. Revised 1885, 1901, 1952, 1973.

Thoma, Clemens and Michael Wyschogrod, eds. 1989. *Parable and Story in Judaism and Christianity.* Mahwah, N.Y.: Paulist Press.

Thorlby, Anthony. 1972. *Kafka: A Study.* London: Heinemann.

Thorlby, Anthony and Alan Udoff, ed. 1986. *Kafka's Contextuality.* Baltimore: Gordian Press and Baltimore Hebrew College.

Tishby, Isaiah, ed. 1948. *Mishnat haZohar* [The Teaching of the Zohar]. Jerusalem: Bialik.

Todorov, Tzvetan. 1967. *Littérature et signification.* Paris: Larousse.

———. 1968. *Poétique.* Paris: Éditions du Seuil.

———. 1970. *Introduction à la littérature fantastique.* Paris: Éditions du Seuil.

———. 1971. *Poétique de la Prose.* Paris: Éditions du Seuil. English translation: *The Poetics of Prose.* Trans. Richard Howard. Ithaca: Cornell University Press, 1977.

———. 1977. *Theories du symbol.* Paris: Éditions du Seuil.

Trattner, Ernest. 1955. *Understanding the Talmud*. New York: Thomas Nelson and Sons.

Udoff, Alan, ed. 1987. *Kafka and the Contemporary Critical Performance: Centenary Readings*. Bloomington and Indianapolis: Indiana University Press.

Unterman, I. 1952. *The Talmud*. New York: Bloch Publishing Co. And reprinted, 1971.

Urbach, E. E. 1975. *The Sages: Their Concepts and Beliefs*. 2 vols. Jerusalem: Magnes Press.

Urzidil, Johannes. 1969. "Cervantes und Kafka." In *Max Brod: Ein Gedenkbuch*. Ed. Hugo Gold. Tel Aviv: Olameinu, 107–126.

Valéry, Paul. 1972, 1974. *Cahiers I and II*. Paris: Gallimard.

Veiser, Raphael. 1988. "*Mamashut ubedayon bebiographiah shel 'Agnon*." [1980]. [Reality and Fiction in the Biography of Agnon]. In *Dyoqno shel Shai 'Agnon: Haromanim shel Shai 'Agnon* [Portrait of S. Y. Agnon: The Novels of S. Y. Agnon]. Ed. Avinoam Barchai. Tel-Aviv: Everyman's University.

Vendler, Zeno. 1972. *Res Cogitans*. Ithaca: Cornell University Press.

Vermes, Geza. 1976. "Bible and Midrash: Early Old Testament Exegesis." In *The Cambridge History of the Bible*, 1: 190–231. Cambridge: Cambridge University Press.

———. 1977. *Jesus and the Jews*. Glasgow: Fontana.

———. 1983. *Jesus and the World of Judaism*. London: SCM Ltd. Press.

Via, O. Dan. 1980. *The Parables: Their Literary and Existential Dimension*. Philadelphia: Fortress Press.

Voegelin, W. 1943. "Der Gottesmord." *Die Diabole bei Lysiass*. Basel: Druck von B. Schwabe. 63–85.

Vuarnet, Jean-Noël. 1971. "Le labyrinth de l'absence." *Europe* 511–512: 73–80.

Ziegler, Ignaz. 1903. *Die Königsgleichnisse des Midrash: Beleuchtet durch die römische Kaiserzeit*. Breslau: Schlesische Verlags-Anstalt v. S. Schottlaender.

Weiman, Robert. 1988. "Text, Author-Function, and the Appropriation in Modern Narrative: Toward a Sociology of Literature." *Critical Inquiry* 14.3: 431–447.

Wellek, René. 1956. *Theory of Literature*. New York: Harcourt, Brace and World.

Weltsch, Felix. 1957. *Religion und Humor im Leben und Werk F.K.* Berlin: Grunewald.

Werckmeister, O. K. 1995. "Kafka 007." *Critical Inquiry* 21.2 (Winter): 468–495.

Wheelock, K. Carter. 1969. *The Mythmaker: A Study of Motif and Symbol in the Short Stories of Jorge Luis Borges*. Austin: University of Texas Press.

White, Alan. 1975. *Modal Thinking*. Ithaca: Cornell University Press.

White, Hayden. 1986. "Historical Pluralism." *Critical Inquiry* 12 (Spring): 480–493.

Wilden, Anthony. 1968. "Lacan and the Discourse of the Other." In *Jacques Lacan, The Language of the Self: The Function of Language in Psychoanalysis*. Trans. Anthony Wilden. Baltimore: Johns Hopkins University Press.

Wilson, Edmond. 1954. "The Fiction of S. Y. Agnon." *New Yorker*, December 12, 186–193

————. 1956. "The Fiction of S. Y. Agnon." In *Red, Black, Blond and Olive.* New York: Oxford University Press.

Wittgenstein, Ludwig. 1963. *Philosophical Investigations.* Trans. G. E. M. Anscombe. Oxford: Basil Blackwell.

Whitman, Jon. 1987. *Allegory: The Dynamic of an Ancient and Medieval Technology.* Oxford: Clarendon Press.

Wolfson, Elliot. 1988. "The Hermeneutics of Visionary Experience: Revelation and Interpretation in the Zohar." *Religion* 18: 321–324.

Wolin, Richard. 1994. *Walter Benjamin: An Aesthetic of Redemption.* Berkeley: University of California Press.

Wright, Georg von. 1951. *An Essay in Modal Logic.* Amsterdam: North Holland Publishing Co.

Young, H. Bradford. 1989. *Jesus and His Jewish Parables.* Mahwah, N.J.: Paulist Press.

INDEX

Narrative segments
  in "Before the Kaddish," 213–215
  in "Cities and Signs," 187–188
  in "The Parable of the King's
      Banquet," 88–104
    first and second, 93
  in "The Parable of the Poor Man's
      Ewe Lamb," 55–59
  phrases forming, 100
Narrative trajectory
  Greimas's view of, 223
  in "The Parable of Cervantes and
      The Quixote," 171–172
  in "The Parable of the King's
      Banquet," 86
  in "The Parable of the Poor Man's
      Ewe Lamb," 59
New Testament. *See* Synoptic Gospel
  parables
Nietzche, Friedreich, 69–70
Nimshal
  connection between, and *mashal*,
      206
  defined, 7, 9
  primacy and actuality of, 20
*Nostalgia and Nightmare: A Study of
  the Fiction of S.Y. Agnon*, 203

Olken, I.T., 180
"On Parables," 34–35, 118, 219
Oppositions, sets of, in "The Parable
  of Cervantes and *The Quixote*,"
  174
Oral tradition
  of synoptic Gospel parables,
      66–67
  and written text, of rabbinic
      parables, 83–85
Other. *See* Doubleness
Overcoding. *See* Coding
Ozick, Cynthia, 29
  on Agnon, 210–211

"The Parable of Cervantes and *The
  Quixote*"
  analysis of, 164–177
    deep linguistic, 157–159

comparison of, to "Cities and
  Signs," 185, 189
text of, 164–165
"The Parable of the Crossroads," 17
"The Parable of the King's Banquet,"
  16
  analysis of, 85–104
    deep linguistic, 88–89, 92–102,
      104
  text of, 85
"The Parable of the Marriage Feast:
  At the King's Table"
  analysis of, 71–79
    deep linguistic, 74
  text of, 71
"Parable of the Palace," 33–34
"The Parable of the Poor Man's Ewe
  Lamb"
  analysis of, 43–60
    deep linguistic, 56
  text of, 42–43
"The Parable of the Sower," 18–19
"The Parable of the Spoiled Son," 20
"The Parable of the Two Kinds of
  Faith"
  analysis of, 112–119
    deep linguistic, 114–119
  text of, 112
Parable(s)
  classic, Kafka and, 144
  delineations of study, 4–6
  and dreams, 26–28, 143
  early, 41–42
    compared to synoptic Gospel
      parable, 12
  etymology of, 8–9
  inherent doubleness of, 6–7
  Kafka's, 127–128
    and dreams, 143
  king, 73
  modern, Franz Kafka and,
      123–124
  pastoral, regarding Moses' plea, 12
  polysemy of, 26
  suitability of, for Kafka, 149
  two versions of, comparison of,
      71–73